Albee
in Performance

Albee
in Performance

Rakesh H. Solomon

Indiana University Press
Bloomington & Indianapolis

This book is a publication of

Indiana University Press
601 North Morton Street
Bloomington, Indiana 47404-3797 USA

www.iupress.indiana.edu

Telephone orders	800-842-6796
Fax orders	812-855-7931
Orders by e-mail	iuporder@indiana.edu

Library of Congress Cataloging-in-Publication Data

Solomon, Rakesh Herald.
  Albee in performance / Rakesh H. Solomon ; [foreword by Edward Albee].
    p. cm.
  Includes bibliographical references and index.
  ISBN 978-0-253-35485-3 (cloth : alk. paper) — ISBN 978-0-253-22205-3
(pbk. : alk. paper) 1. Albee, Edward, 1928—Dramatic production.
2. Albee, Edward, 1928—Stage history. 3. Albee, Edward, 1928—Interviews.
I. Title.
  PS3551.L25Z885 2010
  812'.54—dc22
                           2009049325

1 2 3 4 5 15 14 13 12 11 10

TO
JUNE

for her understanding
while I pursued this project
that devoured time more rightly hers
my debt remains
immeasurable

Contents

Foreword

From the point of view of its predominant subject—Edward Albee as a director—and its predominant environment—Edward Albee's plays—this scholarly work succeeds in its detailed, comprehensive, and intelligent examination of the author and his processes. The fact that the subject is me and the environment is my work as a director could pose problems if my delight at the book's clarity and ultimate objectivity were not doubled by Mr. Solomon's understanding of theatrical process and practical result.

I am seldom grateful in print, but I will be here. In much the same way that Mel Gussow's biography *Edward Albee: A Singular Journey* relieved and nurtured its subject by its intelligence, perception, and critical acumen, Rakesh Solomon's work does for my directorial exploits. Mr. Solomon does not write from theory only; he was *there!* He watched me more or less from the beginning—saw me stumble my way into professionalism—all the while examining and testing the theory that an informed author/director can, more accurately than others, represent his work on stage, and seeming to agree that I have been, at least as often as not, correct.

To understand exactly what Rakesh Solomon has been examining and determining (and what *I* have been), read the pages which follow. They are accurately and beautifully done.

Edward Albee
New York City, 2009

Preface

I owe my first and greatest debt to Edward Albee for allowing me to attend his rehearsals over so many years. Without his generosity in permitting me to observe and record every aspect of his directorial work, this book would not have been possible. I am also grateful to him for giving me numerous interviews—despite hectic production schedules near opening nights—and for access to his drafts of plays, unpublished scripts, and restricted papers at the New York Public Library for the Performing Arts. I also thank him for permitting me to speak without any constraints whatsoever with his actors, designers, stage managers, producers, and directors.

Of these Albee collaborators, my deepest appreciation goes to the many actors who graciously allowed me to observe them at work—a situation of inherent vulnerability for them and thus normally closed. For their numerous acts of generosity and their candid conversations and interviews, I am especially grateful to the following actors: Cynthia Bassham, Patricia Kilgarriff, Stephen Rowe, Wyman Pendleton, Irene Worth, Tony Musante, Frances Conroy, Earl Hyman, Maureen Anderman, Tom Klunis, Shirley Knight, John Ottavino, Bruce Gray, Edward Seamon, Kathleen Butler, Jordan Baker, Myra Carter, and Marian Seldes.

I wish to acknowledge as well my gratitude to several directors: David Esbjornson, Lawrence Sacharow, William Gaskill, and most especially Alan Schneider, for letting me attend his rehearsals of plays by Edward Albee and Samuel Beckett, sometimes even in difficult situations. I am also indebted to several stage managers—most especially to Mark Wright, Wendy Beaton, and Julia

Gillett—for making my day-to-day participation easy and for sharing schedules, production books, director's notes, and their particular insights. Among others who have helped this project in different ways, I am grateful to Ruby Cohn, Tom Postlewait, Glenn Loney, Bernard Dukore, Timothy Wiles, and Gregory Boyd.

Over the years while conducting this project I have accumulated many other professional and personal debts. I am grateful to the East-West Center at the University of Hawaii for an East-West Center Grant that allowed me to attend my first Schneider rehearsals; to the University of California, Davis for two Regents' Fellowships and a Chancellor's Fellowship for academic study and for attending my earliest Albee rehearsals; and to the Office of the Vice Provost for Research at Indiana University Bloomington for several grants to attend rehearsals in New York, Houston, and elsewhere.

Among my many personal debts, it is a particular pleasure to acknowledge my gratitude to Vinita, Amar, and Vikram Singh for making June and me a part of their family and for opening their Menlo Park home not only to us but also to our extended family.

My work has been enriched by the generous advice, support, and friendship of many colleagues in the profession. Of these numerous colleagues I must especially thank Phillip Zarrilli, John Emigh, Farley Richmond, Kathy Foley, Carol Sorgenfrei, Frank Hildy, Daniel Gerould, Tom Postlewait, and Marvin Carlson.

Taking a longer view, I must say this book, ultimately, was only possible because of the support and encouragement of some remarkable people and institutions, foremost among them William Rajpal, Principal of St. Stephen's College, University of Delhi, who made it possible for me to study at that extraordinary institution, took me under his tutelage, and launched my career. I am also indebted to another institution, St. Stephen's School, Dohad, that even with limited resources provided me a fine education and first sparked my interest in theatre.

Finally, I simply could not have completed this project—that required so much time, over so many years, and in all seasons—without the unflagging support and understanding of my family. I am most grateful to my parents, Horace and Gulab Solomon, who, while not quite sure about the wisdom of pursuing theatre studies, nonetheless remained unstinting in their affectionate support of my endeavors that would eventually lead to this book. For their fond indulgence, I remain deeply grateful, above all, to my wife, June, to her mother, Agnes Sequiera, to my sister Rekha, my brother Felix and his wife Susan, my sister Rita and her husband Vijay, and my nephews Raunak and Reuben and nieces Asha and Aneesha, and, it should go without saying, to my mother and father.

Acknowledgements

For permission to use my previously published articles and interviews, grateful acknowledgment is made to:

Cambridge University Press: "Albee Stages *Marriage Play*: Cascading Action, Audience Taste, and Dramatic Paradox," in Stephen Bottoms, ed., *The Cambridge Companion to Edward Albee* (2005), pp. 164–177.

Routledge: "Forging Text into Theatre: Edward Albee Directs *Box* and *Quotations from Chairman Mao Tse-Tung*," in Bruce J. Mann, ed., *Edward Albee: A Casebook* (2003), pp. 79–91.

American Drama Institute: "Crafting Script into Performance: Edward Albee in Rehearsal," *American Drama* 2, no. 2 (Spring 1993), pp. 76–99.

I wish to acknowledge and thank Shoshanna Green for her copyediting.

Albee
in Performance

1

Albee in the Theatre

*T*he burgeoning ranks of playwrights who direct their own plays are impelled by the modern theatre's predominant characteristic and principal ideal—the control of all performance elements by one theatre artist. Although this role has fallen to the director, almost from the time the modern director emerged many theatre practitioners and theorists have argued that this primacy should instead belong to the playwright. Adolphe Appia insisted in 1921 that the ideal artist to regulate the theatre's interplay of light, music, and movement—which was central to his theories that revolutionized modern stage practice—was the playwright-director: "To specialize these two functions . . . is a sacrilege."[1] Even seminal directors of the modern French theatre, Jacques Copeau, Charles Dullin, and Jean Vilar, accused the non-directing dramatist of abdicating his responsibility. Branding him "a master who has let slip the instrument of his mastery," Copeau argued in 1935 that playwriting and directing "are but two phases of one and the same intellectual operation" and called for "a dramatist who replaces or eliminates the director."[2] Even at the height of his career, the distinguished British director Sir Tyrone Guthrie declared in 1962, "The ideal way of putting on a play is for the author himself to direct it."[3]

Theorist Raymond Williams similarly concluded in 1968 that only a "dramatist directing his own play [can] achieve detailed and continuous control over . . . vital elements of performance"; only then "the unity of text and performance is achieved."[4]

Similar reasoning has led some of the most significant playwrights of the modern theatre to direct professional productions of a substantial number of their own works. Insisting that "the art of producing plays . . . is as much my profession as writing them," Bernard Shaw directed nineteen of his own plays between 1904 and 1924, and he continued to direct or advise at rehearsals for another thirteen years.[5] Bertolt Brecht demonstrated throughout his career a determination to stage his own dramas: he became the *de facto* director of his second play, *Drums in the Night,* in 1922 at the start of his career, and after his return from exile he remained the dominant director of the great Berliner Ensemble productions of his plays until his death in 1956. Samuel Beckett gradually came to direct most of his own plays, and his rehearsal supervision and staging instructions dominated several important productions staged by others. Like Shaw, Brecht, and Beckett, several contemporary playwrights also direct their own plays. Even a brief list of just English-language dramatist-directors, in addition to Beckett, would include such important figures as John Osborne, John Arden, Harold Pinter, Edward Bond, Alan Ayckbourn, David Hare, Caryl Churchill, Athol Fugard, Arthur Miller, Maria Irene Fornes, Sam Shepard, David Mamet, and Edward Albee. Except Edward Albee, however, few of these playwrights have matched the frequency, range, and acumen of Shaw, Brecht, and Beckett's directorial work.

Albee's directorial work is clearly not an isolated, occasional activity, but a regular practicing of his craft: he stands alone among leading modern American playwrights in having directed major professional productions of nearly all his original plays. For more than three decades Albee staged premieres or revivals on and off Broadway, in leading regional theatres, in European theatres, for national and international tours, and for radio. As early as 1961 he directed a professional production of his first play, *The Zoo Story,* only two years after its first production.[6] On Broadway Albee directed the world premieres of *Seascape* (1975) and *The Man Who Had Three Arms* (1983) and the revivals of *The American Dream* (1968) and *Who's Afraid of Virginia Woolf?* (1976).[7] Albee also directed the world premieres of *Listening* (1977), *Finding the Sun* (1982), *Marriage Play* (1987), *Three Tall Women* (1991), and *Fragments: A Concerto Grosso* (1993).[8] His American premiere productions include *Counting the Ways* (1978), *Marriage Play* (1992), *Sand* (1993–1994), and *The Play About the Baby* (2000).[9] In addition, Albee directed all but two productions of the Signature Theatre Company's year-long festival of his plays (1993–1994), which included the New York premiere of *Finding the Sun*. Moreover, Albee directed several of his works in Europe, most frequently in Vienna, where, besides the world premieres of *Marriage Play* and *Three Tall Women*, he staged *The Zoo Story* (1984), *Counting the Ways* (1984), and *Who's Afraid of Virginia Woolf?* For radio Albee co-directed the premiere broadcast of *Listening* (1976) for National Public Radio and the BBC. Furthermore, Albee has staged professional productions of plays by fellow dramatists, including Tennessee Williams, Lanford Wilson, Sam Shepard, David Mamet, and, above all, Samuel Beckett.[10] In a significant recognition of his directorial work, in 1989 Albee was appointed an associate director at one of the nation's oldest and most important regional theatres, the Tony Award–winning Alley Theatre in Houston, where he staged numerous productions of his own works as well as some by Samuel Beckett, notably *Krapp's Last Tape, Ohio Impromptu,* and *Happy Days.*

Albee in Performance examines how this major American playwright transformed written drama into dynamic performance as he staged major professional productions of a representative spectrum of his works. It draws on my personal observation and exhaustive documentation of the rehearsals of fifteen Albee-directed productions since the late-seventies. It documents Albee's directorial work, illuminates his dramaturgy, provides insights into the interpretation of his plays, shows how his texts function on stage, and, more broadly, reveals the way directors make scripts come alive in the myriad constituents of performance. To represent the breadth of Albee's dramatic styles, authorial preoccupations, and long career in the American theatre, the book focuses on his acclaimed early plays like *The Zoo Story* (1959), *The American Dream* (1961), and *The Sandbox* (1960); his preeminent drama widely regarded as a classic of the postwar era, *Who's Afraid of Virginia Woolf?* (1962); his most experimental works to date, *Box* (1968) and *Quotations from Chairman Mao Tse-Tung* (1968); and his plays from the 1980s and 1990s, such as *Marriage Play* (1987) and especially *Three Tall Women* (1991), whose New York premiere in 1994—in a production that bore Albee's directorial imprint from an earlier staging—marked the remarkable resurgence of interest in his work.[11] That Albee renaissance was hailed by the *Village Voice* as "one of the happiest events in the history of American playwriting," and the author was proclaimed by the *New York Times* to be the "American playwright who helped to change the shape of contemporary drama here and abroad."[12]

Albee in Performance interweaves theatre history, performance analysis, and textual criticism to illuminate several key areas. First, it offers a theatre-historical documentation and critique of Albee's directing from prerehearsal preparation to first performance, defines his characteristic methods and overall aesthetic, and situates his work within the historical context of practices of leading modern directors. It especially compares and contrasts him with three eminent dramatist-directors of the twentieth century, Bernard Shaw, Bertolt Brecht, and Samuel Beckett, and with his distinguished and longtime director Alan Schneider, relying particularly on my first-hand record of Schneider's Broadway rehearsals of Albee's *The Lady From Dubuque* and his rehearsals of Beckett's *Waiting for Godot.*

Second, the book delineates in precise and comprehensive detail for each play the multiple performance elements Albee devised to embody his original authorial vision. This record of business, delivery, blocking, tempo, props, settings, costumes, sound, and lighting created or calibrated by Albee constitutes crucial information about how the playwright envisioned each play to work in the theatre. Details of rehearsal deliberations about particular staging problems also suggest practical solutions especially useful for other directors and actors. Third, the study analyzes Albee's decisions and comments in rehearsals—often made with uncharacteristic candor because of the urgency of the situation—for insights into the meaning of his plays and into the dramaturgical considerations that guided their original creation. Locating this discussion within the context of critical scholarship on Albee, it examines how his staging corroborates, modifies, contradicts, or sometimes initiates important critical interpretations. Fourth, it illustrates how Albee's directorial work has altered his playwriting and prompted important revisions in the dialogue, stage directions, and settings of his early plays, providing a record of textual emendations not available elsewhere.

Finally, the book offers a substantial section of excerpts from my extensive personal interviews with the playwright-director and many of his important collaborators. The Albee conversations remain distinct from his other interviews in their sustained attention to matters of rehearsal and performance. They reveal his views on settings, properties, and costumes; on textual interpretation, references, and revisions; on situations, characters, and relationships; and on subtext, timing, rhythm, and tone. The author's comments on these matters offer unique insights into his plays and constitute an exhaustive record of Albee commentary, unmatched in its forthrightness, minute analyses, range of plays, and focus on performance. These remarks are complemented by selections from my interviews with his main actors, designers, and stage managers and with Alan Schneider, permitting these principal players an unmediated voice on Albee in performance, a voice invigorated by the immediacy of dialogue. In chapters 3–9, which focus on different Albee productions, information and quotations are taken (unless otherwise marked) from my own first-hand records of the production's rehearsals and early performances. Contemporaneous comments made outside rehearsals—in personal conversations or interviews—are cited, without dates, as "personal conversation or interview" (abbreviated PCI). Personal interviews dating from the time of *other* productions are provided full reference citations, including dates.

In paying attention to Albee's views on the staging of his plays, the book implicitly argues that a playscript, unlike other literary works, is inherently intermediate in nature. It is a written approximation variously analogized as a performance's mere shadow (Tennessee Williams), spirit (Louis Jouvet), dream (Gaston Baty), design (Vsevolod Meyerhold), libretto (Harley Granville Barker), score (Jacques Copeau), surrogate (J. L. Styan), theory (Albee), seed, or blueprint. This partial pre-text must be completed and actualized in another medium, that of a theatrical performance. Its author's ideas about its proper theatrical realization therefore merit careful attention.

Even if a playscript were regarded as a full-blown literary work, its author's opinions about meaning would not be irrelevant. Even the erstwhile New Critics—contrary to what is commonly but erroneously assumed to be their axiomatic position—concede this point.[13] In fact, W. K. Wimsatt and Monroe C. Beardsley, the high priests of formalist poetics, argued only against using authorial intention as a touchstone for artistic success: that is, against its use for evaluation, not against its use for interpretation. Even though focusing on fully finished literary works, namely lyric poems, their first salvo of Modernist aesthetics granted, "The author must be admitted as a witness to the meaning of his work, and one may even grant special validity to idiosyncratic associations of the author, since at least they will be relevant to the total design."[14] In the last quarter century, however, Modernist literary criticism has been supplanted by postmodernist theory and anonymous discourse that reject not only authorial intention but the very notion of authorship.[15] Yet the more recent advent of cultural history and theory has resurrected both authorial agency and authorial meaning. This book regards the playwright as an autonomous individual who shapes the lineaments of his script to embody his personal vision, and his intentions constitute an essential element in the web of contemporary literary and theatrical practice and reception that together determine the script's many meanings. The study thus treats Albee's intentions and his opinions on the staging and interpretation of his plays, not as a yardstick for measuring his success against avowed aims, nor as canonical or sacred pronouncements, but as crucial theatre-historical evidence as well as compelling textual readings that are at least as valid as those offered by directors, critics, and scholars.

Historical and practical considerations, moreover, argue against privileging Albee's productions as canonical. Albee himself recognizes that he must inevitably change as a playwright, a director, and a human being during the years that in some cases intervene between his writing and directing a play. He also understands that although he conceives a play with the limits of stage production firmly in mind, discrepancies still occur between his original vision and a performance shaped by the exigencies of the casting, rehearsal, and production processes. Moreover, Albee regards rehearsals as the process for testing, refining, and perfecting a text for performance. Consequently, during rehearsals he rearranges, cuts, adds, or otherwise revises his original dialogue and stage directions. In sum, he directs in order to clarify and complete his text through rehearsal and performance—not to proffer a sacrosanct model of authorial conception.

Nevertheless, despite all this, a fundamental unity exists between Albee's written texts and his stage productions. This unity derives from the author-director's focus not so much on fidelity as on authenticity and clarity, on the distillation and communication of the essence of character, situation, and meaning. Principally animating his directing is a resolve to create productions that are both theatrically effective and profoundly truthful to his original vision and intention.

Unlike any other book on a director, on a playwright-director, or on a playwright-and-director team, my study is informed by a singular, fifteen-year, eyewitness perspective on a comprehensive body of rehearsal work. I draw on my detailed records made on the spot during rehearsals of fifteen Albee-directed productions. I typically attended every rehearsal, documented every major staging detail in my own production books, photographed selected scenes and rehearsals, copied the stage manager's production books, and taped interviews with Albee and his actors, designers, and stage manager. No other scholar has had such extensive and prolonged access to Albee productions. I have also had access to Albee's unpublished playscripts and to early drafts of published works.

For purposes of comparison, I followed an identical procedure to acquire parallel data on Alan Schneider's world premiere production of *The Lady From Dubuque*. It is difficult to discuss Albee's directing without reference to Schneider's staging of the first productions of several important Albee plays. By 1978 Schneider had directed eight Albee premieres, including *The American Dream, Who's Afraid of Virginia Woolf?, Tiny Alice* (1964), *A Delicate Balance* (1966), *Box,* and *Quotations from Chairman Mao Tse-Tung.* Albee invariably lists Schneider first among the directors he admires. "As opposed to playwriting, which is an affliction you're born with," Albee says, directing "is a craft, and it can be learned," and he acknowledges his debt to Schneider. "I have learned more about the craft of directing from watching Alan work on a play of mine than from any other source."[16] Besides his crucial influence on Albee and Albee productions, Schneider was a major contemporary director who staged the first American productions of the works of some of the most significant playwrights of the mid-twentieth century, including Harold Pinter, Edward Bond, Tennessee Williams, and, above all, Samuel Beckett. My comments on Schneider also benefit from my documentation of his rehearsals for *Waiting for Godot*, his penultimate production of the contemporary classic before his untimely demise in 1984.[17]

I locate Albee's directorial practices and principles within the main currents of modern directing, which, like modern drama and theatre itself, arose in the 1870s but acquired its present contours only in the twentieth century. I thus compare and contrast Albee with several leading twentieth-century directors, among them Konstantin Stanislavsky and especially Stanislavsky-influenced directors like Lee Strasberg, Harold Clurman, and Elia Kazan, who emerged out of the Group Theatre in the 1930s and went on to redefine American acting and directing in the 1940s and 1950s; Jacques Copeau and Jean Vilar, who shaped French theatre practice in the interwar years and beyond; and Peter Brook and Ingmar Bergman, contemporary directors internationally acclaimed for their dazzling and innovative but faithful renditions of Western classics as well as new drama. Above all, I trace parallels between Albee and this century's most distinguished dramatist-directors, Bernard Shaw, Bertolt Brecht, and Samuel Beckett.

These various directors and dramatist-directors represent many different philosophical and ideological viewpoints, yet my comparisons of them with Albee reveal remarkable congruence in their directorial practices and in their basic approach to theatrical art. They all bring a commitment to preserving a text's integrity and rendering its author's philosophical and artistic intent truthfully. This conviction consistently informed Stanislavsky's directing, even at those times when some of his stage effects drove Chekov to delirium, and it is shared even by Peter Brook, the most radical director among them, who also asserts the inviolability of the text: "That line exists, and it helps you; it doesn't change; you change."[18] In pointed contrast to Vsevolod Meyerhold, Antonin Artaud, and Jerzy Grotowski, most of these directors and playwright-directors are unencumbered by grand theories and programs for revolutionizing directorial or theatrical art. They also show a thoroughly pragmatic and eclectic approach to directing, viewing any method that can achieve a desired result in the theatre as inherently valid. Even Bertolt Brecht, despite his theories, remained immensely pragmatic, invariably discarding the theoretical when it clashed with the practical proof of what worked on stage. All of them, moreover, fall within a central stream of Western theatre which regards the art as fundamentally mimetic and representational and directing as fundamentally interpretive and illustrative, a view embodied in Bernard Shaw's definition of directing as "the art of making the audience believe that real things are happening to real people."[19]

Belonging as he does to this main tradition, Albee, as will be evident from the practices and statements examined in this study, subscribes to a theory of the director that defines him as one who interprets, represents, and embodies within a mise en scene a written text and its inner life, and not an auteur who uses a text to create a fundamentally new work, as epitomized by Meyerhold. Albee's theory, predictably for a playwright, rejects the claims of directorial supremacy over the play text made by Meyerhold and his recent American avatars like Richard Schechner, Peter Sellars, and Robert Wilson, who virtually create new works with their own metaphorical, conceptual, or ideological extrapolation from other people's texts, often by radically reconceptualizing, cutting, rearranging, rewriting, or interpolating those texts. In sharp contrast, asserting the primacy of the text, Albee defines directing as a secondary-level imaginative endeavor that must intermediate, translate, and actualize a text on stage—as distinct from playwriting, which he defines as a primary-level imaginative endeavor almost capable of *creatio ex nihilo*—of creating a new work out of nothing.

Albee in Performance also suggests how Albee's directorial practices and preferences hint at the nature of his influence as a playwright on the crucial original productions of his plays directed by others. The *New York Times* pointed out in 1968 that unlike other playwrights—whether "new . . . [or] established"—"Edward Albee has managed to take control of virtually all of the pertinent aspects of the production of his own work."[20] Vigorously exercising the prerogative ensured him by the Dramatists' Guild standard contract, Albee from early in his career has been actively involved in most aspects of production, from the choice of director, designers, and cast—including understudies—to the specifics of staging. "During rehearsals" of these productions, Albee asserts, "I maintain as total control as I can. I always retain final approval over the cast and director. I am consulted about the theatre being used. And I also supervise or exert control over the set, the costumes, the lighting. . . . I retain the right to fire the director."[21] Schneider recounts in his autobiography, *Entrances: An American Director's Journey,* that halfway through the rehearsals of *The Zoo Story,* even though the work was the playwright's first American production, Albee, together with producer Richard Barr, fired director Milton Katselas and took over the directing, a change not indicated in the program.[22] During the casting of the Broadway production of *A Delicate Balance* in 1966, Schneider laments, "My dream of working with Alfred Lunt and Lynn Fontanne vanished" because "Edward was determined to assert his writer's prerogatives."[23] In a personal letter Albee confirmed that he had indeed insisted on casting other actors; he also clarified, however, that he "didn't reject" the Lunt-Fontanne star duo but did demand "to go elsewhere" in view of their hesitancy and delay in making a firm commitment to the play.[24] Even when *A Delicate Balance* rehearsals were underway—with Jessica Tandy as Agnes, Hume Cronin as Harry, and Rosemary Murphy as Claire—Schneider writes that Albee, unhappy with Murphy's work, "threatened to replace her—with or without my approval."[25]

Albee's directing has frequently earned excellent reviews. In the *New York Times,* Dan Sullivan praised Albee's "clean, knowing work" as director of *The American Dream* on Broadway in 1968.[26] Reviewing Albee's staging of *Seascape* on Broadway in 1975, Clive Barnes noted in the *New York Times,* "Albee has directed . . . with self-evident skill and ease," and praised him for resolving "the directorial difficulty" of making the giant lizards simultaneously "strange . . . yet credible . . . by virtually choreographing the sea creatures."[27] Discussing that production in a *New York Times* article, Walter Kerr also observed that "Albee has directed his actors well."[28] Albee's 1976 production of *Who's Afraid of Virginia Woolf?* on Broadway was described by Martin Gottfried in the *New York Post* as a "superlative one . . . directed with finesse. . . . Albee's direction is superb"; the author's staging is "one to watch and not merely to hear"; the direction "join[s] the play and the production into a driving experience."[29] Walter Kerr wrote in the *New York Times,* "He has, in fact, directed very well. . . . [T]he pacing is furious but clean and clear."[30] *Newsweek's* Jack Kroll observed, "Albee's direction . . . brings a new balance" and clarity; the author-director "has given us a definitive reading."[31] *Time's* T. E. Kalem announced that Albee's "revival is triumphant," and the Associated Press's William Glover declared, "Albee scores brilliantly as director."[32]

Albee's directing of *Counting the Ways* and *Listening* at the Hartford Stage Company in 1977 received similarly favorable notices. "Meticulously directed," pronounced Clive Barnes in the *New York Times,* and Mark Boyer of the *Hartford Advocate* commented, "Albee directs . . . with a marked restraint. . . . clarity and simplicity honor the integrity of the text."[33] Malcolm L. Johnson asserted in the *Hartford Courant,* "The playwright shows himself to be a lucid and deliberate director . . . able to get a feeling of spontaneity from his players"; "the playwright has directed . . . with cogency and skill."[34] Albee's directorial work for the Signature Theatre Company's 1993–1994 season of his plays earned high praise from both the *New York Times* and the *Village Voice*. Reviewing his staging of *Sand*—a triple bill that included the New York City premiere of *Finding the Sun* and revivals of *Box* and *The Sandbox*—Vincent Canby concluded in the *New York Times,* "As his own director, Mr. Albee beautifully serves himself with *Sand.* . . . Mr. Albee has directed . . . with skill, humor and an excellent cast."[35] Michael Feingold in the *Village Voice* lauded "Albee's low-key staging" and his "fine cast . . . [with] three standouts" in *Finding the Sun.* Comparing them to Alan Schneider's original productions "three decades ago," Feingold commended Albee's direction of *The Sandbox* for "revealing the script's perfect balance," and rated his *Box* superior to the "1968 Broadway rendition [, which] failed to convey what Albee's simple staging now makes instantly clear."[36]

Such critical acclaim does not, of course, explain what impels Albee to stage his own plays, but his interview remarks suggest several reasons. Albee directs a play in order to recreate with maximum precision and theatrical effectiveness the performance he envisioned when writing it—to convey, as he told the BBC, its "look, sound, feel, and smell."[37] In a personal interview he also reasoned, "I probably have a special insight into the nature of the characters I've created that no other director could have," and he told the *Los Angeles Times,* "I probably can help [actors] with their character's subtext more than an ordinary director. I'm the one who created the subtext in the first place."[38] Albee cites imprecision in the theatre as another reason. Following his Broadway staging of *Seascape* Albee asserted in 1975, "I watched twelve of my plays directed by other people, and I looked at *Seascape* directed by me. I don't think that anybody else comes any closer to my intention than I do as a director."[39] By staging his own plays he eliminates at least one of the many interpreters through whom his vision must be transmitted. He argues that his script has to "filter from the page through the director, through the actor, across the footlights, to the audience, to, God help us, the critic. We can at least cut out one step."[40] In essence, then, Albee directs to convey his conception and intention, his text and subtext, with the precision, detail, and insight that only he as author can achieve.

Most directors build their production on the foundation of authorial conception and intention, which they perforce seek through textual analysis, empirical investigation, and, most reliably, through authorial advice—whether in print or in person. As Louis Jouvet, who staged the plays of Jean Giraudoux, Jean Genet, and Jean Paul Sartre, explained, "To direct a production means . . . finding the spiritual mood that was the poet's at the play's conception and during its writing."[41] Even Charles Marowitz—Peter Brook's co-director for the landmark Theatre of Cruelty season, a radical rearranger of Shakespeare's plays into collage performances, and a fierce asserter of directorial hegemony over all other theatre artists—grants that often "writers . . . can be of invaluable assistance in rehearsals, acting as a kind of Geiger counter detecting false notes and wrong turnings."[42] Elia Kazan had Tennessee Williams, Arthur Miller, or Robert Anderson next to him during rehearsals, receiving from them written notes, whispered responses to questions, blocking suggestions, and even movement demonstrations.[43] Understanding authorial conception and intent were central to Kazan's approach to directing. Looking back at his career, he summed up the essence of his method: "I tried to think and feel like the author. . . . I tried to *be* the author."[44] But this is extraordinarily difficult, if not impossible. Even Alan Schneider, despite years of prior artistic collaboration with Albee and despite countless discussions with him both before and during *The Lady From Dubuque* rehearsals, confessed in a personal interview an hour before the opening night curtain that his production could not be what the author had envisioned. "He sees it differently. He wrote it, and he sees it a certain way."[45] Making a parallel argument, playwright Jean Anouilh, a pivotal figure in the modern French theatre, explained why he began staging his own plays in spite of several successful productions by his distinguished director, Andre Barsacq: "Because whispering into someone's ear every five minutes saying, 'It would be better to do it this way' is not the same thing as to take charge."[46] Similar reasoning drives Albee to direct his own plays, just as it had compelled Shaw to conclude, "The most desirable director of a play is the author."[47]

Although unfailingly gracious in paying tribute to his past directors, Albee, on rare occasions, has also acknowledged that one motivation for his directing is "to set the record straight" on some of his plays first staged by others.[48] Over the years he has hinted at what he found problematic in other directors' staging of his works. Among the lapses mentioned are misinterpretation of character or play, emotional imbalance, distracting or disproportionate stress on sets and props, insufficient comedy, and, above all, lack of clarity. In an interview with me, for instance, Albee offered an unusually explicit appraisal of *Who's Afraid of Virginia Woolf?* as staged by Schneider: "That production got criticized by a couple of critics . . . [who] couldn't believe that a couple as intelligent as George and Martha could believe that they had a child. They never *did* believe it. So either [they] intentionally misunderstood, or the production led [them] to misunderstand. So that's one of the reasons I started directing this play: to correct that misinterpretation of the nature of the play."[49] Albee's 1976 Broadway revival of the play made it crystal clear that while George and Martha feel deeply about the child, they never believe that it actually exists. In other departures from Schneider's production, Albee's directing brought greater focus on Martha's vulnerability and sexuality but downplayed her emotional intensity, rendered Nick and Honey more feisty and equal combatants, greatly speeded up the pace and shed several minutes of playing time, and, overall, revealed a considerably funnier play.

Like Albee, the British dramatists John Arden and Edward Bond both began directing their own plays out of a growing dissatisfaction with productions staged by others. Bond, for example, felt that his early director, William Gaskill, no longer fully shared his perspective or conveyed his vision.[50] Unlike them, Samuel Beckett embarked on his directorial career out of a disappointment with his own early texts, which he declared he had not properly visualized in stage terms. Pronouncing *Waiting for Godot,* for instance, "a mess" and "not well thought out," he resolved in his preliminary directorial notebook for the 1976 Berlin Schiller-Theater production "to give form to the confusion."[51]

Not all playwrights are so objective. Albee understands this, and so he also concedes that not all playwrights necessarily make effective directors. As Harold Clurman reasoned, "one capacity does not necessarily imply the other."[52] Indeed, Albee asserts, "A lot of playwrights shouldn't get near their own plays. They're hysterics; they can't work with actors; they think conceptually instead of practically."[53] A playwright should direct only if he has enough objectivity about his own work so he's not protective of its faults.

Besides objectivity, Albee lists other prerequisites for a dramatist-director: sustained study of the craft of directing, rigorous practicality, willingness to revise the text, skill in speaking to actors on their own terms, willingness to allow actors creative freedom, and a capacity for hard, meticulous, even tedious work. Albee's list naturally reflects his own goals as a playwright-director and also serves as one measure by which to assess his directorial work.

Albee in Performance fills a serious gap in Albee scholarship. Little published material exists on the subject of Albee's directing, other than the occasional sentence or two in reviews, a handful of newspaper and magazine features, and a few of my articles and interviews drawn from the present study. The lack in directorial studies in general results partly from the longstanding academic bias in favor of studying drama as literature rather than as performance, especially in the case of plays of linguistic and literary sophistication such as Albee's, and partly from the inherent difficulty of studying rehearsals, which are ephemeral and almost always private, in contrast to easily accessible published literary texts. Despite the litany of calls within the academy over many years for stage-centered scholarship, studies of Albee have largely followed literary-critical models that

Harry Berger calls the slit-eyed analyses of armchair interpreters.[54] In contrast, *Albee in Performance* offers the first sustained analysis of how a broad range of Albee texts function in the theatre. It is also the first to use Albee's directing for insights into his meaning and his dramaturgy. Its record of Albee's staging, moreover, will allow further consideration of these plays, not simply as literary texts or even as theatrical interpretations by particular directors, but as plays-in-performance created by the dramatist-director. Furthermore, since Albee revises his texts during rehearsals, this study is also the first to document how he has emended his earlier works and how his dramatic and theatrical aesthetic has evolved over the years. Publishers may eventually issue new critical editions of all his works, but currently many published texts of his plays perpetuate details of dialogue, scenic directions, and decor that the author has long since revised or even renounced.

In sum, *Albee in Performance* presents a portrait of the dramatist at work on realizing his plays on stage—a portrait that reveals him as a compleat man of the theatre, with a command of both the playwright's and the director's craft and with a profound awareness that a performance lives not simply through an author's words, but through all the elements of the mise en scene, most especially the actors. Ultimately, *Albee in Performance* delineates how Albee authored *performance* texts, well beyond his verbal-literary texts, and in this double authoring attained the ideal of a "single will reign[ing] in our theatre," which Vladimir Nemirovich-Danchenko, Stanislavsky's principal collaborator and co-director at the Moscow Art Theatre, proclaimed "the first and most significant" characteristic of the modern theatre.[55]

2

Casting Practices and Director's Preparation

*A*lbee's approach to casting logically emerges from his authorial attitude toward characterization. From his earliest manuscript drafts to his final printed texts Albee eschews detailed character description, whether physical, psychological, or sociological. None of his original characters is given more than a first name (Jerry and Peter in *The Zoo Story,* George and Martha in *Who's Afraid of Virginia Woolf?*); a majority are provided generic names (Mommy, Daddy, Grandma, and Young Man in *The American Dream* and *The Sandbox*); some are simply assigned pronouns (He and She in *Counting the Ways* and *Marriage Play*[1]); and a few are identified merely by letters (A, B, and C in *Three Tall Women*). Embodying an exactly opposite attitude, Bernard Shaw delineated his characters in very concrete terms: he not only provided full names for almost all his characters, but specified minute details of their appearance and manners, emotional and mental make-up, personal and social relationships, and political and social views. Albee and Shaw's contrasting attitudes toward characterization determine their distinct casting principles and practices.

When choosing an actor, Albee considers a performer's acting skill and intelligence more important than his personality traits or physical attributes. His philosophy is implicit in his praise of actor Eileen Burns's ability, quite contrary to her real-life personality, to grasp the essence of the Long-Winded Lady in *Quotations from Chairman Mao Tse-Tung:* "Look at Eileen, who comes across off stage as a dizzy, *strange* lady. [Yet] I've never had anybody give, right at the first rehearsal, a more accurate representation of a character. . . . She *was* the character."[2] Such an approach to casting, especially in the context of unanticipated financial constraints, allowed Albee to justify his hiring only five actors, albeit highly proficient performers (including Eileen Burns), to play twenty-two roles when he directed a repertory of eight of his plays (several of which are discussed in detail in the following pages). In that instance, for the purpose of casting, Albee subsumed twenty-two of his characters into four broad stock-company types distinguished only by age and gender: Young Man, Older Man, Young Woman, and Older Woman 1 and 2. Clearly listing these types in his audition announcement, he picked each actor according to how well his talent and craft would enable him to play three or four distinct roles within his broad category, rather than according to how nearly he approached a character's particular personality or physical attributes. Albee thus filled these nearly two dozen roles with only five actors. He subsequently added another actor to mitigate the excessive physical demands of so much doubling, but the essence of his approach to casting remained intact. In a marked contrast, but not an unpredictable one for a dramatist notorious for copious descriptions of his *dramatis personae,* Shaw stressed that when casting, "the director should not be concerned with whether the actors understand the play, but whether their ages, appearances, and personalities are suitable."[3]

Albee's approach finds support in the practices of several more recent directors. Playwright-director Bertolt Brecht declared, "It is pure folly to allot parts according to physical characteristics," and director Elia Kazan announced, "I never cast by looks because looks are false."[4] As Kazan's sometime mentor, Harold Clurman, argued, "An actor's looks will impress an audience initially but after his first five minutes on stage it becomes aware of what he or she communicates (or fails to communicate) through *acting.*"[5] Articulated after more than forty years of directing in professional theatre, Clurman's conclusion testifies to the soundness of Albee's casting practice, which, admittedly, also reflects changed ideas about the crafts of acting and directing since the time of Shaw.

Even when not required by any contractual agreements, Albee likes to use Equity Principal Auditions as far as possible to cast all or some of his actors. Such auditions, most significantly, are open to all members of the actors' union, Actors' Equity Association, and are monitored by the union and follow its audition procedures. For the Signature Theatre Company's year-long season dedicated to his works, Albee cast several plays entirely through this open process. Similarly, for his world premiere production of *Marriage Play* at Vienna's English Theatre in 1987, he picked Kathleen Butler for the play's single female character at an Equity Principal Audition in New York. Butler marveled about it even several years later: "He literally picked me out of a chorus! . . . It was an open call. An open call!"[6] As is common practice, Albee announces his auditions in New York City theatrical trade papers like *Variety, Backstage,* and *Show Business.* In view of the large number of actors at such auditions, he restricts evaluative notes to an absolute minimum. Yet he makes it a point to speak individually to each actor, no matter how briefly. Comments from the Actors' Equity Association office and from actors—including those not called back for readings—indicate that, brevity notwithstanding, such consideration is extraordinary.[7] On the basis of these interviews Albee, as is usual, calls back a few actors for readings—the crucial part of the selection process—during which he focuses on assessing each performer's craft, vocal range, and presence. With resumes, photographs, and questionnaires in hand and with interviews and readings fresh in mind, Albee makes his final selections. His overall judgments, scribbled in nearly illegible writing on pocket notebook sheets or audition questionnaires, remain characteristically terse: representative are such minimal comments as "Very good!! Quite possible," "Fine," "Good reading," and "Of course."

Most New York directors, of course, typically cast from among performers they have admired or worked with previously—even in those few calls nominally open to all Equity actors because of contractual obligations. Albee, like them, often casts actors he has previously worked with, either as a director or as a playwright participating in a production. Thus even for his Vienna *Marriage Play* cast, although he chose Kathleen Butler via an open call, he had precast Tom Klunis as Jack, the play's other character: he had directed him earlier in *Counting the Ways* at the Alley Theatre in Houston in 1986 and in *The Zoo Story* and *Counting the Ways* at Vienna's English Theatre in 1984. Likewise in 1992, when staging the American premiere of *Marriage Play* at the Alley Theatre, he again turned to actors from his Vienna production of that play. When he directed the Broadway production of *The Man Who Had Three Arms* in 1983, Albee cast William Prince as the Man and Patricia Kilgarriff as the Woman, both of whom he had directed in earlier productions. Similarly, for the world premiere production of *Three Tall Women* in Vienna in 1991, Albee turned to actors he knew from earlier work: for A (then called the Old Woman) he chose Myra Carter, who had performed in *The Lady From Dubuque* and *All Over* at the Hartford Stage Company and in *A Delicate*

Balance at the Arena Stage in Washington, D.C.; for B (then called the Middle-Aged Woman) he returned to Kathleen Butler; and for C (then called the Young Woman) he tapped Cynthia Bassham, whom he had directed as Honey in the 1990 Alley Theatre production of *Who's Afraid of Virginia Woolf?*

Even when not directing, Albee sometimes keeps particular actors in mind for specific roles well in advance of auditions. After completing the first draft of *The Lady From Dubuque* in August 1978, he confided that actor Maureen Anderman would be ideal in the role of Carol.[8] He had previously directed her on Broadway in *Seascape* (1975) and *Who's Afraid of Virginia Woolf?* (1976) and at the Hartford Stage Company in *Listening* (1977). When Alan Schneider directed *The Lady From Dubuque* on Broadway in January 1980, Albee was instrumental in having Anderman cast as Carol. Some years earlier, for the film version of *Who's Afraid of Virginia Woolf?* he had envisioned Bette Davis and James Mason, and for the Broadway *Seascape* he had first considered Katherine Hepburn and Henry Fonda.[9] Albee thinks of specific actors, however, only after he completes the initial writing process: "I try to empty my mind of all actors when I write. Otherwise I would be writing a role rather than a character."[10] He claims he has never written for specific performers. "In fact, when I'm writing, and I begin to see, or hear, real actors," he asserts, "I put the play down for a few hours until the real people go away. . . . When the play is finished is the time to cast, and not before."[11]

Albee's casting skills and instincts were developed during his decades of experience as a playwright who actively used his contractual rights to demand the final say in the selection of actors for his plays directed by others. Albee's insistence on "always retain[ing] final approval over the cast" allowed him to overrule Alan Schneider's preferences on several occasions.[12] Despite Schneider's reservations, in 1966 the dramatist prevailed on Schneider to cast Pendleton as Gerard Girard in *Malcolm* on Broadway, and in 1968 he again insisted on casting Wyman Pendleton as Chairman Mao for the Broadway production of *Quotations from Chairman Mao Tse-Tung.*[13] During preparations for *A Delicate Balance* in 1966, as already noted, Albee overruled both director Schneider and producers Richard Barr and Clinton Wilder to seek new leads in place of the proposed star couple, Alfred Lunt and Lynn Fontanne, whose conditional acceptance he disapproved of.[14] In the American premiere of *Three Tall Women,* directed by Lawrence Sacharow in 1994, Albee played a decisive role in the casting of Myra Carter as A.[15] Although Albee and Schneider may have occasionally disagreed about the choice of a particular actor, both agreed on the critical significance of casting, most especially for the first production of a play. Albee would no doubt concur with Schneider's characterization of the importance of casting for a director: "It represents choosing the proper battlefield on which he will win or lose. Casting a new play often determines not only its success or failure but its very nature."[16]

Albee as author actively immerses himself in all aspects of the selection process, unlike Beckett, who even when directing found auditions unnerving and who almost invariably had his plays precast for him.[17] During *The Lady From Dubuque* auditions, for example, Albee not only interviewed actors for principal and secondary roles but spent time in selecting understudies as well. More than a year prior to the March 1981 opening of his adaptation of Vladimir Nabokov's *Lolita,* directed by Frank Dunlop, the playwright searched outside the theatre for an actress to play the title role. His humorous remark contained a grain of truth: "[I] wander around the subways looking strangely at 9- and 10-year-old girls. Mothers are giving me the oddest looks."[18] His intimate participation in casting stems from a belief that the secret of mounting a successful production lies in choosing a good script and a good cast. "Three-quarters of the trick of directing," he once declared to the *New York Times,* "is to start with a good play and good actors."[19] Harold Clurman used to make an identical case: "'Choose a good script,' I sometimes advise students, 'cast good actors—and you'll all be good directors.'"[20] Elia Kazan's famous quip echoed the same idea: "*Streetcar* had no problem, all you had to do was cast it right, and anybody could have directed it."[21]

Albee's actions as a dramatist seem unusual in the light of Clurman's overview of practices in recent theatre. Drawing upon his long directorial experience working with an array of dramatists—from Clifford Odets, Maxwell Anderson, and Lillian Hellman to Tennessee Williams and Arthur Miller—Clurman asserts, "In America . . . the author is contractually the pivot of the organized production"; but, either because of timidity or a lack of practical theatre expertise, "the playwright very rarely exercises his legal right."[22] A practiced theatre craftsman and an assertive man, Albee remains notable among prominent American dramatists in exerting so much control over the casting of his plays.

Moreover, as a director of many of his own plays on Broadway and elsewhere, Albee has further enhanced his casting skill and experience. In the sentence or two that newspaper and magazine reviewers usually devote to specifics of directing, they often laud Albee's casting. Martin Gottfried of the *New York Post* praised the aptness of Albee's "cast[ing] classical actors" like Deborah Kerr and Barry Nelson in *Seascape* to match "his writing[, which] is so literary and poetic."[23] Clive Barnes of the *New York Times* and Henry Hewes of the *Saturday Review* also praised Albee's casting for that production. Barnes commended him for his "carefully picked" cast, and Hewes found the casting "unusual" but lauded him for selecting performers perfectly suited for that work—actors "excellent at keeping a comic tone in a play that is in great danger of slipping into a sober realism."[24] In his *New York Times* review of the Albee-directed *Who's Afraid of Virginia Woolf?* Barnes compared the author's staging favorably with its original production and praised him for clarifying and reaffirming the play's heterosexuality "partly, perhaps largely, by his casting."[25] In his weekly *New York Times* column, "Stage View," Walter Kerr echoed Clive Barnes in praising Albee for scotching, through his casting, the rumor that *Virginia Woolf?* was actually about homosexuals. By selecting Colleen Dewhurst and Maureen Anderman, Kerr argued, Albee demonstrated that "the play's two women . . . are—on the evidence of our eyes and ears—incontestably women." Kerr also found that the author-director gave credibility to the continued presence of the young couple, "given their initial scathing reception"; they "seem to belong on the barricades more than their predecessors did."[26] Also commenting in the *New York Times,* Mel Gussow justified the revival itself by citing the contribution made by Albee's casting.[27]

As a director preparing for a production, Albee chooses not to make any changes in his scripts prior to rehearsals, although he may later depart from his original text and even introduce new performance elements. Especially when directing a revival—a theatrical term he detests and shuns—Albee believes that the text has already been trimmed sufficiently during rehearsals of its first production, whether directed by him or others.[28] Moreover, he claims his texts are already quite "tightly constructed," since he typically keeps a play in his head for a long time in order to mentally "rewrite" it before actually putting it down on paper. During his "three months at the typewriter to write a play," he makes "revisions on each page at the end of each day's work"; later, while doing "an entire second draft," he revises again.[29] In view of these earlier revisions, any additional alteration of lines or business, Albee insists, must emerge from work during rehearsals: "Why would I make a theoretical cut when in rehearsal I can make a practical cut?"[30] Not all playwright-directors share this attitude. George Bernard Shaw often made prerehearsal changes when staging revivals of his plays. As co-director of the 1921 revival of *Heartbreak House,* Shaw deleted over sixty lines from the third act of the 1919 version; for Max Reinhardt's production of *Caesar and Cleopatra,* the dramatist advised dropping the entire lighthouse act (act 3) from the 1898 original.[31]

Albee also differs from dramatist-directors like Bernard Shaw and Samuel Beckett in preferring not to compose a director's notebook when preparing to stage his own plays. He declares, "I keep everything in my head!" Given his habit of a long prerehearsal period of meditation on the play he is getting ready to direct, he claims, "I have a pretty good idea of the way I want the play to look and the way I want the play to sound."[32] In addition, he makes mental notes about specific scenes, problem areas, and the overall blocking. "Even when I am not absolutely sure of the physical placement," he asserts, "I pretty much know the psychology of the blocking that I want."[33] Thus he sees no need for transcription: "I've merely got to try to remember what was in my head."[34] Albee's plunging into rehearsals without a director's book recalls Jean Vilar's proclamation early in his career that "I have no papers, no notes, no written plans. Nothing in my hands, nothing up my sleeves."[35] In contrast, Shaw insisted on a promptbook that specified, in words and diagrams, "every entry, movement, rising and sitting, disposal of hat and umbrella."[36] Beckett too prepared meticulous handwritten director's notebooks—one eighty-five pages long, another in two volumes—marking rehearsal scene divisions and specifying matters that required particular work, ranging from minutiae of physical staging to philosophical patterning.[37] Beckett, however, preferred never to refer to these notebooks during rehearsals.[38] Ingmar Bergman too created highly detailed director's books—"I have to prepare precisely for every little movement, in every little detail."[39] Several Bergman actors have noted that while he "is incredibly good at casting," "above all, he is unique in the extraordinary preparations he goes to. In his proposals for blocking he knows exactly how we will look, what the setting will look like."[40] Although Bergman "work[ed] like hell . . . sitting at home and working things out mathematically down to the last millimeter," he was flexible about changing details to suit his actors, and, like Beckett, he too never consulted his notebooks during rehearsals.[41]

Albee, without a director's promptbook or even a script, accurately recalls not only every line and stage direction but even minor details of textual emphasis and punctuation. But more crucially—beyond familiarity with word, emphasis, or punctuation—Albee as the author claims a "special insight" regarding what a "play is about" and regarding "the concepts he wanted to write into it."[42] Analyses of similar matters are principally what most directors commit to their notebooks. Elia Kazan jotted down such conceptual planning in his notebooks, defining directing as "half-conceptual, the core of it—you get into what the events mean, what you're trying to express," and half "just work."[43] "The producer's business, when faced either with a new script or . . . old," Tyrone Guthrie insisted, "is first of all to decide what it is about."[44] "The first thing I write on the blank pages of my production notebook," Alan Schneider emphasized, is "what the play is 'about,' as well as what its tone or texture should be. . . . [This] is the director's main concern—and contribution."[45] As the author, Albee considers preparing such a director's notebook unnecessary.

Albee does believe, however, that as a director, his "job is to plot out [his] work very carefully."[46] He certainly makes an overall plan and a schedule of what he will rehearse each day, but he likes to be sufficiently open to allow "for improvising, for a certain amount of on-the-spot intuitive directing."[47] Thus, despite preparing a daily schedule, he is prepared "to be flexible enough to revise that schedule every day," as determined by the progress of his work with the actors.[48] Notwithstanding any prerehearsal planning, Albee strives to remain flexible enough as a director "to surprise [himself] with new solutions."[49] How well did Albee's substantial casting experience and expertise—gained both as a supervising dramatist and as a director—serve him as he selected actors for the productions under consideration in this study, how good was his prerehearsal reflection and preparation for effective and creative directing, and how flexible and intuitive did he prove in improvising practical as well as imaginative solutions during rehearsals? These are some of the questions the following pages seek to answer.

3

The American Dream

*T*he first production of *The American Dream* at the York Playhouse, in January 1961, consolidated Albee's reputation as off-Broadway's most versatile and significant playwright. Astonishingly, this estimation had mushroomed during the preceding fifteen months, beginning with the first performance of *The Zoo Story* in Berlin in September 1959, which was followed in quick succession by American and European productions of *The Death of Bessie Smith, The Sandbox,* and *Fam and Yam.* Running for 360 performances, *The American Dream* elicited wide coverage from such major publications as the *New York Times,* the *New York Herald Tribune,* the *New York Post, Theatre Arts, The New Yorker, Nation, Horizon, Saturday Review,* and *Life.* Soon *The American Dream,* together with *The Zoo Story,* ranked among the most frequently produced plays at college and university campuses and at adventurous regional theatres, further contributing to Albee's national reputation.

The American Dream presents a scathing critique of American society through the grotesque portrait of a family devoid of love, decency, and humanity. With an openness unmatched in his subsequent authorial pronouncements, Albee declared his goal in a preface at the time of the play's publication: "The play is an examination of the American Scene, an attack on the substitution of artificial for real values . . . a condemnation of complacency, cruelty, emasculation, and vacuity; it is a stand against the fiction that everything in this slipping land of ours is peachy-keen."[1] Deeply rooted within an American cultural milieu, *The American Dream* nonetheless offers insights into all human behavior. In this satirical comedy Albee principally employs linguistic and social parody, broad exaggeration often approaching farce, and several techniques then most associated with the Absurdist playwrights, especially Eugene Ionesco, such as clichés and platitudes, pointless nuances and stories, bizarre events, and a proliferation of objects. (One side effect of these techniques was critics' frequent mislabeling of Albee as an Absurdist, most prominently in Martin Esslin's influential *The Theatre of the Absurd*.)

As *The American Dream* opens, middle-aged Mommy and Daddy exchange inanities while waiting in their stuffy apartment for Mrs. Barker, whose name and reason for coming escape them. With perverse pleasure Mommy bullies Daddy and brags about how she demands satisfaction as an implacable consumer. When Grandma, her eighty-six-year-old mother, joins them, Mommy is monstrous toward her: she inflicts insults and cruelties and threatens to have her carted away to a nursing home by a "van man." Spunky, witty, and compassionate, Grandma offers home truths that prick Mommy and Daddy's smugness and hypocrisy while she mysteriously covers the living room floor with nicely wrapped boxes containing her belongings. Upon Mrs. Barker's arrival Mommy struggles at playing the gracious hostess, mindful that the visitor is the chairman of their woman's club. Like Mommy and Daddy, Mrs. Barker is clueless about the purpose of her visit. Grandma, however, explains it to her when they are alone in the living room. Mommy and Daddy have summoned her because she works for the Bye Bye Adoption Service, from which they adopted a "bumble of joy" twenty years ago. As the baby failed to live up to their expectations, they had mutilated it part by part until one day "it finally up and died." They therefore "wanted their money back" (101).

While Mrs. Barker, Mommy, and Daddy mysteriously stumble in the kitchen in search of a glass of water, the Young Man walks in the front door and offers Grandma his services—he is willing to do "almost anything that pays" (109). He turns out to be the identical twin of the boy Mommy and Daddy mutilated. Wily Grandma offers him a job, improvising a solution for both herself and Mrs. Barker. Grandma leaves, telling Mrs. Barker to pass off the Young Man as her agency's replacement for the unsatisfactory baby and to inform Mommy and Daddy that she has been taken away by a van man. Mommy and Daddy return, miss Grandma for a moment, but quickly turn to celebrating the happy resolution of their complaint, and Grandma steps out of the fictional stage space to tell the audience that since "this is a comedy," it had better end when "everybody's got what he wants . . . or everybody's got what he thinks he wants" (127).

Albee first directed *The American Dream* in 1968 on Broadway and returned to it ten years later to stage it on a double bill with *The Zoo Story*, as part of a three-evening repertory of his shorter works spanning the first two decades of his career, from 1958 to 1978. The repertory consisted of the other early plays *Fam and Yam* and *The Sandbox*, the stylistically radical and challenging works *Box* and *Quotations from Chairman Mao Tse-Tung*, and his newest plays at that time, *Counting the Ways* and *Listening*, which received their New York City premieres as part of this festival of author-directed plays entitled *Albee Directs Albee*. While *The American Dream* was paired with *The Zoo Story* for one evening's bill, continuing a tradition of joint staging unequalled by any other pair of Albee plays, for the other two bills *Fam and Yam* and *The Sandbox* were grouped with *Box* and *Quotations from Chairman Mao Tse-Tung*, and *Counting the Ways* was matched with *Listening*, with comedies in all cases preceding serious works and separated by an intermission. This repertory constituted the entire roster of his shorter plays up to that date (with the sole exception of *The Death of Bessie Smith*, which Albee called "economically impossible" because it required three additional actors; PCI). These plays, their one-act form notwithstanding, are for the most part serious, substantial works, some seventy to eighty pages long in their published versions. "There's no proper *duration* for any work of art," he stressed in an interview; "what is good in art is that which is inevitable." Albee attaches special significance to the one-act form: he has written almost as many one-act plays as he has written two- and three-act plays. Impatient with some plays that stretch out to three acts, he once quipped, "I don't see any purpose for plays to go on forty-five minutes after they're over."[2] A one-act drama is "not an anecdote, a diminishment," he asserts, "it's an intense statement without pause."[3] Reviewing the *Albee Directs Albee* plays, Sylvie Drake, the theatre critic of the *Los Angeles Times,* called them "an edifying encounter with the writer's mind . . . a perceptible lode of complex thought." Moreover, she asserted, "span[ning] a 20-year period," these plays "reveal Albee's consistent and enduring concerns" as well as tracing the trajectory of his "austere and clinical" style as it becomes progressively distilled and "intensified."[4] In a similar vein, Allan Jalon of the New York City weekly *The Westsider* stressed how well the plays "illustrate every phase of his career so far," and William Collins of the *Philadelphia Inquirer* declared that, since the author was staging them, "the argument for these being definitive interpretations is conclusive."[5] Putting the production in the context of the author's position in the American theatre, Bernard Weiner of the *San Francisco Chronicle* declared, "When an award-winning playwright such as Edward Albee directs eight of his shorter works, which span 20 years in the American theatre, the event is worth serious attention."[6]

The *Albee Directs Albee* enterprise was driven by Albee's desire to showcase these plays on an extensive ten-month national and international tour of major resident theatres, commercial houses, and universities in the United States as well as professional theatres in five countries abroad, and culminating in an open-ended run off-Broadway. It was also propelled by Albee's goal of staging, as he asserted, "reasonably authoritative productions . . . to give [audiences] some idea of how I think my plays should look," especially since he traveled frequently on the national and international lecture circuit, where he often encountered productions of his works that he thought were "way off-base" (PCI). These goals were consonant with Albee's increasing determination, from the 1970s onward, to exercise maximum artistic, especially directorial, control over the production of his plays, or as he put it, "to take other directors' jobs away from them—as far as my work is concerned!"[7] As an extension of this wish for artistic control, Albee originally intended to produce these plays himself—the project's early press material, brochure, and contract list him as the producer.[8] With the enterprise's increasingly complex and time-consuming business details, however, a few months before rehearsals began Albee relinquished the producer's role to his friend Mark Amitin, who was already intimately involved with the project; he was its booking agent and had secured several engagements.[9]

As an author, Albee would have preferred a much larger cast for this repertory, but as a director he became remarkably pragmatic and devised a way to fill the twenty-two speaking parts with only five actors, with each playing multiple roles. For the casting, as briefly noted earlier, he divided the roles into five stock company categories—Older Man, Young Man, Older Woman 1 and 2, and Young Woman.[10] "When I write a play . . . maybe I'm attempting something that's impossible," he explained, "but when I direct a play I've written, my job as a director is to make everything possible."[11] The actual casting for the company commenced a month before the start of rehearsals with announcements of Equity Principal Auditions on July 17, 18, and 19, 1978, in *Show Business, Variety,* and similar professional theatre publications in New York City. For seven hours each day Albee interviewed a total of 450 actors at the Minskoff Rehearsal Studios on 1515 Broadway in the heart of the theatre district.[12] Despite the large numbers involved, Albee sought to speak individually to each actor, even if only for a moment. Typically he made only the briefest notes on the margins of the actors' questionnaires: "#1," "OK," "#1 (for 1 or 2)," "Read," etc. On the basis of these interviews, Albee called back thirty actors for readings, where he made closer evaluations of their acting skill, sensibility, stage presence, and voice, again summing up his decision in tiny one- or two-word scrawls.[13] The final five actors Albee selected were Stephen Rowe (Young Man), Patricia Kilgarriff (Older Woman 1), Eileen Burns (Older Woman 2), Catherine Bruno (Young Woman), and Wyman Pendleton (Older Man).[14] In fact, Pendleton had been offered the role "a full year earlier," because Albee was eager to secure a commitment from this veteran actor, who had performed in seven of his works on as well as off-Broadway, including four that were included in this repertory.[15] At these auditions Albee picked another actor, James Knobeloch, to play two non-speaking roles (the Musician in *The Sandbox* and the Minister in *Quotations from Chairman Mao Tse-Tung*), understudy the Young Man roles, and serve as the assistant stage manager.[16]

At the opening rehearsal of *The American Dream* Albee asked this company of five principal actors and the understudies to sit with him in a circle to begin a reading. Albee as a writer prefers not to discuss what his plays are about, yet as a director he finds it necessary to precede his first reading with some comments, however brief. He introduced *The American Dream* as a "satirical examination of much that is wrong with American society." The play's first director, Alan Schneider, had articulated a parallel summation in his production notebook, calling it "a cartoon sketch dealing with the hollowness of our current existence" and "a charming and well crafted cartoon" detailing the decay of American virtues and values.[17] Albee then offered the briefest information about characters and setting before delineating the opening dramatic situation in simple, concrete terms: Mommy and Daddy are waiting for something, "but they have been waiting so long that they have, or seem to have, forgotten what they are waiting for."

Like Albee and Schneider, director Ingmar Bergman also commenced rehearsals by articulating his vision for the play: "When he meets with everyone . . . at the first rehearsal, he begins by telling what the play is about."[18] Writer-director Beckett, on the other hand, never said a word about his dramas at his first rehearsals, eschewed a reading, and jumped right into scene work.[19] Tyrone Guthrie similarly plunged into blocking, frequently dispensing with opening comments and readings; in several of his nearly ninety articles, commentaries, and books he advised against rehearsal discussions.[20] Peter Brook, also unlike Albee, goes directly into exercises, although he does not shun discussion as a rehearsal technique. For his National Theatre production of Seneca's *Oedipus,* adapted by Ted Hughes (1968), the cast, with Sir John Gielgud and Irene Worth in the leads, began work with a series of vocal and physical exercises and continued with them for three weeks before Brook even showed them the script.[21] For his landmark *Midsummer Night's Dream* (1970), Brook invited only a part of the cast—those playing the clownish Mechanicals—to attend the first rehearsals; they started with improvisational exercises and then shared all the parts for a reading, punctuated by directorial comments and discussion.[22] Even William Gaskill, less radical than Peter Brook, asserted in an interview with me that he rarely asked a cast to read a script in full at an opening rehearsal when he headed the English Stage Company, or when he directed at the National Theatre, the Royal Shakespeare Company, or the Joint Stock Company, or when he staged the first productions of works by Edward Bond, Arnold Wesker, John Arden, and David Hare.[23]

Immediately following Albee's introduction, the reading commenced. "Read with your instincts, let the play happen during the reading," Albee advised, so that the actors themselves would discover the nature of their characters and relationships. In striking contrast, Shaw insisted that *he* first read the play aloud in order that his cast learn "the inflexions of voice peculiar to each character," "how the author wished the various parts to be acted," and "what the author had in mind."[24] Albee remained silent during the reading, except occasionally to correct pronunciation or pacing. Harold Clurman argued for similar reticence: there is "little point in giving the actors at the first readings any instructions whatsoever. They should be allowed to read in any way they will and should not be interrupted unless they become inaudible or strain to produce an effect."[25]

Albee desired no physical movement during the reading. If an actor stood up or moved, he stopped him and reminded him to "read purely to get a sense of the relationships." This restriction, in addition, arose from the importance he placed on the rhythm of his words: he wanted the focus only on the words at that early stage. Shaw had similarly stressed that in an ideal situation actors ought "to get the music right before going on to the stage," even if it meant "a half dozen rehearsals seated round a table, books in hand."[26] Reflecting a parallel emphasis on words common in the French theatre tradition, Jean Vilar, head of the Theatre National Populaire from 1951 to 1963, recommended devoting one-third of the rehearsals to reading, "script in hand with buttocks on the chair."[27] After the reading, Albee spent a few minutes responding to actors' questions, steering them toward matters of performance and away from those of interpretation and authorial intention. Following the questions, Albee began blocking *The American Dream* on the first day itself. His cast's familiarity with this popular play also encouraged the director to quickly put it on its feet.

Within the parameters of his script's explicit as well as implicit stage directions and under his watchful eyes, he allows his performers to improvise the early blocking. He asserts, "Good actors instinctively know when to move, and nine times out of ten they are right" (PCI). Albee spent the first three or four days on blocking, quite unlike Bertolt Brecht, who usually blocked for three or four months. Albee explains, "I try to get the blocking done as soon as possible so that people can begin working on interpretation."[28] As actors walked through the *American Dream* living room—an arrangement of rehearsal room chairs to approximate a center-stage sofa, with an armchair on either side—Albee accepted most of their moves, but altered a few and created several new ones as well. He eliminated visual awkwardness and moves that his actors found uncomfortable, and he aimed for a smooth-flowing movement with adequate variety. He repeated the blocking of each segment and then of the whole play, but he reminded the company that the moves were open to change as needed. Although only a few minor alterations were required in subsequent rehearsals, Albee remained perfectly willing to modify moves in response to actors' suggestions or new staging exigencies.

As with the blocking, Albee was receptive to actors' ideas when working on the interpretation of his lines. Even if an actor hesitated to offer his own reading because of the director's reputation as a major playwright, Albee often provided several alternatives for the actor to select from. When the Young Man momentarily misunderstands Grandma's offer and suggestively leans over her, she warns him to stay away, but exclaims, "I don't mean I'd mind. I don't know whether I'd mind or not . . . But it wouldn't look well; it would look just *awful*." Albee told Catherine Bruno, playing Grandma, that she could choose to deliver the middle sentence as a parenthetical comment, as a thinking aloud to herself, or as an aside to the audience.

Albee also allows his performers freedom in determining the emotional contours of a speech. He let the Young Man "pick one or two moments" when he would permit his deep hurt to well up, even though it was largely with cool indifference that he recalled his lost identical twin brother. In another instance, Albee encouraged Eileen Burns, as Mrs. Barker, to choose her own distinct coloration for each of her five clichéd exclamations that punctuate Grandma's veiled story about Mommy and Daddy. Albee similarly gave his actors considerable freedom in devising appropriate business to express an emotion or idea. Early in the first week of rehearsals, he asked Wyman Pendleton, as Daddy, to be profoundly apprehensive on first meeting the muscular Young Man. What his actors created Albee liked, refined, and retained for performance: on being introduced, the

Young Man so aggressively extends a fully outstretched arm that Daddy stumbles several steps backward and falls onto his sofa.

Finally, however, the director must shape the results of such freedom into a unified and coherent performance. Albee's rehearsal work on *The American Dream* revealed remarkable skill in molding his actors on what David Selbourne has called "the potter's wheel of theatrical direction."[29] He communicated with unusual authority and precision because of his position as the playwright and his professional theatre experience. Albee elucidated his characters with a command and clarity that enhanced the players' understanding of their roles, a prerequisite for conveying a play's meaning to an audience. On different occasions, Albee explained to Mommy, "You love to hear your own voice," "Everything is a bother to you," and "You take it out on Daddy." "You are terrible to everyone," he explained further, "but you are really beastly to Grandma, who has loved you the most"; "You're a destroyer." He quoted one of Daddy's lines to suggest the character's spine: "I just want to get everything over with" (70). Albee intended such comments to help actors find appropriate behavior patterns for their roles.

To help actors grasp his characters, Albee often employed images, although not with the extraordinary frequency of another playwright-director, Edward Bond, known to his actors for a bottomless reservoir of metaphors.[30] Albee made clear to the Young Man, "You're quite an experienced hustler," and though "you're a stick, you don't remain one—you have a tiny hint of sensitivity." To Mommy Albee explained that toward the end of the play she should regard the Young Man as a fine "product," since she thinks, "I am a shopper and this is what I want." Her examination of the Young Man before adoption must not be a light matter: "It is important for you to get your money's worth—he's not a hat; he's a car." During the rehearsals of the 1961 premiere he called Mommy a "tumescent monster" and Daddy "an avocado blob."[31] Albee delineated Grandma's character: "Grandma is a devil"; "She wears sneakers—always ready to run or jump." Fleshing out her character in subsequent rehearsals, Grandma mischievously bounced on her toes, clad in sports shoes, transforming imaged suggestions into telling behavior.

Albee similarly brought verbal exactitude and double authority as dramatist and practiced director to matters other than character elucidation. Albee explained to the cast that rhythm is adversely affected by an inappropriate pause, business, or movement. Consequently, beginning in the second week Albee checked actors for pauses several times each day. "Why didn't you pause after Daddy's 'qualms'?" he asked Mommy. "Why did you take the pause after dropping your boxes on the living room floor?" he enquired of Grandma. Pointing out her unnecessary pauses after an early preview, he exclaimed, "This is not a Pinter play!" On different occasions, in addition, Albee questioned Grandma as to why she had scratched her arm, or shrugged her shoulders, or opened her mouth as if to say something, or turned her head in a certain direction. A few times during each rehearsal he told different actors, "Take a beat," "New beat," or "End of beat." Sometimes after a scene he reminded actors to pick up their cues.

Since rhythm is significantly shaped by the articulation of words, Albee made vocal orchestration a central concern. Such an emphasis invites comparison with Shaw's focus in his rehearsals. In "George Bernard Shaw: The Playwright as Producer," William Armstrong concludes, "This persistent concern with the pronunciation, the articulation, and the music of words was fundamental to the art of directing as Shaw conceived it."[32] Like Shaw, Albee ensured unusual precision in the speaking of his text.

Beyond pronunciation- and punctuation-perfect lines, he attended to exactness in stress, coloration, tone, and pitch. For example, after Mommy's gaffe, her exclamations—"Oooohhhh! What have I said? What have I said?" (92)—should have an extremely exaggerated, "overly unctuous" tone, but without any hint of "sarcasm or irony." At the end of his emotionally draining autobiographical account to Grandma, the Young Man's "And so . . . here I am . . . as you see me" (115) must echo the falling rhythm after a release of pent-up feelings. On first seeing the handsome Young Man, Mrs. Barker's double take—"Well . . . Who's this?" (116)—ought to reflect "first confusion, then sexual curiosity." When she quotes her brother's favorite line, "Of course, I'm married" (84), Albee specified "a hoarse, guttural voice, with a very low pitch."

On many other occasions as well Albee stipulated distinct vocal inflections. To describe the first child's life with Mommy and Daddy, Grandma should switch to an "intimate tone" (99). However, Mrs. Barker, her sole auditor, must not follow suit—a usual actor adjustment. Instead, her voice ought to remain "expansive and social." Later in the scene, in order to ironically "encourage Mrs. Barker's monstrous reactions," Grandma must sustain a "matter-of-fact tone" as she details the child's brutal mutilation (99–101). In other instances, Albee assigned discrete colorations for the same emotion or the same word. Laughter in different scenes had to be "social" (84), "sarcastic" (85), "dirty, private" (110), "quiet" (113), "nervous" (119), or "cheerful" (123); each of Mrs. Barker's three hellos—to Mommy, Daddy, and Grandma—needed a distinctive inflection (76). Despite this concern with vocal precision, which he shares with Shaw and Beckett, Albee, unlike them, did not employ musical terms to indicate tone or pitch.

Albee's meticulous attention to ensuring accurate intonation, however, did not translate into directorial line readings. He believes that a performer should represent in his own way the original impulse of a text, rather than simply copying the director. Consequently, Albee insists, "I hate to give line readings" (PCI). As early as 1909 Shaw had similarly argued, "There is only one effect to be produced"—that specified by the director—"but there may be fifty ways of producing it."[33] Likewise, most directors today generally shun line readings. In spite of his distaste for line readings, however, Albee remained practical enough to offer some as a last resort. During *The American Dream* rehearsals, most of these were directed to the relatively inexperienced performer playing Grandma. Although strict adherents of the Method may disapprove of such line readings, Stanislavsky's own practice supports Albee's pragmatic approach. Asked if he ever read lines for a performer, the Russian director immediately responded, "Of course, whole speeches sometimes. One does everything, anything to arrive at the desired result."[34]

While Albee restricted line readings to a minimum, he readily demonstrated stage business. A few times each rehearsal day, he walked up to an actor, assumed his character's pose, and executed a piece of business in order to communicate his authorial and directorial intention. Standing on his toes, knees slightly bent, and shoulders tilted forward, Albee showed how Grandma, despite her age, must look like a "basketball player—ready to take off." He urged Grandma to remain physically agile throughout the play. To demonstrate her spry entrance in the play's final scene, Albee came skipping in like a happy schoolgirl. When Grandma calls Mommy "a tramp and a trollop and a trull to boot" and proceeds to reveal embarrassing secrets (69–70), he acted out for Mommy an elaborate and progressively more menacing pattern of movement around a center-stage sofa, to convey what he characterized as her "'If Grandma goes any further, I'm going to kill her!' attitude."

Through such demonstrations Albee indicated what effect he desired, but the actors were expected to spontaneously recreate that effect and not merely to mimic his enactment. To preclude imitation, Albee usually exaggerated his demonstration slightly, as did Shaw and Brecht in their demonstrations. According to Carl Weber, an assistant director at the Berliner Ensemble, Brecht "would exaggerate enough so that while [the actors] saw exactly what he wanted, they were never tempted to copy him." Since Brecht "could be a marvelous clown," Weber recalls, sometimes "the actors liked to provoke him to demonstrate something" just to watch him.[35] Beyond directorial communication, such exaggeration is often amusing, and in addition it eases tensions and encourages playful invention.

Albee's demonstrations functioned similarly and, with his recurring witticisms, provided welcome relief during grueling rehearsals.

Demonstrations reveal only a part of Albee's intense concern with stage business. Moving beyond his authorial stage directions, he invented physical action to enrich his text in performance. In addition to the menacing movements he demonstrated for Mommy, he created another, stronger movement for her following her *faux pas* about Mrs. Barker's wheelchair-ridden husband (92–93). Infuriated at Grandma's taunts, Mommy dashes around the sofa toward Grandma—almost ready to attack her physically—forcing her to jump up from her armchair and "scoot" behind it in self-defense.

Whenever they are together, these two characters assault each other verbally. Through movement, gesture, and posture, Albee theatricalized their seesaw battle, as he did the rest of the play's action. During one set of exchanges, for example, he devised a series of minor climactic moves and items of business that took Mommy from her downstage right seat and Grandma from her downstage far left position to a strong upstage center climax (85–89). In the first beat, Albee asked Mommy to sniggeringly imitate Grandma's voice and, toward the end of her speech, rise from her armchair triumphantly with "You see? I can pull that stuff just as easy as you can" (85). In response, he had Grandma turn quickly, advance a few steps toward Mommy to "parody" her brisk gait, elaborately place her hands on her hips to mimic her pose, and retort, "Well, you got the rhythm, but you don't really have the quality" (85). In the next unit, Albee instructed Grandma to cross close to Daddy's armchair, snap her fingers at Mommy, and condescend to her: "You'll learn" (86). To reflect Grandma's determination to continue, he suggested she sweep toward the upstage center sofa that held Mrs. Barker. This forced Mommy to turn in resignation and snap, "Go on. Jabber away" (86). Since Mommy is easily aroused, however, the director soon required her to stride right up to the side of the sofa, shake her finger at Grandma, and shout, "And it's you that takes up all the space . . ." (88). In retaliation, Grandma should rush up to her side of the sofa, lean forward, and hurl a string of personal insults at her. Mommy should then react with a "large gesture" conveying "social embarrassment." For the climax, Albee directed Mommy to close in from the right on Mrs. Barker, who has been sitting on the sofa and savoring every insult, and then to bend over and exclaim into her ear, "You stop listening to her" (89). Almost immediately, Grandma must advance upon Mrs. Barker from the left, lean over, and scream into her other ear, "You stick up for me" (89).

Throughout these exchanges, in contrast to Mommy's and Grandma's vigorous moves, Daddy and Mrs. Barker must remain stationary. Albee required

Daddy to appear almost immobile in his armchair, feebly request an end to the arguing, and merely watch. Mrs. Barker, however, should enjoy the verbal mayhem. Albee asked Mrs. Barker to follow the antagonists advancing from opposite sides by enthusiastically swinging her head from speaker to speaker, like an avid "spectator at a table-tennis match." To parallel Mommy's and Grandma's increasing verbal and physical energy as they approach their upstage climax, her head swaying became swifter and more pronounced—and more ludicrous. Although the printed text offers no stage directions for this four-page duel, director Albee created substantial stage business to physicalize the conflict, intensify the dramatic action, visually underscore character traits, and generate comic effects.

Albee enlivened his script further by inventing other comic business. On Mommy's recollection, "When I was a little girl . . . [and] Grandpa was in heaven" (65–66), he suggested that she momentarily strike "a Sunday school pose" and "point to heaven." A little later, delighted to be "very well provided for" in Daddy's will (68), she should lean toward him and throw an exaggerated flying kiss in an uncharacteristic—and consequently more funny—gesture. Her jaw must soon fall in shock, however, when Grandma points at Daddy and recounts how even as an eight-year-old Mommy had planned to "mahwy a wich old man" (69). In order to point up Mommy's vanity, Albee directed her to squint and crane her head but resolutely refuse to use the spectacles that hung from her neck throughout the play. However, he also picked out one or two occasions where she *should* use them. For example, unable to recognize Mrs. Barker, she exclaims, "Don't be ridiculous. I was talking to the chairman of my woman's club just yester—" (78). Albee asked Mommy to pause mid-word, lean over the sofa that held Mrs. Barker, reluctantly raise her glasses, peer through them for a second, drop them hurriedly, and chirp, "Why, so you are." The rarity of her action rendered it both more comic and more dramatic.

New comic action vivified characters and situations in other parts of the play. When the doorbell first rang, for example, Mommy jumped to her feet, and Grandma, wondering if she was to be carted off, strode stage right to Mommy and then left to Daddy (72–75). Mommy in turn followed Grandma to Daddy, who tried to avoid answering the door. Unable to persuade Daddy even after the third ring, Mommy lifted Daddy from his armchair and thrust him toward the door. For the next dozen lines, Albee choreographed a series of discrete but repetitive movements for Daddy: one or two steps forward—with head turned back toward Mommy—alternating with stops for each of Mommy's reassurances that he is "firm," "decisive," and "masculine" (74). To accentuate the comedy, Albee first ensured that Daddy reached the door just as the bell sounded again. He next excised some dialogue so that this aural effect led directly to the stage direction requiring Daddy to back off from the door with "Maybe we can send them away" (75). Finally, when Mommy's insults prodded him into opening the door, Daddy, with his eyes glued to the visiting Mrs. Barker, nervously traversed the length of the stage—from an upstage right position to his downstage left chair—walking backward.

Albee directed Mrs. Barker, in contrast to the nervous Daddy, to be sunny, expansive, and elaborately social—no matter what the situation. Upon arrival Mrs. Barker cheerily and ceremoniously greeted Mommy, then Daddy, and then raised an arm well above her head to wave to Grandma as if to someone far away. She displayed the same deliberateness and cheerfulness whether she simply crossed her legs or spread her arms to announce, "My, what an unattractive apartment you have!" (77). Albee also devised new business and movement that intensified the comedy and irony in the play's concluding moments. He advanced Grandma's final entrance by one full page in the printed text, so that she came to the apron to watch the stage action several speeches earlier than in the original. No longer offstage, Grandma now listens, watches, gestures, clucks, shakes her head, and maintains conspiratorial eye contact with the audience throughout the section where Mommy expresses shock at Grandma's disappearance, accuses her of running away with something, confesses that she and Daddy had simply made up the van man, weeps for Grandma, and seeks Daddy's comfort.

Besides fresh comic business, Albee employed new direct addresses to theatricalize his text. As playwright he had given Grandma two speeches in the final scene to be spoken to the audience, but as director he quintupled her direct addresses and scattered them throughout the play, redirecting lines that she originally spoke to other characters. Some of her designated lines made up entire speeches (72, 105, 127), and some were only a one-sentence request (122) or question (77). Others began as a response to a character, but after a sentence or two became asides (64 [both speeches], 68-69, 82); in one case, he interposed a direct address to the audience into a speech that was already directed in turn to Mommy, Daddy, and Grandma herself. During these addresses, the actress had to remain in character, and when others were present she had to preserve her relationships with them as well. To indicate clearly to the audience that they were being addressed, Albee specified gestures and movement: Grandma glanced or leaned or turned her head slightly toward the audience, or even crossed to the downstage edge to "look into all sections" of the theatre. Through these addresses and accompanying actions, the director aimed for a sense of immediacy and for sharper audience attention. Stylistically, they stressed the theatrical context for the audience as well as reinforcing the script's presentational elements throughout the performance—something that a few critics had found lacking during its 1961 premiere.[36] These critics felt that Grandma's audience address—limited to the play's final minutes in that production—had switched styles too abruptly.

While theatricalizing and contributing stylistic cohesion to the performance, the new direct addresses also served to channel audience sympathy. All these addresses, except for a one-line question, consisted of generalized comments about old age: "Old people are very good at listening . . ." (72), "People don't say good-bye to old people . . ." (105), etc. All were spoken by Grandma, who, in the author's words, "certainly is an enormously sympathetic character, worthy of a good deal of affection and love."[37] These speeches, when impressed with the force of chorus-like direct address, strongly guided the audience toward an authorial perspective. Even the brief direct address in the original production was similarly intended to regulate audience response: Alan Schneider confirmed in 1961 that with the audience address "Albee was trying to break down the barriers between audience and the play."[38] Albee's textual revisions during *The American Dream* rehearsals probably grew out of his dramaturgic experiments with multiple direct addresses in *Counting the Ways,* composed a year earlier, and in *The Lady From Dubuque,* then being completed.

Direct address—to create dramatic immediacy, encourage closer attention, and steer response—forms an integral part of director Albee's persistent concern with the audience. During eight to ten hours of daily rehearsals, Albee rarely spent more than seven to eight minutes in one spot. "There are audiences all over the theatre," he reasoned, "and I want the thing to be relatable from every area in the theatre" (PCI). Characteristic of his practicality, such continuing awareness of the audience meant that his directorial injunctions almost always took into account the effect they would have on the spectator. Often this reference to the audience was explicit. Albee told Mommy, when Mrs. Barker gushes about her brother, "Don't look bored, or else the audience will get bored too." Following a run-through prior to the opening night performance, Albee reminded Grandma that, during the speech about the child's mutilation, "You can get such a big audience response." Ten days earlier he had scolded the cast after a preview: "It was a curious performance in which the audience was not included."

Albee approaches a production through an audience's eyes and ears. Identifying with them, he spoke in plural first-person pronouns. The Young Man should convey some inceptive danger, he explained, because "We [the audience] have to be able to relate it to the hint that Grandma gave us" about possible violence later that night. The day before the first preview, he advised Mrs. Barker, "Keep your responses big, or we lose interest."

Many times, when specifying a delivery, gesture, or movement, Albee stressed how it would assist the audience. Early in the first week, he told the Young Man that in order to "help the audience" visualize Mommy and Daddy in another part of their apartment, he should turn with curiosity toward the couple's off-stage voices (108). With the same goal, on "Mrs. Barker, I'd much rather you came into the kitchen" (103), Mommy should step toward the stage left exit and point to the offstage kitchen. When Grandma passes off the Young Man as the van man—"Dear, will you take my things out to the van?" (120)—Albee urged conspiratorial head and eye movements, because "You've *got* to help the audience." For Grandma's final good-bye, where the script simply indicates that Grandma "*takes in the room*" (120), Albee directed her to walk slowly to one or two familiar objects, touch them with subdued feeling, and become momentarily "immobile—unable to leave the environment." The amplified business, he explained to Grandma, ought "to show the audience what you're saying good-bye to—the physical room and its contents," not to Mommy and Daddy.

Albee's desire to assist the spectator regularly prompted him to similarly clarify plot and character in rehearsal, although without such explicit reference. To suggest that Mrs. Barker present the Young Man as a replacement for Mommy and Daddy's original "bumble," the text asks Grandma to "*whisper into Mrs. Barker's ear*" (118). Except for Mrs. Barker's surprise and delight, the subsequent dialogue offers no clue to what she whispered until five pages later. In his staging, however, Albee revealed the subject, from the start directing Grandma and Mrs. Barker to turn and point frequently toward the Young Man while he carries the boxes outside. Accompanying smiles and exclamations, animated head-shaking and gesturing spiced this clarification, consistently provoking laughter in performance. When Mrs. Barker presents the new "bumble," according to a scene direction, Mommy "*circl[es] the Young Man, feeling his arm, poking him,*" as she exclaims, "Yes sir! Yes, sirree! Now this is more like it . . ." (124). Although this scene could be interpreted sexually, Albee asserted he had always intended otherwise. He revealed the subtext by urging Mommy to inspect the Young Man's muscles "for toughness" and to convey "not sexual vulgarity, but a vulgarity reflected in seeing the man as merchandise."

Like these textual and subtextual clarifications, practical staging needs caused changes in earlier business. Despite Grandma's loud protests, according to an original stage direction, Mommy "*steps on several*" of her mother's nicely wrapped boxes as she "*walks through*" them (80–81). Modifying this, Albee instructed Mommy instead to kick them out of her way, since boxes sturdy enough to support her 114 pounds would have been too heavy for Grandma to carry. When Mrs. Barker matter-of-factly removed her dress, he had instructed Mommy to place it neatly across the sofa back. But the activity on and around the sofa caused it to slip to the seat or to the floor at unexpected moments. He consequently directed Mommy to hold the dress until, seconds later, her guest's insistence on smoking enrages her to fling it onto the rarely used coffee table. Early in the second week, in another example, Albee had suggested a series of gestures to flesh out Grandma's "sketchy delivery." Despite much effort, she failed to assimilate them into her role; instead her gestural activity began to overwhelm the words and to imply antagonism and complaint in a character the director had described as "entirely without self-pity" and "the only cheerful person in the play." As a result, from the third week onward, Albee persistently urged her to "cut all the physicalization" that he had himself recommended, even telling her at one stage, "Grandma does most of her acting with her eyes."

Albee brought this objective approach to his lines as well. In comparison to changes in business, however, he made only minor textual revisions. "None of these plays is having its first performance," he explained. "I've [already] *done* a lot of cutting. I'm really doing a kind of *honing* at this point" (PCI). Besides the four-line deletion to heighten the comedy of Daddy's retreat at the sound of the doorbell (74–75) and the two-sentence excision to psychologically reinforce Mommy's absorption in the Young Man (127), both noted earlier, Albee made three other cuts. In the first one, Grandma lost her six-line disparagement of middle-aged people, "Look. I'll show you how it's really done . . . You'll learn" (85–86). In this speech the director had wanted Grandma to subtly parody her own delivery style. Apparently her inability to do so led to the deletion. Albee later restored the dialogue when Bruno's Old Woman roles were given to Sudie Bond, who had played Grandma in the original productions of both *The American Dream* and *The Sandbox,* and who was hired later as Old Woman 3 and became the company's sixth actor.[39]

Usually, however, Albee prefers "not to cut to accommodate actors' inadequacies." Instead, he claims, "I try to cut in order to make the text flow"—the rationale for his two other deletions in *The American Dream* (PCI). He pared away a thirteen-line interlude where Daddy repeatedly forgets Mrs. Barker's name. Because this passage lay sandwiched between Grandma's offer, "Now, if you're interested in knowing why these boxes *are* here . . ." (86), and Mommy's response,

"Well, nobody *is* interested!" (87), its deletion smoothened and quickened the movement of the dialogue. It eliminated repetition: Grandma no longer restates her offer, as she needed to at the end of the omitted episode. Since earlier Daddy momentarily forgets Mrs. Barker's name—"Uh . . . Mrs. Barker, is it?" (77)—and struggles with it later—"Why we asked . . . what's-her-name to come here?" (123)—the cut also removed superfluous information. Almost identical reasons dictated the final cut—a sixteen-line comic word play on variations of "implore," from Mrs. Barker's "I implore you!" (95) to her "Well, then . . . please tell me why they asked us to come" (96). This excision of verbal embroidery allowed an immediate response to Mrs. Barker's initial request, removed the need for repeating her pleas, and speeded the dramatic action.

Beyond these deletions, Albee made four textual emendations. He transposed two exchanges so that the Young Man and Grandma's crucial conversation—"And what shall I do now?" "Oh, you stay here, dear. It will all become clear to you. . . ."—now logically preceded (not followed, as in the original) their leave-taking—"Can I get you . . . a cab, or something?" "Oh no, dear . . . I'll take it from here" (120). An addition, indicated here in square brackets, underscored the text's political relevance: Grandma tells the Young Man, "Yup. Boy, you know what you are, don't you? You're the American Dream, that's what you are. [Carter and] all those other people, they don't know what they're talking about" (108). Another established that Grandma recalled the Young Man's words accurately: "Why do you say you'd do [almost] anything for money . . . ?" (113). In the final change, Albee updated one of Grandma's references: the Prix de Rome became the National Endowment (91).

Not textual refinement but skillful acting finally assures effective performance. Actors consequently remained the focus of Albee's directorial attention, and his comments to them reveal a theatre aesthetic significantly rooted in the Stanislavsky-Strasberg tradition. Early in his career, according to Alan Schneider, Albee was "involved, actively and enthusiastically, with the Actors Studio," where the *The Zoo Story* had had its first showing" and where Albee had once planned to premiere *Who's Afraid of Virginia Woolf?*[40] Reflecting the Actors Studio influence, Albee defined the ideal actor as one "capable of using his craft fully and vanishing into the character, not the kind of star who projects his or her own personality at the expense of the character."[41] Bringing an expert understanding of the actor's craft, Albee guided his players toward "becoming" their characters. His notes to actors often contained such remarks as, "I see Trish [Patricia Kilgarriff] commenting on Mommy"; "You *must* not comment on your character"; "Now you are losing your intention"; "We [in the audience] know it;

you don't"; and "You must have great confidence in the lines, in the characters, and in yourselves."

Further revealing his affinity to the Actors Studio approach, Albee urged his cast that even though *The American Dream* is "a highly stylized form of comedy . . . you have to see and believe in yourselves as actual, physical, realistic, naturalistic persons—not stylized characters." Albee maintains such an emphasis throughout his rehearsals and demands naturalistic character portrayals, no matter how stylized, experimental, or non-representational his script. Even when staging *Counting the Ways,* which he had subtitled "a Vaudeville," he called for naturalistic stage behavior, reminding an actor, for instance, to search for movie listings not on his newspaper's front page but on an inside one.

In *The American Dream* Albee routinely justified exaggerated action, gesture, or delivery in naturalistic terms. In one case, he argued that many of his characters deliberately—and fully in character—perform parodies of social stereotypes. Thus Mrs. Barker's extraordinarily expansive gestures result from her desire to perform a parody of the obsessively professional woman, and Grandma's many clichéd and exaggerated responses, including her sexual reaction to the Young Man, arise from her intent to playfully parody the old woman stereotype. Through his emphasis on actors' naturalistic interpretation, Albee presents a humanistic, multidimensional, and balanced view of his characters—not a one-dimensional, abstract, and simplistic reading, even in those scripts that critics term stylized or mannered.

Albee employed the same approach when staging Beckett's *Ohio Impromptu* and *Krapp's Last Tape* at the Alley Theatre in Houston, clearly recalling his debt to Alan Schneider. At the opening rehearsal of *Tiny Alice,* with Albee in attendance, Schneider had told his cast, "Since actors cannot act either symbols or abstractions, we should concentrate . . . [on] who were the people and what were they doing?"[42] Even when staging Beckett's most non-naturalistic plays, Schneider focused on the three-dimensional reality of the human beings and their evolving interaction on stage. Irrespective of the degree to which a script was stylized, Schneider insisted his actors concern themselves solely with portraying the details of what he called the "local situation," that is, "who the characters are as human beings and what their human situation is."[43] In other words, both Albee and Schneider believe that in the theatre actors must understand and play characters in their full human dimensionality, naturalistically. This attitude is not surprising, because Schneider's directorial aesthetic, even more than Albee's, was shaped by Lee Strasberg. In his autobiography, *Entrances: An American Director's Journey,* Schneider portrays himself as virtually a lifetime member of the

Actors Studio and acknowledges Lee Strasberg as the single most important influence on his development as a director: "He made me think differently about the process of putting on a play . . . about what a director does, as well as about how and why he does it. . . . I must credit him fully for bringing me alive as director."[44] Yet neither Schneider nor Albee is a complete adherent of the Actors Studio's aesthetic and methods. Even while paying this tribute to Strasberg, Schneider confessed, "I always knew that what he taught me, though it dealt with the truth, was not the whole truth."[45] Schneider found Strasberg's methods too rigid, particularly when staging his many non-naturalistic and stylized scripts, where he needed to emphasize formal and external elements in the acting, movement, and decor. Both Schneider and Albee admire such non-realistic plays—by Brecht, Beckett, and Pinter, for instance—far more than the realistic plays associated with the Actors Studio, and in different degrees their directing avoids the Actors Studio's excessively and superficially detailed naturalism. Even more than Schneider, Albee both as playwright and director increasingly championed a theatre of simplicity, minimal effects, and symmetry.

Yet Albee's conviction, shared with Strasberg and Schneider, that the actor's art is rooted in the naturalistic depiction of human beings in human situations—or, in Shaw's words, the depiction of "real things . . . happening to real people"—leads to a rehearsal focus on creating believable stage behavior. "Make it real for us" thus is one of his recurrent injunctions. As a first step in achieving this goal during *The American Dream* rehearsals, Albee worked on developing sustained realistic interplay among his actors. Paralleling Ingmar Bergman's belief that "when you are acting . . . you must concentrate not on yourself but always on your fellow actors,"[46] Albee frequently commented, "First of all you *must* listen to each other." He directed them to listen actively, that is, respond with a specific attitude, conveyed through a look, a tiny gesture, or an occasional sigh, grunt, or exclamation. Albee suggested, for example, that Mommy "take an ironic stance" toward Mrs. Barker's narration of her brother's virtues but register "social embarrassment" when Grandma recalls details of Mommy's birth. In reaction to Mommy's "Don't step on the Pekinese; it's blind" (92), Daddy should appear "peevish, almost angry." When Grandma tells Daddy that Mommy "was a tramp and a trollop and a trull to boot, and she's no better now" (69), the director instructed Mommy to interject a distinct vocal reaction after each insult.

To maintain this sense of realistic interaction, Albee reminded the actors of another essential principle: lines should be clearly addressed to specific characters. During Grandma's description of how the newborn Mommy "had a head shaped like a banana" (88), he commented, "Look at Mommy directly and give it to *her;* now it seems you're giving it to the void." Similarly, even when she only recounts the contents of her boxes, she should "share it with the Young Man." Such sharing and animated listening—combined with the substantial reactive business described earlier—made the stage action "real for us."

Implicit in these directions is the concern for depicting psychologically credible behavior. In order to illuminate the underlying psychology elsewhere in his text, Albee devised fresh business as well as altering or excising his original stage directions. He suggested that Mommy's sexual attraction to the Young Man could surface in the play's final minute, when she confides, "You don't know how happy I am to see you! . . ." (127). This was justified, he explained, by his original stage direction preceding the speech: "*her voice already a little fuzzy from the wine.*" Tonal indication of an oncoming inebriety provided the psychological underpinning for the business he devised to illustrate her hitherto submerged sexual interest. In his amplified scenic direction Albee asked Mommy to pull the Young Man down onto her sofa, put an arm around him, begin the speech with "a complete and abrupt change of tone," and "behave as if the others"—Daddy and Mrs. Barker, who freeze behind opposite armchairs—"are not present." In view of such an absorption, he revised his script for psychological consistency: Mommy no longer "*indicates Mrs. Barker*" or talks about her presence or her causing "all the trouble" (127).

In another effort to reinforce a character's psychology through appropriate business, Albee instructed the Young Man to "size up the place" and take a few steps to "look around" when he first arrives, since selling his services is his sole concern. When Grandma claims, "There's more money around here than you'd know what to do with," he reassesses the apartment in exactly the same way before responding, "I'm not so sure" (110). But, drawn to money, he begins to gravitate toward Grandma; taken in by her tactical boast—"Old people quite often have lots of money; more often than most people expect" (110)—he seats himself close to her on the sofa.

Albee also frequently offered explicit psychological motivations for delivery or action. When Mrs. Barker cheerfully discloses her eavesdropping, he told Daddy to "react with great surprise" since "you feel an invasion of your privacy." But soon Mommy should "be *extra* nice to Mrs. Barker," Albee suggested, "because she is the chairman of your woman's club." Advising the Young Man to speak warmly to Grandma, the director indicated, "You begin to like her . . . you enjoy the life in her"; unlike the others, "she's fun." On "I can sense these things" (109) he should step close behind Grandma, for "in his trade" this is what "he would do for other women." This move surprises Grandma, and Albee asked the Young

Man to then move back: "You're pretty subtle; you won't do anything cheap." The usually lively Grandma becomes subdued as she leaves the apartment, he explained, because she is "concerned about how she's going to manage on the street." Such justifications helped actors undergird their characters psychologically, making them more believable in performance.

Complementing motivation derived from characters' psychology, Albee provided external motivation based on staging needs. When altering earlier stage business, as already seen, he had given practical reasons for the new action. Similarly, instructing Grandma to restrict her gestures, he suggested, "Keep it simple; the words need air." To prevent her from rushing on after a comic line, he told her, "Wait for the audience's laughter, or they'll laugh at you"; to generate comedy through contrasting attitudes, he explained, "You must hit each of these metaphorical destructions" of the child, as "this will play nicely against the seriousness" of the literal-minded Mrs. Barker. By furnishing such down-to-earth reasons, the director prevented inessential discussion and communicated his instructions swiftly and efficiently.

Such rehearsal comments also testify to Albee's ability to offer useful acting advice. He proved an able diagnostician and prescribed effective, straightforward remedies. Because "you are not confident," he pointed out to the company after a preview, "you are not listening to yourselves and to each other." Moreover, he added, "instead of having pace, the performance seemed rushed." Following another preview, Albee analyzed Mommy's performance: "You have a speed at which you're working, and you don't seem to care whether others are with you or not." He demanded a serious effort to "listen to others and to yourself." Performing at her own pace, he inferred, was also a symptom that her "physical moves and lines were getting set." He urged her to ensure that "Mommy grows and develops . . . from performance to performance." During a late rehearsal Albee reasoned that Grandma's lines seemed unconvincing, because "it doesn't sound that you as an actor are thinking." He offered a simple prescription: "*Think* about what you're saying." But when the actress began to think about what she was going to say, it undercut her spontaneity and revealed her as an actor getting ready for a line. Albee recommended a solution both practical and apt: "Don't think before your line, think in the middle." Directions such as these often evoked an appreciative "right," "good," or "great" from the cast.

Actors appreciated just as much the playwright-director's unique insights into his characters. Albee believes an "actor has to build from individual truths to a total truth"; his directorial comments consequently supply enlightening "truths" about his creations.[47] Besides the insights he offered in initially delineating characters, inventing business to provide psychological reinforcement, and describing inner motivation, he supplied information in many other remarks. During the hat story—"perhaps the most tedious anecdote ever forced on Battered Man by Dull Woman"[48]—Mommy is very surprised, but not pleased, to find Daddy attentive, because she prefers to catch him inattentive. When Grandma first arrives, loaded with boxes, the daughter treats the mother as if she were a child. As Grandma leaves to get more boxes, Mommy says, "I can't stand it, watching her do the cooking and the housework, polishing the silver, moving the furniture . . ." (67). Albee explained that she says this because she is "annoyed and bothered that Grandma is capable of doing all that." He clarified the subtext in another speech: on hearing Grandma ask for an allowance, Mommy exclaims, "Grandma! I'm ashamed of you" (70), not out of outrage at any impropriety but out of a "concern for the money that she might get from Daddy." Despite these concerns, however, the director told her, "we don't see you vulnerable until the van man comes."

In contrast, Albee suggested, when Grandma hears the doorbell and asks Mommy, "The van people? . . . Have you called the van people to come and take me away?" (72), she should not be "shrill or too emphatic," but should "just say it in the sense that 'you've finally painted the wall pink.'" In fact, Grandma is "happy and eager to have the van man," Albee explained, and her question to the Young Man as soon as he arrives, "Are you the van man?" (105), reflects "not fear but happiness." Nonetheless, toward the end of the play, her last good-bye is "not a happy one," for she does "feel a little sad at leaving life and the world." Still, she neither complains nor feels regret, either here or anywhere else, insisted Albee. Thus her audience address—"Old people are very good at listening; old people don't like to talk; old people have colitis and lavender perfume" (72)—is "not angry, nor cheerful—more a statement."

Albee urged Grandma to make her comment to Daddy elsewhere in the play, "If you'd listened to me, you wouldn't have married her in the first place" (69), "very light" and provided the subtext: "It is probably the first time you've mentioned this to Daddy." Yet Grandma is not misleading anyone when she claims she "can't remember" if she had her mother carted off: "She is really unsure about what happened to her mother." On the other hand, although "subtly and just a little," she does "put the Young Man on" for several minutes—from her welcome, "My, my, aren't you something!" until her recognition, "Hey! You look familiar" (106, 112). Grandma can sustain this protracted ironic stance, Albee explained to the Young Man, because "although you're not dumb, you're too preoccupied with yourself to suspect that Grandma might be putting you on."

In scenes following Grandma's teasing, Albee made definite what is only implied in the text: in order to avenge his identical twin brother, "the Young Man is going to kill Mommy and Daddy that night." Beginning with the Young Man's recollection of his wrenching emotional losses, Albee commented, "I have to see a tiny hint of your incipient violence" in order to prepare the audience for the "hint in the play as to what will happen when the curtain goes down." As a clue, the director instructed the Young Man to visibly register "a small alert produced in his mind" that Grandma may be referring to his brother when she reveals, "I don't know you from somewhere, but I knew . . . someone once who was very much like you" (115). In her next speech, Albee asked Grandma to suggest a causal link between her first sentence, which reiterates the Young Man's resemblance to the child she knew, and the second, which immediately offers him a job. Albee explained Grandma's indirection: "I think Grandma is the sort of lady who would say, 'The Young Man will *think* and if he wants he *will* get back at Daddy and Mommy.' She wouldn't go all the way and tell him to go and kill them."

Albee's observation also clarifies why Grandma remains noncommittal both times that the Young Man inquires about his duties. During her second response, Grandma's somber tone and demeanor as well as her words—"It will all become clear to you. It will be explained. You'll understand" (120)—imply potential danger. Similarly for Mommy's final words—"Something familiar about you . . . you know that? I can't quite place it . . ." (127)—Albee specified "an intimation of danger." In previews and performances these hints effectively foreboded violence. Mommy's dawning recognition usually provoked several apprehensive gasps in the audience. Consequently, Grandma's closing remarks (with Albee's performance emphasis)—"Everybody's got what he *thinks* he wants"—acquired a sharper, savage edge.

Shedding new light on his principal characters and on the meaning of important scenes, this staging also contradicts readings offered by several Albee scholars. Of the dozen authors of book-length Albee studies in English to date, five comment on the outcome of the final scene but misjudge the ironic thrust of the play's putative celebratory ending. Instead of the playwright's avenging angel, Anne Paolucci believes, "the Young Man is . . . the redeemer" who, "assuming the burden" for Grandma, will "satisfy Mommy and Daddy in their vanity and vices."[49] Although Foster Hirsch suggests that the Young Man "represents [a] plastic ideal," he too argues that the new son is "guaranteed to give Mommy and Daddy maximum satisfaction" and that "he has found an ideal home . . . [where] the cycle of parental greed and lust is to be enacted once again."[50] Offering a parallel view, Ronald Hayman comments, "He will let Mommy take advantage of him sexually," while Anita Stenz contends that "like a huge plastic mail-order doll the Young Man will be whatever Mommy wants him to be without offering any resistance at all."[51] Matthew Roudane also concludes that the Young Man will be "a suitable match for the unreal demands of Mommy and Daddy" and provide them "their most tangible form of fulfillment, material satisfaction."[52] In contrast, those reviewers of Albee's production that discussed the matter, like his audiences, clearly anticipated the retribution—what one reviewer termed "the horror of a lifetime"—that awaits Mommy and Daddy that night.[53] Albee's rehearsal remarks and staging, intended to sharpen audience perception in performance, also serve to correct key critical interpretation of the play's dramatic action.

Yet Albee resists commenting explicitly on meanings and implications. In fact, scholarly exegeses devoted to his works leave him "mildly amused," "puzzled," and largely indifferent: "I'm sent numbers of copies of books and scholarly papers, and I read them the way I do fiction."[54] As early as 1967 he had recognized the need for an author to refrain from analyzing his work's history, direction, or meaning: "It is very dangerous for a writer . . . to start examining . . . [his] writing for its implications, its content and its relationship to what he has done before."[55] Just as crucially, he admits, "I can't take myself seriously enough to read all these books about me with a great degree of absorption."[56]

Consequently, he has even less use for such analysis during rehearsals. He advises actors who sometimes come armed with some scholarly interpretation or other that they must concern themselves with the tangible life of the play on stage and not with questions of theme, symbol, or philosophic significance. Albee maintains this attitude even when directing works by other playwrights, including during his rehearsals of Beckett's *Ohio Impromptu* and *Krapp's Last Tape* at the Alley Theatre, where, not surprisingly in view of the proliferation of Beckett studies, such questions arose rather frequently. Beckett, too, when directing his own plays, made the same point to his casts: during his first German production of *Endgame* in 1967 he used to "shake his head at questions that strayed from concrete performance" and insist, "Here the only interest of the play is as dramatic material."[57]

But even Beckett, notwithstanding his legendary reticence, found that on occasion his actors' needs demanded that he discuss such matters as the Eleatic philosophers, the Biblical flood, and the importance of "say[ing] No to nothingness" in *Endgame*.[58] Likewise, Albee, especially because of a severely truncated rehearsal period necessitated by financial problems, sometimes resorted to the shortcut of interpretive remarks in order to ensure that his text and subtext were understood as well as being expressed accurately. For instance, when Grandma tells the Young Man, "Carter and all those other people, they don't know what they're talking about. You . . . *you* are the American Dream" (108), Albee explained, "When politicians refer to the American Dream, they really refer to the Young Man, who is not a flesh and blood person but rather a plastic thing." Physically flawless but drained of almost all feeling and humanity, the Young Man for Albee represents a travesty of the ideals of the historic American revolution. Albee elaborated on the original basis for his conception: "It was my theory at that time, and still is, that the American Dream had been emasculated by a bunch of shallow, self-serving, short-sighted people" (PCI). This authorial conception of the character dictated that the Young Man's demeanor, speech, and movement convey complacency and smugness: thus throughout the rehearsals Albee painstakingly ensured that he always moved and spoke in a characteristic "slow, self-indulgent" manner. But since the Young Man eases Grandma into another world, Albee also compared him to the benign Angel of Death in *The Sandbox,* corroborating a parallel pointed out by some critics.[59] Albee directed him to offer his arm to Grandma and to be "very gentle" as he led her out of Mommy and Daddy's apartment. Unlike the critics, however, as already seen, Albee also regards the Young Man as a retributive angel of death who will avenge Mommy and Daddy's mutilation of his brother.

Albee contrasted the hollow Adonis, the personification of the contemporary caricature of the true American Dream, to the clear-sighted, resourceful, and compassionate Grandma, the personification of the genuine spirit and ideals of the original. In opposition to the Young Man's self-satisfied lethargy, Albee demanded that Grandma's movements and delivery be consistently nimble and energetic—a theatrical counterpart to her moral and mental vitality. As a symbol of an "emasculated" ideal, the Young Man's effeminate narcissism and self-regard were countered by Grandma's almost masculine toughness, a quality that Albee apparently associates with the American revolutionary past. Grandma herself claims descent from "pioneer stock" and twice asserts her resemblance to men: "I don't hardly count as a woman" and "I look just as much like an old man as I do like an old woman" (112, 86, 111). During rehearsals Albee described her as "spunky," "spirited," "playful," and "without complaint," and he had insisted in an early interview, "Grandma certainly is an enormously sympathetic character, worthy of a good deal of affection and love."[60] As a corollary to her moral and emotional strength, moreover, he proclaimed that, no matter what the situation, his conception of Grandma permitted neither self-pity nor sentimentality of any sort. This was a major concern of his, and he remained vigilant right up to opening night to prevent any trace of regret or sentimentality from creeping in, something that can easily happen in the portrayal of a wronged but genial old woman. Albee's comments contradict those critics, as well as actors, who sometimes fall into this trap and crucially misread Grandma: Ruby Cohn, for example, condemns the playwright for creating an "incongruously maudlin" character, and Matthew Roudane cites the playwright's biography to assess her as "an admittedly sentimental character based on Albee's grandmother."[61]

Albee offered other insights into his meaning as well. When Grandma leaves the apartment she is effectively staging her own death, departing one world for another. Yet she enlists the Young Man's help to take with her the famous multiplying boxes that hold a lifetime of objects, because, Albee revealed, "It's an Egyptian burial where your goods are buried with you." Mrs. Barker earlier mistakes the boxes as intended for her: she protests that instead of boxes, she is "in the habit of receiving *baskets;* but more in a literary sense than really" (83). Albee explained to Mrs. Barker, "You're basically interested in baby boys for adoption," and the "baskets" refer to "bastards or illegitimate kids for adoption." Since "basket case" is slang for a quadruple amputee, Mrs. Barker's euphemism also foreshadows Grandma's mutilation narrative, although Albee did not mention this. Albee also offered an uncomplicated explanation for why Mrs. Barker, upon her arrival, takes off her dress: Mommy simply misspoke, saying, "Won't you take off your dress?" when she meant "Won't you take off your coat?" *The American Dream* deals significantly with the breakdown of communication between people, he declared, and characters frequently just do not listen to each other.

As well as offering insights into interpretation, Albee's directorial work becomes a lens through which to gain clues to his authorial strategies. His rehearsal focus on physical, vocal, and thematic contrasts between the Young Man and Grandma points to a parallel dramaturgic method of building an overall structure of oppositions. In this light the text of the play emerges as an arrangement of symmetrical and asymmetrical antitheses—of stasis and movement, gestural immobility and hyperactivity, languid and energetic rhythm, sound and silence, clichéd and vital language, real and artificial emotion, compassion and cruelty, sadness and hilarity, authentic and inauthentic characters, two-dimensional and three-dimensional characters, and short and long speeches. The script's opening scene, for example, appears structured as a series of contrasts. Stationed at opposite sides of the stage, Mommy is domineering, Daddy compliant; Mommy is garrulous, Daddy reticent; Mommy is energetic and fidgety, Daddy limp and motionless. Even the scene's dialogue is a series of contrasting sections of short and long speeches: each section consists exclusively of either short speeches, long speeches, or a combination of short and long speeches in which all the long ones belong to a single character. If we use an "m" or "d" to represent a short speech by Mommy or Daddy (an average of one line of printed text), an "M" or "D" to represent a long speech (three or more lines), and figures to indicate the total number of speeches in a section, then the sections of dialogue can be depicted in the following way: *md-4, mD-4, Md-2, md-8, Md-12, md-10, Md-2, md-4.* The alternating lengths of speeches, moreover, produce corresponding patterns of contrasting aural rhythms in performance. Further sets of aural, visual, and thematic contrasts follow, as in the next scene Mommy and Daddy, glued to their chairs and uttering banalities, are joined by Grandma with her sprightly movement, down-to-earth language, and feisty spirit.

Albee's rehearsals show how this dramaturgy of contrasts also extends to his characterization in *The American Dream*. Beyond conventional characterization based on personality traits, Albee employs four distinct kinds of dimensionality to individuate his characters. In this scheme of contrasting dimensionalities, Mommy and Daddy are inherently two-dimensional—devoid of compassion, unable to communicate, and unwilling to face reality—and their moral choices and values reveal them as caricatures of human beings. For quite different reasons, Mrs. Barker too is two-dimensional. Unlike her hosts, however, Mrs. Barker willfully puts on two-dimensionality: she "assumes two-dimensionality," Albee acknowledged, "because that is her paid function" (PCI). Subsuming humanity and individuality in an occupation, Mrs. Barker justifies all her actions with her signature refrain, "I am a professional woman." In contrast to these characters, Grandma is unmistakably three-dimensional: she is well-rounded, self-aware, compassionate, witty, inventive, complex. Unlike all the others, the Young Man begins as a two-dimensional character but attains three-dimensionality. Upon his arrival he displays initiative and individuality but completely lacks the capacity for emotion: "He cannot relate his groins with his mind," explained Albee. Urging an "impersonal quality" and a "cool professionalism," he often reminded him, "You're a professional." Thus Albee reinforced his connection to the plastic and emasculated version of the American Dream as well as suggesting a parallel between the Young Man and the two-dimensional professional persona of Mrs. Barker. Yet as the Young Man recounts the agony of his emotional mutilation, Grandma's emotional vitality affects him and restores his ability to feel, as is evident in his increasingly halting and emotional speech. Albee clearly outlined his emotional revival during this narrative: "You feel what you underwent in the past; you feel the emotion deep inside." Thus toward the end of the play the

Young Man becomes three-dimensional, contributing an evolutionary dimensionality to the mix.

Hitherto unnoticed by Albee scholars, this unusual interplay of characters of differing dimensionalities within a single play again testifies to Albee's commitment to dramaturgic experimentation from early in his career. In contrast to the scholars, director Schneider clearly saw the different dimensionalities of these characters when staging the first production. Yet even Schneider underestimated the young playwright's dramaturgic sophistication and misread his intent in creating such characters. As a result he sought to water down the differences in dimensionalities and mistakenly faulted the author's "inability to blend the more sombre stylization of the Young Man with the other highly colored comic-strip characters [and with] Grandma[, who] exists on yet another level."[62] Albee's own production restored, and indeed highlighted, his characters' contrasting dimensionalities.

The rehearsals brought into sharp focus another recurring feature of Albee's dramaturgy that has remained unexamined by scholars. Albee's frequent assertion in his public lectures in recent years that the use of metaphor distinguishes man from all other animals reflects his own fascination with metaphors, specifically with giving metaphors physical embodiment in his drama. In an unpublished screenplay of his second play, *The Death of Bessie Smith,* Albee first employed this strategy of making a metaphor concrete. At critical moments in the screenplay, ill omens appeared in the form of a pack of semiwild dogs. "The dogs were both allegorical and real at the same time," Albee explained, "and were used as metaphor."[63] Although Albee insisted that this was "all in all a perfectly straightforward matter," the device led to the death of the project. Albee acknowledged his dramaturgic method in *The American Dream:* "I was interested in the fact that somebody could be a metaphor *and* a character—at the same time" (PCI). The Young Man and Grandma, as already seen, are finely developed characters as well as personifications of metaphors, respectively, of the false and the true American dream.

In fact, Albee often makes his characters wield the same strategy, to great comic or ironic effect. The savage comedy of the narrative of the child's dismemberment grows out of Grandma's dexterous use of this technique: she employs words that are everyday metaphoric expressions but which, in the presence of the tone-deaf and literal-minded Mrs. Barker, become actual descriptions of physical mutilation. Thus during the narrative, since the child "only had eyes for its Daddy," Mommy "gouged those eyes right out of its head"; since it "put its hands under the covers . . . they *had* to cut off its hands at the wrists"; and since "it called its Mommy a dirty name . . . they cut its tongue out!" (99–100). Somewhat like Mrs. Barker, critics have largely read these mutilations as factual. Albee's authorial strategy in *The American Dream* and elsewhere, on the other hand, argues for a dynamic balance between simultaneously metaphoric and actual mutilations. Like the characterization of Grandma and the Young Man, "the dismemberment," in Albee's view, "is metaphorical and yet real at the same time" (PCI).

In another almost authorial turn, Grandma transforms a metaphor into a real person. Mommy's favorite bogeyman with which to threaten Grandma is the van man who will cart her away to a nursing home. Improvising an escape from Mommy and Daddy's apartment, Grandma hits back with Mommy's own metaphor: she presents the Young Man to Mrs. Barker as the real van man and departs in style on the arm of the handsome youth. Mommy's bogeyman becomes absolutely real, as Mrs. Barker assures the incredulous Mommy: "The van man was here. . . . I saw him with my own two eyes" (122). Perhaps reflecting his own authorial fascination, Albee told Grandma, "It's a very important matter for you—show it—you feel *wonder* at creating Mommy's van man into a real human being." Recasting the van man as another metaphor, he clarified, "For you the van man is the angel of death."

Moreover, sometimes characters playfully or naively take as literal what is simply a misstatement, metaphor, or rhetorical remark. Grandma mischievously misunderstands Mommy's exclamation, "Oooohhhh! What *have* I said?" as a literal question and answers by repeating Mommy's cruel reference to Mrs. Barker's husband sitting in a wheelchair all day (92). Mommy "*giggles*" at Daddy's protest, "I'm all ears" (59), and in Albee's production Mrs. Barker reflexively stepped aside and looked around her feet, fearing real mice, when Grandma used the simile "up and down the social ladder like mice" (95).

Characters and events that are simultaneously real and metaphoric recur in many Albee plays. *The Sandbox* presents a character called the Angel of Death as a handsome, athletic, Southern Californian actor, but *The Lady From Dubuque* portrays the angel of death as an elegant duo—Elizabeth, the titular and metaphoric lady from Dubuque, and Oscar, her black companion. Despite the Lawyer's warning not to "personify the abstraction" in *Tiny Alice,* the play lets us understand Miss Alice as Alice, God, or pure abstraction. Extending the metaphoric mutilation of *The American Dream, Listening* shows the Girl actually slitting her wrists but with non-existent glass—the characters and audience alike see the blood but not the glass. "I'm sure," Albee insisted, "she manages to do the real thing with a metaphorical piece of glass. Absolutely certain of it" (PCI). Albee's dramaturgic goal in all these plays is summed up in his comment on the Elizabeth-Oscar angel of death in *The Lady From Dubuque:* "I was attempting having a metaphor and its embodiment simultaneous and levitating it."[64]

Besides illuminating his dramaturgy, Albee's directorial decisions reveal his evolving theatre aesthetic. Albee's wished to underline the Americanness of his play's social and political milieu as well as its theme. Demonstrating his growing preference for a simple and subtle staging aesthetic, however, Albee avoided the original production's ponderous symbolism of a large, gilded, but empty picture frame surmounted by two crossed American flags dead center on the living room's rear wall, with two smaller empty picture frames on the side walls.[65] Instead Albee employed a pervasive but unobtrusive and almost self-consciously playful color scheme that reproduced the colors of the American flag in every element of his stage decor. Albee and his scene designer, Karl Eigsti, had agreed well before the rehearsal period that their eight plays and the tour's varied theatrical spaces demanded a set that was flexible, generalized, and portable.[66] By the early rehearsals they had settled on all the main elements of the set: the main backdrop consisted of three square interlinked aluminum frames, almost white, that stretched across the length of the stage. Each frame was bifurcated by a vertically hung silky cloth panel—a central reddish one flanked by two sky-blue ones. A light blue leather armchair stood on each side of a central deep blue leather sofa and a wooden coffee table, instead of the premiere production's "heavy gilt and brocade furniture.[67] A solitary red cushion lay on the sofa.[68] Costumes also repeated shades of red, white, and blue. Mommy sported a bright red dress and two strings of pearls instead of the original production's "purple velvet suit [and] pounds of gold jewelry."[69] Mrs. Barker, however, retained the original's blue dress and slip—because they fit the new color scheme—and her cream hat, which was dictated by the dialogue. Daddy wore a blue suit and a red bow tie, and the Young Man was attired in a silky white tee-shirt, blue jeans and matching vest, and white sneakers. Albee made Grandma stand out from the rest in a black dress and light grey shawl, but he wrapped her props—the numerous boxes in many sizes—in red, white, and blue. The simplicity of this approach and of the decor in general debunks one reviewer's claim that the play's "caricature of contemporary America" is contingent "on elaborate set and props."[70] On this stage, which Albee asked his lighting designer Stephen Pollock to illuminate with simple, bright, and largely unvarying lighting, the minimal sets and props—whose color scheme reinforced that of the actors' costumes—served to focus maximum attention on his actors during the hour-long performance.[71]

Lavishing maximum directorial attention on his actors, Albee had coaxed excellent performances from them, as is evident in a broad spectrum of reviews.

However, as playwright Albee knows only too well, no writer, director, or actor wins unanimous applause, and his production of *The American Dream* was no exception. Some critics found the staging too "talky," "abstract," and "static," which they felt was only predictable when a playwright directed his own work. In the early performances, when Catherine Bruno played Grandma, many reviewers, even those who were otherwise positive, questioned why an actor in her twenties was chosen to play a character in her eighties: the *San Francisco Examiner* commented, "It is hard to see what Albee had in mind when he asked an actress in her 20s to play an 86-year-old," and the *Los Angeles Times* noted that "Catherine Bruno, an immensely gifted performer . . . [was] inexplicably cast as an old woman. A matter of touring expediency? Probably so, but unfair."[72] Most of the time, however, critics praised the acting—sometimes even while criticizing the script. The *Washington Post,* for example, remarked, "The players manage . . . to create life on stage where none exists in the lines."[73] Assessing the opening night performance, *Newsday* concluded, "Most of the acting is first rate."[74] Other reviews of that performance echoed the judgment: "Excellent acting by Patricia Kilgarriff, Wyman Pendleton and Eileen Burns"; "They all give excellent performances"; "Good to excellent performances by its players"; "Kilgarriff was effectively domineering and emasculating. . . . Pendleton . . . was perfectly cast."[75] The *Washington Post,* reviewing a later performance, praised Wyman Pendleton for "manag[ing] to raise sitting in a chair to an art" and proclaimed Sudie Bond "a more accomplished mugger than any to be found in Central Park."[76] In a second *Washington Post* article, veteran critic Richard Coe also commended the two: "Sudie Bond . . . is a strength of the company, as is Pendleton," who "make[s] passivity interesting."[77] The *San Francisco Chronicle* lauded Albee for "evok[ing] rich comic performances from his older actors—Patricia Kilgarriff as Mommy, Wyman Pendleton as Daddy and especially Eileen Burns as Mrs. Barker," and the *San Francisco Examiner* commented, "Albee cast the play with competent performers who convey the pathetic quality of the characters. . . . Catherine Bruno makes a lively Grandma. . . . And Eileen Burns is outstandingly funny."[78] Several performers earned praise from the *Honolulu Star Bulletin:* "Patricia Kilgarriff, as Mommy, demonstrated a flair for trenchant, rapid-fire comic delivery and a superb sense of timing; Eileen Burns, as Mrs. Barker, displayed grand foolishness in an ideal contrast to Kilgarriff's style. . . . Stephen Rowe, as the Young Man, served up a nice blend of comic conceit and despair."[79] The *Village Voice* commended Stephen Rowe and Sudie Bond as "good performers" and praised Wyman Pendleton "as almost as skilled in the Albee realm as [Sudie Bond]."[80] The *Philadelphia Inquirer* called Kilgarriff and Pendleton "perfect foils for each other" and lauded Bond for "all her old-sweet-and-sour savor" and Burns for "sweep[ing] over obstacles in high clubwoman style."[81]

Beyond these reviews' implicit tribute to Albee's ability to elicit such performances from his actors, many critics offered explicit praise for his directorial skills. (Since *The American Dream* was on a double bill with *The Zoo Story*, some of these directorial assessments also cover Albee's staging of the latter play: conveniently, these inclusive evaluations also provide an additional perspective on his staging of *The Zoo Story*, which forms the subject of the next chapter.) Opening night notices appraised Albee's direction as "crisp and assured," "tight and concise," "clear and confident."[82] One commented, "Albee directs Albee with precision and passion . . . and as much clarity as is possible in an Albee play"; another observed, "Albee demonstrates both in the writing and the direction how he has earned his place in the contemporary arts."[83] Such opening night assessments were echoed in reviews of subsequent performances in major cities like Philadelphia, Washington, D.C., San Francisco, and Los Angeles. Commenting on *The American Dream,* the *Philadelphia Bulletin* observed, "The playwright has directed with the eye and ear of a symphony conductor," and the *Philadelphia Inquirer* applauded the production's "bite" and "intelligence."[84] Departing from the common criticism that playwright-directors merely want actors to stand and mouth their words, the *San Francisco Chronicle* praised Albee's staging of *The American Dream:* "Director Albee spreads the play all over the wide stage."[85] Unusually for a review, the *San Francisco Examiner* began its appraisal of the two plays by highlighting the directing first, praising "the strong purposeful direction of the author." Labeling *The American Dream* "a modern classic," the review noted, "Albee staged the play with skill and precision," and in its conclusion it again turned to the directing: "Albee has certainly pinpointed his intentions with both plays."[86] In the same vein, the *Honolulu Star Bulletin* asserted, "The direction is crisp and incisive," and the *Los Angeles Times* concluded, "Albee emerges as a sound interpreter of his own work, not necessarily the case with all playwrights."[87]

Albee proved an expert director of his own play: he drew out rich, memorable performances from his actors and created a remarkably lucid and fine-tuned production of *The American Dream.* Moreover, he did not rely only on the strength of his written script. Instead he invented much new business, stage action, and movement, and he creatively exploited the comic and thematic potential of his production's necessarily limited costumes and simple set and backdrop. The range of newspapers and critics that lauded the performances further testifies to the strength of Albee's directorial principles and practices.

4

The Zoo Story

*T*he *Zoo Story: A Play in One Scene* (1958) marked
Albee's spectacular debut as a playwright. First
staged in Berlin in September 1959 at the Schil-
ler Theater Werkstatt on a double bill with Samuel Beckett's *Krapp's Last Tape,*
it received its American premiere three and a half months later, again paired
with the Beckett play, at the Provincetown Playhouse, Eugene O'Neill's first New
York City theatrical home. The next three years saw four revivals in New York
City alone, several in Europe, and numerous more in adventurous regional theatres and universities, and it was eventually established as one of the great postwar American plays. Three decades later the distinguished literary and cultural
critic Harold Bloom judged *The Zoo Story* "without any peers among the shorter
works of O'Neill, Wilder, and Williams . . . worthy of such authentic American
visions of the abyss as West's *Miss Lonelyhearts* and Pynchon's *The Crying of Lot 49.*"[1]
A model of dramatic concentration, *The Zoo Story* presents a harrowing portrait
of urban loneliness and alienation and the human need for contact, even if only
through violence. On a Sunday afternoon in New York City, Peter, a mild and
complacent publishing executive reading a book on a Central Park bench, encounters Jerry, a dispossessed drifter living in a squalid Upper West Side room-

ing house. Jerry by turns cajoles and bullies Peter into carrying on a conversation with him. Through a combination of charm, effrontery, and aggression, Jerry gradually ferrets out intimate details of this middle-class family man's unsatisfying personal life and mesmerizes him with sordid tales of his own nightmarish life, devoid of companionship and suffused with sadness and disappointment. Propelling all this is one man's desperate plea to another for some human response and acknowledgment. Faced with Peter's refusal to understand this, Jerry finally goads, threatens, and punches Peter until he is willing to hold a proffered knife in self-defense, and then outwits him by impaling himself on it, sacrificing his life to achieve the only contact possible and changing Peter forever.

As is his custom, at the opening rehearsal for *The Zoo Story* Albee offered only a general introduction to the play, preferring to deal with details of character interpretation when working on specific scenes. Uncharacteristically, however, his introduction acknowledged the play's broad social scope, beyond the merely personal: *The Zoo Story* deals with "the meeting of two unreconcilable aspects of United States society—the settled, acclimated Peter [played by Wyman Pendleton], a fair representative of the status quo, and Jerry [played by Stephen Rowe], the unreconciled and unreconcilable outsider." Calling Jerry a teacher, he noted that "the clash between these two individuals comes from Peter's refusal—or inability, if you wish to be generous—to receive the messages being sent to him by Jerry." Albee concluded by stressing that the play's final outcome must appear "inevitable" and entirely dictated by the two characters' personalities, insisting that "had Jerry met someone other than Peter, the play might have ended differently."

Early in the first week of rehearsals, Albee sought "a barrel or some object" to dramatically block Peter's attempted retreat through the downstage left exit at the play's end. The play text offered no such object, but, after trying and rejecting several possibilities, Albee settled on a "round wire trash basket, metal, tall enough to lean against (approx. 30"–36"),"[2] and guided Jerry to use it on several occasions: for example, to motivate his opening business, and to vary his posture by resting against it. Adding a set piece during rehearsal was unusual for Albee, because his theatrical aesthetic in the late 1970s—reflected in the dramaturgy of plays like *Counting the Ways* and *Listening* and in the directorial choices of these rehearsals—sought a simplified stage picture and limited theatrical effects.

More typically, Albee eliminated one bench of the original two, since the dramatic action did not require its use and since the dialogue referred to it just once. Similarly, even in elaborately staged productions, director Max Reinhardt insisted that there be "no piece of furniture that does not join in the acting, that remains mere decor," and Harold Clurman claimed, "It is my practice to remove virtually every property or piece of furniture which has no function in the play's action."[3] Striving for simplicity and economy of dramatic means, Albee replaced the set piece with a gestural suggestion during the single verbal reference to the second bench. On the line "Listen to me, Peter. I want the bench. You go sit on the bench over there," Jerry merely pointed off stage left to evoke an empty park bench.[4]

The single green bench—located center stage and slightly angled, whereas the original script called for front-facing benches, "one toward either side of the stage"—served to focus greater attention on the protagonists (11). Albee also reduced the text's "foliage, trees, sky" to three plain cloth backdrops, eleven by five feet each—two forest-green drops hung vertically and an aqua one hung horizontally, the latter retained from *The American Dream*. The simplified set and Albee's decision to illuminate it throughout with unvarying, bright, almost sharp lighting further concentrated visual focus on the two performers. Although this was a naturalistic script, Albee's lighting and setting choices approached the "directness and the ascetic simplicity," achieved through a "concentration on the bare minimum," that are characteristic of Bertolt Brecht's epic theatre productions.[5]

Through such concentration of focus, Albee attempts to lead the spectator toward clear perception. When asked about his chief concern as a director, Albee responded, "I'm after clarity, simplicity" (PCI). More accurately, he seeks to provide clarity *through* simplicity. So does Ingmar Bergman in his staging, where his "need for clarity" has similarly led to progressively simpler decor and effects.[6] For the European premiere of *Who's Afraid of Virginia Woolf?* (1963), for example, Bergman radically simplified the detailed, realistic living room of the original Broadway production. On the Swedish stage, "one saw only an uncompromisingly bare gray room that consisted of a primitive wall-screen at the back and an absolute minimum of furnishings."[7]

Once a line reading, gesture, or business—whether contributed by actor or director—was decided upon, Albee worked toward its clear and precise execution. He insisted, for example, on exactness of tone and stress. When he is pigeonholed by Peter's "Oh; you live in the Village!" Jerry's response, "No, I don't. I took the subway down to the Village so that I could walk all the way up Fifth Avenue to the zoo" (21), should show "condescension." In his turn, Peter's tripartite response to Jerry's wanting his bench, "People can't have everything they want. You should know that; it's a rule . . ." (42), should be successively "pompous, complacent, and condescending." In the rooming-house speech, as well as early in the dog story, Jerry's "tone is ironic, rather than angry," specified Albee; toward the end of the dog story, however, his tone must be "direct" and "very calm," since "it's a parable by that point." By the time Jerry sits next to Peter on the bench and announces "The Story of Jerry and the Dog: the end," his tone must convey "friendliness, camaraderie." To elicit the proper stress and intonation in what Albee termed "a very important line," he gave Jerry a virtual line reading for "And *I* am there, and it's feeding time at the lion's house" (40; Albee gave it this emphasis in rehearsal). Correcting his cast for not stressing some italicized words, he decreed, "I have used italics to indicate the high points, words which *must* be emphasized."

Albee was equally particular about pauses: "If you don't pause during an ellipsis, it can alter the meaning." When Jerry tells Peter, "You're a very . . . a richly comic person" (37), explained the director, "you should pause, because you don't know what to say; without the pause it would be an incorrect sentence." Although no such pause was indicated by ellipsis or stage direction, Albee ensured that Peter hesitated for a moment when first asked to fight for the bench. "It's such a preposterous thing," he pointed out; "you haven't fought for many, many years—not since you were seventeen!"

Always practical, Albee does not shy away from offering similar down-to-earth advice on other external aspects of performance. He reminded the actors, for example, that stress on italicized words need not be achieved through increased volume: "You can go very, very soft" and still emphasize a word. "When you say, 'I'll sit down soon,'" he told Jerry, "don't point to the place where you'll be sitting," since this would render the subsequent action too predictable. Again to maintain unpredictability, Albee suggested Jerry imitate the voices in just one or two of the conversations he remembers and recounts. In performance, his re-enactment of the hamburger seller's reaction when asked "not to bother with the roll" (32), for example, became doubly funny because of Jerry's sudden switch to a coarse, uneducated accent.

Frequently Albee directs externally: he specifies the emotion, posture, attitude, or speed required but not the impulse behind it, which may or may not be immediately apparent to the performer. When Jerry talks about the picture frames in his room—"And let's see now; what's the point of hanging a girl's picture, especially in two frames?" (26)—the director advised, "Get a little lighter," presumably because excessive seriousness so early in the encounter would drive Peter away. Late in the play, as Peter recovers from his hysterical laughter, saying, "Oh, my. I don't know what happened to me" (39), Albee indicated that he should be "really puzzled." During the dog narrative Albee told Peter to show "more reaction"; for example, when Jerry pretends to put up signs on a billboard, "you could be a little amused." Jerry, in turn, should "look at Peter" and "see how he's reacting." When he recalls how the dog caught his trouser leg, the director suggested, "Put up your left foot on the bench." At the story's end, Jerry should "wait a little," probably to give Peter time to absorb the fable. Albee suggested that Jerry theatricalize his reference to St. Francis by mimicking the pose common in popular images of the saint, with arms outstretched for birds to perch on. In addition, Albee's notes contained many simple mechanical instructions: "take a beat," "change your pace," "too static," "very slow," "wait for him," "don't sit on the trash basket so often," and so on.

Albee offers such external directions because their precision makes them easy to communicate and provides actors a sense of security conducive to their further growth. With "relentless attachment to technique," director John Dexter at the National Theatre relied almost solely on similar directions, according to Jim Hiley's *Theatre at Work*. Such instruction, "Dexter believe[d], . . . provides a basis of confidence for actors to develop their performances the more freely."[8] Albee expressed a parallel view: these directions should "lead the actor to discover more about the character" and to build upon those discoveries (PCI). In *Peter Stein: Germany's Leading Theatre Director*, Michael Patterson describes how Stein also often "invite[s] an actor to work 'from the outside in' in order to get a move or a line right." He advises his performers, "Don't be afraid to do something externally or mechanically. That way you might arrive at the feeling."[9] The belief that "out of the physical action would come the feeling" was central to Joan Littlewood's initial rehearsals as well, according to Howard Goorney, a Theatre Workshop member for thirty years. In Littlewood's approach (based chiefly on Rudolf Laban's techniques, which were a crucial influence on the company), "the emphasis was always on the physical" action or movement "to help bring out the right feelings."[10]

Given Albee's frequent practice of guiding actors externally and of sharing with them the process of building character and action, he often explains a direction by reference to practical staging needs. He told Jerry, "Ideally, stay behind Peter, where he can't see you," in order to visually convey a sense of "entrapment and manipulation." On a few occasions, Albee wished Jerry to go behind Peter and lean over the bench, so as to suggest familiarity, almost friendliness, as when he wonders about Peter's pornographic cards: "I suppose when you were a kid you and your pals passed them around, or you had a pack of your own" (26). The director explained that Jerry must lean from just behind Peter at center stage, a bit to either his left or right, because that constituted both the most dramatic and the most personal area. Neither a stage left nor a stage right spot, which the actor wanted, could yield the desired effect. Again citing staging effectiveness as the reason, Albee stopped Jerry from moving away from Peter in resignation after completing the dog story, because "such a move would diminish and spoil the tension." He urged Jerry, "Don't sit comfortably on the bench, like Peter is sitting, [but] stay on it, resting on one knee," and explained, "It creates more tension visually." To justify the posture further, he added that it would give Jerry, who was shorter than this Peter, "additional height" and make him more menacing. This directorial logic was reminiscent of his staging of *Who's Afraid of Virginia Woolf?* on Broadway, where, for example, he asked Colleen Dewhurst as Martha to rest her elbows on the mantelpiece behind her, in order to suggest a similar sense of power as well as to make better use of the set.[11]

Much more frequently than Albee, his longtime director Alan Schneider offered external directions and instructions explained in terms of staging requirements. When directing *The Lady From Dubuque,* he peppered his rehearsals with such comments as "I want you to be standing up on that line," "I'm trying to get you down before he arrives," "I'd like you to get away from them—it's too crowded there," "I want to use the cushion at least once to justify its presence—so please sit on it now," "I like you above that chair because I like the image," and so on.[12] He told Oscar (played by Earl Hyman), to rise as he delivered the line "The view from above, to the pit below," since "I want to make this important."(115). In order to accentuate the humor, he suggested, Fred (Kevin O'Connor) should pick up a drink just as Sam (Tony Musante) begins, "Besides, it's my house, and you're drinking my liquor" (5).[13] A few times during act 1, Schneider explained, "I want to repeat this move in act 2, since these lines are echoed there." Thus as Lucinda proclaimed, "Let there be silence!" she had to raise her hands and gesture from a position that could be repeated exactly by Oscar in act 2 on his "Let there be silence; shhhhhhhhhh" (6, 15). Parallel moves for Jo (Frances Conroy) and Elizabeth (Irene Worth) also accompanied their identical requests in acts 1 and 2: "The man asked for silence; give it to him" (4, 5, 115). Albee attended several *Dubuque* rehearsals and in a personal interview soon afterward spoke with approval of Schneider's practice.[14]

Both Albee and Schneider, however, recognized that such directions alone are not adequate. They consequently interspersed them with other directions dealing with character psychology. Thus during *The Lady From Dubuque* rehearsals Schneider consistently complemented his external directions with those intended, as he explained, to "rationalize" or "justify" action and delivery "on the basis of realistic behavior." At least once or twice a rehearsal he would exclaim, "I don't get your intention," in order to point out an actor's lack of clear inner motivation. Just as often he would insist, "We'll need to find a reason for this."

For example, when Sam does not reach out to protect Jo as Edgar criticizes her, the director first encouraged Musante to discover why. "It's strange . . . so we'll have to find a reason for it." He then pointed out to Musante some of Sam's lines to Jo later in the act: "You tell me to ignore you when you get like this, and then you yell at me for . . ." (69). Schneider explained, "Sam wants to help Jo, but she won't let him—even though she wants it." Similarly, he reasoned that during the struggle to untie himself, Sam should refrain from kicking Fred again. "You would have learned your lesson from the first kick, when he punished you with a hard punch."

Paralleling Schneider's practice, Albee sometimes told an actor, "I don't get any motivation for this," and then guided him to communicate what drives his character's words and actions at a given moment, beyond whatever practical considerations of staging that director and actor may have discussed. Albee told Jerry to remain near Peter after finishing the dog story in order to maintain a physical, theatrical tension. But he also provided a character-based justification. Jerry would not "disengage and go off from Peter . . . [but would] stay at the corner of the bench" so as to preserve the almost hypnotic sway over Peter that he had achieved through subtle narrational manipulation. Earlier in the play, too, Albee offered Jerry psychological motivation, although for a nearly opposite action. "Don't get too close to Peter at the beginning," he instructed, "or he would panic and leave." He explained that everyone maintains a circle of space around himself, and its breaching makes one uncomfortable or afraid. Because "Peter's circle is *very* large," Jerry should "move in as large a circle as possible and lighten up and joke whenever it gets a little serious." Albee again cited psychological appropriateness as justification when asking Peter to stop in the middle of preparing his pipe. Peter must put his pipe and tobacco pouch away as soon as Jerry begins, "Well, boy; *you're* not going to get lung cancer, are you? . . . No, sir. What you'll probably get is cancer of the mouth" (13). Given such words, argued the director, "I don't think you'd light up."

Unlike Albee and Schneider, however, some directors refuse to offer such explanations. Shunning psychological justifications, Ingmar Bergman prefers precise external directions: "I can not hand out emotional rubbish to an actor, then he's got me in an instant. I must give him completely distinct, clear technical directions."[15] Even when a performer found a move uncomfortable, Joan Littlewood remained adamant. As Howard Goorney writes in *The Theatre Workshop Story*, "Joan's reply to an actor's 'I don't feel right' was 'You don't have to bloody well feel right, you just have to do it.—DO it!'"[16]

For Albee, though, communicating the psychological motivation behind Jerry's myriad recollections became a crucial directorial concern. "Be very, very careful," Albee advised, to indicate that "you're reexperiencing these experiences in order to transfer them to Peter—to test him and to teach him—not for your own emotional satisfaction." Emphasizing the importance of this distinction, he urged, "Set this up fairly early in the play. . . . I don't want you to seem uncertain" about it at any stage.

From the beginning Albee stressed that Jerry is manipulative. "I want to see you doing things for their effect on Peter." While describing his rooming-house life in graphic detail, Jerry should "test Peter" by moving in semicircles behind him to "see how he reacts—it will tell us in the audience, not too obviously, what you're doing." In performance, during this as well as other scenes, Jerry often paused for the briefest moment to look at Peter and ascertain his response to a facial expression, gesture, or word. Sometimes he registered Peter's reaction with a look of satisfaction, as if to say, "My strategy is working." At times, after confirming Peter's reactions, he glanced conspiratorially toward the audience. Correspondingly, the way Jerry spoke his lines also clearly showed the manipulatory intent of his speeches, which Albee characterized as "words spoken not as information but as a vehicle for testing Peter." Early in the rehearsals, he advised Jerry to shift tonal gears wherever such a shift was implicit in the text, to catch Peter off-guard and determine whether he is "worthy of your attention."

Many stage and critical interpretations of Jerry see him as too uniformly intense. The author's directing, by contrast, revealed a far more complex personality; Jerry's aggression is interlaced with deft manipulation of as well as genuine feeling for Peter. Indeed, more than once Albee warned that Jerry "need[ed] more charm," "a sense of sharing" and "camaraderie." As he explained, "Up to the dog story, Jerry must manipulate him by charm." On several occasions he interrupted rehearsal to stop Jerry from playing the emotional intensity of his lines to the virtual exclusion of their manipulativeness. Following a run-through he observed, "The teaching scene"—the last quarter of the dog fable—"became terribly interior and terribly private—it was more 'me, me, me,' rather than 'you, you, you.'" Jerry must not be self-indulgent: his emotions, although deeply felt, must remain "underneath." Albee pointed out that he had deliberately created a character who was in his late thirties, a man of experience who could not be easily stereotyped and dismissed as an immature, bohemian kid. "The major thing," he explained, "is to see a mature man objectifying his experiences." Two days prior to the first preview performance, he analyzed why the actor's recollections were sometimes too emotional: "You might be playing the reality of the situations much more than the *objectification* of those situations for a manipulation." The diagnosis again stressed that Jerry must diligently control his emotions and actions.

While "there is control and an overall psychology" that motivates the character, Albee clarified, "there can't be a [Stanislavskian] through-line, since Jerry is improvising." An actor working in terms of a through-line might suggest that Jerry knew beforehand not only what he wanted but also how he would speak and act to achieve it. Albee, however, declared, "I don't think he was sitting in his room and deciding that I'll go and do this or any of the thoughts that he expresses to Peter. The whole thing really just happens!" Albee takes strong exception to critics and directors who interpret Jerry as a psychopath. During the play's very first American production, Brooks Atkinson of the *New York Times* branded Jerry "wild, scabrous, psychotic," and Tom Driver of the *Christian Century* characterized him as "a psychotic . . . mad young fellow."[17] During its 1963 revival Lewis Funke of the *New York Times* labeled him a "tormented, psychopathic young man."[18] The characterization survived for years and surfaced in other critical estimations. Because Jerry "cannot relate to human beings or to animals," Robert Heide argues in *Other Stages,* he "embraces despair," "goes into the park [and] seeks out someone who will kill him," someone who will, in Gilbert Debusscher's parallel view, "put [him] out of his misery at last."[19] Reviewing Albee's own production in the *Philadelphia Inquirer,* William Collins recognized the import of the author's staging but longed for earlier readings of "an outcast psychopath," "suicidal" and with a "streak of madness."[20] A few years later a literary scholar pronounced him "demonic and indeed psychotic."[21] Firmly denouncing such readings as "misinterpretation" and "incorrect," Albee pointed out that had Jerry methodically planned the violent events of that day, he would indeed be a psychopath: "he would be crazy, but that's one thing Jerry is not."[22] Albee later mused, "It's conceivable that a future incident or its possibility flashed at the lion's cage," but that does not mean, he insisted, that Jerry made "a decision that he will go to the park and commit suicide" (PCI). Instead, Jerry improvises from moment to moment in a growing commitment to connecting with Peter, gaining our understanding and admiration. Albee concluded, "He is far closer to being a teacher—he's trying to teach Peter like crazy."

To preclude misinterpretation, he eliminated more than half a page—a substantial deletion in a script already fine-tuned in previous productions—to completely remove from Jerry's crucial dying speech all references to his experience at the zoo, his momentary speculation that he might have planned his actions, and his reminder about the face that will appear on TV that night (48). Correspondingly, he also cut Jerry's tantalizing but now unfulfilled promise from earlier in the play, "Let me tell you about why I went [to the zoo] . . . well, let me tell you some things" (27). These textual emendations ensured that Jerry's attack and suicide appeared completely improvised, without a hint of premeditation. Besides revising his script, Albee guided his actor's movements, gestures, and inflections to generate a performance that unmistakably conveyed a man inventing his strategy from moment to moment to suit an evolving encounter.

In another change from the published script, Albee altered his stage directions to stress that although Peter's hysterical laughter and babbling in the tickling scene—"the parakeets will be getting the dinner ready soon. Hee, hee. And the cats are setting the table"—are triggered by Jerry, they bubble up from within Peter. Jerry starts tickling him one line earlier than in the text's version, at "Stay a while longer," and stops fully five lines earlier, at "Oh, hee, hee, hee. I must go. I . . . ," so that Peter's hysteria is manifestly self-generated (38). To further clarify this, Albee instructed Jerry to remove his fingers from Peter's side in a clearly theatrical gesture, with arms raised and spread wide, like a magician finishing a grand trick.

Albee also revised his text to introduce important new business and movement for greater visual variety, tension, and theatricality in his play's already quite vivid last few minutes. In the original script, *"Peter rises"* from the bench only when Jerry throws the knife at his feet and then *"grabs him by the collar"* (46). In the amended version, Jerry physically pushes Peter off the bench, and does so seventy-five lines earlier. During those seventy-five lines, i.e., until the knife throwing, the two men had originally remained seated, sparring only verbally. Now, during those lines, Jerry sprawls on the bench to stake his claim and physically covers each part of the bench as Peter approaches it. In turn, Peter, who now remains on his feet throughout, desperately rushes back and forth and around Jerry, trying to regain the bench. The new staging is not only more dynamic but mirrors Jerry's similar though calmer movement around Peter in much of the play earlier, visually stressing the theme of their essential commonality as human beings despite their many differences. In another change from the original, Jerry steps back four or five feet to the right of the bench to throw the knife, so that he can stalk Peter. And Peter, instead of remaining seated until grabbed by the collar, now flees backward upon seeing the knife but is trapped as he stumbles into the newly introduced trash basket. He then tries to run away from the stalking Jerry, first downstage and then above the bench, where he is caught by the collar.

For the play's final moment, Albee departed from his original text to again create new action that was highly theatrical and thematically redolent. According to an original stage direction, when the dying Jerry reminds Peter to take his book, which is lying on the bench, *"Peter rushes to the bench, grabs the book, retreats"*

(49). But in Albee's staging, Jerry clutches at the book in a painful spasm just as Peter reaches the bench, forcing another struggle until Jerry relents. This new and sudden struggle echoes their earlier fight for the bench and leads to another, more desirable contact, not via a violent act but via a book, the visual emblem of communication and understanding, thus rendering the play's theme palpable through stage action.

Albee made a few other textual refinements during these rehearsals. He deleted a stage direction so that Jerry no longer laughs when Peter threatens to call a policeman but instead maintains his soft tone, and he cut Jerry's insult "Stupid!" from the question to Peter, "Don't you have any idea, not even the slightest, what other people *need*" (43, 45)? He changed Peter's "I must be getting home soon" to "I must be getting home now" (38), telling the actor, "This is your chance to escape," because at this stage Peter feels, "I sense something terrible happening here; maybe I can sneak out!" Finally, he changed Jerry's mention of Peter's likely favorite writers from "those two men" to "both men," replaced J. P. Marquand with James Michener, and updated the publishing executive's yearly salary from eighteen thousand to thirty-eight thousand a year.

When Albee makes such changes in his play texts, he is doing more than fine-tuning. He works to clarify the overall thrust of the play and fundamental matters of characterization (such as the fact that Jerry's actions are improvised, not premeditated), about whose importance he is emphatic. But even then, to translate these matters into the particulars of performance he offers his actors considerable freedom for invention and collaboration. Under his general guidance, he encouraged actors to offer their own individual reading of specific lines and scenes. When Jerry exclaims, "You have everything in the world you want; you've told me about your home, and your family, and *your own* little zoo" (44), Albee reminded him, "These words have been italicized with a purpose," and he suggested, "Consider the fact that Peter has his *own* zoo but *you* had to go to the public zoo in the Park." Beyond this, however, Albee did not demand a specific interpretation; instead, he invited the actor to propose a reading. "See if you can make something out of this line." For another of Jerry's lines—"I'm on your precious bench, and you're never going to have it for yourself again" (43)—Albee simply stressed that it was a "very, very important statement." "Speak it very clearly," he told Rowe, "and if you like, you could have some silence preceding it. A different beat." Specific vocal coloration and timing again was left to the actor.

If an actor's interpretation strays from Albee's basic conception of a character or his overall goal for a scene, he quickly intervenes, but does not dictate what should be done. Instead he often offers the actor several readings to choose from.

As Jerry switches from tickling and poking to punching Peter, the flabbergasted man exclaims, "Stop it! What's the matter with you?" and Jerry retorts, "I'm crazy, you bastard" (41). Early in the rehearsals, Albee stopped Rowe during this response, warning, "Don't say it straight!" "If you do," he explained, "Peter would leave immediately." Instead, he suggested, Rowe could decide either to "mock" Peter or to "joke" with him with that retort. To match the delivery, Jerry should "make a derisive gesture, or take a funny stance," and Albee demonstrated a possible pose—knees bent, arms raised, fingers contorted, eyes bulging wildly, chin thrust forward, and tongue hanging out.

When an actor finds a suggested movement or business uncomfortable or unhelpful, Albee gives him the freedom to change or even reject it. "The wise director recognizes," wrote Harold Clurman, that "not everything the cleverest director suggests is useful to the actor."[23] In *The Zoo Story*, "*as the curtain rises*," according to an original stage direction, Peter "*stops reading, cleans his glasses, goes back to reading*" (11). Albee's actor found handling glasses, kerchief, book, pipe, tobacco pouch, and lighter unwieldy and wondered, "Do I have to clean my glasses?" "If it's uncomfortable, don't," replied Albee. "I don't care whether you do it or not."

Although Albee said this about several of his instructions to the actors, most of the time he did care. But he usually thought it preferable, when an actor could not promptly understand an instruction or comfortably incorporate a suggested action into his characterization, to alter, replace, or delete the instruction. Similarly, in Ingmar Bergman's stage as well as film work "an instruction or a decision that makes no immediate emotional sense to an actor is rarely either explicated or insisted upon. . . . It is simply changed to something else."[24] Remaining willing to change throughout his rehearsals, Albee provided the cast self-confidence for freer creativity.

These practices, individually as well as collectively, offered actors frequent opportunities for active collaboration. Rowe and Pendleton significantly enriched *The Zoo Story* by originating facial expressions, gestures, business, and a host of character nuances throughout the play. In the opening scene, for example, Albee asked Jerry, as he first arrives, to "take all your time and size up Peter," but the actor freely chose movement, business, and property to communicate this, elaborately theatricalizing the simple textual direction "*Jerry enters*" (11). Clad in blue work shirt and worn jeans, Jerry leisurely walked downstage from an upstage right entrance, as he finished a can of Coke; he glanced from the corner of his eye at the man in a tweed jacket, brown slacks, and loafers, sitting on the center-stage park bench. For about fifteen seconds he stopped at the edge of the stage; then he turned briefly to look at Peter and sauntered across the stage as if to throw the can into the trash basket. Instead of discarding it, however, he walked around the basket, so that he could get a better view of Peter while he slowly crushed the aluminum can in his hand, and only then tossed it with studied deliberation. Two or three times during this action Jerry averted his eyes as soon as Peter unconsciously glanced toward him. Finally, he ambled upstage in order to finish studying Peter as well as to speak his first line, out of the auditor's view.

Later in the play, when Jerry recalls how he and his landlady's dog had "looked into each other's face . . . [and] made contact" (34). Rowe and Pendleton, in contrast to their avoidance of eye contact in the opening scene, maintained a dramatic, mesmerizing gaze into each other's eyes for nearly a minute. Visually and thematically, this linked the two encounters and stressed a parallel between Peter and the dog. Albee developed the parallel further in the play's last minutes: he asked Peter not to *"dart down,"* as the text indicated, in order to pick up the knife thrown by Jerry, but instead to scramble on all fours like an animal.

Similarly, an original stage direction called for Jerry to announce, *"as if reading from a huge billboard,"* "The story of Jerry and the dog!" (30). Instead of simply declaiming the line, however, Jerry mimed erecting a sign high above him, as if lifting up bulky boards one by one, each board bearing one word of the title, and as he hoisted a word he mouthed it with exaggerated theatricality. Saddened by Peter's refusal to comprehend the meaning of his dog story, Jerry tells him, "I don't live in your block . . . I am a permanent transient . . . in New York City, which is the greatest city in the world. Amen" (37). Although Jerry delivered this *"in a monotone, wearily,"* as instructed by a stage direction, on his sarcastic "Amen" he made an impulsive, theatrical sign of the cross. An opening night review called it "a stunning, volatile gesture . . . as if to tear open his soul and release the agony within. It is unforgettable."[25] Since Albee had endeavored to provide the freedom that nurtures such creative contributions, he enthusiastically incorporated them into performance. Similarly, even Brecht, who generally "didn't consult actors," writes Eric Bentley in "The Brecht Memoir," "was often happy to accept an idea that was entirely the actor's own."[26] Though working within the European dictator-director tradition, Brecht's actors—even when he used his own *Model Book* for a revival, as in his 1950 *Mother Courage* at the Munich Kammerspiele—frequently discovered that "Model or no Model, they could show what they liked. If it was good it was accepted at once."[27]

Because the degree of Albee's directorial supervision of a play varies in inverse proportion to its performers' skills, *The Zoo Story* received less directorial attention than did *The American Dream,* its companion on the evening's bill. When directing the Broadway revival of *Who's Afraid of Virginia Woolf?* Albee affirmed, "Three quarters of the trick of directing is to start with a good play and good actors," just as Alan Schneider, director of the original production of that play, had observed, "Casting skillfully is more than half the director's battle."[28] Confident that he had cast *The Zoo Story* particularly well, with two skilled and inventive actors, Albee concentrated on *The American Dream,* where Patricia Kilgarriff and the less experienced Catherine Bruno required greater attention. Moreover, he could count on Pendleton to steer himself and Rowe close to authorial intentions because the veteran actor had performed in four Broadway and two off-Broadway Albee productions, in most of which the author had actively participated. Indeed, he had played Peter in an off-Broadway production of *The Zoo Story.*[29]

Albee's choice of Bruno, a relatively inexperienced actor, to play the older roles in *The American Dream* might be judged an instance of poor casting. That was also the view of at least one fellow actor, expressed a few months after the rehearsals. Discussing why Albee had allowed them to rehearse *The Zoo Story* on their own, Wyman Pendleton noted in a personal interview that Albee "had another play he had to get together, with an actor (who shall be nameless) who didn't know what she was doing. And so he took advantage of that."[30] However, many reviews interpreted Albee's choice of a young actor to play an old woman not so much as a casting error but as a private joke or a deliberately mystifying Absurdist touch.

At least in part, Albee's limited supervision of *The Zoo Story* also resulted from stringent time constraints imposed by an already modest budget suffering a last-minute reduction. The new budget allowed only thirty-two days for rehearsing the three-evening bill. During the last sixteen days, moreover, evening previews took up two and a half hours of the average eight-hour workday, and on six of those days matinee previews consumed another two and a half hours a day. Like many directors, Albee regards previews as a crucial part of the rehearsal process, where actors hone their performance in the presence of an audience; nonetheless, the large number of previews took considerable time away from potentially more valuable moment-to-moment interaction between the director and his performers. In fact, Albee confessed privately that he let his actors, especially those in *The Zoo Story,* work without him more often than he liked: although in the professional theatre "you have three and a half weeks for one play, . . . here we've really had a week for each play [i.e., for each evening's bill]" (PCI). In point of fact, however, Albee managed to devote about three weeks to the first two evenings' bill, by reallocating time originally earmarked for the third evening's bill of *Counting the Ways* and *Listening,* which he decided to present initially only as staged readings. (That decision is the reason they are not analyzed in this book.) In view of the truncated rehearsal period, it is noteworthy that Albee achieved the level of performance documented here.

Albee's faith in Rowe and Pendleton was borne out during the rehearsals. In an interview two days after the opening, Albee held up the two performers for special praise: "Look at the interesting things that Stephen tries to do. That's a very intelligent and interesting actor. You just touch him, just a little touch, and the whole thing improves." Commending Pendleton, he recalled that he needed the least amount of directing, because "with a good actor you don't have to" direct much (PCI). Both comments also point to Albee's method when directing good actors. He avoids detailed instructions to good performers, convinced they need only hints to guide them toward an appropriate representation of character. In a conversation during a break he summed up his approach: "A good actor is like an FM band in a radio; you tune it just so slightly."

Conversely, he argues that inexperienced or less skilled actors require continual coaching, as if tuning a short-wave radio. With some actors, he observed, "you've got to do it constantly." Speaking privately about Bruno, particularly about her Old Woman roles, he sighed, "I'll be working with her for another month, trying to get a decent performance out of her" (PCI). Eventually, Albee secured good performances from Bruno, especially as the Girl in *Listening:* the *Los Angeles Times,* for example, called her "an immensely gifted performer whose interpretation of the Girl is the highlight of *Listening.*"[31] Besides paying special and persistent attention to novice actors like Bruno when rehearsing in a group, he also works individually with them for extended periods. In short, he understands that a director "must distinguish between born actors who should be let alone to find their own way," as Bernard Shaw once declared, "and spook actors who have to be coached sentence by sentence and are helpless without such coaching."[32]

Although Albee willingly devotes considerable time to individual work with inexperienced actors and offers them basic acting advice, he is not an acting coach, as some directors are and which such actors need. Without professional acting experience of his own (although he once boasted that he did nothing but act during his brief stint in college), Albee is at a disadvantage in serving as an acting teacher, especially as compared to those directors who began their theatrical careers as actors and thus easily slip into the role of teacher. Some actors view this as Albee's directorial weakness. Albee counters that teaching acting is not his job; the professional actor must be capable of doing his own work, utilizing the training and techniques that best suit him. This attitude resembles that of other playwright-directors, most notably Beckett and Brecht. Despite his respect for actors, "Brecht never cared how his actors worked. . . . He didn't give a damn about the mechanics they used, he just cared about results," insists Carl Weber, one of his former assistant directors at the Berliner Ensemble.[33]

Irrespective of a cast's level of expertise, however, Albee believes that in order to provide an atmosphere of greater freedom for creativity and the discovery of fresh nuances, a director should stay away from one or two sessions, especially later in the rehearsal process. This belief is another reflection of his links to the Stanislavsky–Actors Studio tradition, although several directors outside that tradition hold it as well. Discussing his staging methods, Max Reinhardt observed, "It is best to leave some rehearsals to an assistant. . . . The actor feels freer, less supervised. The assistant . . . leaves the actors as much as possible free to run on in their own manner."[34] It was usual for Beckett as well to "deliberately absent himself from a late rehearsal or two, so that the actors may feel freer in their final discoveries."[35] For similar reasons—although also in part because of a teaching commitment—when directing *The Lady From Dubuque*, Schneider left three rehearsals just before previews to his assistant director, whom he nonetheless telephoned daily to discuss the salient features of each rehearsal. Since Albee's company had access to another, larger theatre as well as to other rehearsal areas in a five-theatre complex, the *Zoo Story* actors worked in one space while Albee rehearsed with others elsewhere. Pendleton confirmed later that, in rehearsing without the author-director, he and Rowe felt "free to develop and grow" and "found it could be of very great help."[36]

But before permitting actors—including Pendleton and Rowe—to work alone, Albee ensured that they had grasped the nature of their characterization and were thoroughly familiar with the blocking. He also often specified whether they should run lines, improvise without book, work on particular problems, redo certain scenes, or have a run-through. With equal frequency, however, Albee gave no such instructions. Instead he told them, "Do whatever you think will be useful—you already know what I want," or "Whatever you like—rehearsal time is for you." Still, the overall artistic intent and the goals to be reached were the director's; the ways of achieving them were left to the actors.

After the actors had rehearsed independently, usually for two to three hours at a time, Albee closely reviewed the results. In the case of *The Zoo Story*, Pendleton and Rowe rehearsed without the director for slightly longer periods—often for half a rehearsal day. He accepted or rejected what they showed him, asked as well as answered questions, and offered new suggestions, then proceeded to re-hearse the scene or play again under his close supervision. In Pendleton's words, "When we had been through the play twice or something," Albee would see if "things [were] going awry . . . see any progression or regression and comment or work with us on it."[37] Returning to *The Zoo Story* after a hiatus of several hours also helped Albee see their work with freshness and greater acuity.

Even when present at a rehearsal, Albee recognizes that sometimes an actor should be allowed to work on a problem independently. Never demanding immediate results, he often tactfully allows performers to discover solutions on their own and to bring them to subsequent sessions for his consideration. In the same vein, Schneider argued that "the skill and tact of the individual director are tested most specifically" in "knowing exactly when to take hold of and when to leave alone."[38] Albee understands when to insist and when to let alone. Soon after the rehearsals concluded, Stephen Rowe praised his ability "to stay out of an actor's way" when appropriate, and James Knobeloch cited his willingness to "allow the actor to do his work" as a major strength.[39] Singling out "one very strong point" when evaluating his directing a year after these rehearsals, veteran Albee actor Pendleton made a corresponding observation: "He knows the moments when to leave . . . the actor alone.[40]

Albee's approach during *The Zoo Story* rehearsals reflects his directorial method in general. Implicit in his practices is the principle that, within general guidelines dictated by a text, the actor must be allowed maximum creative freedom. In personal interviews, conversations, and letters, actors most often cite Albee's willingness to collaborate with actors as his signal strength and the hallmark of his directing method. Rowe praised "his openness to allowing the discovery of nuance that [even he] may be unaware of."[41] Albee is not only "open to actors' suggestions" but "really allows his actors to participate in the creative process," echoed Knobeloch, who played Yam in *Fam and Yam* and the Minister in *Quotations from Chairman Mao Tse-Tung.*[42] Openness to actor collaboration, Albee argues, is an imperative for successful directing, because without it the actor cannot make his proper contribution to a performance. Thus even though, as the author and director, he can exercise extraordinary power, Albee prefers not to; as he quipped, "These are not puppets you're working with . . . they are flesh and blood human beings . . . with interesting intelligences" (PCI). While indicating precisely *what* he wants conveyed, he often tells his actors, "I don't care *how* you show it," in order to foster an atmosphere of creative freedom. As Albee himself describes his method, "I give very few specific notes. . . . I would rather give an actor a general intention note first and hope that he will come up with or invent his own specifics" (PCI). In short, while Albee's vision for a given text controls the broad contours of character and the overall shape of the performance, he encourages the actor to create his own moment-to-moment details of delivery, business, and movement that allow him to simultaneously imitate and inhabit the character. Albee's practice follows Max Reinhardt's precept "Give the actor the widest possible freedom of maneuver," and heeds Harold Clurman's memorable warning "Without freedom the actor remains a stick, no matter how polished."[43] Practices of directors from Stanislavsky, Reinhardt, and Shaw to Brecht, Vilar, Clurman, Kazan, Hall, Schneider, Planchon, and Bergman attest to the soundness of Albee's directing philosophy, which clearly stems from the main text-centered and mimetic tradition of Western theatre directing represented by such diverse artists.

As much as their distinguished historical precedents, so too do the almost universally good reviews of *The Zoo Story* testify to the strength of Albee's directing principles. With one exception, which thought Pendleton too old for Peter, opening night reviews gave unanimous praise to both the director and the actors. One called Albee's production "magnetic," noted "the confidence that he transmitted to the actors," and acclaimed his directorial "precision and passion . . . beauty and . . . clarity."[44] Another hailed "Albee's faultless ability to build and sustain emotional momentum," resulting in "dramatic excellence not to be missed," and lauded Rowe's acting for "conviction, intensity, and electricity" and a "supreme mastery of the character."[45] Several others also commended the directing and acting, often singling out Rowe for his performance, which is not surprising, since Pendleton's role allowed limited scope. Calling the directing sharp and confident and the acting excellent, one reviewer commented, "Rowe admirably captures" Jerry's "revulsion with the world and his sudden bursts of humor"; another found Rowe "superb" and "his monologue . . . spellbinding, frightening."[46] Still others admired Rowe's Jerry as "powerful" and "passionately portrayed" and Pendleton's Peter as "excellent" and "played effectively."[47]

Notices following the initial run were equally strong. Ruby Cohn in the *Bay Arts Review* applauded the San Francisco production as "gripping" and remarked, "Stephen Rowe as Jerry and Wyman Pendleton as Peter built relentlessly to a climax unsullied by stage blood." Lauding Albee's directing as "clear and precise," Cohn reported, "Character, blocking, and pacing meshed excitingly so that half the audience sprang to its feet with applause."[48] Stanley Eichelbaum of the *San Francisco Examiner* described it as a "commendably performed" production where "Rowe does a remarkable job" and "Pendleton is persuasive as Peter." Eichelbaum also commented that Albee's staging was "unfailingly gripping" and had rendered his authorial vision crystal clear.[49] Bernard Weiner of the *San Francisco Chronicle* summed up the production as "a rich theatrical experience" and praised Rowe as "exceptional" for his portrait of "a man poised on the emotional razor's edge," which, he added, was "skillfully developed" "under Albee's direction."[50] The *Honolulu Star Bulletin* judged Rowe's performance "excellent" and found it to be "reminiscent of the young Marlon Brando," a comparison also made by the *Washington Post*.[51] Noting Rowe's "talented performance" and Pendleton's "generous performance," the *Philadelphia Bulletin* compared Albee's directorial precision to that of a symphony conductor.[52] In the same vein, the *Los Angeles Times* remarked that Jerry was "brilliantly performed by Stephen Rowe" and that Albee had proven himself a capable interpreter of his own plays.[53] Cumulatively, such testimonials to the overall strength of Albee's directing and the high level of the acting that he elicited from his cast reaffirm the effectiveness of his directorial principles, whether implicit or explicitly articulated, and of his staging practices.

Edward Albee directs Stephen Rowe as Jerry, *The Zoo Story (Albee Directs Albee)*, New York. All photographs by Rakesh H. Solomon; copyright: Rakesh H. Solomon, except where noted.

Wyman Pendleton as Peter, Stephen Rowe as Jerry, and Edward Albee on the single park bench, *The Zoo Story (Albee Directs Albee)*, New York.

Opening view of the set of *Who's Afraid of Virginia Woolf?*,
designed by Jay Michael Jagim, Alley Theatre, Houston.

Edward Albee gives notes after a run-through to John Ottavino as Nick, Cynthia Bassham as Honey, Carol Mayo Jenkins as Martha, and Bruce Gray as George, *Who's Afraid of Virginia Woolf?*, Alley Theatre, Houston.

Act 1: "Fun and Games." Opening scene with Bruce Gray as George and Carol Mayo Jenkins as Martha awaiting their guests, *Who's Afraid of Virginia Woolf?*, Alley Theatre, Houston. *(above)*

Edward Albee speaks to Bruce Gray as George and Carol Mayo Jenkins as Martha, *Who's Afraid of Virginia Woolf?*, Alley Theatre, Houston. *(facing above)*

Act 2: "Walpurgisnacht." "Violence! Violence!" Carol Mayo Jenkins as Martha, Bruce Gray as George, Cynthia Bassham as Honey, and John Ottavino as Nick, *Who's Afraid of Virginia Woolf?*, Alley Theatre, Houston. *(facing below)*

Act 3: "Exorcism." Bruce Gray as George, Carol Mayo Jenkins as Martha, John Ottavino as Nick, and Cynthia Bassham as Honey, *Who's Afraid of Virginia Woolf?*, Alley Theatre, Houston.

Edward Albee speaks to Bruce Gray as George while Carol Mayo Jenkins as Martha, Cynthia Bassham as Honey, and John Ottavino as Nick take notes, *Who's Afraid of Virginia Woolf?*, Alley Theatre, Houston. *(facing below)*

Act 3: "Exorcism." "Pansies! Rosemary! Violence! My wedding bouquet!" Bruce Gray as George, Carol Mayo Jenkins as Martha, and John Ottavino as Nick, *Who's Afraid of Virginia Woolf?*, Alley Theatre, Houston. *(above)*

5

Fam and Yam and *The Sandbox*

*A*lbee claims that playwrights direct their own plays because "we're . . . interested in people seeing . . . our vision of what we intended."[1] As a result, in his own rehearsals, Albee asserted in a personal interview, "I try to make [a script] work most effectively as a stage piece—as closely as I can to the way I see it working in my head when I write it" (PCI). In the light of such a claim, an examination of Albee's rehearsal work on his productions of *Fam and Yam* and *The Sandbox* offers crucial and concrete evidence of how he makes his texts work on stage or, more precisely, how he creates an aural, visual, and kinetic life for them in performance.

Fam and Yam, subtitled *An Imaginary Interview,* unfolds on a Sunday afternoon in the richly appointed apartment of the Famous American Playwright, Fam, as he meets the Young American Playwright, Yam. Claiming to be seeking "advice" for an article on the state of the American theatre, entitled "In Search of a Hero," Yam adroitly coaxes the successful author—softened by numerous sherries—into acquiescing in his devastating denunciation of every aspect of the American theatre establishment. Yam departs but immediately calls to thank Fam for giving him the "interview," leaving Fam flabbergasted.

The first New York performance of *Fam and Yam* took place off-off-Broadway on October 27, 1960 under Richard Barr's direction at the Theatre de Lys on a bill that included Samuel Beckett's *Embers*.[2] In staging *Fam and Yam* nearly two decades later, Albee made several crucial revisions in his script. In these revisions, his avowed goal of making his text "work most effectively as a stage piece" took precedence over his goal of reconstructing his text "as closely as I can to the way I see it working in my head when I write it." Since his original script was presumably closer to what he saw at the time of composition eighteen years earlier, most of Albee's revisions reflect changes in his conceptions of effective staging, i.e., changes in his dramaturgy and his directorial aesthetic.

The economy and simplicity of stage decor manifest in his 1977 premiere productions of *Counting the Ways* and *Listening* carried over to his staging of *Fam and Yam*. He drastically pared down the set specified in his 1960 original: "*The living room of the East Side apartment of a famous American playwright; a view of the bridge, white walls; a plum-colored sofa, two Modiglianis, one Braque, a Motherwell, and a Kline.*"[3] Instead he chose a plum-colored cushion, a lightweight armchair, and a round table—placed on a small, dull green, faux-marble platform—against a backdrop of two horizontal cloth panels, one light blue and one dark.[4] This simplified and elegant stage guided audience attention toward the characters rather than the setting.

Nearly two decades after writing *Fam and Yam*, Albee as director created theatre through stage action rather than stage effects: he transformed the offstage conversation and sound effects that originally opened the play into more immediate onstage dialogue and action. According to the original stage directions, Fam goes out to an offstage front door, followed by the offstage "*sound of voices whence* FAM *vanished.* . . . 'Well, now, how do you do, sir,'" and returns with Yam (82). In Albee's staging, however, Fam walked to an imaginary but onstage doorway and ceremoniously welcomed Yam with the previously offstage greeting. Correspondingly, as Yam departed at play's end, Fam no longer accompanied him off stage for final leave-taking, nor was this followed by the text's offstage "*Goodbyes—thank yous . . . don't mention its. Sound of door closing*" (95). Instead the two characters bade each other farewell in palpable onstage action.

More radically, Albee excised from the play's final moments the episode where Fam answers his telephone only to hear Yam's voice "*loud—over a speaker,*" as a stage direction indicates. The unseen Yam declines an invitation to return for a drink, thanks Fam a few more times, and only at the very end off-handedly throws in his "Thank you very much for the interview"; the unsuspecting Fam simply responds politely and hangs up (96). Albee eliminated prop, sound equipment, business, and most of the dialogue. He retained only Yam's essential line about the interview and Fam's innocent reaction; more crucially, he converted them into an onstage exchange—a part of their final leave-taking. Conveyed through stage action and dialogue rather than a stage device, the critical information that Yam's conversation had actually been an interview and Fam's failure to grasp its import—now even after being told face to face—became charged with greater theatrical immediacy and comic irony.

As the truth suddenly sinks in, Fam screams with disbelief, "THE INTERVIEW!!! THE INTERVIEW!!!!!" and, according to the original stage directions, *"One of the Modiglianis frowns . . . the Braque peels . . . the Kline tilts . . . and the Motherwell crashes to the floor"* (96). Having earlier dispensed with the walls and paintings, director Albee deleted this final stage effect. Instead of the canvasses frowning, tilting, and crashing, now the actor winced, reeled, and sank in shock, supporting himself against the platform's prominent downstage edge. Albee's directorial revision transformed the play's final moment, replacing falling pictures with a falling protagonist.

A look at these directorial choices also indicates the kind of impact Albee had, as a playwright, on productions of his works staged by others. Only fifteen months after the *Fam and Yam* rehearsals, his preference for simple sets and minimal stage effects and properties influenced Alan Schneider's production of *The Lady From Dubuque* on Broadway. Albee's insistence in rehearsal on a living room *"uncluttered, perhaps with a Bauhaus feeling,"* as the set description indicates, frequently conflicted with Schneider's desire to introduce small objects in order to illustrate information contained in a stage direction or a line, or to impart a stronger "lived-in feeling" to the set. For example, since a scenic direction at the start of the second act says *"OSCAR enters from the library"* (78), Schneider wanted him to enter holding a large book, preferably an encyclopedia revealing a colorful map or chart. Albee opposed this firmly. As he explained later, the "look, I have a book, therefore it's a library" staging was unnecessary, "and so . . . first of all I got the book smaller, and then I finally removed the book."[5]

In another instance, during the first act when Sam *"views the room"* after the party and exclaims, "I don't know how six people can make such a mess . . ." (46), Schneider had glasses, bottles, plates, paper napkins, ashtrays, food, pillows, and some shoes scattered around the stage. Albee found the clutter excessive and complained in a personal interview, "I do think that Alan is a trifle prophappy."[6] Most of act 1 does consist of various party activities in the living room, so Albee reluctantly agreed to the props. Schneider also sought to retain these objects into act 2, pointedly reminding the author that the second act opens on the same living room early the next morning, with the guests having gone to bed without clearing up anything. Albee, however, felt strongly that a simple, uncluttered stage was better. So he improvised a solution that could work at least in the second act: he exercised his authorial privilege to revise the text. To Elizabeth's lines "Do you always leave your lights on? Glasses about?" in act 2, the dramatist added, "I straightened up for you a bit," forcing Schneider to remove most of the detritus (75). Albee's staging aesthetic once again took priority over his original composition. That he included the new dialogue in the published text illustrates how his extensive directing and involvement in rehearsals now impacts the final shape of the printed plays—the versions relied on by subsequent actors and directors as well as readers of his works.

Like the *Lady From Dubuque* script, the *Fam and Yam* text also underwent rehearsal-inspired revisions in its dialogue, besides those in its set, stage effects, and props noted earlier. The deletion of the telephone exchange was the largest change: Albee cut from the ringing of the telephone up to Yam reiterating "and I wanted to thank you again" (96). He inverted the order of the two speeches that followed and moved them back so that they came after Fam's "Oh, my . . . I haven't laughed so much" (95) and thus converted Yam's offstage remarks into onstage speech. To focus on Fam's crucial realization, moreover, his final speech was pruned to just "THE INTERVIEW!!! THE INTERVIEW!!!!!" followed by a "*crisp blackout*" instead of the original "curtain" (96).

Other dialogue revisions aimed for clarity and refinement. Albee modified one of Yam's statements early in the play: since the audience does not know what the obviously important Fam is noted for, Yam's "You . . . along with a few others" became "You . . . along with a few other American playwrights" (85). To Yam's "list of villains" in the theatre, Albee added actors, explaining they were "the only component not present," and wrote an acerbic summation of them, like those that Yam already gave of the other villains: "they talk all proud about the theatre and then run off to television as soon as somebody waves a contract at them" (91–92, 94). To sharpen the jab at theatre owners, who topped Yam's list, "real estate owners" became "real estate operators" (93).

Albee also updated scattered topical references throughout the play. Two allusions to critic Robert Brustein, who was employed at Columbia University when *Fam and Yam* originally opened and was leaving Yale University when this production began, were changed: "What's-his-name . . . up at Columbia" became "What's-his-name . . . just got fired from Yale" (86, 87). Reflecting changed conditions in American theatre, Albee dropped the reference to agencies ("call them assembly lines or something" [94]). The Young American Playwright's work now appeared "off-off-off-Broadway," instead of "off-Broadway" (88). Similarly, Fam's line about the "new generation" of playwrights, "Gelber, Richardson, Kopit . . . (*Shrugs*) . . . Albee . . . you" became "Shepard, Rabe . . . What's-his-name . . . (*Shrugs*) . . . and you" (89). Lastly, to update Yam's list of famous American playwrights, Albee dropped Thornton Wilder and William Inge, retained Arthur Miller and Tennessee Williams, and added his own name. Pointing to his upgraded status, Albee joked as he uncorked French champagne at the opening night cast party, "Would the famous American playwright serve anything but champagne? Would the famous American playwright serve *American* champagne?"

Beyond updating his changed position, Albee wished to poke fun at himself. He instructed Yam to convey "immense disparagement" when mentioning his name and to "just throw it away" with a shrug and a "yeaahh" (85). He also asked that Yam mispronounce the name as "Al-bee" and that Fam interject a correction. Even when his name had been included among the "new generation," as in the first New York production, directed by Richard Barr in 1960, Albee's intent was the same: *Fam and Yam* "demonstrates its author's ability to laugh at himself," Arthur Gelb had remarked in the *New York Times*.[7]

Demonstrating a director's ability to make an audience laugh, Albee created new comic business. Instead of opening the play with Fam seated and reading, as in his script, Albee had him strut in like a dandy, adjust his colorful scarf, balance a cigarette in one hand, daintily step onto the platform, sink into his chair, stretch his feet, and use the cushion as a footstool. Comfortably settled, he then poured himself a glass of sherry, held it to his nose, took a sip, puffed on his cigarette, blew smoke elaborately, began reading, and broke into a chuckle.

Some new business transmitted the subtext. Upon hearing the young playwright ask his advice, Fam replies, "(*Softly, with becoming modesty*), Well, I'd be happy . . . I don't know that I'm . . ." (87). Albee suggested that Fam, despite his tonal and verbal modesty, should wear a patronizing look, throw the cushion from under his feet toward Yam, and gesture to him to sit down, more or less at his feet. Albee's choice of the two-foot-high platform for Fam similarly physicalized his text's image of a condescending man perched on a pedestal of immense self-regard. Sporting a pink paisley smoking jacket over a white shirt, blue denim pants, blue socks, and dark-blue patent leather shoes, Fam remained atop the platform, except to receive and see off his visitor. Since Yam, in contrast, stayed off the platform, except once when he sat at Fam's feet, throughout the play Fam literally looked down on his upstart rival. The platform's theatrical effectiveness was ironically but palpably driven home when a technical mishap prevented its use in one matinee performance. Without Fam's pedestal, the play-long visual contrast of a pompous writer's physical hauteur and disdain toward the lowly neophyte author lost quite a bit of its comic and satiric edge, and this was evident in the audience's relatively milder response that afternoon. Elsewhere in the play Albee similarly built on his written text to delineate character through movement and business.

To clarify his authorial intent as well as to help the actors, Albee embodied his subtext not only in new business, costume, and set pieces but also in one or two new props. For example, when criticizing theatre personnel, the actor playing Yam appeared to improvise his biting labels, but the director advised, "You do not grope for words, you have all the adjectives." Making his subtext explicit, he told Yam, "You're not tentative when listing the adjectives," despite the claim of still writing the piece, "because you've already written the article; you only need confirmation!" Unable to get the actor to rattle the text off as he wished after two rehearsals, Albee introduced a prop: he asked Yam to carry crumpled pages of the article in his sports jacket, pull them out, find the correct page, and then read off the epithets at high speed.

In contrast to this rare introduction of a new prop, Albee more typically explained his characters in more detail and depth than was possible in the written script. "Let's examine the psychology of it all," he told Fam, to reveal why Fam is initially reluctant to accept Yam's condemnation, despite his apparent agreement. Suggested the director, "You resist Yam's putting words in your mouth." Moreover, Albee pointed out, Fam is "worried and discomfited" by Yam's "unconscious condescension," as when Yam characterizes his creative output as "The way you keep writing them . . . one after the other!" (85) or when Yam declines a glass of sherry with his tactless "No . . . no, thank you. But you . . . you keep right on" (92). Helping Fam see what motivated him in another section, Albee disclosed that Fam knows of the budding author's obscure first play only because Yam mentioned it in his note requesting a meeting.

Albee similarly illuminated the character of Yam. When listing the major American playwrights, Albee explained, Yam is "very dogmatic" about Fam, Miller, and Williams, but "uncertain" and "reluctant" about Albee. On the other hand, Yam is "not too impressed" by Fam's trappings of success; he remains "quite cool, not insecure." Yet he has "no sense of humor": Fam's jokes, which are at least mildly funny, fall completely flat to him. The overearnest Yam becomes the source of "unconscious comedy." Having offended Fam by saying, "I don't drink . . . ," according to Albee, Yam actually "tries to retrieve the situation" by adding the disastrous "this early" (86). Albee then guided his actors to translate these comments into appropriate action and delivery.

Such authorial insights, beyond their usefulness in rehearsal, sometimes refute or confirm critical commentary on a play. Without implying any naive intentionalism, Albee's, or for that matter any dramatist's, observations about his own works deserve to be considered valuable interpretations, by theatre practitioners as well as critics and scholars. Thus Albee's censure of Yam's dogmatism, humorless solemnity, and "unconscious comedy" argue against identifying Yam with Albee, as Michael Rutenberg does when he concludes that Yam "sounds very much like the young Mr. Albee" and that, correspondingly, the title of Yam's play, *Dilemma, Dereliction and Death,* "fits the events of *The Zoo Story* rather well." [8] Albee's derisive characterization of Yam and his inclusion of actors among the theatre's villains also counter Rutenberg's interpretation that in *Fam and Yam* "only the actors and new playwrights are left to revitalize the art" of theatre. On the other hand, his instructions to Yam to be "uncertain" about including Albee among the leading dramatists confirm Arthur Gelb's comment, noted earlier, that the author is engaging in ironic self-mockery in *Fam and Yam.*

To complement these character insights, Albee also offered his actors more concrete directorial instructions, specifying, for instance, precise vocal tones and stresses for particular moments. In order to indicate exactly what he wanted, Albee on occasion even imitated the voice or mannerism of a friend or a person the actors knew. Although he is not an accomplished mimic, his imitations—especially given his otherwise serious and reserved persona and his stature as a playwright—also served to put the actors at ease and to release inevitable rehearsal tensions. To great comic effect, he once mimicked his friend and fellow playwright Tennessee Williams's characteristic "heee-heee-heee" so that actor Wyman Pendleton, who also knew Williams from working in the 1974 Broadway revival of *Cat on a Hot Tin Roof,* could accurately recreate it in his own frequent laughter. When Tennessee Williams attended a performance of *Fam and Yam* several weeks later in San Francisco, he recognized and enjoyed the parody, as he cheerfully confessed when visiting the cast afterward. Among other vocal directions, when Fam asks, "What did you want to see me about . . . exactly?" Albee specified a tone that conveyed "I want to shut this man off!" and when Fam feigns humility, saying "You youngsters are going to push us out of the way," the director wanted a transparently disbelieving tone (86, 89). At other moments he told Fam to sound "businesslike," "supercilious," "nasty—a slow burn, though not anger," "pompously gracious," "genuinely gracious," and "*merely* gracious." And Yam, on first noticing the paintings, had to give voice to exclamations that were "really very, very big, but not too loud," "almost a scream of surprise, but not fear," "a *manly* sound," "a mildly envious expression of how great it must be to have originals."

If an actor could not attain a specified voice coloration in spite of such precise directions and explanations, Albee reluctantly offered line readings. In *Fam and Yam*, most of these were directed to James Knobeloch, the young and relatively inexperienced actor playing Yam, during his disparaging mention of Albee as a major playwright and during his sarcastic comments about the state of the American theatre. Besides giving line readings when necessary, Albee even provided basic acting advice and demonstrated suggested action. In the new simplified set, without actual canvasses, Albee wished Yam, at various times during his admiring comments, to walk toward, look up at, or point to the imaginary, offstage paintings. Albee climbed up on stage to demonstrate that once the actor had located the pictures in one spot, he could not point to them elsewhere. He pinpointed a space—"they're always in the theatre balcony"—in order to ensure consistency in Yam's movement and business.

No amount of directorial advice, line readings, or demonstration of business, finally, can sufficiently compensate for an actor's lack of experience and skill. This partly explains the uneven quality of some *Albee Directs Albee* performances, especially during the tour. Albee had originally hired Knobeloch to work as assistant stage manager, understudy Stephen Rowe's five roles, and play two minor, non-speaking parts. Only as a last-minute expedient to lighten Rowe's load without adding additional expense did the director switch the role of the Young American Playwright from Rowe to Knobeloch. While financially necessary, theatrically the change led to a less than impressive Yam, since Knobeloch was a novice actor whose post-university acting experience consisted of just two roles in a small regional theatre. Not surprisingly, as early as a month into the tour, according to a letter from Albee's assistant, dissatisfaction with Knobeloch's work made the director and producer consider replacing him. Knobeloch, however, felt that more personal coaching would solve his problems: "Not having sufficient rehearsal time," he noted in a letter to me, was the element he liked least in the *Albee Directs Albee* project. Another Knobeloch comment in the letter, that Albee is not the ideal director "if an actor must be 'guided' through a role," while phrased in general terms, in fact reflects his own need.

Similarly, limited and irregular directorial attention while touring—although common in the theatre—adversely affected some performers, especially the less experienced Knobeloch and Bruno, during a tour that lasted nearly a year. Albee, however, saw no need for traveling with his actors. When asked by a *Washington Post* reporter if he would join the cast on the tour, he retorted, "It's not an animal act." In fact, Albee could not accompany his actors or work with them regularly, because the tour covered five foreign countries and crisscrossed the United States and thus would pose insurmountable problems given his hectic schedule of lectures and other professional activities; moreover, he was seriously injured in an automobile accident a few weeks after the opening. Without accompanying the cast or at least working with them frequently, Albee could not provide consistent supervision and thus could not ensure consistent performances during the tour.

Without the director, actors occasionally felt tempted to make minor alterations. For instance, Albee had specified that Yam's "AH! And this?" when he looks out the window should echo the surprise and envy of his first "AH!" when he notices the paintings (84, 83). But Knobeloch, apparently in order to feel more comfortable, replaced "AH! And this?" with "OH, my god!!" according to the tour stage manager's promptbook. Knobeloch also inserted an uncomprehending "Huh?" when Yam misses the humor in Fam's comment and "rush[es] on" with "I guess what I mean is 'You're a real pro'" (86). Similarly, Pendleton put in an "Oh, my . . . " after Fam's opening laugh. He also inserted an emphatic new "WHAT?" in place of Fam's confused "Hm?" following Yam's loud exclamation about the paintings (83). Pendleton also changed Fam's gracious reaction to his visitor's request for advice from "Well, I'd be happy . . ." to "Why certainly . . ." (87). In the play's final seconds, as Fam recalls Yam's comments with almost delirious laughter—"The pin-heads! Ha ha ha ha ha!"—Pendleton inserted, "Joan Crawford, Susan Hay-hay-hay-" (95).

These textual interpolations by the actors did not seriously affect *Fam and Yam* performances, but other post-rehearsal departures from directorial instructions did. In rehearsals Albee found Pendleton's desire to accompany words with mimed action and gestures a bit excessive. Consequently, he carefully trimmed away unnecessary physical business. However, in a performance in San Francisco that I attended, Pendleton appeared to incorporate previously deleted actions and even invent new ones.[9] Similarly, his performance in Honolulu, according to Bernard F. Dukore in a letter to me, although "capable in many respects . . . [showed] fruity-personal-actor-mannerisms . . . as distinct from character traits." Pendleton displayed no such indulgences during the initial run that Albee supervised.

The most significant alteration on tour, which appeared in San Francisco, was the decision by the actors or the stage manager to eliminate Fam's platform from the set. The change greatly diminished the comedy in several scenes, since

Fam's verbal condescension was no longer matched by a physically patronizing location. With both actors on the same level, and with Fam on a chair but Yam on his feet through much of the play, it became difficult for the average-sized Pendleton to maintain a pompous demeanor toward the six-foot-tall Knobeloch.

While individually minor, such changes in the plays' dialogue, business, and set often cumulatively lowered the standard of performance achieved during the opening run, undermined Albee's authorial and directorial intent, and temporarily damaged his reputation as a director in the eyes of the many audiences who saw those performances in various cities. In a conversation in 1980 Alan Schneider confessed he "was very unhappy" with the few performances he saw, but since he was also aware of some of the production and touring difficulties, he acknowledged, "It was an impossible situation."

Albee brought even greater exactitude in his staging of the next play on the bill, *The Sandbox: A Brief Play, In Memory of My Grandmother (1876–1959)*. His incidental comments over the years leave a distinct impression that, of all his plays, *The Sandbox* remains his favorite. Not surprisingly, only two years after its 1960 off-off-Broadway premiere at the Jazz Gallery, Albee had taken complete control over its staging by directing its off-Broadway production at the Cherry Lane Theatre.[10] With playful immodesty Albee commented in a 1965 magazine interview, "*The Sandbox* is a perfect play. Fortunately, it's short enough so that I can't make any mistakes in it."[11] Soon after *The Sandbox* rehearsals under consideration here, he reiterated to Dick Cavett, "I don't think there are any mistakes in that play."[12] Since Albee considered *The Sandbox* to be especially well crafted, he concentrated his directorial efforts not on revisions for staging effectiveness, as with *Fam and Yam,* but on controlling all elements of the performance in order to accurately recreate his authorial vision. At the play's first reading, he warned the cast, "*Sandbox* is fundamentally a piece of music—as you direct it, you essentially begin to conduct it."[13]

Albee composed *The Sandbox* in 1959 while writing *The American Dream:* "I extracted several of the characters from *The American Dream* and placed them in a situation different than, but related to, their predicament in the longer play."[14] In both, Mommy and Daddy force Grandma into a living burial—in a seaside sandbox in one play, and in a stuffy apartment room in the other—and in both, a Young Man helps Grandma depart to another world. At the start of *The Sandbox,* as a handsome, bikini-clad Young Man performs calisthenics on a beach, Mommy and Daddy give instructions to a Musician and then carry in the eighty-six-year-old Grandma and dump her in a child's sandbox to begin a death vigil. Grandma mocks their hypocrisy, speaks to the audience about her life, and plays at being dead. When Mommy and Daddy leave, Grandma discovers that she cannot move, and the good-looking Angel of Death gently eases her into her sandbox grave.

During his rehearsals for *The Sandbox*, Albee found little need to revise the text. The most significant alteration involved the physical placement of his characters on stage, possibly reflecting a shift in his dramaturgy or at least in his attitude toward these characters. Primarily in order to increase the stage focus on Grandma, he moved her large sandbox from the text's *"farther back,"* upstage location to a downstage center position. To further strengthen this new, dominant position, he relocated Mommy and Daddy's chairs from *"near the footlights, far stage right,"* as in the original stage directions, to an upstage area near the upper right corner of Grandma's box; correspondingly, he repositioned the Musician from the text's *"near the footlights, far stage left"* spot to an area near the bottom left corner of the sandbox. Albee made no other change in the play's set, props, sound effects, music, or dialogue. This was partly because the original script of *The Sandbox*—unlike that of *Fam and Yam*—had not called for an elaborate set or any stage devices; instead, its minimal set requirements and its overall simplicity and stylization were closer to Albee's theatrical aesthetic at the time of these productions (which is also reflected in his works of this period, such as *Counting the Ways*).

Although Albee's rehearsal work on *The Sandbox,* aimed at representing on stage his original conception for the play, did not lead to any revisions in his text, it did provide authorial readings that amend or confirm some theatrical and scholarly interpretations of the play. Given its comedy, stylization, and self-reflexive theatricality, some critics and directors have conceived productions with a great deal of fast action and movement, especially in the play-long exercises of the Young Man. Thus Michael Rutenberg, for example, criticizes Albee's dramaturgy, assuming that "in performance this physical action would appear to take away much of the focus from Grandma."[15] A few months after these rehearsals, a professional staging of *The Sandbox* in San Francisco pulsated with the tempo of farce throughout the play, and its Young Man exercised to brisk music.[16] From the outset of his own rehearsals, however, Albee had insisted that *The Sandbox* is a "very simple piece" that "should have a dream-like quality," and despite its comedy and parody "this play is never very fast—no sense of racing on and off stage." On his stage Albee urged the Young Man, played by Stephen Rowe, "Don't rush: he does not perform fast calisthenics"; instead he moves his arms in a "slow uniform rhythm" no matter what happens around him. Albee often warned Mommy, played by Patricia Kilgarriff, as well as Daddy, played by

Wyman Pendleton, against their tendency to move too briskly: "Enter slowly," "take your time," "look around," "no hurry." Such injunctions achieved a continuously slow, otherworldly rhythm in performance.

In another important interpretation Albee stressed that the Young Man's relationship with Grandma "is quite straightforward business," without *The American Dream*'s parodic overtones of an old woman's sexual interest in a young man. The author's staging revealed a genial old woman striking up an innocent conversation with a friendly and helpful young man and contradicts Gilbert Debusscher's characterization of the relationship as a "paradoxical bit of coquetry between the old woman and the young athlete."[17] It also denies Anne Paolucci's interpretation of the sandbox as a symbol of "sexual fulfillment." On the contrary, when Grandma questions the Young Man about who he is and then turns to the audience with "Fine; fine" (15), Albee told her to make "no tonal comment on the Young Man, but just a simple, business-like, matter-of-fact statement." Albee's direction also undercuts Paolucci's claim that "listening to [the Young Man] and watching him, Grandma forgets everything else. She is completely taken with him . . . and welcomes his attentions."[18] The polite Young Man's respectful kiss on Grandma's forehead in Albee's production clearly debunks Paolucci's assertion that Grandma "accepts his kiss gratefully, as a mistress might, lapsing into sleep" (28), an interpretation sometimes heavy-handedly embodied on stage in a lecherous Grandma enjoying an on-the-lips kiss. The San Francisco production not only incorporated such a kiss but even added a line in which Grandma moaned nostalgically, "My husband used to kiss me like that."

In contrast to the regret, longing, and easy sentiment of the San Francisco production's version of Grandma, Albee's portrait of her eliminated every hint of sentimentality. When Grandma tells the audience about her life story, *"Anyhow, I had to raise . . . that over there all by my lonesome. . . . I'm not complaining"* (15–16), Albee asked Catherine Bruno, playing Grandma, to deliver the line in an "absolutely straight" and "factual" voice: "no self-pity; let the audience react as it likes." Consonant with the overall style of Albee's production, a touch of irony and theatricality—her charming compliment, for instance, to a *"blushing"* Angel of Death—thwarted sentimentality even in her somber and affecting final moments. Such a staging, moreover, demonstrates the accuracy of Michael Rutenberg's reading of "the final scene [as] quite moving," in contrast to Christopher Bigsby's view of it as "somewhat mawkish" and Gilbert Debusscher's calling it "sentimental."[19] Unfairly envisioning a maudlin ending on the basis of the play's dedication to the memory of the author's grandmother, both Debusscher ("the playwright's concession to his autobiography") and Bigsby ("a concession to her memory") underestimate Albee's ironic resolve, crystalline in his own production.[20] More than once Albee clarified that by and large his authorial goal for Grandma's character was not sentimentality or naturalism but comedy, theatricality, and parody. "Just as Grandma parodies an old woman in *The American Dream*," he explained, "she plays at being a petulant baby" in *The Sandbox*. This parodic goal was integral to his overall non-naturalistic conception of Grandma and contradicts Gerry McCarthy's mention of her "graceful naturalism."[21]

Rather than to challenge critical interpretations, Albee's goal in such rehearsal remarks was to promote accurate and richly detailed character portrayals in performance. He explained, "I try fairly soon to start giving the actors hints . . . that they can use for overall characterization" (PCI). To that end he offered numerous explanatory comments about his characters. The Young Man's character, he suggested, remains largely the "same as in *The American Dream*, but more vapid," and although he objectively watches other characters and their activities, he never looks at them when they address him. Despite Mommy's laughable behavior in moaning for a mother she is herself discarding, her cry after each of the three offstage rumbles must be quite believable and become progressively more moving. Mommy and Daddy, in contrast to their conduct in *The American Dream*, should "be generally gracious. . . . they should be at their best wake behavior," since they are "still in mourning." Albee expects such basic comments to serve as a foundation on which actors can build their own individual portrayals. He encourages actors to create the particulars of characterization—gesture, business, and delivery—by drawing on their own impulses. Under his supervision, the Young Man, for example, conveyed the author-director's description of his character as "vapid" by delivering each of his "hi's" in an identical, flat voice, and with the same dumb, vacuous smile. When necessary, Albee also willingly suggests multiple gestures or bits of business, so that an actor can choose one that matches his own inclination. When Mommy cheerfully welcomes the new day with "Well! Our long night is over" (18), Albee had asked her to show an interest in the Young Man in his sexy black swimsuit. He offered her several ways to do so: a slight head turn to look at him from the corner of her eye, a broad smile, a wink, or a coy wave. In performance Mommy both smiled and coyly waved at the youth. Albee's encouragement of actors' creative contributions and choices would have pleased playwright-director Bernard Shaw, who declared in an essay on Granville-Barker, "The perfect producer lets his actors act, and is their helper at need and not their dictator."[22]

Since Albee directs in order to modulate all elements of performance, when an actor could not accomplish the desired effect, he provided minute instructions on delivery, business, and movement. Dissatisfied with Grandma's cry "Ah-hhhhh! Graaaaa!" when dumped into the sandbox (11), Albee specified that her screams should sound "not [like] the cry of a loveable child, but an angry Siamese cat's cry." On the other hand, Mommy's tone must be well mannered, even when Grandma throws a shovelful of sand at her. Mommy's remonstrance—"You stop that, Grandma; you stop throwing sand at Mommy!" (13)—Albee told her, should be delivered "under your breath, through the side of your mouth."

Albee similarly stipulated detailed business or demonstrated a move when an actor required it. To mark Grandma's end in the play's final seconds, according to a stage direction, *the YOUNG MAN puts his hands on top of GRANDMA's"* (21). But Albee preferred the Angel of Death to seem to "completely engulf" Grandma. For four or five consecutive rehearsals leading up to the first public performance, Albee painstakingly directed the Young Man, who knelt upstage of Grandma as she lay in the raked sandbox, to raise his arms above his shoulders and, like an angel, gently bend over Grandma in order to suggest a "total enveloping quality." Repeatedly, Albee instructed him on precise execution: "Bring your arms down from straight above, not from the sides"; "Lower only your arms and upper torso"; "Allow your hips to bend only as much as is absolutely necessary"; "To prevent your backside from sticking out, bend only your knees and keep the rest of your body straight—use your knees as the axis." To ensure that the actor fully grasped his directions, Albee physically demonstrated the action three or four times during each of these late rehearsals.

Albee demanded similar accuracy in the coordination of action to the music. "I *know* from experience that the music works as it was written," he told the cast, "so I'll have it taped and mold you to the music!" Although he preferred live music—during the play's premiere production Hal McKusick, leader of a jazz trio, played the Musician—Albee settled for a tape recording in order to secure consistent sound for precise timing of cues during a long tour. Besides, it allowed him to fill the Musician's role with a non-musician actor and understudy, James Knobeloch. Beginning as early as the third rehearsal, Albee—music sheet in hand—meticulously reworked the music scenes three or four times each session. He made certain of the proper sequence of events. For example, when Mommy first asks for the music with "You can begin now," the original stage direction simply states, *"The MUSICIAN BEGINS PLAYING; MOMMY and DADDY exit"* (10). Albee clarified that, following Mommy's instruction, the Musician should start getting ready—rearrange the music sheet, extend his arms to bring the clarinet to his lips, etc.—but should not begin playing (and the stage manager should not start the tape) until the departing Mommy and Daddy are "just out of sight."

Soon Mommy and Daddy reenter carrying Grandma, but they do so, Albee specified, "only when the quality of the music changes," and he trained the actors to
recognize the change.

Albee insisted on details with such uncharacteristic exactness because of his
special fondness for *The Sandbox* and because, as mentioned earlier, he thinks the
play is very well crafted, with almost a musical precision. Albee's requirements
did not, however, exceed the practices of other modern playwright-directors, especially when compared to the rigorous rehearsal demands of two of the most
influential dramatists of the twentieth century, Bertolt Brecht and Samuel Beckett. For instance, because of Brecht's "immense care for detail," John Willet notes,
"a single production might demand between sixty and a hundred rehearsals."[23]
"The most meticulous attention was paid to the smallest gesture," writes Carl
Weber. "Brecht spent hours in rehearsal exploring how Galileo would handle a
telescope and an apple. . . . Often paintings or other pictorial documents of the
period were brought into rehearsal for the study of movements and gestures."[24]
Similarly, Beckett's rehearsals reveal extraordinarily precise demands. His directorial notebooks contain diagrams of actors' movements in far more detail
than is necessary for simple blocking, even for some movements invisible to an
audience. These diagrams, according to Ruby Cohn, who attended many of his
rehearsals, dealt "with who faces where at every moment . . . with the total stage
pattern, with the counterpoint of word and gesture, with visual echoes, sym-
metries, and oppositions."[25] He also specified—sometimes in musical terms—the
pitch, volume, duration, tone, and rhythm of line delivery as well as aural effects.
Frequently, Beckett read lines for an actor—even reciting with him—and demonstrated business and gestures, including head and eye movements. Unlike Beckett or Brecht, Albee actually prefers not to dictate minute details of action or
delivery. As a rule, he claims, "I hate to give very specific things. . . . I would rather
give a general intention note," encouraging an actor to create the particulars of
his performance himself (PCI).

However, in matters of practical production that can be physically calibrated, Albee demands minute accuracy. Displaying intimate knowledge of the
technical aspects of production, as he had during the rehearsals of *The American
Dream* and *The Zoo Story*, Albee scrutinized set pieces, props, lighting, and sound
equipment for several hours preceding the dry tech, or technical rehearsal without actors, for both *Fam and Yam* and *The Sandbox*. During this, as well as during
the next day's technical rehearsal with the actors walking through their performances, Albee often asked his scene and lighting designers probing questions
about wattages, gelatine shades, types of lamp, and so on. Sometimes he urged

that lighting be modulated to get just the right effect. At times he even argued with the designers about whether a desired effect was feasible. He insisted, for instance, that an opening, special light on the Young Man could be arranged to illuminate his body only above the waist, despite the actor's location close to the backdrop. Although lighting designer Stephen Pollock argued that "the half-special will wash the drop too much," Albee supervised the crew as they tried different spotlights and different positions, until he got the Young Man's upper half lighted without any stray beams spilling onto the back curtain. Albee also paid thorough attention to costumes, make-up, sound effects, set changes between plays, and other production details. In their mid-size theatre he demanded Grandma use drastically limited or almost no make-up. "In larger theatres," too, he allowed only "*some* aging make-up . . . but not lining, maybe egg yolk . . . which will crack the face." He directed that the taped clarinet music be played only through the stage left speaker, since the Musician sat on that side; in addition, he worked to modulate the three offstage rumbles into deep, long rolling sounds that became progressively louder, more violent, and more frightening.

Albee's practice recalls Edward Bond's scrutiny of every technical detail when staging his own plays. Even when someone else directed his works, Bond devoted the same scrupulous attention to them, as William Gaskill, who directed his early plays at the Royal Court Theatre in London, recounted in vivid detail in a personal interview. During the technical rehearsal of *Lear* for its 1971 premiere, Bond, in the words of Gaskill's assistant director, "went round like a Sergeant Major, inspecting every cranny."[26] Edward Bond's model theatre artist, Bertolt Brecht, similarly paid meticulous attention to technical matters. At the 1950 *Mother Courage* rehearsals in Munich, according to Eric Bentley, Brecht regulated the stage with stopwatch and light meter: "He would run up on stage, light meter in hand, to demonstrate that 'they' [the lighting technicians, whom he called Nazis] had not given him the intensity of white light that he had demanded." In the same way, during scene changes, "when his stopwatch told him 'they' were taking more seconds than [specified], he would have a fit" and "bawl [the stage manager] out in language both harsh and raunchy."[27] In *Bernard Shaw, Director* Dukore describes how Shaw too "supervised every element of production: scenery (construction and painting, as well as design), lighting, costuming, make-up."[28]

Fernando Arrabal, Albee's fellow-dramatist on the four-play bill that premiered *The Sandbox,* represents a sharp contrast to these author-directors. Even though Arrabal has directed a few of his own plays, he confesses, "The technical aspects of the theatre do not interest me at all."[29] Albee, however, argues that a writer staging his own works must be "willing to put up with the tedium" of painstaking, repetitive work on the mechanics of production.[30]

Albee's remark points to his thoroughly pragmatic manner of working as a playwright-director, evident throughout these rehearsals. During technical rehearsals, too, Albee insisted on what he wanted—but always only up to a reasonable point. He first demanded that the set change from *Fam and Yam* to *The Sandbox* occur during a blackout, but observing difficulties during a few attempts, he permitted dim work lights. Similarly, Albee wanted four stage hands in order to ensure an expeditious set change, while set designer Karl Eigsti thought two would be sufficient. Albee agreed to try with two men, saw that they were adequate, and readily halved the crew size. In his work with designers and technical personnel, Albee proved to be both cooperative and pragmatic.

Such a practical attitude to matters affecting his own creations remains one of Albee's signal strengths as a dramatist-director. It is a quality Albee strives for during his rehearsals: "When I direct my own plays, I have serious arguments with myself . . . between me as the author who wants the impossible and me as the director who wants what's possible." The winner of this struggle, Albee explains, is "usually me as director, because I've got to be . . . practical."[31] Albee's statement echoes Bernard Shaw's comment about his own work as a playwright-director. In a letter to Mrs. Patrick Campbell, Shaw claimed that as an author staging his own plays he tried "to get, not what I want, but what's possible."[32] Distinguished French director Jean Vilar's assertion "The staging of a play is always the result of compromise" testifies to the soundness of Albee's pragmatic approach to staging his own plays.[33]

Thus, in his work on *Fam and Yam* and *The Sandbox,* Albee strove to recreate on stage his original authorial vision for these plays while simultaneously making them "work most effectively" as theatre pieces. In the case of *Fam and Yam,* practical performance needs as well as changes in his own aesthetic prompted multiple textual revisions that shifted audience attention from sets to actors, converted sound effects and offstage voices into onstage dialogue and action, introduced a new set piece and prop, clarified ambiguities, and updated references to developments and personalities in the American professional theatre. In contrast, the *Sandbox* script underwent only one important revision. For both the plays Albee devised much new comic business and action to embody his text as well as subtext, and he enunciated his fundamental conceptions of the characters and situations so that the actors could convey his original vision accurately. Some of his rehearsal comments incidentally also corrected or corroborated past critical and stage interpretations, especially of *The Sandbox,* the more frequently discussed and performed of the two plays. While requiring actors to operate within the essential contours of his plays as set out by him, Albee also offered them room to improvise and innovate according to their own artistic and personal instincts. When particular performers needed them, however, he was pragmatic enough to provide highly specific instructions about vocal tone, delivery, posture, movement, and so on. Finally, this overall mode of operation with his actors also extended to his work with his set and costume designers, his technical director, and his production crews: on a few key details he remained insistent, even adamant, but on most others he sought their creative input, invited suggestions, moderated his initial demands, and remained pragmatic. As a practical man of the theatre, Albee understood and acknowledged both technical and human limitations.

6

Box and *Quotations from Chairman Mao Tse-Tung*

*B*ox—a play without an onstage actor—and *Quotations from Chairman Mao Tse-Tung*—a play without dialogue—remain the high-water mark of Albee's experimental dramaturgy, just as they remain the least analyzed of his works. In *Box* the outline of a polished metal cube dominates a bare stage while the Voice, an offstage female speaker, meditates on the decline of art and on the corruption and sense of loss in life. Into this scene, *Quotations from Chairman Mao Tse-Tung* introduces four characters on board an ocean liner, three of whom speak interweaving monologues while the fourth remains silent. Intermittently, the disembodied Voice from *Box* breaks in. At the end of *Quotations from Chairman Mao Tse-Tung*, with characters and cube still on stage, brief ruminations from *Box* form a reprise. Originally, *Box* was then replayed in its entirety and the plays called *Box-Mao-Box*, as at their first public performance on March 6, 1968, at the Studio Arena Theatre in Buffalo, New York.[1] For their Broadway premiere on September 30, 1968, at the Billy Rose Theatre, Albee wrote in his program note that although they had been written as two independent works, *Box* and *Quotations from Chairman Mao Tse-Tung* "are more effective performed enmeshed."[2] Maintaining that view, a decade later the author again staged the two plays together.

Albee introduced *Box* and *Mao Tse-Tung* to his cast as director and actors sat in chairs arranged in a circle on the stage.[3] "No one really interacts with anybody in *Mao Tse-Tung*," he began; "when connections do occur, these are completely accidental, though very carefully arranged by the playwright." *Mao Tse-Tung* is "very fragmented—everyone is exceedingly concerned with himself." Both *Box* and *Mao Tse-Tung*, he further suggested, "flow with a sea rhythm"; and in both, the Voice from *Box* should be "a bit autumnal, very gentle."

As is usual with Albee, following the brief remarks, he asked the cast to read the plays aloud, while he listened without interrupting. Unusually for a first reading, however, this one displayed emotional intensity as well as a close approximation of the characterizations desired by the playwright. Toward the end of *Box*, Patricia Kilgarriff as the Voice dissolved in tears, while Eileen Burns as the Long-Winded Lady trembled with sadness through most of *Mao Tse-Tung*. Three weeks later Albee still marveled at how some of these actors had "become" his characters, to a degree unprecedented at initial rehearsals (PCI). Albee's admiration for this reading suggests that, notwithstanding *Box* and *Mao Tse-Tung*'s non-representational nature, the playwright intends them to have a strong emotional impact. As Albee harnessed and enhanced these strong initial interpretations, both actors broke into tears at every subsequent rehearsal and opening-run performance, creating passionate and moving theatre. Following the first night's performance Albee recalled with satisfaction how a young man, "quivering with rage," had accosted him backstage halfway through *Mao Tse-Tung*. The playwright mimicked the playgoer: "'I walked out! . . . How—how dare you sub—subject me to—to a woman saying things like that! I mean, she's so sad and so awful!'"(PCI) Albee regarded the outburst as a vindication of his directorial strategy. Such an emotional staging, moreover, supports scholars like Gerry McCarthy and Anne Paolucci who argue that "however abstract *Box* may seem . . . it is . . . deeply felt" and that although *Mao Tse-Tung* may seem the "most far fetched of his allegorical compositions," it evokes "intensely *human* feeling."[4] On the other hand, Albee's staging debunks those critics who assume that these plays' formal experimentation necessarily leads to merely cerebral drama.

Even more importantly, this staging encapsulates Albee's authorial and directorial aesthetic for all his plays, including those non-naturalistic works that critics usually label as abstract, allegorical, or symbolist. Irrespective of the degree of stylization or exaggeration in a play's situation or characterization, as a dramatist and director he conceives the characters as whole human beings—linguistically, sociologically, and psychologically credible individuals—not caricatures, symbols, or lifeless abstractions. He therefore believes that no matter how morally, psychically, and stylistically extreme the characters may be, actors must always portray them as flesh-and-blood human beings. Albee's directorial work grows out of this fundamental mimetic aesthetic conviction, as this chapter will make further evident. Even when he created non-human characters, like the sea lizards in *Seascape,* he imbued them with deeply human characteristics—emotions, language, and personal names—and when he directed its Broadway premiere he instructed the actors to portray them to appear as sophisticated and as bourgeois as the play's two human characters (PCI).

In *Box* and *Mao Tse-Tung,* Albee guided his actors meticulously toward a life-like and emotionally rich representation of the characters, shedding light on both his text and subtext. Early in *Box* the Voice comments, with a *"tiny laugh,"* "Nature abhors, among so many, so much else . . . amongst so much, us, itself, they say, vacuum" (5). Albee reiterated his textual stage direction prescribing a *"schoolmarmish"* tone and clarified the meaning: "Nature abhors three things: 1. Us; 2. Itself; 3. Vacuum." During the subsequent lament about the death of seven hundred million babies, corruption, the spilling of milk, and art that hurts, the Voice unexpectedly shifts to "So much . . . flies. A billion birds at once, black net skimming the ocean . . . blown by the wind, but going straight . . . in a direction. Order!" (5-7). For this switch, Albee suggested a simple, realistic motivation, "Suddenly you see the birds," and he offered a revealing subtextual justification for an enthusiastic tone: "You're trying to talk of the saddest of all things, but the wonder of the flying birds keeps breaking in." A little after first sighting the birds, the Voice in *Box* exclaims, "There! More! A thousand, and one below them, moving fast in the opposite way!" (8). Albee required a mixed mood of happy admiration tinged with anxiety, for which he proposed a psychological rationale: "Although you appreciate the order, you're full of wonder about the one bird going in the opposite direction—the only remains of humanism in our society; you're grateful for it, but also worried that it is going in the opposite direction." After a *"two-second silence"* following this speech, the Voice remembers, "What was it used to frighten me? Bell buoys and sea gulls; the *sound* of them, at night, in a fog, when I was very young" (8). Although she recalls things that made her afraid, Albee urged "a childlike eagerness," because, he explained, "You're sort of enthusiastic about what used to frighten you *then*—that is so much better than what frightens you *now.*"

Beyond the unusually large number of emotions already spelled out in his textual stage directions, Albee called for several more. For the line "System as conclusion . . . the dice so big you can hardly throw them anymore" (5), he required irony, but for "And if you go back to a partita . . . ahhhhh" (6), he wanted unconscious self-indulgence, which he conveyed to the actor with a line reading and which he described as the Voice's "favorite point." Although the Voice only proffers an explanation at "Here is the thing about tension and the tonic" (7), he argued, the subject should inevitably "lead to sadness." For "Nothing belongs" at the end of *Box* (10), he urged the Voice to "make it a sort of final statement— a kind of protest," but when the Voice returns to the phrase at the end of *Mao Tse-Tung* (67) he suggested, "Great loss." Such requests for a range of emotional readings epitomize Albee's overall directorial concern in *Box,* best expressed by his often repeated instruction to the actor: "Emotional, not clinical!"[5]

If Albee sought to convey the realistic, human dimension of the invisible character in *Box,* he did so even more with the quartet of onstage actors in *Mao Tse-Tung.* Early in the rehearsals he focused on accurate vocal orchestration (although this was no longer the only available arena for directorial attention, as in *Box*) to ensure a powerful but varied emotional landscape. The Long-Winded Lady delivered her autobiographical recollections to the silent Minister with passion, poignancy, and frequent irony and humor. In order to ensure a lifelike representation Albee advised Burns, "Take all the time in the world—you must try to keep the man's attention." Since she peppers her reminiscences with snippets of past conversations, he directed her to develop discrete vocal imitations of the different people she quotes, to mimic their physical idiosyncrasies, or to address them as if they were actually present. For instance, at "Where were *you* those last six months," Albee reminded her to address the absent daughter: "Let's not forget about your daughter's presence. Make more of her imagined presence." When she recalls and quotes the extended conversation about death and dying that her husband had with an unnamed "somebody" and her "sister's savior," he directed her to employ different voices for the two men, which she did to great theatrical and comic effect (44–49). For many of the Long-Winded Lady's speeches, moreover, he specified different vocal coloration: "excitement," "not pity, anger," "mockery," "sad," "loud," "hysterical," "great loneliness," "wake up from a reverie," and so on. At other times, however, particularly at moments of sadness, Albee warned the actor against becoming "too interior and not having a conversation," a point he reiterated in his notes after the first preview performance.

For the other two speaking characters, the Old Woman and Chairman Mao, Albee ensured that, even though they speak only in quotations and speak them directly to the audience, their delivery should be natural and realistic, never artificial, literary, or declamatory. His rehearsal comments to the Old Woman, played by Catherine Bruno, clarified his textual stage directions and revealed his strong preference for realism, despite the fact that her words are quoted from a poem by the popular nineteenth-century poet Will Carleton. According to his text, the Old Woman's "reading of her poem could have some emotion. . . . It should be clear though . . . she *is* reciting a poem" (14). In rehearsal, however, Albee stressed the recitation quality only in the Old Woman's opening stanza, for which he told Bruno, "I'd like just a suggestion of doggerel—read it in a singsong fashion." For her very next speech, he charged her, "Begin getting more involved now." His next comment, "This is one thing you should always remember while reading the poem," demonstrates the importance he places on an emotional and realistic portrayal of the Old Woman. Albee's overall direction to Stephen Rowe as Chairman Mao was "Hit a conversational tone—interest us; involve us." Mao's speeches had to be primarily "conversational," "measured," and "gentle," but sporadically punctuated by a range of different tones. For instance, he should speak as if "exhorting millions of people" at "Imperialism will not last long," be "speculative" at "If imperialism insists on fighting a war," and convey "absolute certainty," "conclusion," and "finality" at "Whoever sides with the revolutionary people" (21, 51, 44).

Some of these directions resembled Alan Schneider's injunctions during his staging of the Broadway premiere, where he too had sought to bring out the human dimension of the three speaking characters through emotional coloration of their speeches. Wyman Pendleton, who played Mao in 1968, recalled that Schneider elicited passionate portrayals from all three: the Long-Winded Lady often appeared angry and visibly tormented, the Old Woman projected intense suffering, and Chairman Mao sometimes burst into Chinese curses but then returned to his cajoling and soothing tones.[6] Notations in Pendleton's rehearsal script reveal Schneider's goal of creating a "benign uncle—a happy, pleasant man [who] believes it all completely and absolutely" but who is also given to flashes of violent temper and bouts of Chinese-language speeches.[7] Within this broad conception Schneider required a variety of tones: "glee" at "China has six hundred million people"; "beautiful, poetic, and sweet" at "On a blank piece of paper . . . the most beautiful pictures can be painted"; "reassur[ing]" at "Imperialism will not last long"; and "confidential, personal" at "Historically, all reactionary forces on the verge of extinction" (18, 19, 21, 23). But he also demanded "threat" and "danger underneath" for several speeches: Mao should be "pleasant but ice underneath" at "A revolution is not a dinner party"; pose a "challenge" at "As for the vacillating middle bourgeoisie"; convey a sense of "this is *it*" at "After the enemies with guns have fallen silent"; and deliver a violent *This is it!!!!*" outburst at "People of the world, unite and defeat the U.S. aggressors and all their running dogs" (48, 30, 48, 69). Thus, despite the congruence in Albee's and Schneider's overall approaches to portraying a human Mao, there were significant differences. Albee's Mao was pleasant but restrained and cool, in full control of his emotions. Schneider's Mao, in contrast, was amiable but by turns also threatening and furious. Albee considered some elements in Schneider's production extreme and quite unnecessary, such as Mao's angry outbursts and his half-dozen Chinese-language interpolations, which included his opening and closing speeches.

In his own production, to complement Chairman Mao's vocal realism Albee encouraged the actor to incorporate some "characteristically Chinese mannerisms," bowing, for example, before and after certain long addresses. Urging him to imitate the historical Mao as well, Albee cited documentaries, posters, and photographs of the Chinese leader to point out that typically Mao "appears to be doing one of three things—standing, gesturing, or applauding." During certain sections, in addition, the director proposed other specific actions. Following the speech "Communism is at once a complete system of proletarian ideology and a new social system" (20), Albee told Mao to turn away from the audience and "take the stance of a person in thought, with one hand behind your back." On "People of the world, be courageous, dare to fight" (69), he asked Mao to cross center stage right and raise his arm like a leader addressing a crowd. A few times Albee directed him to lean against an upstage pole of the cube as if resting, or to hold an upstage railing as if looking out from the rail of a ship. In dramatizing his original vision of the title character as "basically factual," Albee as the director not only created new realistic vocal tones, gestures, and demeanor but also insisted on a historically accurate physical appearance: The character wore a grey "Mao suit" and black shoes and a realistic facial mask that resembled the Chinese leader's face, although he disallowed as unnecessary and distracting the Chinese-accented delivery that the actor desired. At the same time, however, Albee also regards his dramatization of Chairman Mao as ironic. Consequently, he gave the actor theatrical double masks. Over the Mao mask, the actor held another, identical mask attached to a stick. From time to time, such as before beginning a series of addresses, Chairman Mao would face or walk toward the audience, lower the outer mask, and hold it behind his back. After that set of speeches, he would raise it again and turn away, usually to an upstage railing. Besides theatricalizing the text, the mask behind the mask reflected the play's essentially non-representational dramatic situation and also suggested the possibility of more similar-looking faces underneath—"a joke about a box-within-in-a-box and Chinese duplicity," confirmed Albee (PCI).

To further humanize and enliven the character in a play largely without traditional stage interaction, Albee devised many movements for Chairman

Mao. In doing this, he departed from his text's opening stage direction, *"He may wander about the set a little, but, for the most part, he should keep his place by the railing"* (13). During an eight-line monologue that begins "Riding roughshod everywhere, U.S. imperialism has made itself the enemy of the people" (25–26), Mao began a cross from an upstage center location behind the cube, slowly strolled diagonally across to the down right corner of the stage, and sat on his heels in dramatic proximity to the audience. During one of Mao's briefer homilies Albee instructed him, "Do the Judy Garland bit!" and directed him to come from behind the Old Woman at stage left, walk straight to the stage edge, step down, push himself back up to sit on the stage with his feet dangling, and proclaim, "All reactionaries are paper tigers" (33). When Mao stresses that imperialists always "make trouble, fail, make trouble again, fail again . . . This is a Marxist law" (37), Albee instructed him to step right on to the auditorium floor and traverse the length of the orchestra. For his next speech, "When we say 'imperialism is ferocious' . . . this is another Marxist law" (37). he climbed onto the center steps connecting the stage to the auditorium and spoke as if from a podium. After his address—and as the Long-Winded Lady began her lines—Mao bowed, stepped back on stage, and traveled all the way back to the right rail.

In a parallel and simultaneous movement stage left, the Long-Winded Lady sauntered from the cube's upstage pole to its downstage one, achieving a stronger position during her speech. Just as he did for Mao, Albee created new gestures and movement for the Long-Winded Lady, who ranged throughout the cube (though not outside it). Again he was defying his own textual stage direction: *"She should, I think, stay pretty much to her deck chair"* (13). When the Voice from *Box* speaks for the first time in *Quotations from Mao Tse-Tung,* Albee directed the Long-Winded Lady to react by rising slowly from her chair, remain standing lost in thought for a moment, and then begin her lines by turning toward the Minister to indicate that she is addressing him. As her speech recalls her standing by the rail of an ocean liner, Albee suggested she stroll diagonally across to the downstage right pole and mime holding and moving along a rail at the cube's downstage edge. In contrast, Albee did not allow the Minister, played by James Knobeloch, to move out of his deck chair, placed right of center stage, and he restricted the Old Woman to her perch on the downstage left steamer trunk. In their cases he preferred to follow his original stage directions: the Minister *"stays in his deck chair"* and the Old Woman *"should stay in one place"* (14).

When asked about his departures from his text in the cases of Chairman Mao and the Long-Winded Lady, Albee stressed that he had controlled those and reaffirmed his essential dramaturgical goal of restricting stage movement in certain kinds of plays: "If your play is basically interior action, then you have less physical movement." Clarifying further, he confessed, "I don't like unnecessary movement. I don't like movement to get in the way, especially with plays that are fairly complex in their ideas, plays like *Listening* and *Quotations from Chairman Mao Tse-Tung.*" In other plays, like *Who's Afraid of Virginia Woolf?* and *The Zoo Story*, when "you have exterior action, mostly, then, of course, you have a great deal of physical movement" (PCI).

In conjunction with these comments, a comparison of Albee's staging with that of Schneider's original production explains the nature of the rift that had developed between the playwright and his longtime director. In contrast to Albee's Mao, Schneider's Mao roamed around the theatre throughout the performance. According to Pendleton's notations in his rehearsal script, Mao walked up and down the two aisles, went twice into the stage left box and twice into the stage right box, "circle[d] stage left box via the mezzanine," went "around up above the balcony," crossed to the "top of the stairs," walked "close to one audience member," gave a lollipop to a young audience member, placed his hand on the shoulder of another, and periodically sat down in an empty seat in the first few rows. Albee thought so much activity had disturbed his play's aural and visual rhythms and distracted from its interior action; he had therefore restricted his Mao to a single stroll in the orchestra. Similarly, Albee allowed his Minister no movement and confined his Long-Winded Lady's movements to within the cube, whereas Schneider had permitted his Minister to walk once or twice and his Long-Winded Lady to wander all over the set. In addition, as noted earlier, Albee ruled out the Broadway Mao's bursts of temper as excessive and his Chinese-language speeches as superfluous. In a major departure from the original production, Albee represented the deck of an ocean liner with a simple, symmetrical one-level set consisting of only two pairs of steamship railings and two deck chairs, because he regarded as too elaborate Schneider's realistic set consisting of three different levels connected by steps.[8] Albee, in addition, replaced Schneider's (and his original script's) realistic sound effects of bell buoys and seagulls with the simple clarinet dirge from *The Sandbox*.

Such differences illustrate the aesthetic divide that had developed between them and explain why Albee preferred that he, rather than Schneider, direct his plays, especially their first performances. Especially in his non-naturalistic plays, Albee preferred a theatre of simplicity and restraint, of minimal means and effects. He therefore demanded limited rather than constant physical activity, distilled rather than extravagant emotions, highly selective—almost emblematic—props rather than the clutter of everyday life, suggestive and evocative rather than naturalistic sound and lighting, and pared-down—almost stylized—rather than naturalistic sets. Such preferences conflicted with Schneider's theatrical aesthetic, deeply rooted as it was—despite his admiration for Beckett, Pinter, and Albee—in his early experience with and continuing affinity for Lee Strasberg's and the Actors Studio's naturalistic acting and production style. Albee had grown increasingly distant from this style in the late 1960s and the 1970s, as is evident from his plays of that period, such as *Box, Mao-Tse-Tung, Counting the Ways,* and *Listening.* Further exacerbating these differences was Albee's belief that Schneider had failed to sufficiently appreciate and convey the comedy in his plays. Albee once dubbed him "humorless" and confessed, "It was finally getting to me. Because my plays are, I find, rather funny!" (PCI).

Reflecting his artistic evolution, during these rehearsals Albee made several textual changes in both *Box* and *Mao Tse-Tung.* In a radical revision he excised more than two-thirds of the *Box* segment that follows *Mao Tse-Tung:* he deleted everything from the opening to "you cry from loss . . . so precious," from "No longer just great beauty" to "in a *direction.* Order!" from "Instead of the attainable" to "it no longer relates . . . *does* it," and from "Look! More birds! Another" to "Well, we give up something for something" (71–74). In the years since he had created these works, Albee had come to favor whittling things down: consequently he now felt his initial version was "too long," in fact "a strategic mistake." "I just wanted essences from [*Box*]," he said, and thus he now questioned his earlier aesthetic: "Why go into a whole recapitulation? We've heard the play at least twice. Why do it a third time? . . . I was just being greedy back in 1967" (PCI). With similar logic, he took out eight lines each from two of the Long-Winded Lady's longest speeches in *Mao Tse-Tung,* cutting from "God!, and he looks, and he says" to "we *show* we are?" and from "Straight In The Eye!" to "Don't talk like that!!" (45, 46). Albee also made a few tiny deletions and additions, which he termed "honing" and "refinement." From the Long-Winded Lady's recollection "Circumcised . . . well, no . . . but trained . . . like everything; nothing surprising, but always there," he purged "like everything," in order to clarify that not all was trained or predictable in her experience with her husband (42). Wishing to de-emphasize the Long-Winded Lady's sense of regret at the end of the play, he expunged "Well; yes; I'm sorry" from her crucial, self-defining last speech (70). For accuracy he changed "burn" to "burning" in her "What I mean is: the burn; sitting in the dim moon," and he added "by it" to her "Be *taught*?" to clarify that she means "be taught by death," a subject of her previous speech. For greater thematic stress on the Voice from Box during *Mao Tse-Tung*'s concluding moments, he introduced two refrains from *Box:* "If only they had told us . . . clearly" preceded Mao's final speech, and "If only they had told us" preceded the Long-Winded Lady's final speech.

While these revisions arose from changes in his aesthetic, Albee, as a man of the theatre, made them only on the true testing ground of a rehearsal process, not in the isolation of his study. He insists that he never makes prerehearsal changes in his texts. "I would rather that the cuts . . . come out of the rehearsal process"; "Why would I make a theoretical cut when in rehearsal I can make a practical cut" (PCI)? Revisions, most especially substantial ones, that result from Albee's auto-encounter—of himself as author with himself as director—thus lead to essentially new dramatic-theatrical texts. These rehearsal-tested revised versions of his plays are what Albee regards as the correct texts—texts that best represent his vision and his craft and texts that he wants his theatrical as well as his reading audiences to experience. Until new editions of his works appear in print, however, the current editions perpetuate for a large audience of readers as well as scholars the uncorrected older versions that the author has long rejected.

When directing a play, whether his own recrafted text or someone else's, Albee frequently advises actors to mime an activity referred to in the dialogue. Such directions help to theatricalize the narrative elements in a speech, as well as assisting actors in concretizing their character's reality for themselves and for the audience. "Show us all the things you mention in the lines," Albee told Burns, as she began another walk from her deck chair to the front edge of the cube during the following speech:

> But if you've been sitting on a chair, that is what you do: you put down the Trollope or James or sometimes Hardy, throw off the rug, and slightly unsteady from suddenly up from horizontal . . . you walk to the thing . . . the railing. It's that simple. You look for a bit, smell, sniff, really; you look down to make sure it's moving, and then you think shall you take a turn, and you usually do not . . . (58)

Guiding her to physicalize the described action, Albee skillfully recreated on stage the crucial moments before the Long-Winded Lady's brush with death. He urged similar action during several speeches, encouraging her at one stage, "Do this as often as you can."

In the same way, during each of the Voice's three references to a net of flying birds, Albee instructed all four characters, "Look up in the sky—no matter what direction you're facing—and follow the movement of the birds a little." Each character observed a different area of the sky, individualizing their similar actions. At the same time this tableau, which in its last occurrence also became the play's memorable final image, graphically stressed the thematic point that each character, although part of a group, was so locked in his or her individual consciousness as to perceive the same event idiosyncratically.

Albee also specified other gestures for the Minister and for the Old Woman. He directed both to continue their respective activities, and not freeze, during other characters' monologues. Giving the deck chair–bound Minister a book and a pair of spectacles in addition to the text's tobacco pouch, pipe, and matches, Albee instructed him to use those props to devise different bits of business to occupy himself with throughout. He also reiterated the play's original stage directions: the Minister *"must try to pay close attention to the Long-Winded Lady . . . nod, shake his head, cluck, put an arm tentatively out, etc."* (14). Although he must also *"doze off from time to time,"* the director clarified that he should do so only momentarily, "or we'll fall asleep" (14). Albee encouraged the actor to respond as often as possible to convey a mostly "professional solicitude." Sometimes, though, his gestures and expression could suggest a "snide" attitude, as during her "Bag of crullers" speech, and sometimes "a little bit of genuine concern," as during her "That dreadful death" speech (26, 36). Albee did warn him against extreme reactions, such as the thigh slapping and loud laughter indulged in by Richard Barr, the playwright's longtime producer and friend, when he played the part in Spoleto. This excessive response cost Barr the opportunity to reprise the role in New York City; "I told him absolutely no!" recalled Albee (PCI).

Probably in view of *Box* and *Mao Tse-Tung*'s experimental form and his cast's relative unfamiliarity with the subject matter, Albee provided several uncharacteristically explicit comments on the meaning of the text. Even more frequently than the Voice, the Long-Winded Lady talks of the past, often betraying the poignant unreliability of human memory. Albee elucidated one of her reminiscences about falling off an ocean liner. The Long-Winded Lady remembers, "And me up here, up *there*—this one? No.—and being burned! In that—" (41). Albee explained what her lines mean: "On this deck? On this boat? Or the other one?— She doesn't know on which boat it happened." On another occasion the Long-Winded Lady summons up a long-ago conversation: "Death! Yes, my husband would say . . . Bishop Berkeley will be wrong" (47). Albee explained his reference to the eighteenth-century Anglo-Irish clergyman and philosopher: "Nothing exists unless you're aware of it, said Bishop Berkeley; since you aren't aware of death, death does not exist—only dying exists." As a director, he provided these insights into authorial intent and subtextual import in order to help his actors grasp and convey the surface as well as the subsurface life of his dramas.

Outside rehearsals, however, Albee as a dramatist shrinks from commenting on such matters. Asked what effects on the audience he had contemplated when creating *Box* and *Mao Tse-Tung*'s unusual dramatic structure, he answered, "I don't remember, [but] I was aware that I was making a fairly complex experiment." On being pressed he disclosed some information about the genesis of these plays. Albee first wrote *Box,* then he "decided to write a play with Chairman Mao in it, and . . . started writing the Long-Winded Lady," writing the part "as one entire speech" (PCI).[9] After selecting quotations from Chairman Mao and clipping them, he "discovered this poem," which he put into quatrains, just as he "clip[ped] the Long-Winded Lady's speech into arias." Finally, he started arranging the approximately one hundred and fifty cards on which he had written bits of dialogue into what he "ultimately thought was a proper order" (PCI).

Far more than such cryptic comments, Albee's directorial decisions illuminate his dramaturgy—his rationale for the "proper order." From the first rehearsal, he insisted that the speeches, although disconnected, were "very carefully fragmented." A passage early in the play provides an example:

LONG-WINDED LADY
You never know until it's happened to you.

VOICE, FROM *BOX*
Many arts: all craft now . . . and going further.

CHAIRMAN MAO
Our country and all the other socialist countries want peace; so do the peoples of all the countries of the world. The only ones who crave war and do not want peace are certain monopoly capitalist groups in a handful of imperialist countries which depend on aggression for their profits.

LONG-WINDED LADY
Do you.

VOICE, FROM *BOX*
Box.

CHAIRMAN MAO
Who are our enemies? Who are our friends?

LONG-WINDED LADY
Do you. (29–30)

Albee asked Chairman Mao to enunciate carefully repeated "do" in his speech, to the point of slightly stressing the words. The director then ensured strong emphasis on the Long-Winded Lady's first "do," aurally suggesting a connection between the two speeches. Thus the Long-Winded Lady seemed to ask Chairman Mao, "*Do* you want peace?" or "*Do* you depend on aggression for profits?" Albee also explained that "the Long-Winded Lady's second '*Do* you' is an extension of the first" and demanded an "identical" delivery, thereby reinforcing the impression that the Long-Winded Lady is questioning Chairman Mao. On one level, the Long-Winded Lady's words simply dovetailed into her previous speech: "You never know until it's happened to you. . . . *Do* you." But Albee's staging clarified his original intent of ironically subverting Chairman Mao's political certitude with the Long-Winded Lady's questioning uncertainty.

Both dramaturgically and directorially, however, Albee wished to avoid making too heavy-handed a connection. Consequently, he eschewed interrogation points, which also explains his statement appended to the published text: "There are one or two seeming questions that I have left the question mark off of" (16). As he staged the scene, the Long-Winded Lady did not look toward Chairman Mao as she asked her questions. While Chairman Mao remained upstage and left of the cube, the Long-Winded Lady stood at the cube's downstage right corner, facing out. Since she looked directly into the auditorium, his staging also implied the possibility that those questions—"*Do* you want peace?" "*Do* you depend on aggression for profits?"—were being addressed to the audience as well.

The directing revealed several other instances of Albee's dramaturgic strategy of encouraging connections between juxtaposed but apparently unrelated speeches. For example, speaking of Hitler and the reactionary rulers of Russia, China, and Japan, Chairman Mao ends with, "As we know, they were all overthrown" (34). In the speech that follows, the Long-Winded Lady exclaims, "All that falling," recalling her own fall, which she mentioned two speeches before. Albee linked the Long-Winded Lady's comment to Chairman Mao's in order to undercut his public and ideological gloating with her deep, personal feeling: the director instructed her to cut in with unusual speed and shake her head in sadness, as if at the historical events. This staging also corroborates the linkages noted by such critics as Ruby Cohn and C. W. E. Bigsby.[10]

In a script crafted out of juxtaposed speeches, pointing up such linkages remained a crucial directorial concern. Beyond the structural and stylistic demands of the script, however, rhythm received particular attention. Albee regards rhythm as an especially significant element in his work: "My plays are rhythmic in ways that a lot of people's are not."[11] His concern with his play's rhythms commences at the time of composition. He uses a typewriter, as he has explained in print and television interviews, because "when you're writing a play, you're very interested in rhythms and sound. And you get those a lot from the typewriter."[12] In the case of *Quotations from Chairman Mao Tse-Tung*, he was so concerned about its rhythm that in his published text he appended a special note for future actors and directors. He stressed that in performance the play will work as conceived, as "musical structure—form and counterpoint," only by achieving his "speech rhythms" "indicated . . . by means of commas, periods, semi-colons, colons, dashes and dots (as well as parenthetical stage directions)" (15). During his own rehearsals on the first day's reading he proscribed all movement because he wanted actors to concentrate on his words' rhythmic properties. In subsequent rehearsals too he focused especially on "the sound of the sounds," that is, on the aural rhythms of the words spoken by his cast. At one session he asked Patricia Kilgarriff, who played the Voice, as well as the entire cast to listen to the rhythm that he felt was superbly achieved by Ruth White as Voice in an audio recording from the original production. Albee did not, however, follow Beckett's example of sometimes reading a part aloud or taping his own rendition of a speech "to explain the rhythms," as Beckett did for actor Jack MacGowran as Lucky in *Waiting for Godot*.[13] Dissatisfied with a preview performance, Albee offered a mock imitation of the actors' somewhat similar speech patterns and tempi and then devoted a morning rehearsal entirely to work on rhythm: "I want to get a separate sense of each of your rhythms . . . to establish . . . distinct rhythms."

Even as playwright, Albee urges his directors to emphasize rhythm. During the original production of *Who's Afraid of Virginia Woolf?* director Schneider asked the actors to simply read the script for the first several days, in order to grasp "a basic structure, just vocally," since "Edward was terribly concerned with . . . the basic rhythm."[14] Eighteen years later, again reflecting the playwright's emphasis, Schneider urged his *Lady From Dubuque* cast to read intuitively, "because half of the play's meaning is in the rhythm."[15]

Rhythm is equally stressed during Ingmar Bergman's rehearsals. Discussing his methods after nearly forty years of "continuous activity as a theatre director" in addition to film directing, he insisted, "Rhythm is always the most important thing."[16] Consequently, when staging a play, "usually I begin by giving the actors the rhythm of the whole thing."[17] Similarly believing that actors should apprehend a play through its rhythm, Peter Brook concentrated his early rehearsals of *A Midsummer Night's Dream* on finding "the shape and rhythm of the lines."[18]

Because of the importance Albee attaches to rhythm, he argues that for a director it is necessary "to *listen* a great deal to the text—not only to watch it—because he can tell a great deal about how well he is directing just by the sound of it" (PCI). Following his own prescription, in the rehearsals for these and other plays he listened intently to his actors' vocal rhythms—he often sat far in the back and at times lay down and even closed his eyes in order to pay exclusive attention to vocal patterns. Roger Blin, one of the leading postwar French directors (of Beckett and Jean Genet, among others), offers a parallel: John Fletcher's "Roger Blin at Work" describes how he "stands watching [his actors] sometimes . . . . More often he sits . . . his eyes closed."[19] Even when others direct his plays, Albee often sits and listens with his eyes shut, as he did many times during Schneider's rehearsals for *The Lady From Dubuque* on Broadway. During preview performances, he sometimes focuses on the spoken rhythms by listening to the actors from backstage or, as he did during *The Lady From Dubuque,* on the intercom in the large work area under the now demolished Morosco stage.

The Lady From Dubuque rehearsals also marked the return of the Albee-Schneider collaboration after nearly a decade. Albee turned to Schneider partly out of practical necessity. A falling out between the playwright and the actor Irene Worth made them unwilling to work with each other, but Richard Barr, the play's main financial backer, deemed the much-admired actor indispensable to the success of the production. Albee later relented, but Worth did not, leading to the search for another director. Albee chose Schneider from among other available directors because, despite their mutual differences, he still believed that, along with Peter Hall, Schneider had been one of his best interpreters. Schneider was aware of the situation and confessed on opening night, "It was very tough for [Albee] . . . because he wanted to direct. He had me more as a kind of intermediary. . . . I thought I'd have to fight hard, tooth and nail. [But] he was marvelous." [20] Schneider also recognized the trust Albee demonstrated in turning to him. "I felt very good about his coming back to me, not sentimentally, but I mean just in terms of professional respect."[21] This collaboration turned out to be their last; Schneider died tragically in a road accident three years later.

As the first public performance of *Box* and *Mao Tse-Tung* neared, Albee made a few final changes, again approaching his creations pragmatically. "When I write a play," he explained, "maybe I'm attempting something that's impossible, but when I direct a play I've written, my job as a director is to make everything possible" (PCI). Since some actors felt insecure because they were not yet line-perfect, Albee decided, "Let's make a virtue of it!" and improvised new props. He reasoned that each character could habitually carry a book in a play where two of its three speaking characters quote from books and the third spends her time reading one. (Albee had already given a book to the non-speaking Minister.) But Albee also had the stage manager paste each character's lines in each book. Thus, while remaining completely in character, if necessary, Chairman Mao could read from a collection of his own sayings—Albee gave him his personal copy of Chairman Mao's Little Red Book, what he termed "the real *Quotations from Chairman Mao Tse-Tung*"—and the Old Woman could read from her beloved book of Will Carleton poems, rather than reciting from memory. Since the Long-Winded Lady immerses herself in Trollope, James, and Hardy on her voyages, she could just as fittingly glance at a book. Although it had no practical utility for the silent actor, a copy of the Bible became an emblem of the Minister's profession. Albee's new props thus provided his actors a sense of security, enabled them to develop new bits of business, and visually underscored character traits. Albee also decided to introduce the haunting music from *The Sandbox,* playing it at both the beginning and the end of *Box* as well as throughout the "Reprise from *Box*" following *Mao Tse-Tung.* The music linked a family wake on the beach in *The Sandbox* with a civilization's vigil on the ocean in these later plays and heightened their sense of loss and their apocalyptic mood.

This account of the *Box* and *Mao Tse-Tung* rehearsals shows how this practical approach is of a piece with Albee's focus on performance. He fleshes out his written words by providing actors with an array of emotions and a spectrum of tonal colorations. These he augments with new expressive gestures, postures, business, miming of recollected actions, and other movements to create credible and life-like portraits. While guiding his actors toward a desired result, his justifications and explanations, moreover, offer insight into the author's conceptions of his text and subtext and into his overall vision and intent for each play. Testing his scripts in rehearsal, he sometimes cuts substantially, but customarily only distills his lines for precision, lucidity, and thematic emphasis. Once in a while he also introduces new properties or music or eliminates a sound effect or set piece. Orchestrating all these elements, Albee strives for the right vocal, physical, psychological, and thematic rhythm with which to stamp his distinctive directorial imprint on each production.

7

Who's Afraid of Virginia Woolf?

*W*ho's Afraid of the Tanks?" proclaimed the headline of the Lithuanian daily *Lietuvas Rytas,* in its glowing review of Albee's staging of *Who's Afraid of Virginia Woolf?* at the State Theatre of Vilnius in April 1990, six weeks into the nation's tumultuous declaration of independence that had brought Soviet tanks onto city streets. Seizing the fundamental point of the play—the need to destroy illusion and face reality without fear—Vilnius audiences saw a distinct analogy with their national situation: "The play is important for us because it is about discovering reality again."[1] A local actor known nationally for her poetry recitations at anti-Soviet political rallies observed after the opening night performance, "We have been living in a surreal world, putting our hopes in some future—and now we must begin to live it."[2] The Lithuanian audience's grasp of the play's central thrust, despite cultural chasms and vagaries of simultaneous translation, testified to the clarity of the author-director's staging of his classic. Almost presciently, only a few weeks before this response from people in the midst of a battle for political and national freedom, Albee had stressed the play's political dimension in an interview. "I was suggesting . . . that people who are wise enough to un-trick themselves may be better off. . . .

Self-deception leads not only to personal trouble but to political malaise and social irresponsibility" (PCI).

This production of *Who's Afraid of Virginia Woolf?* had begun life seven months earlier at the Los Angeles Music Center under Albee's direction, with John Lithgow and Glenda Jackson as George and Martha, and Brian Kerwin and Cynthia Nixon as Nick and Honey. Produced by the Center Theatre Group/Ahmanson Theatre, it played at the Doolittle Theatre in Hollywood from October 5 to December 17, 1989. The extensive film and television commitments of this star cast, especially John Lithgow, permitted only a limited engagement. Albee therefore conceived this production with unusually high-caliber actors as standbys who could capably take over as the principal cast after the initial Los Angeles run. He also arranged for this new principal cast—Bruce Gray and Carol Mayo Jenkins as George and Martha, and John Ottavino and Cynthia Bassham as Nick and Honey—a second three-and-a-half-week period of rehearsals and previews at the Alley Theatre in Houston, where the production's next run was scheduled.[3] After a three-week run at the Alley Theatre this production was fine-tuned for a short U.S. tour and a three-city engagement in Lithuania, as well as performances at the Maly Theatre in Leningrad and the Sovremennik Theatre in Moscow.[4] Albee retained not only his original Los Angeles Music Center production's understudies, now the main cast, but also its set, costume and lighting designs, which were minimally modified for the Alley Theatre's Large Stage, a thrust stage, by its resident designers in consultation with their California counterparts. At the Alley Theatre—where Albee held the title of associate artist for direction and playwriting for several years—he reminded his cast and the resident designers on the first day of these new rehearsals, "I'd like it essentially the same as the Los Angeles production, except where you might have a serious question or objection," but he also cautioned the actors, "Not just copycat; make it your own."[5] As he explained in a letter, his overall goal was to build on and refine his Los Angeles staging, taking full advantage of these actors' familiarity with "the lines of my directorial intention."[6]

Set in the small campus town of New Carthage, *Who's Afraid of Virginia Woolf?* begins at two in the morning as George and Martha return home from a Saturday night party hosted by her father, the president of the college where her husband teaches history. In act 1, entitled "Fun and Games," unbeknownst to George and despite the late hour Martha has invited the newly hired biology professor, Nick, and his wife, Honey, to stop by. The handsome young Nick and the giggly hapless Honey are initially well mannered and eager to ingratiate themselves with the college president's family, but, with their own private baggage and endless drinks, they are soon sucked into the turbulent and miserable lives of their hosts. George and Martha fight in bristling and dexterous wordplay, sear each other with venomous humor, and both unnerve and captivate their guests with bitter and hideous details of their sadomasochistic relationship. George feels wrenched by Martha's public lashings about his personal and professional failures in what he labels a parlor game of "Humiliate the Host." This quartet descends into the nightmare of the second act, called "Walpurgisnacht," as George nudges and cajoles Nick into revealing intimate particulars of his relationship with Honey, including the fact that their marriage was mandated by a hysterical pregnancy and the glow of her father's wealth, which he amassed by stealing from his church. Bristling at his humiliation and armed with such dirt, George forces everyone to play another party game, "Get the Guests," during which he reveals Nick's intimate confession, sickening Honey and disgusting Nick. Martha goads George by being brazenly seductive to Nick, but George persists in feigning indifference, even as Nick and then Martha move to the offstage kitchen on their way to the upstairs bedroom. In the final act, "Exorcism," George returns from a walk outside and pelts Martha with snapdragons he has plucked in the dark. Soon he browbeats everyone into playing a last game, "Bringing Up Baby," to mark the eve of their son's twenty-first birthday. He talks Martha into a long, familiar, yet anguished recollection of their son's growing up, and toward its end he inexplicably begins an antiphonal reading from the Latin mass for the dead. George then announces that he has received a telegram with news of their son's death. Devastated, Martha begins howling, while Honey and Nick incredulously realize that all the talk about the son referred merely to a fantasy they had concocted to fill the void in their lives. With demons acknowledged and exorcised, their long evening culminates in a new but dim and grey Sunday dawn, as Nick and Honey leave and George and Martha contemplate a life without fantasy and lies. The curtain falls as George gently sings, "Who's afraid of Virginia Woolf?" and Martha cries, "I . . . am . . . George. . . . I . . . am . . . ," confessing her fear of living without illusions.[7]

Albee was returning to his masterpiece after thirteen years, having directed its critically acclaimed Broadway revival with Colleen Dewhurst and Ben Gazzara in 1976.[8] Although he had written the play more than a quarter-century earlier, he saw no need to reconsider his script. "I don't think people walked in a different way in the sixties than they do in the eighties," he quipped, "or even thought in that much of a different way. . . . I've not tried to update this play" (PCI). Besides, he argued, "all good literature is supposed to anticipate the future" (PCI). While he granted that audience perception does change, he insisted,

"You can't go around trying to second-guess audience perception, because you distort your work" (PCI).

During rehearsals, however, other considerations led to textual revisions and shed light on his changing dramaturgic aesthetic. From the standard Atheneum edition of the play, Albee deleted several references to the child in the first scene. The largest omission—a page and a quarter long—began with George's "All right, love . . . whatever love wants. . . . Just don't start on the bit, that's all" and ended with Martha's "Yeah . . . sure. Get over there!" (19–20). It contains George's six insistent warnings to Martha not to mention their son when their guests arrive, and Martha's defiant claim to a right to bring up any subject. Also deleted were George's cryptic caution to Martha as she leads Honey toward the bathroom, "Just don't shoot your mouth off . . . about . . . you-know-what," Martha's retort, "I'll talk about any goddamn thing I want to, George!" and after George's "O.K. O.K. Vanish," her final reiteration, "Any goddamn thing I want to!" (30). Albee's explanation for the cuts—that the references were "unnecessary"—reflected his growing desire for an economy of means, characteristic of the dramaturgy in his later works, such as *Marriage Play*. Reflecting on his career since writing *Who's Afraid of Virginia Woolf?* Albee himself acknowledged in an interview with Peter Sagal of *Theater Week,* "I would hope to have learned . . . to do things more efficiently. I think my plays are more economical now."[9]

Yet the simplicity of Albee's explanation also belied the deletions' dramaturgic import. George's repeated warnings to Martha not to bring up the child imply that she may have done so in the past. In spite of this, however, the text does not explain why George destroys their child on that particular night and not during any previous infraction of their private rule. The possibility of past breaches also casts doubt on George's explanation for his action—tendered during the couple's most honest and intimate moment in the play—"You broke our rule, baby. . . . You mentioned him to someone else" (136). The script, moreover, provides no alternative reason for George's action, nor for the urgency of his warnings that evening. Consequently, by deleting the poorly motivated warnings, Albee eliminated the ambiguity surrounding the play's pivotal action.

Through his revision Albee also argued against the kind of interpretation offered by Anita Stenz, who reads George's cautionary references to the child as a surreptitious "planting of an idea in Martha's head" and a deliberate attempt to goad Martha into a defiant revelation of their secret.[10] Furthermore, with the elimination of George's warnings and of Martha's refusal to be bound by them, George's shocked reaction—*"wheeling, as if struck from behind,"* upon hearing that Martha has mentioned their son to Honey—became more credible (44). (Stenz does not explain why George would be so shocked if he had instigated the event.) When rehearsing the scene, Albee categorically told George, "Martha's mention of the child is a *new* one—until now it's been the old one-two."

Albee made another crucial revision in a scene that resonates with the play's central concern: the distinction between truth and illusion. When George returns with the snapdragons at the beginning of act 3, he playfully but earnestly probes what happened in the bedroom, whether Nick is Martha's "houseboy" or "stud." Because Nick implores Martha not to reveal his alcohol-induced impotence, she reluctantly admits, "No; you're not a houseboy" (202). But despite the transparency of her lie, George accepts it as truth. In the original, Martha pleads, "Truth and illusion, George; you don't know the difference," and George responds, "No; but we must carry on as though we did" (202). While staging this scene Albee reasoned that the exchange was a dramaturgic error: George, who is clear-sighted enough to destroy his and Martha's twenty-one-year lie that night, *would* know the difference between truth and illusion. He explained, "I wrote it incorrectly. . . . I miswrote myself" (PCI). Albee altered the lines so that Martha now appeals, "Truth and illusion, George; you know the difference," and George replies, "Yes; but we must carry on as though we did not." The new version clarifies that George accepts Martha's infidelity "as though" it were true in order to "carry on" with his plan to end their fantasy parenthood. To avoid making the actors self-conscious about matters of interpretation, however, Albee underplayed the reversal of truth and illusion as "a very minor matter." Yet privately he confessed, "It's a major matter," echoing the thematic focus of Alan Schneider's production (PCI). As part of his own private directorial preparation for the premiere, Schneider's first comment on the title page of his script read "Truth and illusion (through illusion to truth)," followed on the next page by "A dark legend of Truth and illusion."[11]

Moreover, Albee explained that Martha's statement that Nick is not "a houseboy" "is a lie, and the audience has to know that it's a lie." To clarify that Martha's statement is merely a response to Nick's *"intense pleading"*—and not the truth that George seeks—Albee urged Martha to convey compassion rather than information, as had the play's first director, Alan Schneider, whose rehearsal notes asked Uta Hagen, the original Martha, to make her statement "an act of kindness."[12] For even greater clarity, Albee brought forward Nick's *"tender"* "Thank you" and Martha's "Skip it" (203). Now this exchange occurs nearer Martha's kindness—without the interposition of Martha's "Amen" (which Albee deleted) and George's "Snap went the dragons!! (NICK and MARTHA *laugh weakly*) Hunh? Here we go round the mulberry bush, hunh?" (202–203).

Albee also excised one of George's lines in order to steer the actors away from concern for its thematic implications. "I don't want you all to get any ideas," he joked, as he deleted the first three words of George's "Pow!!! You're dead! Pow! You're dead!" which he cries out as he pulls the trigger of his fake gun to reveal a red and yellow Chinese parasol (57). Dramaturgically, Albee wished to avoid a too heavy-handed thematic stress on death, a crucial motif in the play, as well as to achieve his goals economically: "Once is enough," he insisted, even though his George begged to retain the whole line.

In reviewing his text during rehearsals, Albee also preferred to de-emphasize Martha's unreasonableness. He consequently deleted the exchange where Martha suddenly and flagrantly denies Nick and Honey's presence in their living room and then without explanation and just as quickly accepts their existence—Martha: "We're alone!"/ George: "Uh . . . no, Love . . . we've got guests."/ Martha (*With a covetous look at Nick*): "We sure have" (121). As well as making Martha seem unreasonable, the author-director thought that her behavior here was not credible. Similarly, although a comment in another scene sounded clever, Albee felt it lacked logic. Accusing Nick of planning to make babies in test tubes, George wonders, "What will happen to the tax deduction? Has anyone figured that out yet?" (40). Albee reasoned that couples would get tax deductions no matter how their babies were made and cut the comment, joking, "The playwright got better!" (PCI).

While downplaying Martha's unreasonableness, Albee stressed her loquaciousness. To "make it clearer and nicer," Albee substituted "mouth" for "nose" in George's retort "In my mind, Martha, you are buried in cement, right up to your neck. No . . . right up to your nose . . . that's much quieter" (64). And to clarify that Nick's remonstrance "Honey, do you think you . . . ?" is a reaction to Honey's impolite question "When's the little bugger coming home?" Albee moved up Nick's line to come immediately after her rudeness, without the intervening comment by George (70–71).

These revisions must be regarded as substantial, considering how minimally Albee changes his texts—even during rehearsals for their first performances. Albee asserted, "I don't think I've ever cut more than 5 percent of the play. I remember in 1962 with *Who's Afraid of Virginia Woolf?*—a two-hundred-and-fifty-page text—I think I cut, what? About nine pages."[13] Alan Schneider, who directed that production, confirmed this estimate. "I have eleven pages of *Virginia Woolf?*—terrific eleven pages—that he cut." Schneider also recalled that Albee wanted to excise more, including the now famous Bergin story, which he coaxed the author to preserve. Over the years, however, Albee has cut a little more than

5 percent of his texts during rehearsals of some of his other plays, including *The Lady From Dubuque,* where, as its director Schneider acknowledged on opening night, "he cut much more deeply than I would have thought, more deeply in this play than any play he's ever done."[14] Nonetheless, Albee's 1989–1990 changes in *Who's Afraid of Virginia Woolf?* are considerable and reveal significant changes in the author's view of his masterpiece. These revisions, moreover, were impelled by his dramaturgic principles and predilections. Most were driven by his concern for clarity and an economy of dramatic means. These he achieved, as is evident from the above examples, by sharpening character motivation, strengthening internal logic, correcting inaccurate writing, accentuating character traits, stressing connections between speeches, minimizing thematic iteration, and eliminating redundant information, ambiguity, obvious comments, and awkward aural rhythms. Together such emendations both streamlined and strengthened his play.

Albee's fine-tuning extended to the set as well. Although he wanted his Los Angeles and Houston scene designers to largely follow the design that William Ritman, his favorite set designer, had created for the original Broadway production, he also sought some crucial changes. In keeping with an aesthetic that eschewed obvious thematic stress, Albee eliminated key elements from Ritman's setting that were too obviously symbolic, such as a metal colonial eagle, an inverted American flag, and early American period furniture that a critic had labeled the "rough-hewn tokens of the revolutionary past."[15] Although Albee had approved these details in 1962, he now thought that they suggested too blatantly the parallel between George and Martha's fantasy child and the failure of America to keep faith with its revolutionary ideals. This reflected a new dramaturgic desire for greater subtlety, not a denial of an analogy he had acknowledged from the beginning: "I named the couple George and Martha after General and Mrs. Washington."[16]

Similarly, according to Alan Schneider, in 1962 Albee had "wanted the image of a womb or a cave," which Ritman conveyed through "all kinds of angles and planes that you wouldn't ordinarily have."[17] Indeed, Norman Nadel of the *New York World-Telegram* described Ritman's living room as having "been roofed by an architect with hiccups."[18] But in 1990 Albee preferred a setting without such symbolic distortions: whereas Schneider had characterized his set as "not real," Albee labeled his own set "naturalistic." Shunning excesses of architectural torsion, Albee instead accomplished his original goal—economically and subtly as well as naturalistically—through strategic lighting. To evoke a confining, cave-like space, according to the Alley Theatre's lighting designer, Robert P.

Hill, Albee demanded "darker edges around the set."[19] In addition, he required two areas along the edge of the set—one near an upstage left bookshelf and one near a stage right fireplace and mantelpiece—to be lit extremely dimly in order to extend and accentuate the dark circumference.

The naturalism of Albee's set grew not only out of perfectly angled and leveled architecture—with the author-director even employing an actual level to ensure accuracy—but also out of an accumulation of fine details. For the first few minutes of the play audience attention focused on numerous set pieces and props in the unremarkably furnished New England living room, as George and Martha turned on lamps, hung their coats on the rack behind the front door, straightened up sofa and chairs, removed glasses, cigarettes, and matches from end tables and coffee table, picked up books, magazines, and newspapers from the floor and chairs and placed them on the magazine rack or bookshelf, made drinks at the well-stocked bar, emptied ashtrays, and so on. The set consisted of a raised upstage area along the width of the stage, with a large central archway that led to the rest of the house and revealed a partial view of a staircase. Wooden bookshelves flanked walls on both sides of the archway, and in front of the right bookshelf, a well-appointed trolley served as the bar in an area separated by a low railing. On the lower level, to the right of the bar, stood a fireplace and mantelpiece with photographs, ashtrays, a working clock, and an abstract painting on a pale green wall above. In front of the fireplace a leather chair, footstool, and rocking chair formed a small seating area, and slightly below it on the left was the main seating area with a downstage center sofa, chair, ottoman, and coffee table framed by an oval, earth-hued rug. Along the left stage edge and extending to the upstage front door ran a bay window with sheer curtains, hanging plants, and a window seat with pillows and a leather basket. Wooden panels and hardwood flooring provided warmth and unified various areas of the set.

Because of the detailed naturalism of this mise-en-scene and the length of the play, Albee provided a nearly full but unfinished set, a complete group of furniture, and many of the props for the first rehearsal itself, and he had the rehearsal studio's floor marked off with tape to indicate the various spaces of the performance area on the Large Stage, to which rehearsals moved in a few days. Although rehearsing in the performance space was much more unusual for Broadway productions, Schneider had similarly rehearsed the original production of *Who's Afraid of Virginia Woolf?* at the Billy Rose Theatre. Twenty years later Uta Hagen asserted, "To me, this was one of the unique experiences of my entire life in the theatre, starting with the things that are food for the play being alive on the stage."[20] Albee was thus building on a rare but sound precedent and greatly helped these actors to make the stage environment their own and move quickly to matters of blocking and characterization.

With this detailed set, Albee blocked his play speedily. Given his cast's recent experience as understudies in the Los Angeles production, Albee skipped the reading usual at his first rehearsals and completed the initial blocking for his three-act play within three days. In contrast, in 1962 Schneider needed nine feverish rehearsal days to block the unfamiliar script. Albee puts a play on its feet early, quickly, and always with input from the actors. As in most aspects of his directing, he readily accommodates actors' reasonable requests for modification in this initial blocking or its subsequent refinement and correction. Drawing on his experience in several of the author's productions, John Ottavino commented that although Albee plans out movement precisely, "he's loose about it. . . . Unlike other directors, I've never heard him say to an actor who says, 'I'm not comfortable here,' 'Well, tough darts, *get* comfortable.'"[21] Albee's practice matches Ingmar Bergman's approach in his rehearsals: veteran Bergman performers display "surprising unanimity" in stressing his combination of "precise" and "exact" blocking with an openness to actors' suggestions.[22] Gunnel Lindblom, one of his longtime collaborators, concluded, "He's always . . . proposing very distinct blocking. But you're always able to discuss changes."[23] Albee too typically asks an actor to show him an alternate movement he desires, and, if it does not seriously clash with his overall intent for that scene, accepts it freely and occasionally even compliments the actor on the improvement. Nonetheless, Albee's overall stamp on the blocking remains unmistakable. In the highly stylized *Box* and *Quotations from Chairman Mao Tse-Tung* Albee had, unusually, restricted movement to a minimum, but in *Who's Afraid of Virginia Woolf?* he filled the stage with physical action to match the dialogue's often frenetic energy and constant back-and-forth. His blocking made optimum and varied use of the elaborate set, moving the actors between the two levels and through the different areas of the living room. Such blocking belies the charge sometimes hurled at Albee—and at other playwright-directors—that he only wants actors to face front and mouth his precious words.

Even before a play is fully blocked Albee begins to offer hints about his characters, so that actors can build upon them from early in the rehearsals. From the start George became the center of directorial attention, partly because, as Albee acknowledged, he has the largest number of lines and remains on stage the longest. More significantly, Albee asserted in a postrehearsal interview that he thinks George "is in control of the entire arc of the play the entire time" (PCI). This view of George's dramatic function and agency in *Who's Afraid of Virginia*

Woolf? goes well beyond most critical estimates of his role in this widely studied play and aligns George with Jerry, who similarly determines the shape of the action in *The Zoo Story*.

In the opening scene, Albee suggested that George is more weary than angry when Martha announces the imminent arrival of guests. As soon as he meets the couple, he should start sizing up Nick as a potential threat because "he is good-looking, young, and ambitious." Beginning with George's "That what you were drinking over at Parnassus?" (30), nothing should be "simple conversation," Albee urged. "You're probing him to see how much he'd allow you to put him down—after all it's 2:30 fucking in the morning and it's your house." Just as Jerry keeps Peter off balance through verbal dexterity in *The Zoo Story*, George throws Nick off with ambiguous and ironic remarks, and, like Jerry, George tests a stranger for his worthiness as both antagonist and pupil. When George mentions that he is "*in* the History Department . . . as opposed to *being* the History Department" (38), Albee told him, "You should be contemplative but not remote; don't let regret creep in; you're too clever to let Nick see it; you keep hitting the emphasized words to show your engagement through irony." Similarly, the emphasis in "Your wife *doesn't* have any hips" (39) was intended to "keep Nick off balance." George, again like Jerry, is pleased by his interlocutor's capacity for vigorous response, confirmed Albee.

In the "Get the Guests" scene Albee worked meticulously to convey the precise tenor and purpose of George's verbal attack on Nick and Honey. Although he called for "a necessary relentlessness" in George's thrusts, he warned him, "If you're smug or pleased, it would make you appear cruel towards Nick and Honey. Even the slightest smile will mean cruelty." At another rehearsal, he demanded, "Avoid the smug expression; it can then seem ugly." He kept urging the actor to play the scene without any comment or self-consciousness: "Rid it of everything but the destinations." He suggested that George narrate the story implicating Nick and Honey as if it were a fairy tale. Stressing that "fairy stories are for children. . . . Fairy stories are very simple stories," he advised him, "Keep it simple; no comment." Also, conceding that playing in this way is "a tricky business," he confessed, "Maybe it's the author talking" in that segment. Overall, he explained, there is a "fine line between enthusiasm in what you're doing and pleasure in causing Nick and Honey pain." Toward the end of the scene, he suggested George "take out the sneer, the ugly triumph," because it must be "a sad triumph." Recommending "a sad sigh, not pride" for George's final line in the scene, "And that's how you play Get the Guests" (148), Albee explained, "It's mercy killing; no one is pleased doing it."

Albee clarified, for example, that some of George's speeches remain private musings in spite of the presence of others. When George warns against a science-dominated future, Albee instructed him to "go private" from "There will be a certain . . . loss of liberty" up to "I will not give up Berlin" (67). But George should not be heavy in these private moments, cautioned Albee, because "George is like a man who would cut off your head, and you'd turn—not realizing what he's done to you." Yet George's emotions must well up in certain scenes. At the end of act 2, after George hurls a book with immense fury at the chimes, his "I'm going to get . . . Martha," Albee indicated, should "inform everything in this scene" and culminate in his "When people can't abide things as they are" speech, with its Chekovian echoes that also reverberate in *The Lady From Dubuque* (175–178). This "quiet, philosophical statement" must reveal "the intense rage and utmost dogmatism of a philosopher gone mad." His reaction to Honey in this scene should be "intense loathing, almost vomiting [because] she *can* have children and she keeps killing them," Albee explained, shedding light upon the character's inner logic. Despite this emotional intensity in the final scene of the act, Albee maintained that George has not yet absolutely decided to kill the son, though he has intellectually considered it—"He's trying it out to see how it will work out." This firm authorial assertion challenges those critical interpretations that see George as planning the son's destruction from the beginning, as illustrated by such comments as, "From early in Act I onward most of George's social and psychological strategies center on one goal: to exorcise the son-illusion."[24]

Even in act 3, after George commits himself both intellectually and emotionally to killing the son, he—like Martha—must not lose the role-playing that is inherent in his character. Branding George and Martha inveterate "comedians," Albee demanded they continue their "performance . . . despite everything going on underneath." Thus, notwithstanding their bloody duels, they burst into singing "I'm nobody's houseboy now. . . ." (96). Insisting that "the song must not appear to have been done earlier," Albee guided them to look at each other for a moment, take cues, and on George's "Now!" start singing in unison, with "an absolute sense of simultaneous invention." A few lines later the two banter about whether the moon was up or down when George stole snapdragons from his father-in-law's greenhouse: "There's no moon; the moon went down." / "There is a moon; the moon is up" (197–199). Always referring to this scene as the Alfonse and Gaston routine, Albee required that it be performed with the speed and formality of a manic vaudeville act. At one rehearsal he analogized, "You are playing a Noel Coward scene—you need actors' poses"; at another he told George, "Often Martha asks you for a word, and you give it to her—it's comic set-up and response." Even at the play's tragic climax, in the speech beginning "Sweetheart, I'm afraid I've got some bad news for you . . . for us, of course. Some rather sad news" (229), he required hints of theatricality. Bruce Gray, playing George, asked if he should convey the news of the son's death to Martha as an actual father would. Albee specified "a fairly straightforward delivery, but with a tiny hint of parody." He pointed out that he had not "written the lines as a single, long speech—it's in small bits, with pauses and hesitations because George does not want to do the punch line too soon, just as a comedian knows how to hold off." Such a performance focus on role-playing corroborates critical commentary about the play's self-conscious theatricality. C. W. E. Bigsby comments, "George and Martha are role-players" in a play with a "self-conscious theatrical air"; "two actors . . . behind mask[s]" who "play their characters" and "perform and praise one another for the qualities of their performance."[25] Forster Hirsch similarly argues, "The two of them have a rich sense of theatre, skillfully arranging the long evening as so many exercises in psychodrama."[26]

Bigsby further suggests that, despite his theatrical posturing, George is firmly a political liberal, a label Schneider also used for George (but not Martha) in his director's script in 1962. Albee saw both George and Martha as liberals and introduced framed pictures of Franklin Roosevelt and Mahatma Gandhi into their living room bookshelf. He observed, "It occurred to me that George and Martha are two people who in their growing up in the 1940s, in their innocent liberalism, admired both Roosevelt and Gandhi very much" (PCI). He also conceded that George's pacifism might have made him a conscientious objector who skipped the war to run the college's history department.

Despite the couple's shared political convictions and shared personal fantasy, Albee asserted that Martha relates to the world much more emotionally than does George. Thus Martha's "involvement with the son is more personal and emotional," whereas George's relationship to the son—and everything else— is intellectual. Moreover, he allowed that Martha occasionally "slips into believing" the son is real, "probably because she's a woman; women and their relation to children, their wombs, and the whole thing" (PCI). Consequently, when she understands the finality of George's decision to kill their child, her great howl, "NOOOOOOooooooo," Albee indicated, must be directed not to George or Nick or Honey but "to the whole world." Albee's production revealed a Martha who earns the right to feel such profound grief.

Albee's staging sought to elicit both profound empathy and profound distaste for Martha. On the one hand, he directed Martha to come across as selfish, skirting reality, cruel, and obsessive—as he explained to Carol Jenkins, Martha is "*not* crazy," but she is single-minded to the point that people think, "Wow! She's *obsessed*." On the other hand, Martha must simultaneously also appear genuinely funny, intellectually agile, passionate, and, most importantly, capable of both compassion and love. Schneider's rehearsal notes to Uta Hagen sought a similar balance and warned against the pitfall of playing a harridan: "Martha is an educated, very sensitive woman. . . . If we are given only vulgarity, camp, drag . . . then the whole thing is thrown so out of focus that it can never recover."[27] This contrasts with many directorial and scholarly interpretations which depict her as a detestable shrew. Critics like Anita Stenz and Michael Rutenberg excoriate Martha wholesale. Stenz's description of Martha, for instance, as a "virago, harridan, termagant wife," who "wallows in disillusionment with nothing to do that interests her and nothing to live for," comes across as caricature of the complex and haunting figure the playwright presented in his production.[28] Albee's rehearsal statements serve as important corrective testimony, although they grew out of a need to elicit accurate performances from his actors, not out any desire to rectify critical scholarship, which, in any case, he almost never reads. When asked during a rehearsal break if he had seen a new book about his work by a major Albee scholar, he responded, "I *may* have," but confessed, "I don't read all of that!" (PCI).

Since some actors often find it more convenient and more enjoyable to play a stereotypical villain than a complicated and contradictory character embodying both detestable and estimable traits, Albee concentrated in rehearsal on balancing Martha's foul-mouthed aggressiveness and cruelty—aspects easy enough to perform—with a countervailing frankness, mental agility, passion for life, and robust humor. Especially important to the playwright-director was underlining Martha's wit and spirit of fun. Early in the rehearsals he clarified what Martha means when she tells Nick, "You think I'm kidding? . . . I never joke. . . . I don't have a sense of humor. I have a fine sense of the ridiculous, but no sense of humor" (76). Albee told Carol Jenkins, "Martha says what she says because she *does* have a sense of humor. A sense of the ridiculous is a highly *refined* sense of humor. You are making a joke!" Martha even enjoys many of George's insults, taunts, and attacks because of their wit and humor. When George mocks her with "Your father has tiny red eyes . . . like a white mouse. In fact, he *is* a white mouse" (75), Albee guided Jenkins to find amusement in the insult's inventiveness and detail. He devised new business and even added a new line, asking the actor to rise in mock disbelief, cross to the mantelpiece, pick up her father's framed photograph, challenge the assertion with the new line ("Let me see"), remain unconvinced, carry the photograph to a nearby lamp, hold it up under the light for further mock scrutiny, begin her next speech ("You wouldn't dare say a thing like that if he was here!") to the framed picture in her hand, replace the frame to the mantelpiece, and cross toward George to finish the speech with "You're a coward!" (75). Albee told Jenkins, "What gets you going is that the story builds like a snowball," and it also offers Martha a chance to retaliate—with greater humor—through the added stage business and through her own subsequent story about George's "inadequacies" and their getting married. Many more stories later, when the two of them are mocking Nick, Albee suggested she and George perform a kind of musical revue, singing in unison and imitating their guest's protest "I'm nobody's houseboy now" (197).

Albee devoted particular directorial attention to conveying Martha's sheer enjoyment of life, especially in the first two acts. As Martha tells her story about Miss Muff's Academy, he advised her, "Remember it with great *pleasure:* it's about you, not about George." His meticulously detailed comments while rehearsing Martha's tale of knocking George off his feet in a surprise blow during a boxing match arranged by her father best illustrate this attention. As Martha begins her story, George slams down his glass and strides out *"with a sick look on his face,"* prompting Honey to enquire, "Is he alright?" (54). For Martha's response, "Him? Oh, sure," Albee precisely specified the needed quality: "Don't worry about him! Let's do story. What fun! Everything subsequent is propelled by the fun in telling the story." At another rehearsal, he demanded "real joy" and "great enthusiasm," explaining, "This is a wonderful anecdote—you're a little kid in a toy store!" When hints of retaliation or self-pity crept into Jenkins's performance, Albee insisted, "No ulterior motive whatever in the telling of it—not to hurt George, or anything else." "Don't let these scenes become angry," he reminded her another time. "Concentrate on the pleasure." Since Nick and Honey's incredulous exclamations punctuate this hilarious story, Martha occasionally responds to them as well, although in quick asides, such as "No kidding" (55). Jenkins accompanied those asides with tiny gestures and looks, but Albee thought even those deflected from his emphasis: "Don't do double takes, and don't spend time on asides . . . keep the focus nicely on the fun in telling the story." Two of his key rehearsal comments to Jenkins—"Effusiveness and joy is what I'm after" and "I'd rather not see a tragic Martha till act 3"—best sum up Albee's overarching authorial and directorial intent for Martha. In contrast, Schneider's distillation of Martha's character, jotted down next to her name in the cast of characters in his director's book, reads, "To destroy, lash out/hurt and be hurt. Anger/*drives.* Action. Instinct."[29] Despite its necessarily telegraphic and bald style, this summary shows that although Schneider too sought a balance between distaste and sympathy for Martha, he did not consider Martha's sense of humor and zest for life anywhere as significant as Albee did in his own staging.

As he did for the actors playing George and Martha, Albee clarified pivotal character traits for the actors playing Nick and Honey. He delineated an intensely self-seeking, "cool," and feisty Nick—an equal combatant for George. When John Ottavino wondered if Nick would find the phrase "musical beds" tasteless, Albee asserted, "Nick *doesn't* think that way." "Avoid things that make him a prig," he advised Ottavino, whose initial tone and "facial reactions [he found] too naive—those of a naive kid," inappropriate even though Nick is the new kid on the block. He also instructed Ottavino in the early rehearsal to remove all earnestness. "Don't be so sincere!" the director insisted, for example, during Nick's statement that he "rather appreciated it [the faculty party thrown by Martha's father]. I mean, apart from enjoying it, I appreciated it" (26). Instead, "try something else," he advised. "You could do it as teasing or repartee." But Albee praised Ottavino's use of a "scrappy street fighter" image for his character. Similarly, Schneider's primary image for Nick in his director's book was an "intellectual hustler" whose goal was "to get what's coming."[30] Albee helped Ottavino develop his Nick into a spirited antagonist who frequently aligned himself with Martha to discomfit George (for instance, during her recollection of the boxing match) and who enjoyed the battle as much as George and Martha did. During the seduction scene, Albee clarified, "You're not a total victim . . . merely a compliant victim," and so after George returns, "I should see you walking on eggshells." Overall, the Nick that emerged under Albee's direction was much tougher than that envisioned by critics who sees him as "a caricature . . . an innocent Midwesterner . . . no match" for George, and more coolly calculating and less prudish than imagined by those who view him as "conceited" and "self-righteous."[31]

Albee paired this street-smart and scheming Nick with a wife who is dumb and tactless. "Honey is so gauche," he told Cynthia Bassham as she began building her character. "She is not at all subtle or socially adept," he added; "she will openly try to further her husband's career . . . because she is not clever enough to disguise things." Her maladroitness as well as her drinking that night cause her to gloat transparently over her hosts' troubles and, when George grabs Martha's throat during their deadly fight, to gleefully and repeatedly shout, "Violence . . . violence!" (135–137). When the fight ends, a textual stage direction called for Honey to moan, "Oh . . . oh . . . oh . . ." with *"disappointment in her voice,"* but Bassham struggled to grasp the cause of her regret (138). Albee clarified his authorial intent: "You have no fear of violence; you're enjoying it; you're disappointed when it stops." Moreover, he pointed out that while Honey is not afraid of

violence, she is very afraid of having children and thus keeps aborting her pregnancies. That fact, he told George later, drives his extraordinary fury against her
during the speech that culminates "And you, you simpering bitch . . . you don't
want *children*?" (178). Toward the end of the play, upon hearing Martha's long
recitation about her son's birth and growing up, Honey thrice cries out, "I want
a child. I want a baby" (222–223). This sudden announcement despite Honey's
long history of willfully terminating her pregnancies, Albee suggested, reflects
the effects of the long, drink-soaked evening at George and Martha's rather than
some gradual, life-affirming realization. "It's irrational," he asserted, "because
by listening to a story, she decides to have a baby." Thus, he concluded, "What
she really means is 'I want my Mommy.'" Albee offers such advice because he
knows from his directing experience how much actors appreciate this kind of
clear and authoritative character delineation. Yet such explication in rehearsal
sometimes also exposes scholarly misreadings, such as those by critics who regard Honey's wish for a child as indicating the beginning of a personal regenera-
tion: one claims, "Honey's conversion . . . seems to be sustained," and another
asserts, "With her epiphanic moment . . . her life with Nick has undergone the
first change of a profound reformation.[32]

Albee regularly interweaves advice about individual characterization with
guidance on how actors should reveal the complex interrelationships between his
characters. Albee calls this network of links between his characters their "connective tissue." From early in these rehearsals he demanded to see such links, especially between George and Martha. At one rehearsal, during the act 1 scene where
Martha insists, "Our son does *not* have blue hair . . . or blue eyes" (74), Albee asked
Jenkins, "What is your feeling about that?" and suggested, "You're back to *possession* now." He then reminded her, "I thought there is a connection between this . . .
and a lot of other things. I want to see the connective tissues between George's
'chromosomological' lines [two pages earlier] and this." He instructed Martha to
be "private rather than conversational" despite the presence of her guests, quip-
ping, "You're not talking of slipcovers!" Toward the end of act 3 Martha finally
succumbs to George's relentless prodding and agrees to perform the recitation
about their son. For her speech "Our son. You want our son? You'll have it" (216)
Albee suggested "a fuck-everything recklessness—if that's what you want, I'll give
it to you" quality. As Martha summons memories of their son's early years, Albee
wanted her to convey to the audience how these recollections emerge from years
of both cherishing and battling over a jointly created fantasy. Reminding Bruce
Gray that his text clearly indicates that George's corrections of Martha should
be "*quiet asides*," he reiterated that they are "not comments on Martha" but "really

asides, which she should be hearing only peripherally." Furthermore, the audience must also sense Martha's confidence and her command—as a co-creator of them—over the story's details. Consequently, Martha should treat George's corrections with impatience, as if they were "annoying mosquito bites," and "put them off more definitely." Martha must feel, "It's *my* story!" and "dismiss his corrections" because for her they are "an absolute violation of the truth." Through such orchestration of his actors' stage interaction, Albee aims to bare the distinct "connective tissue" that he as the playwright implanted when he created his characters.

Such conscious authorial linking also means he can offer unique and highly persuasive subtextual guidance to actors when he directs his own plays. "When I'm doing a play that I've written," he remarked in an interview outside the rehearsal, "the subtext comes to my consciousness. I'm already aware of it" (PCI). Virtually every rehearsal of *Who's Afraid of Virginia Woolf?* offered instances of authorial insight into subterranean meaning, as Albee told his cast, "I want to hear the engines of your mind working," and then guided them to grasp what propelled their words and actions. Many of his comments stemmed from his central concern in this staging, as in his earlier Broadway revival, to clarify that George and Martha are grieving over the death of their cherished private metaphor, not the death of a real child. Albee believes the play's pivotal first production fell short of clearly conveying this point, and asserted that "one of the reasons [for] directing this play [was] to correct the misinterpretation of the nature of the play." "One of the things that I tried to emphasize in the [Los Angeles] production and finally got Glenda [Jackson] to do—and I'm getting Carol [Jenkins] to do here . . . is to understand that they are exorcising a metaphor. Something they both realize is a metaphor" (PCI). During the rehearsal Albee also spelled out for his actors precisely when George decides to destroy their fantasy child. "Out there in the dark," he told Carol Jenkins and Bruce Gray, "as George wanders outside in the early morning hours—between acts 2 and 3—he has come to some conclusions about what he's going to do." When he returns in act 3 his rage at having to take that action impels a "kind of manic recklessness in George's behavior" toward both Martha and their guests. Overall, Albee reiterated, "The play for me is more touching and chilling if it is the death of a metaphor" and consequently in this production he focused painstakingly on "getting the through-line of the exorcism of the fantasy-child metaphor a little clearer" (PCI).

During these rehearsals Albee once remarked that sometimes "subtext is more important than text, even," and that ideally in his directing "the first two weeks are basically subtext work. So they really understand why the character behaves the way the character does in a certain section" (PCI). The incidents discussed here are a small but representative sample of how he helped his actors understand and play the subtext at particular points. When Martha discreetly places George's hand on her breast, the author explained, she intends it as "a very private kind of apology, but George makes it public," which motivates her line "You . . . prick!" (59). She means, "I was trying to apologize to you." On the surface George's remark "Well, you just hold that thought, Martha . . . hug it close . . . run your hands over it" (168) appears merely to refer to Martha's insulting thought that his life is going nowhere. Albee clarified, however, that George is actually employing sexual double-entendres to mock her lust for Nick, and therefore the actor should infuse his delivery with a sexual charge. George's Oriental jokes are "meant to be intentionally in bad taste—he's doing a parody of barroom or locker-room talk," but Honey's comment "Two grown men dancing . . . heavens!" (124) contains "a touch of homophobia."[33] As Martha proceeds to seduce Nick in George's presence, "the whole thing should appear grotesque," because, instead of desire, "rage—enormous rage—impels her to avenge herself through Nick." Later, George's declaration "Care? You're quite right. . . . I couldn't care less" (172) should be "passionate," Albee told the actor, "because you do care." Similarly, when George announces nonchalantly, "Lord, Martha, if you want the boy that much . . . have him" (173), he is merely camouflaging "a desperate wounding at what's going to happen."

For Martha's "Deserted! Abandon-ed! Left out in the cold like a pussycat!" speech that opens act 3, Albee offered several subtextual readings. Irony should suffuse this speech, because "Martha is doing a self-mocking bravura performance for her own amusement—she invents ice cubes from tears and all that for effect." Consequently, even though she is isolated, calls out to her absent father and absent husband, and speaks about crying all the time, her speech is free of self-indulgence and self-pity. Although he conceded that she feels sad and disappointed about the events of that night, he insisted that her regret remains submerged. "You have a father you love and respect and wish your husband were like him," he told Carol Jenkins, but Martha's "feelings about her father include denial" as well. Yet he cautioned, "She is not crippled by lack of attention from her Daddy" or by her unhappy marriage. "Martha has always been a tomboy. The way Martha moves—her expansiveness, her bravura, her boisterousness (which comes out of her exuberance), her sexuality—is not the result of any emotional crippling." She would have had the same qualities even if her relationship with her father or her husband had been better, he reasoned. Occasionally, however, he steered clear of subtextual explanation, especially if an actor's request strayed toward matters of authorial meaning or critical significance. For instance, when Carol Jenkins wondered if there was some significance to Martha's claiming to be an atheist, Albee responded, "Naaaah!" When she persisted and rephrased her question, "What does it mean?" Albee deadpanned, "It simply means she does not believe in God." After a pause, he joked, "I thought the *author* was going to get into intellectual trouble!"

When he did explain the subtext, he cautioned the actors that no matter how important it may be, it must by definition remain cloaked in their performance. Thus at various times he interrupted one actor or the other with such reminders as "Oh, but that's subtext!" "Keep it covered—this is subtext!" "Simplify and underplay!" "Unload the delivery!" "I hate symbolism," he once declared as he warned Gray, "Don't play the symbols!" Another time he confirmed Gray's suggestion that in George's novel the confinement of the boy in an asylum may be a metaphor for George's own personal and professional confinement, but found the actor's manner "too portentous." For similar reasons, he objected to John Ottavino's subtextual underlining during Nick's confession that Honey can no longer become pregnant. "Don't play the death of all future children!" he cautioned.

Since by staging his own work Albee seeks to realize in moment-to-moment performance his original blueprint for a play, his rehearsal decisions illuminate his authorial strategies and aesthetic. His directing of *Who's Afraid of Virginia Woolf?* demonstrates how central his insistence on psychologically and sociologically credible stage behavior is to his theatre aesthetic. He has regularly declared that *Who's Afraid of Virginia Woolf?* is "absolutely naturalistic," and his directing concentrated on ensuring that every detail of delivery, gesture, and business was psychologically believable. Several times each day he demanded, "Make it real"— a refrain that echoed, in inverse, Stanislavsky's directorial refrain, "I don't believe it," and Elia Kazan's distillation of a director's craft, as he jotted it in his director's notebook for *A Streetcar Named Desire:* "Directing finally consists of turning Psychology into Behavior."[34] Albee's practice also owes a debt to his early experience with Alan Schneider, who essentially followed Stanislavsky and Kazan but also slightly broadened the definition of directing in the light of his work on the non-naturalistic plays of Beckett and Pinter, as evident in his statement that a director "tries always to translate psychology of whatever form or persuasion into observable behavior . . . in sum, concerning himself with the revelation of human life on stage."[35] So important was Albee's stress on psychologically and sociologically plausible speech and action in his directorial aesthetic that he revised his text when on rare occasions an actor could not believably execute it. Declaring, "I hate ineffective slaps," Albee demanded that the act 3 slapping be so credibly "violent that an actor could get hurt." After several rehearsals, however,

Albee concluded, "I have never believed the slapping" and replaced George's five slaps, indicated in his textual stage directions, with a violent push that threw Martha almost off her feet. Albee's highly naturalistic staging, besides reflecting his directorial strategies and authorial aesthetic, counters critics who insist that *Who's Afraid of Virginia Woolf?* can work well only as a non-naturalistic text. Ruby Cohn contends that the play does not cohere "as realistic psychology," because only "credible motivation drives psychological drama, and Albee's motivation is designedly flimsy."[36] According to Hirsch, the metaphor of the child does not work, unless one views *Who's Afraid of Virginia Woolf?* as a "marginally realistic domestic drama."[37] Gerry McCarthy faults critics as well as Alan Schneider for forcing Albee "into a naturalistic . . . mold," which "in a number of crucial ways he does not fit," and McCarthy predicts that "Albee is likely to suffer at the hands of American actors whose tradition is fundamentally naturalistic."[38] On the contrary, the naturalistic tradition of Albee's actors perfectly suited his naturalistic production, in which a private fantasy, understood as such by two inventive characters, worked convincingly.

Another fundamental feature of the Albee aesthetic that is clear in these rehearsals is a focus on vocal, behavioral, emotional, physical, and kinetic contrasts, both within and between scenes. He frequently demanded, for instance, contrasts in vocal volume, speed, pitch, and tone. At the end of act 2, when Honey staggers in from the bathroom, he told George to remain "contemplative" and "disengaged," but then in a flash to become "engaged," "ruthless," and "withering" (though not loud) when he realizes that she has been aborting her pregnancies. In that scene, Honey too should shift from a soft "dreamy" whisper to a "very loud," "very theatrical," and "nightmarish" scream when she confesses, "No! . . . I don't want . . . any . . . children . . . I . . . don't . . ." (144). In another scene he directed George to shout out, "Ho-ho! Not by a long shot," but then to deliver his next sentence, "We got a little surprise for you, baby" (228), in a "really soft, almost purring" voice. Similarly, when Martha openly seduces Nick in George's presence, Albee suggested that George swing from a false lightheartedness, to "venom," to a confidential whisper. Offering a rare line reading, he told George to speak "no longer light[ly]," increase both volume and intensity, "*lurch* out of your chair," tell Martha, "No. Show *him*," but then lower his voice dramatically and casually ask Nick, "You haven't seen it yet. Have you?" (172).

Albee complemented such vocal oppositions with a variety of behavioral contrasts. Especially in the early scenes, he used them to further accentuate the differences already pronounced in his text: George and Martha's vulgarity and shock tactics and Nick and Honey's formality and Midwestern manners. More interestingly, he introduced jarring instances of gross private rudeness within Nick and Honey's overall mutual public civility. For instance, he rendered their "Dear, you mustn't . . . you mustn't . . . you mustn't" exchange as an outrageously loud and shrill domestic dispute, which, in a further contrast, was being observed by a cool and bemused George and Martha (69). Also set in opposition were the ways that George and Nick laughed: George's laughter was instant, soft, muted, and brief; Nick's was unsubtle, began slowly, grew in volume and intensity, and lingered. In some cases, in addition, Albee opposed words with behavior. For instance, Nick actually thrust the empty ice bucket toward George to reiterate his request for ice, but his host—despite what he heard and saw—continued to feign non-comprehension. When George finally announced that he understood and offered, "I'll get some," instead of doing so he turned away from the proffered ice bucket, walked to a chair, and sat down comfortably. Similarly, as Honey demurred, "I don't drink," Albee asked her to raise her glass and take a large, un-ladylike gulp of brandy.

Just as pronounced as these contrasts and disjunctions in the Albee aesthetic is a schematic for generating audience surprise and shock, an effect toward which he urges his casts regularly. Referring to both his characters and audiences, he once confessed, "It's nice to keep people off balance," and went on to explain, "That's part of dramatic intensity."[39] That reasoning guides his playwriting as much as it does his directing. Thus, at least once every rehearsal, he pinpointed where his actors might astonish the audience. For instance, during George's vehement "No! No! No! No!" asking Martha to stop revealing the parallel between him and his novel's protagonist, Albee urged, "I want to be surprised by your violence—go under the 'No's,' so the violence startles." Elsewhere, he demanded that George's "mercilessness" in relentlessly hurling the snapdragons at "Snap went the dragons!!" "must startle us." Honey's turnaround on "I want a child," he insisted, "has got to be more startling." When George screams "Silence!" to begin his game of "Get the Guests," Albee reminded him to pause first, because the scream "must startle us." His dramaturgy had already established a pause, indicated by closing the preceding speech with ellipses, but he had to justify it during rehearsal because most actors tend to disregard textual punctuation and stage directions—even in plays by dramatists notorious for their pauses and silences, like Harold Pinter and Samuel Beckett, and even with those authors present at rehearsal.

Albee's rehearsal work on the concrete details of physical performance also clarifies and illustrates his authorial aesthetic of planting elements, usually thematic or linguistic, early in a work and then repeating or elaborating them later, in a pattern roughly analogous to musical structure. A central motif in his production of Who's Afraid of Virginia Woolf? that was repeated and amplified throughout the performance was an image of George as a magician, deftly manipulating people and events and keenly assessing his impact on them. Several times Albee positioned George in a shadowy area upstage and one level higher than the others as he charmed, cajoled, tricked, pushed, or forced one character or the other into doing his bidding or acceding to his plan. In four mutually resonating scenes, from almost identical positions upstage left of center, George dexterously manipulated Nick and Honey into staying on, pried extremely private details from Nick, forced Martha and Nick and Honey into playing "Get the Guests," and orchestrated the evening's final, pivotal events by compelling Martha's acceptance of the death of their fantasy as he read from the Latin mass for the dead. In a minor key George's manipulation was also conveyed and repeated through his hovering unseen over those he was controlling, usually as they sat on the prominent center sofa. In another instance of prefiguring or echoing, toward the end of act 2 Albee blocked George and Martha to come face to face at center stage during their bitter fight where George declares, "And you'll wish you'd never mentioned our son!" (154). Immediately upon "son," he directed them to take "a little beat," "break" their position, and "move away from each other." He called this a "very important moment" and explained his strategy: "I want this [move] to be a precursor of [their] later, big break" in the fight's culminating exchange, when George asks, "Total war?" and Martha responds, "Total" (159). For that final declaration of war Albee amplified both the volume and intensity of their exchange while pictorially repeating their previous physical action of a center-stage face-to-face confrontation, a short beat, an emphatic break of positions, and their walking away in opposite directions. A few other scenes duplicated George and Martha's emblematic living-room battle formation: always George at stage right of the sofa and Martha at stage left, both thrusting their bodies toward each other and holding their positions for several lines, while hurling arguments, accusations, and insults. This recurring image stressed the habitual element in their hostility, most poignantly in their last combat when Martha's contests George's right to decide on his own to end their long-cherished mutual fantasy. In other cases Albee asked actors to repeat a particular vocal quality, physical gesture, or business in order to stress a parallel or anticipate a situation or character attitude. He suggested that George's line "Go clean up the mess," when asking Nick to look after Honey, should be delivered in a dismissive tone that would echo Martha's tone a little earlier when she told Nick, "Go look after your wife" (150, 149). When Martha fails to rouse George from his feigned reading despite her impending infidelity, Albee suggested she grab George's book and hurl it across the room, prefiguring George's flinging the same book violently against the chimes a few lines later.

Such assiduous attention to modulating these details—prefigurations, resonances, and parallels as well as contrasts, disjunctions, and sudden surprises—ultimately demonstrates the importance Albee attaches to rhythm in his directing. He asserts that by orchestrating these elements he creates the appropriate rhythm—both the moment-to-moment rhythms and the overall rhythm of his plays. During a rehearsal conversation he declared that rhythm was pivotal for accurately conveying the essence of his plays and for intensifying audience experience, since, he argued, his theatre (like that of many others, especially Chekov, Beckett, and Pinter) operates as a pattern of alternating "tension, release of tension, passive and active moments" (PCI). Albee has often made such a link between his theatre and musical form: "I only feel the play's going well when it's moving like a piece of music: in the sense of both structural order and the interweaving of voices."[40] His directorial concentration on modulating the various elements that determine the rhythm of a play shows how seriously he takes this patterning during his rehearsals. Alan Schneider had astutely noted in his director's book for *Who's Afraid of Virginia Woolf?* the significance of its "musical structure & rhythms—tones," but it took his considerable analytical skills, consultations with the playwright, and much rehearsal work, as he noted, to "find Albee's inner rhythms, how they balance each other, set off each other, to find [his] contrapuntal movements."[41] One of Albee's inherent advantages as a playwright-director is that he already has an unmatched understanding of his text's moment-to-moment as well as overall rhythms and does not have to laboriously discover them the way, for example, Alan Schneider had to in 1962. However, he recognizes that his original textual rhythms must necessarily be fine-tuned or even modified during the rehearsal process to suit the particulars of physical staging and especially of the actors' personalities and instruments.

Albee focused his directorial attention on numerous other performance elements as well. These additional aspects of his work on the nearly three-hour production can be noted only briefly here, but they will suggest the range and nature of his concerns. Albee regularly devoted concentrated, sometimes even exclusive, attention to precisely regulating the speaking of his dialogue. Frequently he specified exact tones and coloration. A selection of his advice for the four characters' various speeches illustrates the specificity he demanded: "Triumph," "Rue, not groan," "Fait accompli, not urgent," "Smooth, cool," "Quivering intensity" for George; "Vulgar girl," "Chuckling," "Teasing, light," "Irony, less loss,"

"No kidding!" for Martha; "Whining, girl-like," "Idiotically cheerful," "Giddily funny" for Honey; and "Tough," "Begging," "Fuck you!" for Nick. Sometimes he indicated the precise word to emphasize within a line: "He can't *be* a floozy"; "*We* couldn't"; "I've been *told*"; "That's *not* what he said." At other times he specified a word's regional or foreign pronunciation or a sentence's rhythm and speed of delivery. He avoided line readings, however, except as a last resort; occasionally he paraphrased a speech to convey the shape of the desired delivery. In three or four important scenes, moreover, he undertook painstaking line-by-line work to orchestrate the actors' delivery and build appropriate rhythms and arcs.

Besides close attention to delivery, Albee devised extensive new business to sharpen character traits, clarify relationships, convey subtext, heighten comedy, and generally enliven and theatricalize his written text. To justify a required delivery or business, Albee usually cited a character's psychological motivation, but from time to time he cited some pragmatic staging need as well. As is typical with him, from as early as the second rehearsal Albee commented on matters of speed and tempo: "pick up speed," "speed is not tempo energy," "*leisurely* tempo," "pick up tempo," "lacked energy," "underenergized—you've got to propel," "nice energy arc," "quicker interjections," "came down emotionally," "build," "much faster," "twice the speed," and so on. To achieve good pacing, he sought to vary tempo, speed, energy, mood, volume, movement, and business. Some of this variation his dramaturgy had already built into the written text, and some he created to meet the needs of this particular theatre space and this group of actors.

In dealing with this cast Albee used the directorial qualities and approach he had employed on earlier productions, although he seemed more assured and authoritative and his demeanor was less strict. Overall, his directorial manner and methods fostered an environment conducive to the actors' creative collaboration. He offered very precise instructions and answered actors' questions incisively and forthrightly, always in their language and always with a focus on performance feasibility. He consulted his actors often about suggested movements and delivery and sometimes even about which area they wished to focus on at a given session. Once or twice almost every day he gave them notes in private, speaking confidentially and quietly to build a sense of trust and closeness. He also praised his actors regularly and publicly, and from time to time he reassured them about their performance and the progress of the rehearsal process. In addition, he readily acknowledged his own rehearsal misstatements and misjudgments. Frequently, instead of simply supplying answers, he employed a sort of Socratic method to help actors make their own discoveries. Most impressively, he was adept at zeroing in on why a performer was finding something difficult to accomplish or developing unsuitable traits or habits. When faced with occasional dissatisfaction, sarcasm, or friction, he did not become defensive but remained—considering his temperament outside rehearsals—surprisingly patient, though also firm, and usually defused the situation with humor. Like many of his characters, he deployed wit and humor frequently and expertly, relieving inevitable rehearsal stresses and maintaining a pleasant and generally unhurried atmosphere where actors felt free to try different things and contribute ideas. Occasionally he even accepted suggestions he did not quite care for.

He remained averse, however, to offering acting advice or to coaching actors on preparing for their roles, which less experienced actors sometimes desire or even need; Cynthia Bassham, the youngest actor in this cast, might well have benefited from more extensive and one-to-one directorial instruction, notwithstanding her postrehearsal assertion that she was happy with the degree of guidance she had received. Still, Albee did not hesitate to offer actors fundamental or technical advice when it was needed. Some of his oft-reiterated commands included "Keep destinations in mind," "Inform the present with the past," "Avoid anticipating," "Do not telegraph prematurely," "Simplify and underplay," "Unload delivery," "Less Baroque," "Less present-tense anger," and "Quiet is as explosive as loud." These injunctions are noteworthy because they illustrate how Albee helped actors regulate their performances, and since they were given regularly they also furnish further insight into his directorial aesthetic.

Through such expertly conducted rehearsals Albee finally transformed his best-known text into a dynamic, hilarious, and intensely affecting theatrical performance with a crystalline thematic thrust that was grasped by audiences as varied as those in Houston, Vilnius, and Leningrad. His production especially played up the script's humor and theatricality, portraying George and Martha as two incorrigible comedians who are always performing. Martha emerged by turns as immensely attractive—passionate, witty, fun-loving—and immensely unpleasant—nasty, foul-mouthed, shunning reality. George appeared as the play's driving force, a man with sparkling wit and sharp intelligence who is in command of himself and of others. Nick came across as surprisingly feisty and combative, and Honey as profoundly gauche but just as complicit as Nick. Albee's production gained from a few brief but crucial textual revisions that eliminated some inessential iteration and information, minimized ambiguity, and corrected some inaccurate and inelegant phrasing. These revisions also suggested the way his dramaturgy has evolved toward greater clarity and directness and an economy of means. The rehearsals demonstrated, moreover, how Albee provided meticulously precise and compelling advice to help actors underline character traits, sharpen psychological motivation, uncover networks of character interrelationships, embody subtext in credible behavior and delivery, convey the text's rhythms of speech and action, and collectively and comprehensively vivify his text. Some of his rehearsal remarks and actions revealed his authorial implanting of patterns—of foreshadowing and resonance, contrasts and disjunctions, and surprises and shocks—and thus shed light on his playwriting strategies and theatre aesthetic as well as correcting some scholarly and directorial misinterpretations. In sum, Albee's directorial comments and decisions during his rehearsals for *Who's Afraid of Virginia Woolf?* constitute a compendium of authorial insights into this contemporary classic—insights into the key elements of characterization, action, subtext, and structure and the effective realization of these elements in performance—and illustrate in substantial detail his main directorial practices and his essential theatre aesthetic.

8

Marriage Play

*M*arriage Play portrays Jack and Gillian unflinchingly dissecting their thirty years together. They recriminate and reminisce—often in witty, allusive, and literary language—about their years of affection and betrayal, attention and neglect, passion and distance. With several linguistic echoes of Samuel Beckett, the play is also a marital *Waiting for Godot:* it begins as it ends, with Jack's declaration to Gillian, "I'm leaving you," but with no indication of his doing so. Bracketed between those identical declarations, Jack and Gillian—an educated, stylish, and comfortable couple—battle in anger and in sorrow, in savage verbal duels, and once even in actual physical combat. *Marriage Play* recalls not only Beckett but also Strindberg and Albee's own *Who's Afraid of Virginia Woolf?* as it paints a somber picture of a marriage in extremis. Jack and Gillian's unremitting self-examination, however, moves beyond their marriage to encompass their entire lives, and their despair, finally, resonates with the existential anguish expressed in Jack's realization "We come to the moment we understand no matter what we have done . . . nothing has made any difference."[1]

The degree of Albee's directorial imprint on *Marriage Play's* most important productions is remarkable. He staged the first three (and most important) productions of *Marriage Play*—its world, American, and East Coast premieres—and he collaborated closely with the directors who staged the play's New York City and London premieres. At Vienna's English Theatre, which had commissioned the play, he directed its first stage performance in 1987, with Kathleen Butler as Gillian and Tom Klunis as Jack.[2] He next directed the first American performance of the play at the Alley Theatre in Houston in 1992, with Shirley Knight as Gillian and Tom Klunis again as Jack.[3] Later that year he directed the play's first East Coast performance—again with Shirley Knight and Tom Klunis—at the McCarter Theatre in Princeton, New Jersey, restaging the Alley Theatre's thrust-stage production for the McCarter Theatre's proscenium stage.[4] This Albee staging was seen by many theatre professionals from nearby New York City. Among them were members of the Signature Theatre Company and its artistic director, James Houghton, who devoted his company's entire 1992–1993 season to Albee plays. For that season's opening production, Houghton staged the first New York City performance of *Marriage Play*. Albee exercised considerable influence on that production, too. As is his standard practice, he amicably but firmly took full advantage of his authorial right, guaranteed by his contract, to participate in all aspects of that production: he served as an advisor, attended selected rehearsals, and ruled on myriad details of the setting, furniture, props, costumes, and even publicity.[5] Furthermore, Albee was available to Houghton and his cast for consultation much more than is usual for playwrights, since during that period he was also serving as an advisor on all the other plays being readied for the theatre's Albee season as well as serving as a fellow director, staging his own newly titled work *Sand,* comprising *Finding the Sun, Box,* and *The Sandbox.* Most crucially, Albee insisted that director Houghton cast Butler and Klunis, thus ensuring that his original molding of these actors' portrayals would continue in, or at least strongly color, the New York City staging. Again, in his authorial role, Albee exerted influence on the London premiere of *Marriage Play,* performed on a double bill with *Finding the Sun* at the Royal National Theatre's Cottesloe Theatre in 2001. He was active backstage, offering guidance and feedback to director Anthony Page and his actors Sheila Gish and Bill Patterson, and even making some textual changes to transform Jack and Gillian into a British couple living in Richmond, Surrey.[6] Between Albee's Vienna and Houston productions, *Marriage Play* had also seen two other European productions, the first at the Lilla Teatern in Helsinki and the second at the Pikku Lillian in Stockholm.[7]

The Alley Theatre's production of *Marriage Play* had four weeks of rehearsals and early previews, from December 3, 1991, to January 4, 1992.[8] When planning these rehearsals, Albee decided that, since *Marriage Play* is a two-character play where both actors have to be on stage all the time, he would not have them work more than four to five hours each rehearsal day. His schedule provided for a total of twenty-four days of rehearsals, including technical and dress rehearsals, and five days of previews. Uncharacteristically, he began the *Marriage Play* rehearsals by devoting two full sessions to reading the script; as described earlier—and unlike many directors—he usually spends only half a rehearsal day on an initial reading. Following this extended reading, he spent three full days on blocking act 1; the next five days were spent on run-throughs of act 1 and on blocking act 2. The next eleven days were devoted to work on specific scenes and daily run-throughs, followed by three days of dress and technical rehearsals before the first public preview.

During the early sessions Albee guided the actors to understand the overall thrust of the play by telling them how he had considered some alternate titles for it. He had first thought of naming it "The Old One-Two" and later "News from the Front," but, he confessed, "I hate plays that are too neatly tied up," and thus preferred the more neutral and ambiguous "Marriage Play." Albee also stressed his play's ambiguous ending and quipped that the title was not "Death of a Marriage" but could be "Illness of a Marriage." These humorous comments served to relieve the tensions and anxieties common in early rehearsals, while simultaneously conveying his broad authorial intent to his actors. Prior to these rehearsals, the characters in the script were simply named He and She. Unless a play requires them for some reason, Albee typically prefers not to give his characters proper names. During the early rehearsals, however, Shirley Knight and to some extent Tom Klunis felt a need as actors to know each other's names, especially since they were portraying a married couple. So the author reluctantly bowed to the actors' wishes and named them Jack and Gillian. In a conversation outside the rehearsals, he admitted that the names were also a private joke, evoking the Jack and Jill of the nursery rhyme. Some months later, Albee told an interviewer from *American Theatre* that another reason for his going along with the actors' request for names was to preempt critical symbol mongering. "If you don't give them names, people say, 'Ah, they're symbolic.' So you have to waste names on them."[9]

In only its second production, the *Marriage Play* script was radically cut during these rehearsals. The bulk of this chapter consists of an interview in which I probe Albee in some detail on his rehearsal-inspired revisions. Such was the extent of Albee's cuts that at one stage he assured the actors, "I promise you these are the last changes!" In a good-humored acknowledgment of the amount of trimming his original text had required, he scribbled the subtitle, "A play &

a half," when inscribing a typescript copy of the play for me at the end of these rehearsals. He carefully reconsidered almost every aspect of his text in order to translate it into effective performance. Thus his explanations for his cuts, modifications, and rare additions to the dialogue and stage business provide insights into his dramaturgy and his overall theatrical aesthetic. More starkly than did rehearsal work on any of the older scripts, Albee's work on *Marriage Play* reveals how the demands of performance alter the idealized vision of a play contained in the author's original, literary version. His comments, made toward the end of the rehearsal process, are also unusual in that Albee uncharacteristically discusses the practical considerations underlying his textual revisions.

In these *Marriage Play* rehearsals Albee paid an unusual level of attention to verbal and performance rhythm, elucidating in greater detail than before what he means by rhythm and how he modulates it in his writing and in his productions. Rhythm is a matter of critical significance in Albee scholarship and performance, and it has received only general, superficial, and almost exclusively textual analysis so far.

Because of his cast's relative unfamiliarity with this new script, Albee provided considerable explanatory comments on character subtext, meaning, and authorial intent to coax an accurate performance from them. Albee also showed that he is an astute handler of actors of different temperaments. Faced with his two actors' significantly different personalities and approaches to acting, Albee proved patient, deft, and diplomatic as a director. With Tom Klunis anxious to establish delivery, business, movement, and overall interpretation as early as possible and Shirley Knight compulsively experimenting until opening night (and beyond), Albee preempted several potential problems and smoothly and economically navigated unavoidable differences.

As well as refining the script, elucidating the characters and situations, and handling both the actors and myriad practical concerns, Albee concentrated on fleshing out this domestic drama with a cumulation of business that translated character psychology into credible stage behavior. Directors from Stanislavsky and Shaw to Kazen and Schneider consider this the essence of stage directing, or in Shaw's words, "making the audience believe that real things are happening to real people," and argued that it was "the beginning and end of the business" of directing.[10]

In the following discussion Albee offers detailed insights into his work as both author and director of *Marriage Play*. Reviewing his rehearsal decisions, Albee ranges from such broad topics as the dramaturgic function of each scene and beat within the larger movement of a play to pragmatic considerations about the lengths of acts within two-act and three-act plays and the distinction between revisions for dramaturgic refinement and those meant to serve audience needs and taste. Albee, of course, devotes most of his comments specifically to his work on *Marriage Play* and explains his rationale for his many textual revisions, the linguistic self-consciousness of these characters and their resemblance to some of his friends, the practical considerations for foregoing a stage slap in favor of an attempted blow with a briefcase, the inherent difficulty of staging physical combat, the paradox of the play's final tableau, his requirements for the set and lighting, his dealings with casting directors, his strategies for ensuring himself sufficiently prominent billing as author and director in publicity material, and his loyalty to his actors.

RS: During these *Marriage Play* rehearsals you have made several substantial cuts. Could you talk about one or two major deletions and your reasons for cutting them?

Albee: In the "Why would I put in a fucking garden?" speech that section was just a long thing, holding it up.

RS: Now you always say, "That's holding it up."

Albee: It's the old rule. Any scene in the play has got to do two things: reveal character further and advance the action. The two things that I've cut, the south of France thing and the thing about the difference between men and women and courtship and all the rest, weren't doing anything. They were interesting. They were nicely written. I liked them a lot. I'm not gonna lose them, no. I can use them somewhere else. I probably will. But they had nothing to do with moving the action of the play forward. They were static moments. The illusion of the static is O.K. But those were just really static; they were set pieces. So I cut them. [Albee managed to incorporate these deleted speeches into his next play, *Fragments: A Concerto Grosso,* which premiered a year later under his direction at the Ensemble Theatre of Cincinnati.]

RS: Well, some of the deleted passages did reveal character a little.

Albee: They must do *two* things, both of them. If they only do one of them, then you've got to look at them carefully. Because maybe they can go.

RS: Well, theoretically it sounds good, but in practical terms I think some lines do not necessarily . . .

Albee: Well, not lines, no. You can't apply that rule line to line. It's scene to scene. Beat to beat. The top of the play has to cascade downhill at that particular point to its ending. It started cascading, then there was this long plateau, and then it cascaded a little further. I was watching the audience for five nights.

Coughing and rustling, and this started to happen. Now that's my fault, because I as director was not being as tough with me as writer. But I have to learn things, and I have to figure them out. I knew at the end of last night's performance. That's why I went and stood on stage and wrote to myself what went wrong. It came to me. I knew exactly what I had to do, and what the lines were, and no more fooling around.

RS: You gave me two absolutely essential reasons for all those large cuts, i.e., for cutting of scenes. But there were several other line cuts, too, and some of them were significant ones, it seems to me. What other specific reasons compelled you to make those cuts?

Albee: Well, I have to relate to what interests me and to what bores me. If something's starting to bore me, who's the author and the director, I can assume that the audience has been bored too. At the same time, I'm *not* trying to suggest here that I am trying to accommodate the audience's taste, the audience's lack of desire for complexity and unpleasantness. No. But I don't think that one should give the audience the opportunity to disengage. I think you've got to make the play as sturdy and as involving as it possibly can be. So that if they want to turn off, it's their fault rather than mine.

RS: Both your major cuts were in the second act.

Albee: Because I had a first act about forty-two minutes long, and a second act about fifty-four minutes long. There was an imbalance—not only a time imbalance but a psychological imbalance. Two major sections I cut bring the second act down, I imagine, to about forty-two minutes. I bet I cut about twelve minutes altogether.

RS: What's the rule of thumb? That the first act is a little longer?

Albee: Oh, I don't think there is a rule of thumb. First acts . . . in a three-act play, first acts tend to be the second in length. The second act tends to be the longest and the third act tends to be the shortest. In a two-act play, oh, some equivalency is usually nice. And if anything, the first act would usually be a little more. Here they're just going to be about the same.

RS: It's always, I would imagine, a little nice to surprise the audience with an earlier-than-anticipated ending.

Albee: But I didn't shorten the second act to make it shorter than the first act. If I was going to do that, I would have put those two scenes somewhere in the first act. The fact is, that would have made the first act tedious.

RS: When you directed *Everything in the Garden* at the Ensemble Theatre of Cincinnati, I remember you changed your two-act play into a three-act work. Was that for similar kinds of reasons?

Albee: It was better in three acts. In Cincinnati it just seemed better with two intermissions.

RS: So you obviously had just one intermission in the original New York City production?

Albee: Yes, with only one intermission in New York, I felt the first act was too long.

RS: Any other reasons why you change things? Were there things that you thought this particular actor or actress could not do?

Albee: I never do that.

RS: Yes, you claim that. But sometimes you do cut and then you say, "I'll put it back in when I publish the play."

Albee: Well, I don't think I've done that here! You have to strip down to essentials without losing anything. But I would rather overwrite than underwrite. You can always cut. Some passages cut here were set pieces—they were not inherent to those two people. Maybe that's one of the reasons I could cut them so easily.

RS: Yes, without trauma.

Albee: Because they're set pieces.

RS: What about your short, one- or two-line cuts here and there?

Albee: I'm sure they were cut for the same reasons, and for the rhythm. A scene goes on for thirty seconds too long; a speech goes on for five seconds too long or five seconds too short; you adjust it.

RS: What about changes in movement and business? Obviously, that's what you do in rehearsal. You had Jack sit down earlier yesterday, stay on the bench. Why? Was it because it repeated Gillian's movement too much and was predictable, a bit like a set movement?

Albee: Yes, exactly. Because what I had done was very stagey. It was not good directing. It was bad blocking. You don't hold to something you have done just for the sake of holding to it. That's stubbornness and foolhardy.

RS: At the end now you have them holding hands.

Albee: I like it.

RS: Does it mean they are closer now?

Albee: No. I like the paradox. It's the first time in the play that they are touching each other. Except in violence. And it's interesting to me that they're holding hands when he repeats the fact that he's going to leave her.

RS: Could it be interpreted that now that he has made up his mind to leave her, his touching is out of pity for her, especially since there is a calmness in his voice?

Albee: No, I'd say it's a lonely decision that he's making. A terrifying decision.

RS: Well, pity for her.

Albee: Mm . . . No. Pity for himself. Two kids in the dark.

RS: It works fine, but it really stresses the positive aspect of the relationship.

Albee: It doesn't do any damage. I think it's sort of a nice little touch.

RS: Yeah, it also wakes people up to thinking that he may not be leaving. Those in the audience who have decided that Jack is leaving.

Albee: Makes it more ambiguous. Paradox does that sometimes.

RS: Overall, how different is this production from the one you directed at Vienna's English Theatre?

Albee: Well, when you have a different actress, you have a different wife; and so you have a different production. I think this is probably a better production, only because I've learned from the Vienna production. I added some things after the Vienna production. There was about a page and a half that I added. The "Do you still care, by the way?" area; "Aren't we wives rational people"; "What are we going to do?"—that wasn't in the Vienna production. I wrote all that stuff. And also seeing it in Vienna and seeing it in Stockholm, I suppose both gave me the opportunity to make this a little richer. During rehearsals for Vienna I cut out a lot of stuff. Just too much writing.

RS: Any changes in staging?

Albee: There's no fundamental shift.

RS: Did the Vienna production have just two chairs?

Albee: That's right. And a little side table. Small stage; that's all that it allowed for.

RS: What about the Stockholm set?

Albee: It was a terrible set. A sofa, a footstool, and a rocking chair. I didn't care for the set.

RS: What about the backdrop?

Albee: Just curtains. Inexpensive production. They did it in one act, which was their big mistake. And the play became much too long. Much too long.

RS: Did you originally write *Marriage Play* as a long one-act play?

Albee: No. I don't think so. I don't remember . . .

RS: I can't imagine such a long play as a one-act.

Albee: It would be. I think I realized early on that there were going to be two acts and that act 1 was going to have to end with the fight. The only difference is that originally I began act 2 at the beginning of the fight [rather than at the end of the fight, as now]. But I realized that that was not a good idea—I couldn't have the actors duplicate the fight.

RS: It's very nice when act 2 shows the actors still fighting. It certainly surprises the audience.

Albee: The intention was to make it seem like they hadn't had an intermission.

RS: In effect, to give an illusion of the continuous action of a one-act play.

Albee: The story thus far, so to speak. Do you remember it an hour back into it?

RS: What did you tell the actors about the implication of the "Don't you care" speech?

Albee: He still cares. It's a dreadful irony. "You used to care enough to pay attention to the fact that you were hurting me, and now you just do it without even thinking about it."

RS: Obviously you're interested in themes about people listening, communicating, not listening. Is that why in *Marriage Play* quite often your actors look out when speaking to each other and often speak while behind their listener's line of vision?

Albee: You don't have to look at somebody to talk to them.

RS: Did the actors feel the need to look more toward each other?

Albee: Maybe a little bit more than I would like. You don't have to look at them to listen to them. Maybe a little bit more. Not as much as the awful problem I had in Los Angeles [directing *Who's Afraid of Virginia Woolf?*].[11] Ah, what's her name? Glenda Jackson, who said, "I can't act unless I can see the eyes of the person to whom I am talking." So I had to restage a whole bunch of things. And then as soon as she got on stage in front of an audience, she never looked at anybody else. That was her attitude during rehearsal. She decided to do a solo performance.

RS: With your actors in *Marriage Play*, what areas needed particular attention during these rehearsals?

Albee: Well, I don't want to get into things that you have to stop the performers from doing. Because the only things you stop the performer from doing are things that you've been critical about. No need to talk about that. But there are certain things that one tries to get out of a performance. Personal attributes or attitudes of an actor sometimes show . . . traits that you don't think belong to the character. I mean, just subtly work them out.

RS: Did you suggest Jack's using the briefcase to threaten Gillian with?

Albee: Well, I originally issued no more than the slap, in spite of the "Oh, it's best to put blood on stage." So I thought that I would try the briefcase. I think it is going to work just as effectively as the slap.

RS: In the script I think it was a slap.

Albee: It was. In a movie I could have a slap.

RS: But you recently did use slaps in your production of *Everything in the Garden*. Two of the actors slapped each other twice, but I think those did prove a bit problematic.

Albee: Oh yes, yes.

RS: I know it is daytime in the play, and I also know that you don't like any dramatic light changes. But is the lighting a bit too harsh and unchanging now?

Albee: Well, you have to be able to see the actors. It was harsher, and I brought the levels down a little bit. I might want to bring them down yet further. I prefer the light the way we rehearsed it this afternoon—a much gentler light. You have that in small theatres. But you can't have that here at the Alley; you have to have things brighter in a huge theatre.

RS: Could the lighting on the glass windows be a little muted?

Albee: Well, yes, but I can't fuss about that now.

RS: Did you select the set and costume designer, Derek McLane, or did you have to use whoever the Alley Theatre provided?

Albee: He was recommended to me. We had some talks, and then I said, "O.K."

RS: Do you like the set?

Albee: It's very nice but I want one more thing on it.

RS: What is that?

Albee: I don't know. Some African piece somewhere.

RS: Did you talk to the actors about it?

Albee: Maybe I mentioned it. I would like something on it. Something more. It's a little sparse overall.

RS: Coming from you, I'm pleased to hear it because it allays some of my own concerns.

Albee: I insisted on having that big tree. That was mine. I insisted on that. And I insisted on the Southwestern rug. Now I need one more thing up there.

RS: At least a sculpture.

Albee: A sculpture or a painting. An abstract painting. I have an abstract painting, perhaps, that could work.

RS: With this experience of directing *Marriage Play* here at the Alley in this particular set, what changes are you planning for your production of the play at the McCarter Theatre in Princeton?

Albee: We have to use a different set. The McCarter Theatre, of course, is a proscenium theatre. This set was built specifically for the thrust stage here. I imagine if we go into a small theatre in New York City I'll try to accomplish a combination of the two sets.

RS: In contrast to your wanting a bit more than what the designer has given you here, I remember that on the set of the Broadway production of *The Lady From Dubuque* you kept wanting less and less while your director, Alan Schneider, wanted more and more. You dubbed him prop-happy for introducing so many props. He also wanted much more color and kept bringing in those color prints, which you didn't think worked with that Bauhaus-style drawing room set. In that context, and given your long working relationship, how would Alan have directed *Marriage Play*?

Albee: I don't know. I don't know. It's a very hard question to answer. I think Alan would have had a problem only with the wit and sophistication of the characters. Perhaps a little bit.

RS: What do you mean?

Albee: These people are upper middle class. Alan's background and taste were different. I mean, it's not Alan's milieu. He would have had a little problem with them, but he would have done fine.

RS: Most of your characters tend to be upper middle class.

Albee: Yes. But that would have been where the problem was.

RS: Many of your characters also are very self-conscious about language and often correct themselves and others. You know a lot of people like that?

Albee: Probably only me. Oh, some other people. Howard Moss is good that way when he has other close friends around.

RS: You do that with your friends?

Albee: Probably.

RS: But you're very precise yourself.

Albee: Also those people! That's the way these people behave.

RS: I have got to know you a little more over the years. In this play you seem to be drawing quite a bit on the traits of people you know and on who you are.

Albee: Maybe I'm beginning to become like some of my characters. Consider that possibility!

RS: All the publicity material announces the title of your play as *Edward Albee's Marriage Play*. When did you add "Edward Albee's" to the title?

Albee: That's the only way to guarantee at a regional theatre that you're going to get your name in the proper size and place it's supposed to be.

RS: At first glance it seems somewhat redundant. I know that you are very self-aware, so I thought you were instead trying to make some point.

Albee: No, no. I'm getting tired of incorrect billing. Most regional theatres don't pay any attention. My contract has always said—all of my contracts from the very beginning have said—the author's name shall be 100 percent of the title [i.e., his name and the title should be the same size]. But they just ignore it. And the only way that I found to get around that is to say that the title of the play is *Edward Albee's Marriage Play*. That's the only way that they can't fuck up the billing.[12]

RS: What size of letters do you ask for the name of the director?

Albee: That has to be 50 percent. It's either 50 or 75 percent. I think 50 percent. It doesn't have to be very big. That's by contract also.

RS: The program lists two casting agencies—what role did they play in your selection of the actors?

Albee: Everybody has casting directors these days. They make suggestions. I can turn them down.

RS: I heard that you had considered Ben Gazzara for the role of Jack in this production.

Albee: I've heard all sorts of things.

RS: You didn't consider him?

Albee: Well, one considers the possibility of everybody. I must confess, though, that I can't imagine anybody really doing it better than Tom Klunis. They wanted another name. They wanted a bigger name. So they kept throwing people at me. But I wasn't happy with any of them. Didn't seem right. And I had seen Tom do it, and I knew that he was right. Might make it more difficult for Broadway later. I don't know. But A: you can't betray people; and B: You go with the best performance you can get. There's too much compromise in the theatre as it is.

Edward Albee gives notes to Gordon Green as Jack and Ginny Hoffman as Mrs. Toothe, following the final dress rehearsal of *Everything in the Garden*, Ensemble Theatre of Cincinnati, Cincinnati.

Shirley Knight as Gillian and Tom Klunis as Jack,
Marriage Play, Alley Theatre, Houston. *(above)*

Edward Albee speaks to Tom Klunis as Jack and Shirley Knight
as Gillian, *Marriage Play*, Alley Theatre, Houston. *(below)*

Edward Albee with Shirley Knight as Gillian and Tom
Klunis as Jack, *Marriage Play*, Alley Theatre, Houston.

Shirley Knight as Gillian and Tom Klunis as Jack,
Marriage Play, Alley Theatre, Houston.

Edward Seamon as Krapp, *Krapp's Last Tape* (*Albee Directs Beckett: Krapp's Last Tape and Ohio Impromptu*), Alley Theatre, Houston. *(above)*

Edward Albee directs Edward Seamon as Krapp, *Krapp's Last Tape* (*Albee Directs Beckett: Krapp's Last Tape and Ohio Impromptu*), Alley Theatre, Houston. *(below)*

Edward Albee speaks to Edward Seamon as Krapp,
Krapp's Last Tape (*Albee Directs Beckett: Krapp's Last Tape
and Ohio Impromptu*), Alley Theatre, Houston.

Edward Albee gestures toward Lou Ferguson as Listener/Reader, watched by Charles Sanders as Reader/Listener and stage manager Wendy Beaton and director's assistant Kevin Cunningham, *Ohio Impromptu* (*Albee Directs Beckett: Krapp's Last Tape* and *Ohio Impromptu*), Alley Theatre, Houston. *(above)*

Lou Ferguson as Listener/Reader and Charles Sanders as Reader/Listener at opposite ends of a stark white table, *Ohio Impromptu* (*Albee Directs Beckett: Krapp's Last Tape* and *Ohio Impromptu*), Alley Theatre, Houston. *(below)*

Lou Ferguson as Listener/Reader, *Ohio Impromptu* (*Albee Directs Beckett: Krapp's Last Tape* and *Ohio Impromptu*), Alley Theatre, Houston. *(above)*

Charles Sanders as Reader/Listener, *Ohio Impromptu* (*Albee Directs Beckett: Krapp's Last Tape* and *Ohio Impromptu*), Alley Theatre, Houston. *(below)*

Howard Nightingall as Boy, Cynthia Bassham as C, Myra Carter as A, and
Kathleen Butler as B, *Three Tall Women*, Vienna's English Theatre, Vienna,
Austria. Photograph courtesy of Vienna's English Theatre.

9
Three Tall Women

*I*n 1994 *Three Tall Women* earned Albee extraordinary and nearly universal acclaim, unmatched even by the critical reception accorded his most celebrated play, *Who's Afraid of Virginia Woolf?*, which had received only mixed reviews. *Three Tall Women* won Albee his third Pulitzer Prize for drama—more than any other playwright except Robert E. Sherwood and Eugene O'Neill. It also received the Drama Critics Circle, Lucille Lortel, and Outer Critics Circle awards for best play. That a work of such excellence was not considered for the Tony Awards, simply because it was playing a few blocks north of Broadway at the Promenade Theatre, generated a lively controversy. With 582 performances in New York, *Three Tall Women* became Albee's longest-running play since *Who's Afraid of Virginia Woolf?* and the London production, starring Dame Maggie Smith, became Albee's first West End show in over two decades. In the light of such honors, it is amazing that for the play's first production three years earlier Albee had had to turn to a European theatre, Vienna's English Theatre, just as three decades earlier for his first play, *The Zoo Story,* he had been forced to turn to the Schiller Theater Werkstatt in Berlin. Albee directed the Vienna production with actors and set and costume designers from New York, and his rehearsal work on this world premiere forms the core of this chapter.

Examining Albee's Vienna staging is especially important because of its fundamental role in shaping the look and feel of the play's three most crucial subsequent productions—productions that led to the extraordinary resurgence in the playwright's critical reputation.[1] Through persuasion, assertion of his authorial rights, and, above all, through the cooperation of a director who had long admired his plays and who largely shared his theatrical aesthetic, Albee managed to exercise unprecedented and detailed artistic control over almost every aspect of these later productions, all directed by Lawrence Sacharow. Thus essential contours of Albee's Vienna staging were recreated in these first American productions of *Three Tall Women*. Sacharow, the founding artistic director of River Arts Repertory, had sought the rights to stage the play at his summer theatre in Woodstock, N.Y., while Albee was still in Vienna in the summer of 1991.[2] After some delays and further negotiations in New York, Albee agreed to allow a Woodstock production, but stipulated that publicity be limited and review invitations restricted to local publications. River Arts Repertory also had a post-summer project-by-project presence in New York and was known for producing new plays that often went on to off-Broadway theatres. Through a series of prerehearsal meetings with Sacharow and close collaboration with him during the Woodstock rehearsals, Albee ensured that this American premiere of the play would largely follow his Vienna staging. (The only real exception was greater movement, which Sacharow favored.) The play that opened on July 30, 1992, hewed so closely to his original production that Albee insisted on essentially moving that production, rather than mounting a new one, when some months later New York producers decided to take the play off-Broadway. With the same cast, director, and set designer, and with Albee still intimately involved, the Woodstock production was restaged for the three-quarters-in-the-round space of the enterprising off-Broadway Vineyard Theatre in Lower Manhattan, where it opened on January 24, 1994, and became the biggest hit in the Vineyard's history. Several weeks later that production was transferred to the thrust stage of the Promenade Theatre, moving from the Vineyard's 130-seat house on West Fifteenth Street to the 399-seat house on Broadway and Seventy-sixth Street. It opened at this uptown but still off-Broadway theatre on April 13, 1994, and ran until August 26, 1995.

The script that the Vienna, Woodstock, and New York productions fleshed out, Albee claims, had had its beginning sixty-three years earlier—at his first moment of conscious awareness, when he was only a few months old. In effect, he asserts, he had been writing the play all his life. A distillation of his life experience and the most openly autobiographical of his plays, *Three Tall Women* presents a ruthlessly candid but compassionate portrait of his adoptive mother, one of the tall women of the title, with whom he spent a miserable childhood until he left home at eighteen. The three tall women of act 1 are A, the mother figure at ninety-two; B, her secretary and caregiver, aged fifty-two; and C, a twenty-six-year-old lawyer, summoned by B to sort out A's papers. As the ancient matriarch struggles with her failing body and mind, she is waited upon by B, the slouching, solicitous, but sometimes sinister companion and nurse. In contrast, the cold, callow, and humorless C tries to maintain a safe professional distance and a focus on resolving A's muddled affairs. A mesmerizes both B and C with alternating flashes of humor and charm, temper and guile, regret and prejudice. Battling her failing memory with growing desperation, A lashes out, weeps, bullies, cajoles, throws calculated tantrums, but most of all enjoys salvaging bits of recollections from her long life. During one such reminiscence toward the end of act 1, as she rambles on while lying propped up in bed, A suffers a stroke and falls into a coma.

Act 2 opens with what appears to be the comatose A still in the same bed, with the same clothes on, and in full sight of the audience, as B and C enter wearing very different clothes and discussing her plight. In a *coup de théâtre* a hail and hearty A in an elegant new dress suddenly walks in and joins their conversation, as the stunned audience realizes that the figure in bed is actually a life mask of the actor. In act 1, B and C had teased A that she could "fall and shatter in . . . ten pieces. . . . Or five, or seven."[3] In act 2 A literally splits into three women, each at a different stage of her life. The three actors now switch roles: the senile and doddering dowager becomes a rational and feisty A at ninety-two; the nurse-companion becomes A at fifty-two; and the lawyer becomes A at twenty-six. In a stylistic reversal from the naturalistic dramaturgy of the preceding act, this act in effect stages the near-death out-of-body experience that the bedridden A is going through. We see and hear three As at different stages of life but, surreally, in the same space and time, talking about and with themselves, and remaining invisible to the prodigal son when he arrives to sit beside the dying figure. What the time-warped, fantasy conversations of this trinity reveal are the details of the life of a remarkable, privileged woman and her family—a life of immense wealth, success, and strength but even more of recurrent betrayal, ugliness, resentment, despair, and loneliness. Given such an existence, the ninety-two-year-old A appropriately closes the play with her existential conclusion that the moment of greatest joy in life is the end of it. Rooted firmly in the fascinating particulars of this singular life, *Three Tall Women* develops into a psychological portrait of the life cycle of all women: three of the four ages of woman (omitting childhood).

In etching this portrait *Three Tall Women* reveals Albee's most personal meditation on regret, disillusionment, and mortality, which is simultaneously a distillation of themes that reverberate throughout his oeuvre. Indeed, the play resonates not only with these Albee preoccupations but also with recurring character types, like the domineering mother, spineless father, alcoholic aunt, absent child, and live-in grandmother. This late work, moreover, furnishes mature examples of many stylistic hallmarks of his dramatic prose, such as the musically structured long monologue, set memory piece, train of thought interrupted by a qualification or clarification, idiomatic or metaphoric expression taken as literal, and direct audience address. As in many of his plays, in *Three Tall Women* Albee again pays private homage to dramatists he admires, offering subtle echoes of such works as Thornton Wilder's *Our Town* and more extensive references to numerous works by Samuel Beckett, most notably *Waiting for Godot* and *Krapp's Last Tape*. In fact, *Three Tall Women*'s trifurcation of a character into different ages recalls Becket's tripartite division of the taped persona in *Krapp's Last Tape*.[4]

The process of writing and staging the first production of this complex work, however, was hardly seamless. In fact, the performance dates already agreed upon with Vienna's English Theatre forced Albee to cast the play, and even begin rehearsals, before he had finished writing act 2. Before leaving for Vienna, which he dubbed "off-off-Broadway," Albee picked Myra Carter as A, Kathleen Butler as B, and Cynthia Bassham as C.[5] In New York (and initially in Vienna), these characters were named the Old Woman, the Middle-Aged Woman, and the Young Woman, as noted in chapter 2.[6] Without act 2, of course, the character of the Boy did not yet exist; he was written and cast later in Vienna, where he was initially called the Young Man.[7] As was often his practice, Albee had chosen actors he had worked with previously. Just prior to leaving New York, Carter, Butler, and Bassham met in Albee's Tribeca loft and read through act 1 while he listened raptly. After the reading Kathleen Butler asked the author, "How does it sound—it's the first time you've heard it?" According to her, Albee offered a telling response: "No, I've heard it before." He meant that he had heard the words in his head while writing. "The way he writes his script," she commented later, "everything—emphasis, italics, quotations—is written down as he hears it. And he wants it done so."[8] Like her, all experienced Albee actors understand that the way his words sound is unusually crucial to the proper portrayal of his characters.

On the day of his arrival at Vienna's English Theatre, Albee quipped, "I've worked here so often it has almost become a habit." He had already directed several of his own works there, most recently *Marriage Play,* as well as works by David Mamet, Sam Shepard, and Lanford Wilson.[9] Vienna's English Theatre is a critically acclaimed Austrian venue for major international plays and theatre artists. With five thousand subscribers, it offers year-round productions in English as well as in French, Italian, and German, having expanded since its establishment in 1963 to incorporate the Theatre Français de Vienne and the Teatro Italiano di Vienna. Founded by Franz Schafranek, it has featured such leading European actors as Vittorio Gassmann, Andrea Jonasson, Jean Paul Belmondo, Jean-Louis Barrault, Jeanne Moreau, Siobhan McKenna, and Judi Dench. It has, moreover, presented world premieres of plays by Albee, Tennessee Williams, and William Saroyan, as well as numerous Continental premieres of American and British plays, including, most recently, Albee's *The Goat, or, Who Is Sylvia?* and David Auburn's *Proof*. Austria's ambassador to the United States, Friedrich Hoess, had declared of Albee's directing, "For us, Mr. Albee cannot be too thought provoking. . . . The [Austrian] public loves him as one of its great idols." Albee's production of *Three Tall Women,* the *New York Times* reported from Vienna, "has been widely anticipated, even in this bicentennial summer of Mozart's death, as a major cultural event."[10] It was because of his reputation and his record at Vienna's English Theatre that artistic director Franz Schafranek had been willing to sign a contract to produce *Three Tall Women* even before its script had been completed.

Rehearsals for *Three Tall Women* began on May 14, 1991. The schedule consisted of four weeks of rehearsals, two dress and technical rehearsals on June 10 and 11 (lighting problems, however, caused the cancellation of the rehearsal scheduled for June 10), two previews on June 12 and 13, opening on June 14, and a six-week run ending July 27. On the first day of rehearsal, sitting around a table, the actors read act 1 while Albee listened intently. Typically, following the reading he praised the actors. "I can't imagine anyone but you three doing this," Bassham remembered him saying, and just as typically, after a dramatic pause, he added, "yet." He wanted to encourage them but also to keep them on their toes: "I don't want your heads to swell."[11] Again characteristically, he avoided giving too many directives on the first day. "He certainly didn't talk about his goals . . . didn't give us many overall instructions," insisted Kathleen Butler.[12] Instead of detailed directions, he provided a preview of act 2 (which was still in draft) and some background information. He told the actors that in act 2 character A of act 1 would be replaced by a mannequin in the bed and that the three would become A at different stages of her life. He revealed that it would include many direct addresses as well as a young man, whom he planned to cast the next week. Bassham was excited by the author's outline of act 2, especially since she thought the C of act 2 seemed warmer and more self-aware.

As is usual with Albee at his first rehearsals—and what is one of his signal strengths as a director—he provided crucial overall guidelines in concrete, simple, and practical terms that actors, designers, and other practitioners find most meaningful. He told Bassham that the young lawyer C "should be brisk, efficient, business-like, but shouldn't race," and that she "would be wearing a business suit" in act 1 and "something 1920s" in act 2.[13] To Myra Carter Albee explained that although A was a store model who modeled clothes and mingled with customers, "she was not a fashion victim." Anticipating the actor's predisposition toward making her character charming, he cautioned Carter that A in act 1 must not be likeable: "We've got to really hate her."[14] Albee concluded by telling the cast that overall *Three Tall Women* should be played "like a chamber piece or a string quartet as opposed to a full-blown orchestra."[15]

Albee displayed skill in communicating with fellow theatre artists a few months later as well, during his first meeting with Lawrence Sacharow, who was preparing to stage *Three Tall Women* in Woodstock. Sacharow marveled at the "very telling . . . very personal . . . enormously helpful" comment Albee made in response to his question "What is the play about for you?" The playwright told him simply "that for him the play was about a woman who you don't like a lot in act 1 and who you get to like a little bit better in act 2." As Sacharow explained, "All the themes in the play are so clear: it's about death and identity and personal transformations over many years. . . . So it's not as interesting for the playwright to restate that." Instead, for Sacharow the answer that Albee provided "illuminated the whole nature of that character, and not only the character but the environment and the context of the tensions between them . . . [and] the subtext of the play."[16]

In order to ensure that his characters are accurately portrayed, one of Albee's rehearsal strategies is to sometimes employ overstatement—to the point that he may subsequently disavow a comment or exclude it from the stage directions in the printed edition of his plays (as he did with his hyperbolic injunction to Carter, "We've got to really hate her.") Thus, although Albee always viewed *Three Tall Women* as one play of two acts, he told his Vienna actors that these were two discrete plays. He intended to steer them away from the pitfall of treating B and C in act 1 as the same or similar characters in act 2, since they have identical names and ages in the two acts. Cynthia Bassham, who played C, kept a journal in Vienna and recorded his advice, "You need to imagine these as two plays," and Kathleen Butler, who played B, confirms it: "He did tell us that; he absolutely did."[17] Albee clarified in an interview with me much later what he was really after. "I wanted B and C to remember that they were different people in acts 1 and

2; not that these were different plays, but that they were different characters."[18] Albee's guidance in Vienna helped the actors portray B and C as entirely different people—psychologically and visually—in the two acts. Albee resorted to the same strategy in Woodstock and New York. At their first meeting, Albee told Sacharow that the two acts "were two separate plays" and advised him even "not to think about the characters in the first act when doing the second act."[19] Jordan Baker, who played C in Woodstock and New York, observed that Albee kept "saying over and over again that these are two separate plays. . . . He was very, very adamant."[20] That Albee's tactic achieved the desired result is evident in Sacharow's comments about the two acts as rehearsed and staged in Woodstock and New York: "Their whole physical life was totally different." "We just kept them totally separate. We never, never tried to connect them at all."[21]

In Vienna, as well as in Woodstock and New York, Albee was unusually concerned with the physical life and look of *Three Tall Women*. At the very first rehearsal in Vienna he brought in sketches created by his costume designer, Ruth Bell, and had the actors measured. Similarly in Woodstock Albee gave his actors the set design and costume sketches at the first reading of the play at director Sacharow's home. In Vienna, Butler noted, "He was very particular about our costumes," and "he just knew exactly the colors."[22] Even though the actors had not yet received act 2, he specified the hues, fabrics, and designs of its characters' clothes: the three women would wear silk dresses reflecting identical taste but different period styles, and, Bassham observed, "he wanted lots of pastels and related colors in act 2 to join us visually." Bassham mused in her journal entry on the opening rehearsal that, given such concern for visual matters, it was only fitting that during their break "Edward was walking around the rehearsal room straightening the paintings!" Color remained a crucial concern for him during the subsequent rehearsals, too. Bassham noted midway through the Vienna rehearsal period that it had been "a long struggle to find the right colors for the second-act dresses" and that "it was very important to him that we look like we belong together."[23] Butler added that "he knew exactly what he wanted" the set and costumes to look like, and that he was "absolutely right on the nose."[24]

One reason Albee devoted such meticulous attention to the visual aspects of this and subsequent productions of *Three Tall Women* was to stress a kind of iconography of WASP wealth that was physically elegant, but spiritually and morally deforming. As a man of the theatre, he wanted audience members not only to hear the dialogue but also to see the physical environment clearly and experience it palpably, so that they would understand how the protagonist's milieu had determined her character and actions. Such an approach parallels Bertolt

Brecht's practice and explains Albee's decision in the Vienna production to illuminate the set with bright, fairly clinical, and unvarying lighting, both during the play and before and after the curtain and during intermission. As Albee later confirmed, in his sometimes oblique interview style, "I don't remember any vast adjustment going on."[25] All three actors in Vienna remarked on the lighting, which some of them found too stark. Albee employed similar lighting in Woodstock and New York, and his actors in those productions, too, commented on this aspect of the performances, as did several New York critics. Most critics merely observed that the lighting remained constant: representative is L. C. Cole's comment, "Phil Monat's lighting stays honey-colored . . . throughout."[26] In a feature essay in the *New York Times*, however, Vincent Canby sensed the strategy behind it: "When you take your seat . . . you have no choice but to examine the handsome, apparently realistic set. . . . [which] is as brightly lighted as it will be during the performance. . . . There's no way of escaping this set, which may well be the intention."[27] Through this device Albee forced the audience to share, both theatrically and viscerally, his protagonist's experience and to understand his play's prominent theme: once one chooses to enter a particular environment, that environment dictates one's behavior.

To realize the set for *Three Tall Women*—which he considered critical and which he had visualized in great detail beforehand—Albee collaborated closely with Claire Cahill, his American set designer (and stage manager); Ruth Bell, his American costume designer; and Hans Georg Jobst, his Austrian lighting designer. He also took full advantage of the limited but quite adequate technical, financial, and staff resources of Vienna's English Theatre. Albee usually likes to press his designers and the producing theatre's technical personnel to their limits in order to recreate on stage the picture he envisioned at the time of writing. It was no different in Vienna: he was "very, very demanding and fussy. *Very!*" noted Butler. The Vienna staff rose to the challenge posed by Albee's punctiliousness about the color, shading, and texture of the costumes, sets, props, special effects, and lighting. For A's death mask in act 2 they sought assistance from the technical staff at the Vienna State Opera. Astonished at the extraordinary efforts of the design and technical personnel, Butler exclaimed, "People were standing on their heads to get things right."[28]

The beautifully decorated but simple bedroom set that finally emerged from these labors largely conveyed the sense of wealth and good taste that Albee sought. With a marked French flavor and dominant blue hues, it consisted of an upstage center bed, two light armchairs covered in silk, a footstool, a window with silk swags, and two doors with archways. Although the set included most elements specified in his script, a few items were simplified, replaced, or eliminated: for instance, the bench was replaced by a footstool, and the "pastel-carpeted floor" and "nineteenth-century French paintings" were eliminated, although wooden moldings like the one over the bed implied framed art on the walls. While it exuded the desired sense of money and taste, it also felt a bit plain and cold—especially to American actors, who thought it lacked the necessary opulence, sumptuous detail, and warm lighting. Butler wondered if the set was "more as the Viennese would do it," and Bassham thought the room "was not warm at all."[29] They also felt the "lights were very bright and very hot" and in need of gels and some variation. But, always practical, Albee understood that his design and technical collaborators had made extraordinary efforts, and also that all performers need encouragement as a production opens: so he proclaimed satisfaction with both the set and the lighting, even though he probably wished for more realistic detail. Much later in New York he conceded, "We didn't have as much opportunity for complex lighting in Vienna"; nonetheless, he insisted, "it was enough; it was all right."[30] The set and lighting choices were partly a result of the constraints imposed by a very small proscenium stage, limited lighting equipment, and a relatively modest budget. But they were also partly due to Albee's recognition and acceptance of a different aesthetic: theatre practitioners and audiences at Vienna's English Theatre seemed to prefer decor with less detailed realism, cleaner lines, and greater overall simplicity. Albee may also have intended the simple stage decor as a stylistic counterpoint to that auditorium's much-admired lavish Austrian Neo-Baroque painted ceiling and gilded stucco.

In contrast to the simple decor in Vienna, the first American productions were decidedly more sumptuous, with remarkably realistic detail. As noted earlier, these productions—at the River Arts Repertory, the Vineyard Theatre, and the Promenade Theatre—were fundamentally the same, having been transferred, refined and restaged at each successive venue with the original cast, director, and set designer. Jordan Baker, who played C in all three productions, asserted that their set basically "stayed the same," although "we had a little bit more money on each production, so it would get dressed a little bit nicer."[31] In order to avoid unnecessary duplication, I describe here the decor and staging of the final production at the Promenade Theatre. James Noone, the set designer, recreated a wealthy socialite's luxurious bedroom, with walls covered with lavish blue watered-silk wallpaper and nineteenth-century French paintings in gilded frames, a glimmering two-toned parquet floor and a handsome carpet, two windows with brocade drapes, and two imposing archways. Dominating upstage center was a large bed made with luxurious sheets, a striking bedspread, and pillows with fringe and braid. Louis Quatorze furniture filled the room: side tables with brass lamps near the bed, a padded bench covered in lush striped fabric at the foot of the bed, upholstered chairs below each window, an armchair and table with a silver tea service, a desk and chair, and tables near each archway. The ample size of the Promenade Theatre's thrust stage—twice as large as the one in Vienna—suggested a grand living space furnished with impeccable taste. Albee enthusiastically approved this sumptuous set because he felt strongly that *Three Tall Women,* despite its stylized tripartite splitting of a character in the second act, should have a detailed, realistic set wherever economically feasible. With a substantial budget for a major off-Broadway production, Albee demanded and got an elaborate and intricately detailed set.

Albee argued, however, that the obvious differences between the Vienna and New York sets were nonetheless differences of degree and not of essence; the two sets, he insisted, were "basically" similar. Soon after the play opened at the Promenade he declared in an *American Theatre* interview that the Vienna production was "really not very different from what's on the stage now."[32] A few years later, he reiterated in another interview that the production in New York "was not all that different" from the one in Vienna.[33] His claim has some merit because, even with larger off-Broadway budgets in New York, he had instinctively shunned the minutiae—especially the clutter and frequent congestion—of a classic naturalistic staging. He initially resisted the inclusion of certain pieces of furniture, such as the desk for the young lawyer that both actor Baker and director Sacharow strongly desired. Communicating through the director, as always, he quizzed them, "If I didn't have a table in Vienna, why do you need one?"[34] He relented on the desk but refused to allow the legal papers, books, and adding machine that Baker also longed for. "My dream production," Baker later fantasized wistfully, "will have *lots and lots* of papers." Similarly, she said, Albee remained firm against Myra Carter's entreaties for additional personal effects such as glasses, medicines, and cream and sugar bowls; his denial of a box of Kleenex to Carter "drove her nuts . . . because she has to weep every four lines!"[35]

As is clear from these examples—and as is typical of Albee—even though he was not directing these productions, he exercised his rights as a supervising author actively and extensively. He not only ruled on important elements of the setting, props, lighting, and costumes, but even controlled matters pertaining to style, color, fabric, and texture. When asked about this wide-ranging influence, he replied quite matter-of-factly, "I have that in my contract."[36] Sacharow confirmed Albee's intimate participation: "Edward had approval of all the sets and costumes and designs. So he was very instrumental in how the production looks visually." As early as the design stage, Albee offered the set and costume designers and the director vivid and detailed descriptions of the matriarch's house and her taste in clothes and furnishings. After the designs came in, he suggested minor modifications or refinements, and then "pretty much had the final decision—on the fabrics, materials, all that kind of thing." Sacharow concluded, "We basically got whatever he wanted."[37] And earlier, during casting, Albee had successfully pressed for Myra Carter, his lead from Vienna, to reprise her role, overcoming what Carter and Jordan Baker saw as Sacharow's reluctance.[38] Sacharow later insisted that he had only resisted casting her "automatically" on the basis of her Vienna experience; once she auditioned, he asserted, "She was the best . . . so I cast her."[39] Albee had also managed to have another actor, Kathleen Butler, hired as an understudy for B, the part she had originated in Vienna.

Albee's strategy in getting his Vienna actors included in the New York cast is clear from remarks he made during the run of the play to explain his collaboration with Sacharow. He asserted, "Larry Sacharow and I work *very* closely together"; in addition, "we had Myra Carter, whose performance remained consistent from . . . Vienna till now," and, consequently, "Larry had double guidance as to the nature of the play, the rhythms, the moods, everything."[40] Kathleen Butler corroborated Albee's assessment of Carter's consistency. "She grounded this in Vienna. . . . She has enhanced it, but she is still true to exactly what . . . Edward wanted her to do."[41] Sacharow was quite amenable to such "double guidance" from the author-director and the leading lady because their advice arose from their practical experience of the play's original production. Thus Albee's directorial work in Vienna clearly exerted fundamental influence on this major work's first New York performance.

The Vienna rehearsals are therefore doubly important. They offer insights into Albee's authoritative readings of his characters and situations, into the thinking behind his textual revisions, and into the nature of his directorial craft and aesthetic. One of his recurring concerns in Vienna was to prevent sentimentality from creeping into Myra Carter's interpretation of A. Bigoted, paranoid, and monstrous, A is also a wily survivor, a victim of circumstance, and suffering from the ravages of physical and mental disintegration. Carter, who describes herself as a radical feminist, was "horrified by this sexist, racist, Republican old pig." Yet Carter, like most actors and especially those playing unsympathetic or villainous parts, tried to build her character by seeing the world through A's eyes. Identifying with her character, she regularly stressed A's sympathetic aspects in order to make her likeable, and, she claimed, "three-dimensional." Albee argued that A as written was already multifaceted and had some sympathetic traits, but that Carter's emphasis rendered A too sympathetic and endearing, especially given the actor's exceedingly charming stage presence. As a result, one of the most frequent admonitions during the Vienna rehearsals was "Don't sentimentalize her!" Carter complained that Albee "badgers me all the time not to sentimentalize her," and once she even threatened, "If you say it again, I'll leave!"[42] Out of his rehearsal tug of war over the correct balance between sympathy and condemnation, Albee eventually elicited a fascinating performance from Carter in which A appeared by turns—and sometimes almost simultaneously—as dauntless and sniveling, charming and repellent, admirable and detestable.

Albee's directorial policy with seasoned actors like Myra Carter and Kathleen Butler, who brought decades of experience and preferred to do their own preparation, is to minimize elucidatory comments, subtextual information, and specific instructions and concentrate instead on any problematic interpretations or unsuitable individual propensities. In contrast, with less experienced actors—like the young Cynthia Bassham, who played C—his procedure is to provide considerably more character-specific guidance. After their first run-through he explained to Bassham that C as the young attorney is "not prissy" and her comments should never be "construed as squeamish." On different occasions he suggested that C should be "aloof," "colder," "brisker," "bitchier," and "very tense, emitting electric pulses." He advised her to convey "more and more iciness" and at a few places to be "really as nasty as [she] can get." Overall, "it was really important for him that he not like her"; as Bassham confirmed from her diary notes, "He stressed that many times!"[43] No doubt because of Albee's advice, Lawrence Sacharow demanded a similar interpretation from Jordan Baker, his C in Woodstock and New York, whom he instructed, "Take charge and don't put up with any of their stuff." In a similar vein, Albee told Baker at their first reading in Woodstock that C is a tough young professional, "a Harvard graduate but one who didn't come from a privileged background and had made it that far on her own." The performance that Baker developed in the rehearsals, however, Albee found too severe and even harsh; so after a run-through he gave her a note through Sacharow that seemed the opposite of what he had advised Bassham. He questioned the strident portrayal, asking, "Why is she so nasty?" and suggested, "She's just a nervous little attorney." That note prompted Baker to adjust her performance to convey, as she put it, "a little bit of this nervous attorney and a little bit of this bitch."[44] Albee recognizes that even when seeking the same result a director must vary his instructions according to individual performers' needs, or, as he later mused, "You tell different actors different things."[45]

If Albee notices an actor has a persistent tendency to overstress an emotional quality or behavior, he usually works doggedly to first completely eliminate it. Once the actor is freed from that particular propensity, he allows him the freedom to reintroduce it, judiciously and selectively, in one or two places. Thus in Vienna Albee's repeated demands for a frosty performance arose in part from Bassham's tendency to make C vulnerable. Albee was right in his assessment: Bassham later granted that she had indeed sought to soften her character, because she feared that otherwise the audience would be "put off by her too much."[46] The director kept insisting, "I still see moments of vulnerability that I don't need"; "Get rid of all the vulnerability!" When Bassham asked why C continues to assist the old woman, if she is so unfeeling, Albee explained that she is there simply "to do her job." Finally Bassham found a justification for suppressing her vulnerability: she told herself that C is simply taking on the "ice bitch" persona as a "cover." Her new performance, free of hints of a softer side, was then applauded by Albee as her most interesting and fascinating yet. Nonetheless, he waited a few more days to ensure that her old tendency did not resurface; then he invited her to choose one or two key moments to give a glimpse of a gentler self, within the parameters he had now fixed. This bolstered the actor's confidence and made her feel validated while simultaneously allowing the director to precisely calibrate her performance. Two days before the dress rehearsal he showed further willingness to collaborate with her. He declared that Bassham's earlier problems with playing an icy character might in fact have been caused by his own text. He faulted C's line in the rehearsal manuscript "Why am I being nice?" and rewrote it as "Why can't I be nice?" to suggest that at least on occasion C wants to be pleasant. Generously, he also suggested that on the new line she "could really take that moment and show vulnerability." Bassham confided in her journal that the revision "really did help" because she felt "it clued the audience in on my cover."

Reversing her first-act portrayal of a chilly professional, Bassham was to exude youthful charm and warmth as the twenty-six-year-old A in the second act. Albee described her as "earnest" and "fresh" in everything she does, someone who "looks forward" to every new experience. He directed Bassham to speak almost exclusively to the audience and from time to time to step right up to the lip of the stage to address them. Yet he clarified, "It's not a formal address" and advised her to be "almost chummy with the audience." In the play's final scene he thought Bassham was too emotional, recommended "the coda is to be thrown away," and steered her away from playing a "scared adult" to more of a "little girl lost." He even shared parts of his family's history—something he is generally loath to do—to help Bassham understand why the maids did not complain when A's penguin-shaped husband chased them into the cellar: they dared not, he explained, "because they were illegal immigrants from Ireland."

By and large, however, Albee downplayed the autobiographical aspects of the play, so that the actors would not feel inhibited in his presence, nor stray too far from the fictional core delimited by his text. When questions turned to details of his life, he usually dismissed them by suggesting that *all* plays, after all, are autobiographical. The actors, though, saw this as a dodge and sometimes attributed it to touchiness on his part, "as if somehow," recalled Bassham, his work's autobiographical origin might be "taking away from his creative genius."[47] Discussing this aspect of the Vienna rehearsals, he later insisted, "It is a portrait of my adoptive mother. There's no question about that, and I never denied it."[48] Yet he felt compelled to make a fine distinction: the play, he insisted, was based on his "biography, not autobiography." By the time of the Woodstock and New York rehearsals the autobiographical origins of the material had become well known and sometimes, as Albee had feared, led the cast temporarily off course during director Sacharow's rehearsals. In Albee's absence some actors explored the implications of biographical details they gleaned from hearsay, such as apocryphal stories that Albee sat in his dying mother's bedroom and "took notes," and on occasion even "recorded [her] on a tape recorder."[49] When asked about this anecdote, he fumed, "Goodness, the things people remember. You know, I didn't even know I was going to write that play until after my adoptive mother died. . . . So, obviously, while she was alive I wouldn't take notes."[50] Albee could not control or correct such conversations, however, because generally when someone else is directing his play he absents himself from daily rehearsals and only attends run-throughs.

Thus Albee's comment to Bassham about his family's illegal immigrant maids during his own rehearsals in Vienna was atypical. What was typical, however, was the great amount of directorial guidance he offered the relatively inexperienced actor: the preceding paragraphs' small sampling merely hints at the extent of this advice. Nonetheless, Bassham, like many young performers under Albee's direction, wanted more guidance. Typically, Albee first provides broad but clear-cut guidelines to both young and veteran actors, and then allows them considerable autonomy to build their performance during the early rehearsals, intervening only to correct serious deviations or idiosyncrasies. In subsequent sessions he helps to further develop, clarify, and fine-tune those performances. Most experienced actors praise this practice, welcoming the freedom to invent but appreciating the author-director's helping them steer close to his characters and vision. In contrast, the relative autonomy it allows actors leaves many with more limited experience feeling insecure and wanting more detailed, individual directorial guidance. Despite receiving substantial attention, Bassham, the youngest of the three performers in Vienna, wanted more, especially since she was creating two quite different characters in the two acts and since she was wrestling with a new script and originating a character in a world premiere production. Particularly in developing the young attorney role, she confessed, "I was floundering a bit just because I didn't have a sense of this character yet." Eventually she discovered how to "love [her] character in act 1," which she regarded as critical for playing a relatively unsympathetic part, but she regretted that she had to achieve that without "a lot of prompts along the way." Most critical to her was the need for advice on inner motivation for the emotions and actions called for by the director: she found it "really difficult" to "justify them" on her own. Referring to his demand for "iciness," for example, she noted in her journal, "*Where* the ice comes from is *my* problem." She chose not to approach the director about her desire, however, because she granted that "all the acting work [needed] to justify it is mine." She was also objective enough to acknowledge that when she played a long-established character like Honey in *Who's Afraid of Virginia Woolf?* she had in fact appreciated the creative autonomy Albee had provided: "I was happy for the freedom. I was happy for the form and structure and then him leaving me alone. I really enjoyed that."[51]

Kathleen Butler, Bassham's fellow actor in Vienna and a seasoned Albee performer, echoed this praise in describing her own experience: "He does give tremendous latitude to actors he trusts. . . . He let us pretty much find things . . . which is great." Yet, Butler noted, he never hesitates to reject, modify, or calibrate readings that actors bring to rehearsal: if he saw "something popping up or a line or even an emphasis that wasn't ringing the way he wanted to, he would certainly bring it to our attention." Still, she singled out Albee's allowing his actors to collaborate freely as his great strength as a director. She asserted, "He's very open to creative contributions," though she added the proviso "if he trusts you," and also noted that "he usually works with actors he trusts." Early in the rehearsals Butler had turned to him for guidance on how A feels in act 2, when she talks about her trip to the doctor with her badly broken arm. Instead of offering a specific reading, subtext, or background detail, he suggested a simple external action: "She's just shaking her head about that." That was just the right advice, exactly the hint that Butler needed. On her own, she then explored whether that head shake was motivated by tiredness, desperation, disgust, or something else, until she found the right emotion "to bring it alive." As she prepared to understudy the part again in New York, she recalled, "That was a very good direction. . . . That gave me the clue to how to do it. . . . It stuck with me." If an actor wants to privately discuss some subtext he has come up with, Albee willingly offers advice to correct or modify it. If, as it sometimes happens, an actor cannot function without the director providing subtextual justification for a scene, Albee improvises background incidents and information, often in colorful detail. Overall, though, as Butler asserted about her Vienna experience, "As a good director he let us find most of it." As with subtext, so with movement: he encourages collaboration and asks the actors to come up with movement that feels organic to them. "He doesn't direct your movement," Butler confirmed; "he lets you find your own physical language." In general, Albee believes that actors should do most of such work on motivation, movement, and body language on their own rather than in rehearsals, and so, as Butler concluded, "Edward tends more to leave actors alone."[52]

Myra Carter, the most experienced actor in the Vienna cast, also praised Albee as a director for allowing actors the requisite creative space to develop their performance.[53] Her commendation was especially noteworthy because it came in spite of her recurrent disagreements with the director. She declared, "If anybody asks me what Albee gave me as a director, I would say . . . that he did somewhat trust me and let me work." Although, in inimitable Carter fashion, she added, "I don't know that he valued it too much." She explained that he allowed her the freedom to concentrate on her own acting process. "He left me alone, largely speaking, to try and make what I could of it. . . . Not 'left alone' in the sense of not helped." Expressing her approbation for Albee's fostering an environment conducive to creative collaboration, she cited another director's philosophy: "I agree with Peter Brook that directing means setting the right atmosphere for the actors. That's a good director."

Unlike Bassham, who wanted more subtext, Carter wanted none at all: she preferred instead to preserve sufficient "space between the text and the director." Resisting any motivation suggested by the director, she asserted, "Subtext has to be your own." However, she appreciated factual background and biographical information that the author-director offered. Moreover, whereas many actors cross out all stage directions in their scripts, Carter valued Albee's textual stage directions: "I hang on to those line readings . . . his comments, his adverbs. . . . I pay scrupulous attention to those because it's all heard" in performance. As part of her preparation, of course, she internalized the readings indicated by the stage directions and made them her own, but she declared, "If you don't produce the sound of him, you don't have Albee." That she succeeded in her aim was evident in numerous reviews. The *New Yorker,* for instance, observed, "Carter hits every vowel and consonant of Albee's words, filling each with lucid thought and wonderful music."[54] In the same vein, the *Nation* wrote that Carter's "phrasing of Albee's half-naturalistic, wholly calculated incipient-Alzeimer's talk is impeccable; her voice dwindles to an Edith Evans warble, ascends to a helium keeling, erupts abruptly into lacerating sobs as required."[55] Carter even recalled how over the years she had steadfastly resisted other directors of Albee plays who had "tempted and ordered and threatened and cajoled [her] to change his line readings."

Such punctiliousness about his stage directions might have afforded Albee some comfort during his rehearsals, but overall Carter's temperament made her the most difficult actor he had worked with in decades, if not his entire career. More often than not she argued about directions, routinely labeled them impossible to execute, failed to learn lines, and complained about every detail, and yet she gradually carried out his directions—usually with great skill and even brilliance. Albee retained immense faith in her ability to finally deliver a superb portrayal of his protagonist, which was why he had cast her in the first place and why he persevered through their endless struggles. His trust was borne out by her extraordinary performance in Vienna, which, in turn, made him insist on her reprising the role in Woodstock and New York, where she won superlative reviews. In the Vienna rehearsals, however, problems with Carter sometimes reached such an impasse that he cut rehearsals short. At other times his focus on her frustrated Bassham and Butler and reduced the guidance he could give them. They did not yet know Carter, and thus did not quite share the director's trust in her. Bassham found this aspect of the rehearsals "excessively difficult . . . just excruciating," and Butler, with her usual tact, described it as "a very difficult period [where] Cynthia and myself didn't get as much work as we would have chosen to."[56] On at least one occasion they jointly took their concern to Albee, who assured them he was aware of their anxiety; he presumably spoke to Carter about her negative impact, for she subsequently moderated her argumentativeness, albeit briefly.

Albee later acknowledged that Carter "was a problem. Yes, of course—not learning her lines and being argumentative about everything." Yet he insisted, "But she's such a good actress that it was worth it." He also granted that at times he ended rehearsals early: "I would have to, if I couldn't work, of course. And since she was on stage the entire time it was impossible to work without her." Nevertheless, he argued that Bassham and Butler "got enough attention to play the roles properly."[57] Despite some reservations, Butler asserted that she understood why Albee had to devote so much attention to Carter. She even commended Albee's handling of Carter: "He was wonderfully skillful personally. . . . [Carter] wasn't well, and it was very difficult for her. . . . He showed great patience and restraint."[58] Although iron-willed and used to having his way, Albee proved practical, flexible, and self-disciplined over a sustained period in coping with an extremely hard, tedious, and wearying situation. He also demonstrated his astuteness in judging correctly that an actor with a long but hitherto unremarkable regional theatre career had the potential—in that particular role—to offer a great performance. John Lahr's comment about the "unknown" actor's brilliant performance was quite typical of the New York reviews: "Ms. Carter, who is sixty-four and is new to me, gives one of the finest performances I've ever seen on the New York stage."[59]

As he had done with his actors in Vienna, Albee allowed his director and designers in Woodstock and New York considerable creative autonomy within the broad guidelines he initially laid down. Although, as noted earlier, Albee as the playwright retained ultimate approval and exercised control over key elements of the staging, including the set, costumes, props, and lighting, final decisions were reached through a process of artistic give and take, not through authorial diktats. The particular phrasing employed by his director, Lawrence Sacharow, to sum up their teamwork encapsulates the nature of a partnership where one member was the senior partner: "It was a real collaboration between Edward, the set designer, and myself, with Edward having a lot of input."[60] Albee first sketched out the crucial contours of the performance he envisioned, but then invited his director and designers to realize its details according to their respective sensibilities. What was brought to him, he often accepted fully or with modifications; sometimes he suggested important changes; and only rarely did he reject anything completely. In all cases, he typically justified his decision on the basis of the script or another aesthetic or staging imperative. In keeping with this practice, Albee held a number of meetings with Sacharow prior to rehearsals, where he presented an overview of his characters and their environment, answered questions, and offered his reaction to the director's ideas about specific details of interpretation and staging. He also confirmed that he would be available to the cast at the initial reading, thereafter attend only run-throughs, and communicate with the actors only through the director. In addition, he readily agreed that he and the director should present a "united front in rehearsals." Sacharow confirmed that, as he commenced his directorial preparation, Albee kept him artistically unfettered. "He didn't give me a lot of information prior to rehearsal, which I felt was very good." Even when the rehearsals got underway, as far as possible Albee favored general comments and advice over detailed instructions on staging. Sacharow appreciated this approach: "I loved it that he never told me what to do and how to do it; instead he always opened up possibilities, and that was very enriching."

After run-throughs, Albee reviewed the director's work and provided "extensive notes privately about what he liked and what he didn't like, and what he felt was successful and what wasn't successful." For instance, in one note Albee remarked that B was "hovering around the back of [A's] chair too much. This woman is a battleaxe; she can take care of herself." He then offered "a general outline of the characters and how they live in that house" and suggested that as a live-in companion B "should be relaxed. She can lie on the bed." Sacharow characterized such straightforward and concrete notes about characters and situations as "very, very helpful," "very clear comments" that "gave me ideas . . . freed my imagination to then create [appropriate] physical actions" for the actors. Thus, following Albee's comment about B, Sacharow explained, "I basically restaged a lot of the middle character's stuff in act 1 and made it much less formal, which helped a lot."

At other times, Albee's incisive questions about directorial choices stimulated more effective staging. In early rehearsals of act 1 Sacharow found that Baker and Seldes, as on-the-job professionals, accomplished their respective tasks with excessive businesslike briskness and reacted to every little comment or demand from their employer. The director, however, preferred a "settled-in quality" that suggested a sense of routine work without haste or emotion. He therefore directed them to move slowly, with precise gestures and movements, and to imagine themselves as figures settling into a succession of changing snapshots. Like many directors, Albee, too, creates stage movement and pictures to visually tell a story or convey a theme, but he was unhappy with Sacharow's scenes when he saw them during a run-through. Like another seasoned author-director, Bernard Shaw, who rigorously "eschewed beautiful compositions when they called attention to themselves as pictorial effects,"[61] Albee judged these scenes self-conscious and posed. He quizzed Sacharow: "What's going on? What are you trying to do there?" After pondering the rationale Sacharow offered, Albee responded, "The problem is I *see* the pictures." Sacharow thought that "was a great comment—just a wonderful note for a director." In response, Sacharow introduced distinct "transitions in and out of the snapshots" to suggest continuous activity and thus make the images less obvious. Albee's note led him to transform those static photographs into dynamic moving pictures. "He gave me his perception," Sacharow observed, "and then I was able to solve the problem."

In assessing his work with Albee during the Woodstock and New York productions, Sacharow offered high praise for the comments Albee offered after run-throughs, both for the kinds of issues he raised and the way he framed and communicated them. Summing up Albee's overall contribution and method, Sacharow declared, "His comments were astute and telling—without his telling me what to do or how to do it." Albee always raised matters of staging appropriateness and effectiveness but never matters of authorial intent or interpretation. Sacharow understood perfectly that although the play may raise many philosophical issues, "you can't act them." So he appreciated that the author's comments concentrated on "what you can act[, namely] what's happening in the dynamics between the people." In this area he found Albee's "perceptions and his insights . . . enormously useful" because they helped him translate the script into a stage performance. Even though Albee had directed the Vienna production only a few months before, he told Sacharow what end results he desired but never told him how to achieve them. Sacharow compared Albee favorably with Derek Wolcott and Richard Nelson, two other playwrights he had recently worked with, and praised him for providing "a lot of time and space" and for being "a real collaborator." Having his ongoing counsel during the rehearsal period, he thought, was "like having a dramaturg." Overall, he declared, "I loved his notes, and I loved it when he would come and watch run-throughs." Sacharow concluded by asserting that Albee is "a real artist [who] knows how to talk about art . . . in terms of unlocking creativity rather than dictating how it should be done."

One key to Albee and Sacharow's successful collaboration was the relative similarity of their theatrical aesthetics. Both men shared a fundamental preference for a simplified and spare staging that kept set pieces, properties, and effects to the essentials required by a script. Although the *Three Tall Women* set in New York, as noted earlier, fully conveyed the opulence dictated by the play's milieu, it was achieved with relatively few set pieces, properties, and lighting effects—much fewer, for example, than what some of the actors explicitly, and in a few cases frequently, requested. In the face of such demands during his rehearsals, Sacharow once even announced that ideally he "didn't want any props." With Albee, however, he had no such problem. Recalling his discussions with Albee about props and other objects on stage, he asserted, "We never had a disagreement about that, because I [too] hate cluttered stages," and "I never use objects . . . to support the text." Almost echoing Albee's own directorial aesthetic, he summed up his approach with, "Everything I direct is spare and clean." In addition, Sacharow brought great respect for the text, as does Albee when he directs other authors' works. Furthermore, Sacharow apparently also shared with Albee a taste for symmetrical stage configuration and actor placement, which can be seen in many Albee-directed productions. Thus Sacharow and Albee's respective stagings in Vienna and New York shared many examples of visual symmetry. For instance, both opened with three actors sitting roughly equidistant from each other and looking out, and both closed with three actors standing equidistant, hand in hand, and looking out. Such a shared artistic taste for simplicity, minimal effects, and visual formality was a key to the successful collaboration between author and director.

In view of this shared aesthetic, Albee did not have to contend with one problem he periodically encountered in his collaboration with his long-term former director, Alan Schneider. In contrast to Sacharow, Schneider preferred, especially when directing contemporary realistic plays, to populate his stage with many set pieces and properties, causing Albee to object and sometimes, as noted in an earlier chapter, even prompting him to compose new dialogue that would clearly preclude such objects. Schneider's directorial habits stemmed in part from his early training and his continuing, if much modified, commitment to the principles and customary methods of the Actors Studio. When Schneider staged *The Lady From Dubuque* on Broadway, he and Albee frequently disagreed about the set and props. Pushing for a more naturalistic staging, Schneider regularly introduced stools, cushions, pillows, books, and similar everyday items to suggest a conventional suburban living room and to provide his actors objects to incorporate into their action and movement. Albee, on the other hand, resisted the new objects and fought to retain the sleek and spare Bauhaus look of the living room set that Rouben Ter-Arutunian had designed and furnished in consultation with him. When pressed to respond to Schneider's argument that the set Albee preferred was too abstract and stylized to adequately create the reality of everyday life, the playwright retorted, "I don't see how he can say that and at the same time admire Brecht's staging concepts as much as he does. . . . If he was doing *Galileo,* would he insist on doing it in a cluttered living room? Perhaps he would. It would do violence to Brecht's style."[62] Albee was plainly arguing then—and he would still do so today—that many of his plays, like most works by Brecht, Pinter, or Beckett, suffer when staged with the excessive physical clutter of naturalism. Albee's practice and comments echo those of Peter Hall, a preeminent Pinter director as well as director of several Albee works, from whom Albee asserts he has learned the most. Hall is blunt on the subject: "You can't litter a . . . Pinter performance with any kind of naturalism."[63]

While Ter-Arutunian's set for *The Lady From Dubuque* projected the taste of the room's occupants, it also reflected Albee's personal taste in art, architecture, and interior design: the set shared such an uncanny resemblance to the high modernist style of the playwright's own spacious, museum-like Tribeca loft that he bought (at a good discount) the production's black leather sofas for use in his living room. Following the opening of *The Lady From Dubuque,* Albee conceded that the bulk of his rehearsal arguments with Schneider had been "about why there were so many props on the stage." He also confirmed, "Alan and I always have that argument. Constantly." Furthermore, Albee contended that Schneider's choices of decor ran counter to the taste and social environment of his characters. "Alan is happiest if all the plays that he directs are in his own living room, which tends to be very cluttered and folksy. And that's not what I was after." Clearly, since Albee acquired some of the production furniture for his own home, he was happy to have at least some of his plays, like *The Lady From Dubuque,* staged "in his own living room."[64] Thus, while the primary cause for the rift that developed over the years in the distinguished Albee-Schneider collaboration may have been a disagreement about the degree of naturalistic stage detail appropriate for Albee plays, a secondary cause may be glimpsed in differences of their taste and even social and economic class. The characters, settings, and language of many, if not the majority, of Albee plays mirror a social and cultural milieu more or less like the author's own wealthy, upper-middle-class background. He has confessed that audiences sometimes become "impatient with [his] wealthy, self-indulgent people who seem to be most interested in the precision of their language," and that "the problem that many of my plays have" is that they are "about an almost extinct people."[65] In a lighter vein, he has claimed, "I know that my characters would never wear 100 percent polyester. . . . Maybe 70 percent cotton and 30 percent polyester, but never 100 percent."[66] Alan Schneider, as Albee himself once very reluctantly acknowledged in a personal interview, came from a "different background" and thus occasionally "had a problem . . . with the wit and sophistication of the characters."[67] As a result, Albee sometimes found Schneider less than fully equipped to handle his characters' linguistic and intellectual style and social and cultural nuances, or the physical particulars of their milieu. By the early seventies, such differences in staging aesthetic and personal taste made Albee turn to another director, John Gielgud, to direct the first performance of *All Over,* and by 1975 he had decided to direct most of his plays himself, beginning with the Broadway premiere of *Seascape.* In 1994, when he worked with Lawrence Sacharow on *Three Tall Women,* he found the director's approach in some respects closer to his own than Alan Schneider's had been in the sixties.

Yet Sacharow had long admired Schneider, with whom he had first studied directing professionally and whose career he had hoped to emulate. Moreover, like Schneider at an earlier period, Sacharow had spent considerable time at the Actors Studio learning and employing its naturalistic, properties-heavy staging methods. During the decade preceding his *Three Tall Women* production, however, Sacharow had moved away from the naturalistic acting and staging style of the Actors Studio and embraced a simple and spare style closer to Albee's own aesthetic. Sacharow's gradual but clear transition grew out of his study and collaboration with Jerzy Grotowski and his work on Stanislavsky's post-1933 phase, which had switched focus from the actor's psychology to his physical action and movement. Sacharow explained that he came to recognize, through his own work, the accuracy of Stanislavsky's later theories, in which the Russian director "chucked all of his psychological work—sense memory, emotional recall, and all that—and said physical action is really the most important thing for the actor to do."[68]

In his own new directorial phase, Sacharow liked to first give his actors a traditional note on intention, but then to complement it with a note for a physical action or movement. He believed that the actor's physical life in performance truly completes his psychological intention. "It's really through physical actions," he insisted, "that you find the meaning of the situation and the scene." "My whole approach is a physical approach—orchestrating energies to support the text." Sacharow's new emphasis on communicating through the actors' patterned and expressive physical movements, however, also meant in effect a tendency toward stylization—a moving away from relying exclusively on realistic, psychologically propelled everyday behavior. But for Albee—as for mainstream professional theatre—scripts that present human beings in sociologically, psychologically, and linguistically credible dimensions demand commensurately believable stage embodiment, especially since a majority of contemporary plays are dialogue-driven works that, more often than not, focus on psychological undercurrents beneath everyday utterances and actions. Not surprisingly, one of the few reservations that Vincent Canby of the *New York Times* had about Sacharow's production of *Three Tall Women* concerned its perceived lack of behavioral credibility. "At the beginning of the play he arbitrarily moves the characters around the stage. . . . Shifts in tempo seem equally artificial."[69] Also predictably, this element of the staging led to the only serious problem that the Albee-Sacharow collaboration encountered: a disagreement about naturalistic versus stylized movement, especially in the second act. (As was implicit in the earlier description of the decor and effects for this production, Sacharow did not desire any parallel stylization of the physical environment.)

During his rehearsals for *Three Tall Women*, Sacharow experimented with a series of patterned movements—primarily circles, diagonals, and triangles—to suggest the emotional and psychological dynamics of the characters. He thought that each character in act 1 repeatedly probed the others' weaknesses and remained ready to attack or defend. To convey this, he "wanted the actors' bodies to sculpt the space and create rhythmic patterns that defined the action."[70] Accordingly, he blocked the act as a succession of stylized circular movements: each actor moved in a variety of circular trajectories, both watching and being watched by the other two, a choreography that suggested animals circling and watching, characters as predators and quarry. In act 2, since A, B, and C are three aspects of the same person, he connected them by moving them along the diagonal lines of a shifting triangle. He wanted to suggest, visually and kinetically, a linear attachment among them at all times, "so that there's always an energy line that connects them in the space." Moreover, each character's movement caused a compensating motion in the other two, at the triangle's other points, suggesting a rippling effect along each edge, so much so that Sacharow hoped "you could be looking at one and listening to another." These movements were intended to generate energies, evoke connections, and hint at interior dynamics—but only at a subconscious level in both the actors and the audience. They were not intended to create conventional stage pictures or representational physical activity, which he also created in addition to these core kinetic patterns. Since he wished to stimulate responses only subliminally, he kept to himself his reasons for orchestrating these movements. Sacharow declared during a personal interview seven months after the play opened at the Promenade, "I never articulated what I was trying to do to anybody . . . I never said it to the actors or to Edward. No, I never spoke to anybody about it because it's not anything that anybody is conscious of. This is the first time I'm actually ever saying it to anybody."

Since Albee did not know the reasoning behind such non-naturalistic choreography and since he prefers to keep movement to a minimum, he "cringed" when he first saw this staging during a run-through. Thereafter he regularly objected to it: "I would come in and see something new had been added, and I would complain about it."[71] Sacharow confirmed that Albee had pressed him to reduce the amount of stylized movement, but, probably because of the author's tact in dealing with fellow artists, Sacharow did not feel that his interventions were persistent or dogmatic. According to Sacharow, "Occasionally he would say that they were moving too much. I would just tone it down and keep the movement but not as exaggerated." In fact, he praised Albee for his understanding. "He never said don't do any movement. He always felt if the movement gets over, goes overboard, it's a problem." Overall, Sacharow thought that Albee "did sort of pull it in . . . [but] it still communicated what I felt was important about the play but in a more subtle way."

The outcome of this disagreement between the author and the director—by their own account, their only one—testifies to Albee's skill in communicating with other artists and his willingness to meaningfully collaborate by allowing creative freedom and by acquiescing, despite his veto power, to elements he may largely disapprove of. This aspect of his work, however, often remains hidden if one relies exclusively on his public pronouncements, which often tend to rhetorical overstatement. Thus he declared in *American Theatre* that he used to "cut off" Sacharow "when I thought he was veering too much towards originality."[72] Similarly, discussing their differences over stylized movement, he proclaimed in an interview, "We had some arguments about that, but I won my point," and "by the time we opened in New York, at the Promenade, anyway, I think we had gotten most of that nonsense out."[73]

During rehearsals there was less disagreement about the movement in act 1: Sacharow understood Albee's rationale for naturalistic movement in an act that depicts a relatively straightforward, everyday situation. But he failed to see the need for it in act 2. That act operates on a highly stylized premise that smashes the restrictions of naturalistic space and time: A lies unconscious in bed but the internal monologue she is experiencing becomes flesh as her old, middle-aged, and young selves enter the bedroom, watch her, move to her bed, discuss her condition, and assess her/their entire life. Thus Sacharow was surprised that the playwright still wanted only minimal and realistic movement, even though he knew that, as he put it, Albee "doesn't love a huge amount of movement."[74] But Albee continued to assert that act 2 was perfectly naturalistic and to ask Sacharow to minimize movement. "For some reason he thought that act 2 wasn't as naturalistic as act 1," Albee recalled. "I kept saying it's naturalistic. And then he tried to make it more stylized!"[75] Sacharow also admitted, "My first impulse was to do something more stylized, and he felt 'no, that's wrong; it has to be realistic.'"[76]

A part of the difficulty arose from what Albee means by "naturalism" and "stylization." Through much of his career he has offered idiosyncratic, playful, much-qualified, shifting, and paradoxical definitions of naturalism as it applies to his plays. In 1979 Albee responded to a question about the style of his play *The Lady From Dubuque:* "I can't get that objective about my own work."[77] But then he went on to compare its style to those of several of his plays he had just directed and which were then touring as part of the *Albee Directs Albee* project: "It probably gives the illusion of being as naturalistic a play as *Who's Afraid of Virginia Woolf?* I don't think that's a particularly naturalistic play either. None of my plays is, and all of them are, depending on the approach you take to it. It's not a highly stylized play like *The American Dream;* it's not a terribly experimental play on the surface of it like *Quotations from Chairman Mao Tse-Tung;* it's not vaudeville like *Counting the Ways;* it's not theoretically opaque like *Listening.* It's a fairly devious play with a fairly easy-going surface." In 1994, while *Three Tall Women* was playing at the Promenade, Albee offered another opinion about the naturalism of his plays: "All of my plays are stylized, to one extent or another, but all drama is artifice. Within those parameters, all of my plays are absolutely naturalistic. Some are less what the audience expects than others, which is my definition of stylization."[78] To communicate with his director or actors Albee would, of course, never resort to such definitions or such paradoxical pronouncements. What he meant when he urged Sacharow toward a naturalistic staging for act 2 may be clearer from a look at Albee's own directorial work.

In his productions of such stylized, abstract, and non-naturalistic works as *The American Dream, The Sandbox, Quotations from Chairman Mao Tse-Tung,* and *Counting the Ways,* Albee's staging was impelled by a basic mimetic aesthetic, so far as the actors' speech, behavior, and movement were concerned. No matter how abstract or stylized the characters, setting, or premise of his script, he wanted the actors to portray three-dimensional, living and breathing human beings who spoke and behaved naturalistically, without a hint of stylization or self-conscious acting. During his rehearsals of *The American Dream,* as discussed earlier, he had advised his actors explicitly about this: "You *have* to see and believe in yourselves as actual, physical, realistic, naturalistic persons—not *stylized* characters." Thus when he told Sacharow that the second act of *Three Tall Women* should be naturalistic, he meant that A's three selves should behave with each other and with the dying A in a completely normal, everyday manner, without any artificiality, self-consciousness, or stylization. In his own production of *Three Tall Women* in Vienna, as in his productions of his other stylized plays, irrespective of their non-naturalistic dramatic premise, the characters' stage embodiment was always naturalistic.

Albee's view that the art and craft of acting require that actors always incarnate real human beings anchored in plausible language, psychology, and sociology stems, ultimately, from his coming of age as an artist between the late 1940s and the late 1950s, a period when the American stage was dominated by actors and directors who firmly espoused and practiced the mimetic acting and directing principles of the Group Theatre and the Actors Studio. In this adherence, moreover, Albee had a far greater artistic affinity with Alan Schneider than with Lawrence Sacharow in his post-Method phase. Albee's belief in mimetic characterization and acting even within non-mimetic situations parallels his dramaturgic interest in balancing contradictory genres and styles and real and metaphorical characters within the same work. Quite early in his career he declared, in a 1966 *Paris Review* interview, "You must expect the audience's mind to work on both levels, symbolically and realistically," and he elaborated on the matter in a 1967 Canadian Broadcasting Corporation interview, saying that "a play, to be at all interesting, has got to move on two or possibly three or four levels."[79] Predictably, critics over the years have failed to grasp his experimental intent, and some have castigated him for muddling style and genre boundaries. Among the few to write appreciatively about this aspect of his work was the distinguished director and critic Harold Clurman, who as early as 1966 argued in the *New York Times* that his "peculiar veering from quasi-realism to stylization . . . is integral to Albee's psychological tension."[80] Albee does not veer so much as he balances and levitates different styles and genres and thus also generates an aesthetic tension that enriches the theatrical experience. This dramaturgic and directorial intermingling, furthermore, reflects his taste for paradox and shock and his penchant for confounding audience and critical expectations.

For Albee, given his long dual career as a playwright and director, dramaturgic and directorial concerns go hand in hand. Thus, both when directing his own plays and when working with other directors, Albee refines his texts during rehearsals as a matter of course, using the litmus test of practical performance. Accordingly, he made several textual revisions during the Vienna, Woodstock, and New York rehearsals of *Three Tall Women*. Albee was still writing parts of act 2 when the Vienna rehearsals began, and he gave it to his cast only at the start of the second week.[81] This just-completed script was particularly eligible for refinement in rehearsal. The majority of revisions were made during the Vienna rehearsals; they were, in fact, the final stage in bringing this script to completion, as is implicit in Albee's own remark that "the play was completely finished by the time we got to the New York production."[82] Compared to the published script, the original one in Vienna had a considerably longer act 1: A spoke at greater length about her horses; B went into considerably more detail about their weekly visit to A's surgeon in the city; and A's bracelet-on-the-pee-pee story continued much longer. Also unlike the published play, the script included references to several events and offstage characters, especially an Uncle Bob "who was coming to the house and taking control of things."[83] There were so many references to him that in late rehearsals and even in early performances, if Myra Carter could not remember a line, Kathleen Butler would simply ask her, "Well, what about Bob?" allowing Carter to ad-lib.[84] Carter was so frustrated by the question, which her frequent memory lapses recurrently elicited, that once she completely flustered her fellow actors during a performance by retorting, "I don't want to talk about him!" Uncle Bob also became a figure of mirth during rehearsals in Woodstock, where he was eventually eliminated as not germane to the dramatic action.

Albee made most of the cuts in order to streamline the dialogue by minimizing repetition, whittling away linguistic embellishment, and eliminating minor narrative details. As Carter remarked about some revisions, "So much can be said a different way; then it must go." Sometimes an actor sought some deletions. Carter felt the pee-pee story should stop quickly once the bracelet slides off into A's lap: "You shouldn't go on too long after that. And he went on too long." She subsequently boasted, "Cut myself; cut my own role. Very few actors would." Several cuts, however, were made to accommodate Carter, although Albee almost never likes to make changes for particular performers. Carter was having difficulty learning such a large and difficult role, and he thought it expedient to make an exception to his own rule, especially in view of her age and her frequent complaints. Carter, however, saw it differently and blamed the writing, especially in act 1: "You couldn't learn it. It is virtually unlearnable. . . . Technically speaking, he asks for things that can't be done by the instrument. . . . I would rather do *Medea*."[85] A final section of the original play was cut substantially, in part to assist Carter and in part because of last-minute time constraints. Although there is no such division in the published text, in the initial script A's speech that ends with "I'm *here,* and I deny you *all;* I deny every *one* of you" (107) was clearly marked "end of act two," and the subsequent audience address by the three characters was called a "coda" (107–110). In Vienna the coda's 132 lines were reduced to 23, but 69 of those were restored in New York and in the published version. Discussing the cuts in Vienna and in other Albee-directed productions she had acted in, Kathleen Butler observed, "As a director he's smart enough. . . to know what's playing and what isn't," and when "it's not playing, there's no fiddling around with it, he just yanks it."[86]

Among the other changes in Vienna, two were small but quite significant for character delineation. As discussed earlier, C's "Why am I being nice?" became "Why can't I be nice?" Her self-correction "It's tangible proof . . . that we're valued . . . (*embarrassed*) . . . that we're valuable" was reversed to correct authorial miswriting: "It's tangible proof . . . that we're valuable . . . (*embarrassed*) . . . that we're valued" (11, 103). In the Vienna program, moreover, the characters, instead of being named A, B, and C, were called Young Woman, Middle-Aged Woman, and Old Woman. In Woodstock Albee deleted the reference to a "kike" but then, at the actors' request, restored it in New York. In another case, though, despite many pleas from the actors—Jordan Baker remembered she and Marion Seldes "wept for days"—Albee refused to undo a set of deletions made in New York in A's final speech. Originally this speech deployed the word "surcease" six times, to great evocative effect. In Vienna and Woodstock, however, Albee sensed that many audience members found the word unfamiliar and thus focused on deciphering it rather than fully experiencing the play's critical final moments. So he replaced "surcease" with the less poetic phrase "coming to the end of it." Thus "The happiest moment? Surcease, I think. Surcease; a succession of surceases, a line of them" became simply "The happiest moment? Coming to the end of it, I think" (109). Similarly, "that blessed one—the last surcease" became "that blessed one—the end of it," and "I was talking about . . . what: surcease" became "I was talking about. . . . what: coming to the end of it" (110). In addition, he deleted the word entirely from the play's second-to-last line, "Surcease. When it's all done. When we stop. When we can stop" (110). On the other hand, one crucial new action introduced into the play by his New York cast and director—the three tall women's collective deep breath in the play's final moment—was so perfect that the author assumed it was actually in his original script, when, in fact, there is no such stage direction in the rehearsal manuscripts used in Vienna, Woodstock, and New York, nor in the *American Theatre,* Dramatists Play Service, or Plume printed editions of the play.

This look at Albee's rehearsal work on *Three Tall Women* demonstrates his typically immense impact—as director or supervising author—on the first performances of his plays. In the case of *Three Tall Women,* he not only directed the first stage performance in Vienna but soon afterward also supervised the pivotal first American and New York performances, staged by Lawrence Sacharow, thus exerting even greater influence. Albee's work on staging the world premiere significantly shaped the Sacharow productions, since the author relied on his recent experience to tailor his demands about fundamental features of the new staging and since he ensured that his leading actor from Vienna reprised her role as A in these productions. At the same time, however, he also permitted Sacharow substantial room for invention and genuine collaboration. Albee's interactions with Sacharow offer many examples of wide-ranging artistic collaboration as well as an overall congruence between the two men's theatrical aesthetic, especially in their mutual preference for simple and spare staging; the latter, moreover, explains Albee's earlier frustration with director Alan Schneider's more naturalistically cluttered staging. On the other hand, the playwright's dislike for Sacharow's stylized physical movement, which he used to parallel stylized characterization and situation, confirms a longstanding Albee aesthetic that revels in the paradoxical presence of multiple styles within a single play, act, or scene. Albee's work as a director and consulting dramatist on *Three Tall Women,* in addition, reveals how he brings seasoned instincts to his communications with fellow artists—whether actors, director, or designers—and how he allows them creative autonomy while simultaneously providing clearly demarcated interpretive parameters as well as authoritative insights into characters and situations. Furthermore, these rehearsals show his readiness to revise even the most autobiographical of his texts in order to meet the practical needs of performance. Finally, Albee's extraordinary attention during the *Three Tall Women* rehearsals to the minutiae of stage decor—particularly to the myriad details of setting, properties, costumes, and lighting—shows him not as some word-obsessed writer but as a complete theatre artist who mobilizes all stage elements to communicate his vision.

10

Albee's Double Authoring

John Arden, one of the leading British dramatists of the mid-twentieth century, in his essay "Playwrights and Playwriters," stresses etymological and theatrical distinctions to argue that an author "who requires someone else actually to produce [direct] the play once its text is completed" is merely "a playwriter, a semi-skilled sub-contractor to the theatre." A playwright, on the other hand, is "capable of presenting a complete artistic vision upon the stage"; he is the "overall artistic governor."[1] Edward Albee's comments and practices over the last several decades show how an identical conception of the role of the playwright impels him to stage his own plays. In this endeavor he is also prompted by a complementary conception of the script—a conception that parallels the ideas of the dramatic theorist and scholar J. L. Styan, who defines a script as "the arrangement of *words* [a playwright] must substitute for his conception," and of the great Russian director Vsevolod Meyerhold, who declared, "Words in the theatre are only a design on the canvas of motion."[2] Thus Albee directs in order to exercise moment-to-moment control over all constituents of performance, eliminate one intermediary through whom the script must filter to the stage, and realize his authorial vision on the stage with clarity, precision, and completeness.

In an interview with me Albee offered a long rumination about what he regards as the art of directing. An extended quotation of those comments nicely encapsulates the wide range of performance elements he seeks to modulate as a director of his own plays.

> You must have an overall vision of the piece. With any production, 90 percent of it is casting. . . . Directing, of course, is a lot of knowing how to work with actors. The first two weeks are basically subtext work, so actors really understand why the character behaves the way the character does in a certain section. . . . You have stage pictures that you create in your mind. You do have rhythms that you're after. There's tension, release of tension, passive and active moments. And you've got to populate the stage properly in all of those, in all of those times. There's a tie-in between the visual picture and the psychology of the piece, of course, always. Who is moving? Who is standing still? Who's sitting? The tempo of the speeches. The intentions. All of that has to be put together. So it is a combination of music and painting and literature at the same time. [3]

These are precisely the kind of details this book has sought to illuminate by documenting and analyzing Albee's staging of a representative range of his plays over an extended period of time and in a variety of professional theatres in the U.S. and in Europe. In so doing, this scrutiny demonstrates how central staging and performance are to Albee's conception and practice of his art.

This study of Edward Albee's translation of his written texts into full-fledged theatre preserves a minutely detailed and contemporaneous record of the crucial but evanescent process of this eminent theatre artist's rehearsals and performances, testifies to his command of directing, offers insights into the meaning of his plays, illuminates his overall theatre aesthetic, and provides a performance component hitherto largely missing from Albee scholarship. Comparisons with other leading playwright-directors like Bernard Shaw, Bertolt Brecht, and Samuel Beckett firmly place him within a major tradition of twentieth-century stage practice. Parallels between his work and that of eminent modern directors like Elia Kazan, Harold Clurman, Alan Schneider, Peter Brook, and Ingmar Bergman testify to the fundamental strengths of Albee's directorial practices and principles as well as contextualizing his work within the main traditions of stage directing after the Second World War.

Broadly eclectic in his choice of directorial methods and fluent in the vocabulary of acting, Albee efficiently provided actors with precise instructions, practical advice, technical diagnoses, a sense of security, and considerable creative freedom. Many of his instructions stemmed from his conviction that actors must "'become' rather than . . . 'indicate'" their characters, that they must "vanish" into their roles. "No matter what style the play is," he advised an actor, "you must not comment on your character." This conviction led to believable portrayals of his characters, whether the Angel of Death in *The Sandbox,* the Long-Winded Lady in *Quotations from Chairman Mao Tse-Tung,* or the realistic Jack and Gillian in *Marriage Play.* A related injunction, "Make it real for us," propelled his demands for interplay through actors' listening and reacting to each other—either aurally by small vocalizations or interjections or physically by a look, stance, or bit of business—and his insistent requirement that stage behavior be psychologically credible, irrespective of the level of stylization in the written text. Albee praised Schneider for his similar emphasis during *The Lady From Dubuque* rehearsals on Broadway, and it is from his collaboration with him that Albee learned the value of depicting what Schneider used to call "the realistic . . . truthful . . . human situation" in all plays, even in his staging of the highly stylized works of Samuel Beckett.[4]

In this directorial emphasis, remarkable for a playwright with a considerable body of non-naturalistic work, Edward Albee showed himself firmly linked to the mainstream of postwar American directing and acting, as represented by Elia Kazan and Lee Strasberg, especially at the Actors Studio. Alan Schneider, too, unequivocally acknowledged his roots—even though attenuated—in the Actors Studio tradition. Working with actors typically trained in the Method, Albee was adept at employing the system's language to ensure a psychologically driven performance. At the same time, Albee often directed externally, without reference to any subtextual underpinning: he offered down-to-earth directions in terms of practical staging needs and intended results. This pragmatic approach minimized unnecessary discussion, allowed precise execution of movement and action, and, crucially, fostered in actors a sense of security that was conducive to creative exploration and crucially important at sensitive junctures in the rehearsal process.

Albee did not shy away from furnishing practical acting advice and diagnoses when they were needed. He urged actors to think in the middle of their lines and not before, to hold for laughs, to pause before a punch line, to "play" the audience, to listen to themselves and to each other, to have complete confidence in their lines and characters, to wait for laughs, to create emphasis without increasing volume, to guard against the danger of rote performance, and to be prepared for changes in performance in response to their first audiences.

Most often Albee offered specific intentions and goals but allowed actors the freedom to achieve them in their own way. His rehearsals bore out his contention

"I would rather give an actor a general intention note first."[5] When an actor could not figure out how to convey the suggested intent, Albee provided "little hints." Only when a performer failed to build upon these hints did he specify particulars of delivery or movement. Even then, he usually proffered several alternatives, so that the actor could choose what suited his own impulse. Within the clearly defined parameters of his authorial vision, Albee encouraged actors to use their own personalities and sensibilities to embody his characterizations.

Always practical, Albee recognized that some performers needed detailed, specific guidance. To them he willingly supplied directions on vocal tone, pitch, and volume, and on posture, movement, and business. Several times a day, he demonstrated an action; if necessary, he even assisted with line readings. Whether they needed explicit directions or brief, indirect suggestions, the actors remained at the center of Albee's directorial work. However, Albee had neither the personality nor the requisite professional acting experience to help a novice actor if he needed personal coaching. Nonetheless, Albee demonstrated considerable skill in handling actors with different backgrounds, personalities, and working methods.

Alan Schneider, not surprisingly for a director, believed that most playwrights should not direct their own works. In a personal interview on the opening night of *The Lady From Dubuque* he cited a playwright to bolster his view: "Arthur Miller once said it very well—he said, 'When an author directs, he directs the words. When a director directs, he directs the actors.'"[6] And Albee himself has argued that not all authors can be pragmatic and skilled directors. "Some perfectly good playwrights shouldn't be allowed in the theatre during rehearsals. They can't have any objectivity about what they've done."[7] But unlike Schneider's and Miller's generic author-director, Albee demonstrated his objectivity by attending not merely to his words but to all elements of the mise en scene, with a particular focus on the actors. He created substantial new stage business and movement in order to physicalize action implicit in his words, to visually underscore character traits and subsurface meanings, to generate comedy, to comment ironically, and to intensify emotion.

With similar goals Albee expertly marshaled props, costumes, sets, sound, and lighting not merely to decorate but to convey meaning and widen resonance. He placed Fam's chair, table, and cushion on a podium and costumed him as a dandy to visually stress his vanity and pomposity. In *Quotations from Chairman Mao Tse-Tung* he invented a hand-held Mao mask for an already masked Mao to playfully theatricalize the character's essential duplicity and ironically undermine his political homilies. The introduction of haunting wake music in *Box* deepened the play's sense of loss and suggested an apocalyptic, post-death world. Jaunty sneakers, combined with gestural animation, visually reinforced Grandma's emotional and mental agility in *The American Dream,* where, moreover, sets, costumes, and props based on the colors of the American flag comically signaled the play's broad thematic and satiric sweep. Numerous such instances reveal a seasoned playwright-director who relied not just on words but on all available performance elements.

A few rehearsal choices betrayed a desire to modify past staging and counter critical interpretations. Albee deleted Jerry's momentary premonition about imminent bloody events in *The Zoo Story,* so that his subsequent attack and suicide clearly appeared improvised and not premeditated and psychopathic. Albee's revisions in *The American Dream* highlighted the likelihood of the Young Man's avenging his twin brother's dismemberment by killing both Mommy and Daddy later that night, thus revealing the comedy's violent, dark side, which was rarely grasped by critics or directors. In *Who's Afraid of Virginia Woolf?* Albee deleted eight references that suggested that Martha might have previously mentioned their son to outsiders: this ensured that the play's pivotal action—George's destruction of the son—is driven by Martha's infraction that evening and not, as some critics suggest, by her cumulative breaches or her attempted infidelity.

Albee's directorial work on the first stage production of *Three Tall Women* and the first American production of *Marriage Play* showed how carefully he reconsidered almost every aspect of his written texts in order to translate them into effective performance. During the *Marriage Play* rehearsals he was remarkably incisive in analyzing the ebb and flow of his scenes and ruthless in cutting lines and even scenes that did not work, despite his authorial fondness for the literary quality of some of the deleted passages and despite the pleading of his actors, who were loath to lose such poetic speeches. Even in the case of his most autobiographical play, *Three Tall Women,* Albee remained unsentimental and clear-eyed in cutting his script for the sake of effective performance.

Albee's staging of his more recent plays, including *Three Tall Women* and *Marriage Play,* also confirmed his marked preference for an economy of theatrical means and an overall minimalist theatre aesthetic. That artistic impulse has been evolving over the years, and was evident in his recent directing of some of his earliest plays. Thus in his production of *Fam and Yam* he got rid of the tilting paintings, telephone, sound effects, and offstage conversation. Similarly in his staging of *The Zoo Story* he excised one of the play's two benches, and in *Box* and *Quotations from Chairman Mao Tse-Tung* he deleted more than half of the reprise that ends those interconnected works. Other emendations in other productions offered concrete evidence of how Albee has distilled his dramaturgy. Strategic textual revisions in *Who's Afraid of Virginia Woolf?* clarified character motivation and logic, pointed up connections between certain speeches, eliminated thematic heavyhandedness, smoothed awkward aural rhythms, and jettisoned redundant information.

Over the years at various venues during rehearsals his approach has been consistent: he is precise, direct, open, flexible, practical, patient, firm but never arbitrary, a bit reserved but with flashes of humor and wit. Actors find him immensely reassuring: they feel they can trust him completely because he is the one who created the characters they are trying to fathom and embody. With the production personnel at major professional theatres, such as the Alley Theatre in Houston where he regularly directed his own works, he is exacting, insistent, and fastidious, sometimes becoming a challenge to work for. He believes in pushing the producing theatre close to its maximum capabilities in order to, as nearly as possible, represent the play's physical world as he envisioned it while writing. In contrast, when a theatre is small or a producing organization lacks adequate financial resources or technical facilities, as was the case during the Albee season at the off-Broadway Signature Theatre Company in New York or during some productions at the Ensemble Theatre of Cincinnati, Albee turns accommodating, flexible, and generous, making concessions and devising pragmatic solutions.

Overall this study illuminates how Edward Albee, one of the giants of the American theatre, constructs his scripts, how he envisages them working in performance, and how over a period of almost three decades he created detailed mise en scenes for some of his most important plays, revealing through his staging choices and rehearsal comments his distinct theatre aesthetic. This documentation and analysis of Albee's directorial work demonstrates his skill in transforming his authorial vision into dynamic theatre—in transforming himself, in Vsevolod Meyerhold's phrase, into "the author of the stage performance." Edward Albee's double authoring fuses script and performance in an ideal artistic alchemy—"not conventionally, but in the phases of the work of one mind," as envisioned by the distinguished theatre scholar and theorist Raymond Williams—to reveal a precise, vibrant, and complete artistic vision.[8]

11

Albee and His Collaborators on Staging Albee

FROM *THE ZOO STORY* TO *THE GOAT, OR, WHO IS SYLVIA?*

For each production I observed, I typically tape-recorded extended interviews near opening night with Albee and with his principal collaborators, including actors, scene designers, lighting designers, and stage managers. I sought their comments on matters I had observed during the rehearsal process or discussed informally in conversations with Albee or others between rehearsal sessions. The comments of Albee's collaborators grow out of their distinct perspectives and thus provide an excellent counterpoint to Albee's directorial and authorial views of issues relating to each production. In the three productions directed by others—but with Albee participating in his authorial capacity—I followed a roughly analogous procedure of taping interviews with the director, author, and actors. Thus I provide additional perspectives on the staging of Albee plays via in-depth interviews with three important Albee directors: Alan Schneider on his Broadway premiere of *The Lady From Dubuque*, Lawrence Sacharow on his American and New York City premieres of *Three Tall Women*, and David Esbjornson on his Broadway premiere of *The Goat, or, Who Is Sylvia?* With two exceptions, the following interviews appear in print for the first time here.

Albee's comments about his texts and productions in this chapter are part of an ongoing dialogue that I have carried on with him for nearly three decades. Journalists and scholars have sought and received more interviews from Albee than from most other contemporary American playwrights, both because he continues to provoke interest and because his frequent lecturing, teaching, and directing oblige him to grant interviews. My long professional relationship with Albee and my thorough acquaintance with the particulars of his rehearsals, however, allow me to press, persist, and probe much further than others. More than most subjects, Albee comes armored against the interviewer's probes: he brings to interviews deeply ingrained, almost reflexive habits of defense through deft deflection, shrewd rationalization, too-simple explanations, and opaque comments. His caution stems partly from his temperament and partly from a distrust of authorial or critical paraphrase as a substitute for the essence and experience of a work of art, a distrust he shares with many writers in what Nathalie Sarraute terms the "age of suspicion." During our conversations over the years, however, Albee has become progressively less guarded, and I have had to nudge him less. It is still difficult, nonetheless, to elicit from him a candid, blunt, or spontaneous response, especially about matters of subtext, allusion, or interpretation, subjects on which all interviewers have found him adroitly evasive or uncooperative.

Albee's assertions in the following pages deserve attention because they are grounded in more than three decades of broad practical experience in the American theatre and because they reveal the thinking of an eminent playwright about several of his important works. The way Albee articulates his artistic concerns, moreover, offers a glimpse into his personal sensibility. Above all, without suggesting some naive intentionalism, I argue that Albee's views about his plays and their appropriate realization in performance constitute important testimony about his dramaturgic and directorial aesthetic.

Albee Directs Albee
(New York City, national and international tour, 1978)

EDWARD ALBEE

September 14, 1978

RS: What kind of preparation do you make for directing? For example, I see you don't have a book.

Albee: I keep everything in my head. Of course, it's rather special when I direct my own plays because I don't have to investigate what's going on in the playwright's head in exactly the same way I would if I were directing Beckett or

Chekov or somebody like that. I've merely got to try to remember what was in my head. So I have a pretty good idea of the way I want the play to look and the way I want the play to sound. At the same time, the director's got to be so much more concerned with what is possible. The playwright's concerned with what is theoretically possible. I as a director, you may have noticed, will cut my text, if I don't think the author is as sensible as he should be. I try to cut in order to make the text flow. To make the overall psychology of the piece work.

RS: You said you already had the text in your head, but in preparation for directing do you at all reconsider any of the text before coming to the theatre?

Albee: No. I would rather that the cuts, like the cuts I've made—I've made a few cuts in the past three or four weeks; not many—come out of the rehearsal process. Because why would I make a theoretical cut when in rehearsal I can make a practical cut?

RS: If you had to make theoretical cuts, you would have made them while writing. However, given the number of years since you wrote these plays (*The Zoo Story* was done twenty years ago), you don't cut too much.

Albee: Some of these plays already have their cuts made. But I don't really cut that much. I don't think I've ever cut more than 5 percent of the play. I remember in 1962 with *Who's Afraid of Virginia Woolf?*—a two-hundred-and-fifty-page text—I think I cut, what? About nine pages. And when I directed the revival on Broadway in 1976 I wanted to cut it a bit more because I'm fairly impatient these days. But I found that before I had cut the text down to the point that I could only cut about a page and a half. None of these plays is having its first performance. I've done a lot of cutting. I'm really doing just sort of honing at this point. A refinement of cutting. Or cuts that I just hadn't had time to make before.

RS: The large cut in the Voice at the end of *Box* seems a substantial cut.

Albee: It was a substantial cut . . . it was a strategic mistake before. It was too long. I just wanted essences from it. I mean, why go into a whole recapitulation? We've heard the entire play at least twice. Why do it a third time? I was just being greedy back in 1967.

RS: Do you make a schedule at all?

Albee: Yes, but you mustn't be inflexible. But I do make a schedule of what I'm going to be rehearsing each day. I have an overall plan. But, then again, depending upon the speed with which the actors are learning and where the various emphases are . . . You have to be flexible enough to revise that schedule every day.

RS: You begin with a reading, and usually begin blocking the first day. After that, do you have any particular aspects that you like to start focusing on?

Albee: It's different with each play. I try fairly soon to start giving actors little hints that they can use for overall characterization, to stop them from going wrong too early. And if you notice that bad habits are creeping in, then you can start harping on the bad habits.

RS: At one stage very early in *The American Dream* rehearsals you started talking about pacing, energy level, and speed.

Albee: I did that only because I knew that bad habits are very easy to get into in farce, and also I knew that we had a very short period of time.

RS: How much of your directing would you characterize as improvising during rehearsal? I can sense a lot of things happening in your mind which, of course, you don't indicate to the actor that you've just decided on that.

Albee: A lot of these theoretical improvisations should come from the nature of the actor you're working with. Each actor is going to require different solutions to different problems. And the interrelation of two actors may very easily change your staging concepts.

RS: I see you cleaning up the stage picture and making things clearer.

Albee: I'm after clarity. I don't like unnecessary movement. I don't like movement to get in the way. Especially with plays that are fairly complex. A play like *Listening* or a play like *Quotations from Chairman Mao Tse-Tung,* which take a fair amount of listening to: I would rather have the audience listen than watch a great deal going on on the stage, if the action of your play is interior as opposed to exterior. If you have exterior action, mostly, then, of course, you have a great deal of physical movement. But if the play is basically interior action, you have less physical movement.

RS: I see you do a very minimal amount of directing with good actors.

Albee: Well, with a good actor, you don't have to. I've noticed something very interesting about good actors. They instinctively know when to move. And nine times out of ten, they're right. A good actor, you can just give a hint to, and the whole performance will change, as with Eileen. I just give her a hint, and she can do the whole thing right. Somebody like Catherine, you've got to work with constantly. And I'll be working with her for another month trying to get a decent performance out of her. A good actor instinctively knows when to move. I'll tell you something else about directing that's interesting. It's important for a director, when he's directing, to listen a great deal to the text, not only to watch. Because he can tell a great deal about how well he's directing just by the sound of it. And he can tell a good deal about the shapes he's created just by listening to the shapes that he wants to create and then going back and looking and seeing if the shapes that he has physically created relate to the psychological shapes that he wants to create.

RS: Do you close your eyes?

Albee: I go and sit in the back and listen. I lie down and close my eyes and listen a good deal to the text. And you may have noticed, I'm all over the theatre all the time. Because there are people all over the theatre—there are audiences all over the theatre. I want the thing to be relatable from every area in the theatre.

RS: I don't think I've ever seen anyone move around as much as you do. For a playwright, you seem very flexible, very practical.

Albee: You have to be practical if you're going to be a director. And if an author's going to be a director, he has to be practical. Because if he's going to hold on to every word and every authorial idea, then he's not doing his proper job as a director. The director's job is to make what the author wrote effective on stage, at the same time being faithful to the author's intention. But there are lots of ways of being faithful to the author's intention. As long as the intellectual and emotional and psychological honesty of the play is preserved, there are many different ways of doing it. You see terrible things that have happened when somebody like Andrei Serban gets *The Cherry Orchard* and destroys the honesty of the play for his own glory as a director. That's a great misuse of the directorial function. I have a couple of thoughts about *Uncle Vanya,* if I get at that play one day, but I hope I'll be honest to the play.

RS: Do you give specific notes only when you think that it's absolutely necessary?

Albee: I give few very specific notes because I would rather hope that if I give the actor a general note, he may be able to adjust physical specifics. I'd rather give an actor a general intention note first and hope that he will come up with his own specifics. I hate to give line readings, and I hate to give very specific things. I hope the actor will find something that is interesting within guidelines that I set. If the actor can't find those things . . . then I will pick and choose very carefully one or two physicalizations which I think will lead the actor to discovering more about the character and finding equivalent physicalizations on his own. I mean, these aren't puppets you're working with. Even if they're actors, they're flesh-and-blood human beings, and they do have interesting intelligences.

RS: Have you studied directing at all?

Albee: No. I never studied playwriting, either. I watched other plays being directed in the same way I've watched other plays being performed. I suspect I probably have a special insight into the nature of the characters I've created that no other director could have. Well, it's not a theory that the Society of Stage Directors and Choreographers agrees with, because they think authors should not direct their own work. An author shouldn't direct his own work unless he knows how to direct. I've learned how to direct, and so I know how to do it. I'm after clarity, simplicity. I like to think I get those things. I try to look upon my own work very objectively. To try to make it work most effectively as a stage piece, as closely as I can to the way I see it working in my head when I write it. And that's something that no other director really can do. I suspect that in that sense I probably end up with a different kind of production. There must be, though I don't know what it is, there must be a slightly different look and feel to a production of mine of my own work than of a production by somebody else.

RS: Which of your directors has given the most honest form to your plays on stage?

Albee: Alan Schneider's done a lot of good work with my plays. We stopped working together for a variety of reasons. He's slightly pedestrian. He's humorless. It was finally getting to me. Because my plays are, I find, rather funny. Including lots of lines that nobody else in the world finds funny, but I do. Peter Hall, I think.

RS: What kinds of effects on the audience did you have in mind as you were writing *Box-Mao-Box*?

Albee: I don't remember. I don't know. I was aware that I was making a fairly complex experiment. I always make the assumption that any virtue that accrues to my plays is what I intended. I think I decided to write a play with Chairman Mao in it and I think I started writing the Long-Winded Lady. I wrote that whole speech as one entire speech. Then I took my quotations from Chairman Mao, put them in a certain order, clipped them. Then I had discovered this poem. I put it in quatrains. Then I started clipping the Long-Winded Lady's speech into arias. I had about one hundred and fifty different cards. I started arranging them. I'd look at them, and I played around with them and put them in what I ultimately thought was the proper order.

RS: Does the Young Man's self-awareness, by extension, apply to the historical American Dream that he in some way symbolizes?

Albee: It was my theory at the time, and still is, that the American Dream had been emasculated by a bunch of shallow, self-serving, short-sighted people. I still feel like it has. The personification is a complex matter. I was interested in the fact that somebody could be a metaphor...

RS: And a character.

Albee: At the same time. And most of his destructions were metaphorical. The dismemberment is metaphorical and yet real at the same time.

RS: It also works in *The Sandbox* very effectively.

Albee: It's going on a lot in *Listening* too. I am quite convinced that the Girl manages to slit her wrists by finding a metaphoric piece of glass.

RS: Yes, she says most kids have lots of broken glass.

Albee: I'm sure there's no glass, in fact. I'm sure she manages to do the real thing with a metaphorical piece of glass. Absolutely certain of it.

RS: She never answers whether there was glass or not.

Albee: That's right.

Wyman Pendleton, actor

Peter, *The Zoo Story, Albee Directs Albee,* 1978

Daddy, *The American Dream, Albee Directs Albee,* 1978

Daddy, *The Sandbox, Albee Directs Albee,* 1978

He, *Counting the Ways, Albee Directs Albee,* 1978

Man, *Listening, Albee Directs Albee,* 1978

Chairman Mao Tse-Tung, *Box* and *Quotations from Chairman Mao Tse-Tung,* 1968 (dir. Alan Schneider)

February 20, 1980

RS: What are Albee's strong points as a director?

Pendleton: One very strong point is that he knows the moments when to leave you alone—to leave the actor alone—and just let it grow and watch it. As you may recall, during the rehearsal of *The Zoo Story* he left us alone a very great deal. Not—I don't think—completely because he wanted to: he had other work he had to do on *The American Dream,* as you also know. But then he would come in after maybe we'd been working for three or four hours some days, or after we might have been through the play twice. He would see it, and it would hit him fresh, and then he would make a comment. After all, he first had blocked us thoroughly, and there was not that much blocking, per se, in *The Zoo Story.* Therefore, I found he could be a very great help to us because he *would* go away and we could work on it alone. He wouldn't go away for an entire rehearsal day, but a good part of it—some hours of it, very often.

RS: But how does a director's going away help you?

Pendleton: He leaves you free to develop and grow yourself. Then, if he should see things going awry. . . . In other words, a great many good directors like you to bring something to them when you rehearse. I don't mean just at the beginning of rehearsals. I mean all the time. And that's why you hear directors saying, "I hope you've done your homework! I hope you've done something besides go out and have a lot to drink and something to eat between rehearsals." By leaving us alone that way, he was able to see. He wasn't having his nose rubbed in it by being there every single, living minute. He would see any progression or regression and comment or work with us on it.

RS: Of course, he could do that with you because he trusted you and Steven [Rowe].

Pendleton: That's true. And he was forced into that. I don't think he might have done it anyway. But he had another play he had to get together, with an actor (who shall be nameless) who didn't know what she was doing. And so he took advantage of that.

RS: Are there other strengths?

Pendleton: He knows his own work very well. One of his strengths becomes a weakness. I think he wants to be extremely sure—as all playwrights do, I'm sure—that all his words are heard. So he may want all his words to be heard, to the loss of other dramatic values, I sometimes feel, in some of the plays. He knew that he could trust us, as you said, in *The Zoo Story.* We knew the play very thoroughly, so he would give notes very generally. But in making something like *Listening* be clearly heard, he made it so static that maybe his strength became almost a weakness to people other than those who were just determined to hear everything and study Albee. He does know—many directors don't—how to talk to actors. There is a whole segment of actors that I don't think Mr. Schneider knows how to talk to. Not the right way. He can talk to them, but it's like giving them orders. Some actors you should needle and some you should coddle into what you want, and you'll get it. Give them orders, and you won't get anything.

RS: What are Edward's weaknesses?

A. One of them is a failing common to *all* directors who have never done any acting of their own. All completely fine directors have done some acting themselves. And Edward hasn't. But he is better than a great many on that. He seems to understand acting, because he's seen his own work so much—especially many of the plays that we were doing—that he knew what they should look like. He followed Alan Schneider's original directions *almost* to the letter in *The Zoo Story,* although there were a few tiny changes. I think you could say the same thing about *The American Dream,* although I think in *The American Dream* he was at fault until I was finally joined by Sudie Bond here in New York. If you just gave it a little more depth instead of just straight across the stage. The set and the furniture was straight across the stage. It was in the original, too, but all the movement was not. But he does know his own plays very well.

RS: You mentioned he hasn't acted. He told me once that all he did in college was act.

Pendleton: That's the first I've ever heard of it. I went to Choate Rosemary Hall, and I saw a photograph of Edward in *The Pirates of Penzance* as a little boy hanging on to a spar of the ship! I mean very little acting, and I'm not talking about high school and college, anyway. He didn't stay in college more than— what?—two years. He went to more schools than you and I can name. But he understands, and for a director who has not done a lot of acting, I find he is able to communicate with actors a great deal better than many, many directors.

RS: One thing I found while observing Alan direct is that, comparatively, Edward offered fewer directions.

Pendleton: Yes, he did. To the great detriment of *Box* and *Quotations from Chairman Mao Tse-Tung.* I thought he gave them no help. It was a lot of saying, "Learn your lines and sit there and do it!" Now, that is not what Mr. Schneider did when we did it on Broadway. It had energy and pace and variation and so forth. I think Edward was tired and just let it happen. And it didn't happen.

RS: What about his casting?

Pendleton: A good director, among other things, must be able to cast well. And I don't know whether Edward knows how to cast well or not. I'm not sure. And the reason I'm not sure is that he took on that actor—what's her name—I don't understand that at all.

RS: Why did he not fire her?

Pendleton: He said, I'll give her one more chance. And I'll say one more thing: in *The Lady From Dubuque* I do not understand why Alan, who's my friend, or Edward allowed one actor to still be there when the play opened. I think it threw the whole first act out the window. I don't know whether to blame the actor or the director or Edward—or all three—but something was very wrong.

The Lady From Dubuque
(Broadway, 1980, dir. Alan Schneider)

Edward Albee

February 14, 1980

RS: Which cuts in *The Lady From Dubuque* were made at Alan Schneider's request?

Albee: Every cut and change was made by me. There was one reordering of things—
of the sequence at the very end—that Alan suggested after I made my cuts, and
that I thought was a good idea.

RS: You are referring to the transposition in the scene where Oscar comes down
in Sam's shirt?

Albee: Yes, that was the only alteration that Alan suggested. No. I always make
my own cuts.

RS: But there was so much discussion between you and Alan during the rehearsal for a while.

Albee: That was basically about interpretation. We were arguing about why there
were so many props on the stage. That's why I put that line in at the beginning
of act 2, "I straightened up for you a bit," to get rid of all that stuff.

RS: I know you were both doing that. Alan tried to change bits of business and to
get rid of the downstage cushion in act 1.

Albee: Alan and I always have that argument. Constantly. So he had his way in the
first act. I had my way in the second.

RS: What prompted the major changes? Lack of clarity?

Albee: I think so, yes. There's a difference sometimes between that which works in
theory and that which works in practice. I have to concern myself ultimately
with what worked in practice. I think I only took out repetition. I don't think
I took out any essences.

RS: Well, you took out, for example, the references to the Vietnam past of Sam
and Fred.

Albee: Yes. Because I thought they were unnecessary. I had enough references to
our society, our short-sightedness, and things that were happening too late.
It wasn't essential for character delineation, and it got in the way of the other
political theses that I had running through the play.

RS: Still, that Sam was Fred's captain in Vietnam was such an important reference.

Albee: Well, if I wasn't going to follow through, why have it?

RS: You also cut your original manuscript's last scene, where all the guests returned and Sam announced, "Jo's dead"—in effect a replaying of bits of the earlier scene. You first deleted it, then resurrected it after you spoke with Alan, and finally you deleted it again.

Albee: Yeah, I had restored it, then I decided I didn't like it and took it out.

RS: Did you think that its inclusion might have fostered the idea that act 2 up to that scene had taken place in Sam's mind?

Albee: Yes, of course. That was the whole point . . . the concept . . . as it turned out . . . to make it easier for them. Then I decided it was dishonest.

RS: But you still leave the possibility of that interpretation open.

Albee: The possibility. Yes, of course.

RS: Some changes you resisted because, as Alan once said, you thought it would be kowtowing to the audience. And yet the changes you made, as you just said, were to make your intent clearer.

Albee: Clearer, without oversimplifying. Clarity without compromise, I hope.

RS: You mentioned about Irene not being happy for a time about some rhythm and Alan once said, "Half the play's meaning is in its rhythm." Moreover, you've often talked about musical structure and sometimes focused on just listening to the words, closing your eyes. What do you perceive as rhythm? Is it primarily oral, as it comes out in the speaking of the lines?

Albee: Well, that's that, of course. I suppose a certain intellectual rhythm, too. The meaning and also the sound of the sounds. Each actor makes a sound differently. It's a different instrument. It's a difficult thing to talk about. Well, you just have to listen very carefully.

RS: So you do include stage business and thematic repetitions—everything, the totality?

Albee: The two playwrights that I think interest me most from the thematic point of view are Chekov and Beckett, because they do most effectively do that.

RS: Apparently, there was considerable disagreement about the set between Alan and Rouben [Ter-Arutunian, the scene designer].

Albee: No. That's not true. The original concept that Alan wasn't happy with was, the staircase was where the entrance was. Alan didn't necessarily mind the staircase, not at all. The original model had the only entrance far upstage, and all entrances had to be made from behind the staircase, which was, indeed, impractical. You couldn't see the entrance. So two things that basically changed were, first, the front door was moved downstage of the staircase and the entrance was made from right to left; and, second, the upper walkway was made smaller. That was the only fundamental difference. It was a practical consideration only.

RS: I had a feeling that Alan preferred a more conventional, traditional living room setting, a little more cluttered than you liked, and also one with a more suburban look.

Albee: Alan is happiest if all the plays that he directs are in his *own* living room, which tends to be very cluttered and folksy. And that's not what I was after.

RS: What did you say to his argument, though, that the set does not help create the reality of an everyday situation? He told me that it seemed a little too abstract and stylized, though he understood that the Bauhaus style was okay for the occupants.

Albee: Well, I don't see how he can say that and at the same time admire Brecht's staging concepts as much as he does. Would he direct all of Brecht . . . if he was doing *Galileo,* would he insist on doing it in a cluttered living room? Perhaps he would. It would do violence to Brecht's style.

RS: Alan was also trying to get more color into the set. I think the costumer was trying to do that, too. Whereas your intent apparently was to . . . ?

Albee: No. The background is neutral, that's fine. But the peoples' faces and their clothes stand out. That's fine.

RS: Did you decide to replace the colored Jasper Johns print with the black-and-white one?

Albee: I didn't like Alan's choice at all. So I changed it for another one.

RS: What did Andy Warhol say about the "None of that Warhol shit" reference when he came backstage?

Albee: Oh, he found the remark quite funny. He likes publicity.

RS: Alan repeatedly gives very practical, pragmatic reasons for stage business, movement and so on. Do you think it would help an actor grow more if he had more organic, character-derived reasons for his moves?

Albee: I don't think those two are separate. I think Alan tries to help the actor develop the total organism of the character through his specific instructions. You can't talk to the actor about what the character portrays or represents or about the implications of the character. You've got to deal with the actor getting at the truth of the nature of the character. You may have noticed, when you watched me direct, that I would interfere with what an actor was doing in overall terms only when I thought that the actor was misunderstanding the nature of the character. I would try to get at it by specific truths. An actor has to build from individual truths to a total truth.

RS: But I felt while sitting at the rehearsals that it tends to make an actor's work very mechanical after awhile. "I want you there because I don't like you standing up," or "I want you to be on the ground because you need to pick up the book after a while." Things like that.

Albee: I do think that Alan is a trifle prop-happy. You may have noticed that sometime in rehearsal Oscar appears from the library with a book, so it will look like he's come from the library. "Look, I have a book, therefore it's a library." And so Sam can take the book away because it's his house and what is Oscar doing with one of his books. And I suppose that's fairly interesting, but I find it tedious. And so, you'll have noticed that first of all I got the book smaller, and then I finally removed the book.

RS: There's a certain fragmentation of thought in the play (as in most of your plays, actually), where an idea is broached, interrupted, then picked up again. Is it for reasons of rhythm? Or an attempt to recreate what sometimes does happen in everyday speech? Is it also to keep your intent oblique?

Albee: I never try to be oblique! I think everything works cyclically and is intermeshed. The straight line is often the least interesting distance between two points. In short, it's not necessarily virtuous.

RS: When you visualized these characters, were their exchanges comic?

Albee: Oh yes. I know something's funny when it occurs. And I love things to be funny. If the humor is organic and grows naturally out of the situation, I'm delighted to have it.

RS: You think funny. You said in your preface to *Box* and *Quotations from Chairman Mao Tse-Tung* that it's important for a playwright to experiment and to change people's perceptions. How conscious are you of such a goal?

Albee: I don't set out with a thesis to try to either change people's perceptions of themselves or revise the standards of playwriting. I don't set out to do that. Sometimes I know that a play will make certain experiments that other people aren't making with any frequency, and maybe every once in a while one can expand some boundaries. One is grateful if one does. I don't set out to do it.

RS: Were you aware of doing certain things when you were writing this play?

Albee: I was attempting having a metaphor and its embodiment simultaneous and levitating it so that one wasn't supposed to ask questions about its literalness. Apparently, in the minds of a lot of people, I didn't succeed.

RS: Several people I spoke to had difficulty empathizing with Jo's portrayal. Did you have any reservations about it?

Albee: It's a complex matter. I know she came across in the minds of a lot of people as being too shrill. I wanted the pathos to be always evident, and I wanted it clear that she was lashing out at people because she was in pain. Maybe that lovely actress's voice is a trifle too strident. Everything she said seemed to be on one tone, and maybe the voice irritates. The performance, I thought, was accurate. I could see, intellectually, everything that was meant to be happening, but it may be that she couldn't get the variety because of her voice. She didn't seem sympathetic. I think that's the voice rather than the interpretation. A person who's in terrible pain, with close friends, doesn't bother to be nice.

RS: That's not it. Perhaps, if the audience had more reason, more information about why those close friends were so close and why they would stay on, then it would make it easier to accept her harshness as well as their staying on.

Albee: How much information does one need about people? One has one's friends. There they are. I mean, doesn't Jo say, "Why do we have them over?" And she says "Because we love them. They love us."

RS: But I don't think people take that statement at face value, given the situation that they perceive on stage.

Albee: Well, we're lucky if all of our friends are as wonderful as we hope they are.

RS: The play had to close partly because of an insufficient opening budget. Is it a question of principle for you as a playwright not to put in your own money?

Albee: Neil Simon puts in his own money. The theatre is a very risky business. Let other people put their own money on it!

ALAN SCHNEIDER, DIRECTOR

The Lady From Dubuque, 1980
Box and *Quotations from Chairman Mao Tse-Tung,* 1968
A Delicate Balance, 1966
Malcolm, 1966
Tiny Alice, 1964
The Ballad of the Sad Cafe, 1963
Who's Afraid of Virginia Woolf? 1962
The American Dream, 1961
(all premieres)

January 31, 1980

RS: When did you first get the *Lady From Dubuque* script, and what changes were made before the rehearsals began?

Schneider: I got the script in August. I'd never read the previous versions of the script. There had been several. The only changes that Edward made with me before rehearsal were a few changes of words and one or two very small cuts. He doesn't like to rewrite until he gets into rehearsals. And I didn't have any specific things. The only thing that happened was that I had written in the script, in front of the second act, "Is this all a hallucination, possibly?" I remember when he saw that in my script he immediately said, "I've got the answer." He then went and rewrote the ending in which the Lady from Dubuque exited [at the end of the play] and then the guests came in again and restarted the second act. I was happy with the idea, but I wasn't happy with the actual scene. It also diminished the impact of the Lady in terms of not having the curtain fall on *her*. And I spent some time trying to dissuade Edward from this version, but I didn't succeed until a few days before we went into rehearsal, with the help of Miss Worth.

RS: Apparently there was a third act which you never saw.

Schneider: I mean I've only heard this, I have never read it: the old second act ended with the guests grabbing Sam, so you never saw the actual tying up, and then the old third act began where he was found tied up. I am not sure what Edward's point was there in eliminating it. I think it had something to do with the length of time. The first act would have had to be longer than either the second or the third, and that's not a good idea.

RS: I know when you start working you always write down the concept that you articulated for yourself and for the production. Did you do that here? And what was it?

Schneider: It's a play about the nature of reality, I think. I mean illusion and reality. Truth and illusion are the same thing, the nature of it, and how it's defined by our needs, and each person coming to accept that or not accept it. That's what I mean, without going into great detail. I don't remember everything I wrote down; I kept writing it down in different ways for myself. But I kept saying to myself, "It's not about death, and it doesn't matter who Jo's mother is. Jo's mother is whatever is necessary for Jo." And as I said in that *New York Post* thing today, the important thing is how they accept it or don't accept it. Some people can't accept it. Some people don't want to accept it. Some people accept it but don't admit it, and so on. There's also a great musicality in terms of the repetition of themes, from the first act to the second act, which is very deliberate, which nobody pays any attention to, but which I was very aware of. In fact, I tried to do it in the production; then I finally gave up trying to point up the parallels between the two acts. I couldn't do it. I didn't want to punch it. I kept trying not to make the play symbolically heavy or portentous. But it's about reality, about what reality is, how reality is what gets us through.

RS: Similarly, did you articulate some tone and texture for the whole production?

Schneider: Well. You see, I was stuck with this set. I really fought tooth and nail about this set, and I had no way of changing it, except in detail. I did change the floor plan: I couldn't do anything with the old floor plan. I just couldn't do it.

RS: When the stairs were in the center?

Schneider: Yes; it was ridiculous, in my opinion. I think the set is incorrect for this play. I know Edward sees it very clearly as being correct. So I disagreed firmly about this set. I know it's a real house in *his* mind, but it doesn't seem to the audience to be a real house. Even though it's Bauhaus and all that, it seems a kind of abstract, symbolic set. I would have had a normal, nice, suburban interior. Could have used the *Virginia Woolf* set. I want a window, and I want a sense of light and life and living. I almost didn't do the show because of the set. But I wanted to do the show. Partly for the show and partly for Edward. Because I haven't done a play of Edward's in ten years, and it just seemed to me that it was necessary. I felt very good about his coming back to me, not sentimentally, but I mean just in terms of professional respect and so on.

RS: From what I could glean during the rehearsals, you suggested very few changes to Edward, and all the changes seem to have come from him.

Schneider: Well . . . I talked to him every day, almost every day, about clarifying the second act. I thought that second act was constantly being interrupted, ambiguous, and would always deviate from the main drive. I tried like mad to get him to cut the Russian thing. I hated the Russian thing because I thought it had nothing to do with anything. That's not true, but it was totally oblique. I would keep after him on different things. My real contribution came a couple days before we opened, with that reversal, with that transposition of the scene with Oscar in Sam's shirt. I think that was something that was gradually coming to my mind. I felt that the second act simply went up and down too many times, whereas I wanted it to have some rising action. The cuts, the specific cuts, came from him—the desire for cuts came from me. Because he resisted the clarity, originally. He didn't want it to be too clear. But then, when the audience isn't clear, he sees it. He is very sensitive, and he listens to it. And he watches the audience. He's very aware. He cut much more deeply than I would have thought, more deeply in this play than any play he's ever done.

RS: In the past when you worked with him, did he always make cuts during rehearsals?

Schneider: Yes, in all of them. I have eleven pages of *Virginia Woolf*—terrific eleven pages that he cut. He wanted to cut the Bergin speech. I reminded him of that. But he always cuts. I think he realizes that what may be in his mind doesn't communicate. For example, the real tip-off to me is that he finally cut all that stuff on the sofa with Jo and Elizabeth [toward the close of the play], which Irene wanted him to cut from the first rehearsal. I kept saying to him, "I don't understand this, why the hell is it repeated?" Then he would say, "It isn't repeated. It's different." Then he would explain to me why it's different. But I would say, "But the audience doesn't get that." Then he'd say, "Yes, they will." And then, of course, they didn't. Then he would cut it. But Irene's instincts, when she said, "We've done all that," were right. He catches on. Edward has a fantastic mind. He thinks very cogently. He has an abstract mind, and he has a conceptual mind. He has a philosophical mind, and he has an artistic mind. All those different kinds of temperaments are operating, and he gives the audience much more credit. He's reluctant to kowtow to the audience. But I said to him many times, on this play you are not kowtowing, but you've got to make it clear to the audience—they're not going to work at it the way you and I are. I would say to him over and over again. That's just an idea—it's an idea. You must deal with the human situation. The idea is not enough. So he cut much more than I thought he would.

RS: Therein lies part of the success of your collaboration with him, because of your special emphasis on behavior.

Schneider: It was very tough for him—it must have been tough for him—because he wanted to direct. He had me more as a kind of intermediary. I mean he behaved much more compassionately towards me in that situation than I really expected. I thought I'd have to fight hard, tooth and nail. He was marvelous about that. I mean he didn't like all my blocking, and he kept some of it. I gave in on when I didn't really feel it was necessary. But some of it I held on to, and he eventually accepted it. I mean, obviously, he sees it differently. He wrote it, and he sees it a certain way. But whenever he was dissatisfied, I would try to understand why he was dissatisfied. If he could tell me, then I would deal with it. But not if he couldn't tell me why, or if he simply said he didn't like it or it's not right. If someone says, "It's not right," I don't know what's not right about it. But I think he feels reasonably redeemed in terms of the production. It isn't that much different than it would have been, let's say, in his mind.

RS: What do you think of Edward directing his own plays?

Schneider: I think it's bad for a playwright to direct his own plays. I'll tell you why. Arthur Miller once said it very well—he said, "When a playwright directs, he directs the words. When a director directs, he directs the actors."

RS: Doesn't Beckett direct his own work well? You have seen several of his productions.

Schneider: Well. If the actors give themselves totally to him, which they are in some societies more apt to do, as in Germany. It works okay because Beckett has a very clear idea, and Beckett's plays are more abstract, anyhow. When they don't give themselves to him, as in the American production of *Godot* in Brooklyn, where Beckett's assistant came and simply reproduced it—to me, it was a total, complete disaster. It got good reviews, but I don't care. Absolutely without a heart. Sam is so specific in his demands that in effect the actors are irrelevant. They are simply puppets. I wouldn't say that to him, but I think that that's so. It would not work with American actors.

RS: But Rick Clutchey is American.

Schneider: Rick Clutchey has done *Krapp's Last Tape,* that Sam directed. Rick is such a lousy actor—excuse me. Everyone who has seen that production—and who was objective and was not simply trying to please Sam—has told me it was an awful production. But Sam likes Rick because of all that Sam Quentin stuff, and he lets him get away with murder. That's what he does. Sam becomes intensely loyal to everybody, including me. . . . It's hard to know.

RS: Can you say something about rhythm in Albee's work?

Schneider: Rhythm's the hardest word in the theatre to define, next to reality. The word "reality," I don't know. Rhythm is just where the form and the content serve each other, I suppose. When Edward says the rhythm isn't right, I never know what he means. When I say the rhythm isn't right, then it's either too fast and I can't understand it, or it's too slow and it doesn't seem to be spontaneous. So, I suppose, that's what I mean. But basically, you know when it's off. You know when it jangles. It's like music. It needs to somehow seem unified, or coherent or building or organic.

RS: But is it largely oral for you?

Schneider: For me it's a relationship of the life of the character with the circumstances. To me speech is the result of life. It creates the life or it stimulates the life or it influences the life, but it's not, alone, the life. For Edward, it's entirely oral. But when Edward goes downstairs and listens to the play over the squawk box, I'm sorry, that's not enough. It's not enough.

RS: I was doing that the other day, and all you hear is sound going in a certain pattern.

Schneider: Yeah. Even if you remember where they are and all that, it's not the same. But my gesture to you on "it's not the same" has something to do with the way I'm saying it. If you just *hear* "it's not the same," it can mean a hundred different things. Rhythm has to do with the life, the beat, the heart of the scene. Not just the words. To Edward, the words may be more the heart of the scene. It doesn't mean that I don't respect the words. But they're not all there is.

Who's Afraid of Virginia Woolf?
(Alley Theatre, 1990)

EDWARD ALBEE

January 6, 1990

RS: You have spoken of the importance of subtext in the rehearsal process. Did you reexamine the subtext in *Who's Afraid of Virginia Woolf?* prior to your rehearsals in Los Angeles?

Albee: No. I don't prepare that. When I'm doing a play that I've written, I just say it, and the subtext comes to my consciousness. I'm already aware of it.

RS: Did you work on the actors' getting to understand the subtext?

Albee: Oh yes, of course, when they don't; but if they're very bright, they do to begin with. Subtext is more important than text, even, sometimes. So long as they understand subtext. I'm trying to think of one specific thing with Glenda Jackson in *Virginia Woolf* that she didn't understand. Now, I can't remember the very specifics of it. One of the things that I tried to emphasize in the production and finally got Glenda to do—and I'm getting Carol to do here for the most part—is to understand that what they're doing is exorcising a metaphor. Something they both realize is a metaphor, and that it is not the death of a real child. There is a distinction between the death of a metaphor and the death of a real child. And the play for me is more touching and more chilling if it is the death of the metaphor. That's one of the things I'm trying to emphasize in this production. And I think I am getting the through-line of the exorcism of the fantasy-child metaphor a little clearer this time.

RS: Have you seen productions where the intellectual experience is totally absent?

Albee: Yes, I have, and I don't like them at all. They're terrible.

RS: Where was the emphasis in the original production that Alan Schneider directed?

Albee: I thought it was a little bit toward the emotional. Just a little bit too much.

RS: Compared to your present production?

Albee: You see, that production got criticized by a couple of critics . . . I remember Walter Kerr saying he couldn't believe that a couple as intelligent as George and Martha could believe that they had a child. They never *did* believe it. So either he intentionally misunderstood, or the production led him to misunderstand. So that's one of the reasons that I started directing this play: to correct that misinterpretation of the nature of the play. Now it may be the play that way—not my way—is a more wrenching emotional experience. I don't know. I tend to think not. I think the mind and the gut together are better involved than one at the expense of the other.

RS: Compared to the 1962 production, have you cut the playing time much more here?

Albee: I don't remember what those timings were. I think this may be a little brisker.

RS: Reviews of your 1976 production mentioned how much faster everything seemed.

Albee: Seemed. I don't imagine that the difference was more than two or three minutes in each act. But that adds up. This production is just as brisk as the one in 1976.

RS: The 1976 production was much brisker than Alan's 1962 production.

Albee: Well, yes. That's true.

RS: And funnier, too.

Albee: But none of the lines were changed.

RS: Talking of changes . . . you made several changes in your text for this production.

Albee: Oh, very few. The major change that I made was cutting out the reference to the child in the first scene of the play, which is unnecessary. The other cuts I've made here—what? A word here, two or three words there. That's all. Just for rhythms.

RS: One change does seem to be a big one. Martha's "Truth and illusion, George; you don't know the difference" has become "Truth and illusion, George; you know the difference." Correspondingly, George's "No; but we must carry on as though we did" has become "Yes; but we must carry on as though we did not."

Albee: Oh, well, that's because I wrote it incorrectly to begin with.

RS: How come you didn't notice it earlier?

Albee: I don't know. A mind lapse.

RS: Not a change of mind?

Albee: No. No, no. No. No, no. It's just that I miswrote myself—I didn't put it down correctly.

RS: In your discussion with the actors about it, you kept saying, "That's a very minor matter. That's a very minor matter." Do you really think so?

Albee: No, it's a major matter. But what they meant by "major," they wanted to go back to doing it wrong.

RS: Why did you cut George's comment "What will happen to the tax deduction? Has anyone figured that out yet?" when he speaks of the time when people will make babies in test tubes?

Albee: The playwright got better! Logically, couples with children would get tax deductions no matter how their babies were made.

RS: You also deleted the exchange between George and Martha where she suddenly and flagrantly denies Nick and Honey's existence in their living room but then without explanation accepts their presence.

Albee: It made Martha too unreasonable.

RS: Did you wish to stress Martha's loquaciousness by substituting "mouth" for "nose" in George's retort "In my mind, Martha, you are buried in cement, right up to your neck. No . . . right up to your nose . . . that's much quieter?"

Albee: Yes, and it makes it clearer and nicer.

RS: Why did you cut one of George's two identical announcements, "Pow!!! You're dead! Pow! You're dead!" when he pulls the trigger of his fake Japanese gun?

Albee: Once is enough. Besides, I didn't want the actors to get any ideas!

S: Did you think the cuts in Mike Nichols's film version of *Virginia Woolf* were major ones?

Albee: Yes, of course. They took out the whole historical-political argument of the play. They took out the business about science and a number of other things that the play happens to be about.

RS: When directing this 1962 script in 1989–1990, did you reconsider things?

Albee: No, I don't consciously do that. I've not tried to update this play. I don't think people walked in a different way in the sixties than they do in the eighties. Or even thought in that much of a different way.

RS: In many ways Nick's values resemble those associated with Yuppies in the eighties.

Albee: All good literature is supposed to anticipate the future. True; it does, you know. What I was suggesting was that people who are wise enough to untrick themselves may be better off. I think the least self-deception that people can live with, the better. Well, what does change is audience perception. But you can't go around trying to second-guess audience perception, because you distort your work.

RS: Because of changed audience perception, when I taught *Zoo Story* at the University of California at Santa Cruz, I had to defend Jerry and his viewpoint.

Albee: Well, of course. We're a nation of conformists now. I find that self-deception leads not only to personal trouble but to political malaise and to social irresponsibility. The self-deception that this country has been dealing in for many years now is preferring to be lied to by political leaders, preferring to be conned by short-term values. We may find ourselves in a much greater state of decline than many people realize now. Audiences, when they were a little freer with themselves, used to think *The American Dream* was very funny. But now you do *The American Dream* for a middle-aged audience, and they sit there in silent hostility.

RS: Hostile towards the playwright?

Albee: They don't like examining themselves any more. They get very angry about it. Shocking to me.

RS: Why is George so angry at Martha's story about his career—more angry than he is when she mentions the child?

Albee: Attrition. Time, time, time, time. It's something—the career—about him being a flop and a failure and not living up to . . . This is something that she—every time she gets a few drinks in her and a little audience—she starts on it. After twenty-three years you get fairly tired of it. You just can't stand it anymore.

RS: Still, I was comparing that anger to the anger that I expected and the anguish I expected when Martha reveals the son to the guests.

Albee: Well, George's involvement with the son has never been as emotional as Martha's has. Neither of them literally believes it, but Martha slips into believing it, probably because she's a woman. Women and their relation to children, their wombs, and the whole thing. Her involvement with the son is more personal and emotional than George's is.

RS: But George's greater passion about his career throws me off because I thought the emotional focus would remain on the betrayal of the closely held, private arrangement.

Albee: That's interesting. I must look at that. Maybe I'm doing something wrong.

RS: The import of Martha's disclosure seems to get submerged under George's fury.

Albee: Mm. I'll look at that. Maybe I have changed my mind about a few things over the years.

RS: In the opening scene, when Martha mentions that Honey, the guest they are expecting, has small hips, John Lithgow used to add with some relish, "Oh, God!" It got laughs. It's a small joke, but I'm sure you didn't eliminate it without some reason. Why did you cut that out? Do you think there's a lack of logic?

Albee: I think it's a cheap joke. It's a cheap joke. And also it doesn't make any sense. Because George—

RS: George says he likes "everything in proportion," and he is not attracted to Honey when she arrives.

Albee: Yes. And he does not like women without hips. Martha has hips. Martha's ample. It's illogical. John Lithgow and Glenda Jackson liked it. It was a cheap joke, and they liked it. John and Glenda also barked at each other, "Woolf! Woolf!" on George's "You'll crack your big teeth." I hated that too. You have to give them little things every once in a while.

RS: You were thinking aloud about how George knows that Martha has been talking about him, when he returns with the liquor from off stage. I think George knows because he comes in on Martha's line about him, "along come George."

Albee: If he's heard that coming in, then it's all right. Let's see: "But then George came along . . . along come George," and George reenters. I guess he knows. I guess he knows. I guess it's clear. I believe in being my own devil's advocate from time to time.

RS: If you want to be objective when directing your own work.

Albee: Exactly.

RS: After Martha's great howl, "NOOOOOOoooooo," at the finality of George's decision to kill the child, in this production George tells Nick, "She'll be all right now," I think rather quickly.

Albee: I gave him a note two days ago not to do that so quickly.

RS: It kept happening.

Albee: Yes. I'll remind him. Thank you for reminding me.

RS: Such a quick comment suggests much more premeditation on George's part.

Albee: Yes, it does. I should give him that note almost immediately.

RS: I've often wondered about the reference to Crazy Billy, "some little boy about seventy," when George announces the telegram regarding their son's death.

Albee and His Collaborators on Staging Albee | 219

Albee: Oh, a friend of mine, Bill Flanagan, the composer; he and I worked at Western Union together, and I used to always kid him about how much older he was than me. So, a "little boy about seventy." It's just a private joke.

RS: Another question about a topical reference and possibly subtext. George tells Nick that the abstract painting in their living room was done by "some Greek with a mustache Martha attacked one night." Is that a reference to the Greek-American artist you know?

Albee: Theodoros Stamos.

RS: Do you own any of his works?

Albee: Yes. A couple.

RS: And what was the subtext you suggested to George? During a rehearsal you told him that one evening Martha went to that painter's home and kept . . . ?

Albee: Kept putting the make on him, and then he gave her a painting to get rid of her.

RS: Why did you introduce a picture of Mahatma Gandhi?

Albee: Well. . . .

RS: Why Gandhi's picture on the living room bookshelf?

Albee: It occurred to me that George and Martha are two people who, in their growing up in the 1940s, in their innocent liberalism, admired both Roosevelt and Gandhi very much.

RS: I sense a degree of pacifism in George. Though he doesn't say it, it's probably because of his pacifism that he didn't go to fight in the war. He stayed back and ran the history department.

Albee: I don't know why he didn't go. Maybe he was a conscientious objector. It never occurred to me. That's interesting. You do not find Gandhi worthy of admiration?

RS: Oh, I do, yes.

Albee: Yes. Well, I do too.

RS: Certainly. I was just curious—after all your Oriental jokes!

Albee: That Oriental joke is meant to be intentionally in bad taste.

RS: On George's part, of course.

Albee: Yes. It's meant to be a parody of the sort of barroom, you know, locker room talk that jocks do together.

RS: How can Honey recite the Latin mass for the dead when she grew up in a fundamentalist home?

Albee: I don't understand that. I don't know why. There are depths to that girl that I haven't figured out yet.

RS: All throughout the rehearsals, it seems to me, you gave many more directions to the actor who plays George than to the actor who plays Martha.

Albee: Well, George is on stage almost all the time during the entire play. He has many more lines. He also controls the psychological arc of the play. He is in control of the entire arc of the play the entire time. And therefore I have to be more concerned with making sure that his performance doesn't deviate from my intention, more than I have to be with the other actors. Last night, the notes that I gave him, I want to talk to him about them again because I didn't do that quite as well as I might have. It's just that more can go wrong. And it has to be more tightly controlled. I think the notes I try to give to all of them are fundamental notes as to the nature of characterization. And also I try to give people notes when I see danger signals. When I see they're doing things that I know are going to get them in trouble later in the play. Or distort the character. Now, Bruce Gray [George] is a highly inventive, highly shrewd, and highly skilled actor. And therefore he's more apt to go astray.

RS: And Carol Mayo Jenkins [Martha], in contrast, is . . . ?

Albee: Well, no . . . There is less opportunity for Martha to go astray than there is for George. Let's put it that way.

RS: It must be so since you are saying it, but it is surprising, nonetheless.

Albee: Also they're very different kinds of actors. Carol sets performance. We see the gold of the performance. Bruce is constantly shifting his characterization. And now he's gone to the point where I have to bring him back. He's gone too far. He's become baroque and mannered and artificial. And I have to bring him back to truth. And every actor—no two actors work the same way. No two actors work at the same speed. No two actors have the same way of working. So you have to work differently.

RS: Why no rehearsals the last three days [i.e., before one evening technical rehearsal and two evening performances for invited audiences]?

Albee: There comes a certain point in rehearsal where, if you think the actors know pretty much where you want them to be and what you want them to be doing, you have to let them play the role for a while. And play with the audience. And then, after a few days of watching them with the audience, then you can see whether they're going in the right direction or not. You can overrehearse in theory. I mean, theoretical rehearsal should stop at a certain point, and real rehearsal should start.

RS: What are real rehearsals?

Albee: Well . . .

RS: Rehearsals after they've played in front of invited and preview audiences?

Albee: Yes. That's a different kind of rehearsal.

RS: So you plan to do more work.

Albee: I'll do some work next week [with three scheduled previews]. I'll do some work after they open, too.

RS: I haven't noticed you rehearse short scenes in painstaking detail, orchestrating every element. I know you like to give actors general intention notes, and you expect them to come up with the specifics. You used to do that in 1978 when I first saw you; these are more experienced actors, by and large, and you can do that more safely. However, sometimes I wonder whether detailed scene work might not benefit this production.

Albee: All you tell an actor when you do that, ultimately, is how *you* would do the scene. That doesn't tell them how *they* should do the scene. Then you're asking them to imitate rather than be. That's a last resort. If you can't get it any other way, then you do that. But you've noticed that I *am* very specific, when they miss a beat, or I tell them to wait a beat before they say a line, or accent this word rather than that word. That's very specific stuff.

RS: I understand you give specific notes as well, but I was thinking of sustained moment-to-moment work on selected segments. After the two invited audiences, too, you haven't addressed matters of tempo, speed, and so on.

Albee: I didn't find them shifting all that much. I did tell them that the top of three was slow, which it was again. I think they generally know what they're supposed to be doing. Generally.

RS: You've worked with other directors—Alan Schneider, Peter Hall, Franco Zeffirelli—when they've staged your plays. Did you come across closer scene work in their rehearsals?

Albee: No, not really.

RS: Not really? Do you have an overall rhythm that you are working for?

Albee: I must. I must. Yes, of course. I mean each two-minute section has its rhythms. And these rhythms combine to give the whole rhythm of an act, and the three acts give the rhythm of the whole piece.

RS: Do you build towards certain tempos . . .

Albee: Most you establish at the very beginning. Now you must remember, with these actors here, they sat in from the very first day of rehearsal with Glenda Jackson and John Lithgow. And I spent a lot of time with them the first week discussing character motivation. Everything that I didn't have to discuss here because those actors were there.

RS: You will remove that carpet in the living room?

Albee: I would love to, but I can't find another one. I don't know what to do about it.

RS: You could replace it with the smaller rug that you've hung near the bay window. Just have that on the floor and have nothing near the window.

Albee: It's quite possible. I may do that. I mean, I hate that carpet. It's terrible. It's dreadful. Maybe if they could dye the whole thing. I'll talk to them about that.

RS: Instead of the yellow plastic stool you could perhaps use an ordinary wooden stool with its seat covered with a piece from the third rug, which is not being fully used?

Albee: I can't cut that; we're renting that rug! We can't afford to buy it. That yellow stool is being changed to a green of some sort, which I'll probably hate too.

RS: Do you find the reflection in the bay window somewhat distracting? Couldn't they spray something on the panes?

Albee: I gave a technical note for that to be gotten out somehow. They haven't been able to, yet. Maybe it cannot be gotten rid of. May have to spray something?

RS: While directing, were you tempted to include a few asides to the audience?

Albee: In this play? No. It's an absolutely naturalistic play. None of my naturalistic plays has direct addresses to the audience. It's only the stylized ones.

RS: I thought there was an aside phase in your career when you introduced asides into earlier texts while directing, as you did with a few plays I saw you stage a few years ago.

Albee: In some of my plays, maybe eight or ten of them, people speak to the audience. But those are mostly the stylized plays. It doesn't happen in the naturalistic ones. This is a naturalistic play. All the . . . classical . . . unities and everything. The whole thing.

RS: Why don't you write another one with classical unities and all that?

Albee: I have. It's called *Marriage Play*.

RS: From observing you rehearse *Who's Afraid of Virginia Woolf?* I could deduce some of your directorial ideals. When you teach, what kinds of goals and principles of directing do you posit?

Albee: You certainly should have a vision of the way you think the play wants to be performed when you start directing it. Yet, at the same time, you must also be ready to shift when you find that the play is somewhat other than you imagined it, or there are other values that you hadn't seen. But you must have an overall vision of the piece. With any production, 90 percent of it is casting.

Albee and His Collaborators on Staging Albee |

If you cast properly, if you cast correctly—intelligent, gifted actors—your job is so much easier. You don't have to do the line-by-line thing. Directing, of course, is a lot of knowing how to work with actors. The first two weeks are basically subtext work, so actors really understand why the character behaves the way the character does in a certain section.

RS: What about visual matters? What about rhythm?

Albee: Well, there's always a visual thing. You have stage pictures that you create in your mind. You do have rhythms that you're after. There's tension, release of tension, passive and active moments. And you've got to populate the stage properly in all of those, in all of those times. There's a tie-in between the visual picture and the psychology of the piece, of course, always. Who is moving? Who is standing still? Who's sitting? The tempo of the speeches. The intentions. All of that has to be put together. So it is a combination of music and painting and literature at the same time. You have all three of them.

John Ottavino, actor

Nick, *Who's Afraid of Virginia Woolf?* Alley Theatre, 1990
Young Man, *The Sandbox,* Vienna's English Theatre, 1986
Intern, *The Death of Bessie Smith,* Alley Theatre, 1985

January 6, 1990

RS: Did Albee revise his text much for *Death of Bessie Smith* at the Alley?

Ottavino: He said at the beginning of *Bessie Smith* that he usually doesn't rewrite, he'll just cut. He made several very small cuts, he didn't say why. He did say at one point, in another situation, when someone wanted to cut out a phrase, that it screws up the rhythm. "It just doesn't sound right to me. It sounds right to me when I put that phrase there."

RS: What was your impression of the *Virginia Woolf* rehearsals in Los Angeles, where you were understudy for Nick?

Ottavino: I remember thinking that Edward was directing the hell out of this play. I understood the play most clearly. I was sitting there thinking, there's not a word he said that I don't agree with. But there was one thing that I am not sure I agreed with. He sat and spoke with Glenda [Jackson] and John [Lithgow] about the nature of this imaginary child as an extended metaphor. That affected both of them: they cued into his rationality, that these people are not mad and deluded. But they lost their original feeling of a great, crushing, emotional blow. I am not sure if this was a mistake or not. He also treated

Glenda maybe with more kid gloves. But you're talking about a consummate actress. She was able to deliver anything he asked for.

RS: Does Edward allow you enough creative room as an actor?

Ottavino: He's a very generous director because he has such confidence in his vision: he knows the core of his play; he has all the keys to each play. As long as you're not violating that, you get your freedom. He has tremendous respect for good actors. The best actors in his plays are the actors who know how to take care of themselves, know how to do their homework, have experience, and come in very prepared. The more you give him, the more you'll get back. But if you don't give him anything, he feels, rightfully so, that he's not there to teach you how to act. And he's not here to hold your hand when you go through your emotional memory. You're a pro, that's your job, go do it at home, and bring it in.

ROBERT HILL, LIGHTING DESIGNER

Who's Afraid of Virginia Woolf? 1990

January 5, 1990

RS: What kind of lighting did Edward require in *Who's Afraid of Virginia Woolf?*

Hill: One of the first few things I did was that I talked to Martin Aronstein, who had lit the show in Los Angeles and had also worked with Edward quite a bit, about what Edward had wanted with the show. Marty said, "Remember, Edward is very interested in keeping one look throughout the entire show." He didn't want any variance at all. Once the lights were up he very much wanted one state of lighting for the first act, the second act, and the third act. Towards the end, for the sunrise, he wanted a change but not a very big one. It was very much the idea that the sunrise was more just a glimmer of light than a sunrise. In L.A. Marty did some very subtle cues, where he moved the light around a little bit. Here in Houston, I decided basically not to do that, but to basically get us into a look for the beginning of the acts and then just sort of ride up some of the selective fill, the front fill, and up some more once we were in that very, very slow fade. I think people cue things more these days. But if you look at it, there's really no reason, or any logical reason, why there should be heavy cuing in the shows.

RS: What you're saying is true only at one level. But what about mood and trying to control those kinds of things?

Hill: He's more interested in lighting the reality of the room, which wouldn't change. Once you have this look established, you wouldn't be lighting the mood or the emotion of the play. I think he's much more interested in letting the actors take care of all of that work, rather than trying to enhance it with lighting.

RS: Edward obviously requested realistic lighting for the home interior. Were there times when he said, "This is wrong" or "This is right"?

Hill: He didn't want too many shadows for the actors to go into. There are some darker edges around the set. When we were doing the sunrise, I sort of over-estimated what the morning glow was. I was going a little bit further than a glimmer of sunlight. But he said, "No, no, no, that's not right." He had a very firm idea of what is right on that.

RS: What's the reason for the central arch and the staircase being lit? It looks very nice, even romantic. Since he's talking naturalism, did he offer a realistic explanation?

Hill: Edward said that they left a light on up the stairway and in the arch. He wanted the rest of everything sort of dark, very dark—only a central light coming through the arch, so that you have a sort of light against dark when the audience first sees the set. As the play begins, the door opens, we get this dramatic image of George and Martha silhouetted in the dimly lit doorway. Then there is an explosion of light when George and Martha begin to turn on lamps in their home—a very high, startling contrast from darkness to light. There are parts of the play that are startling: why shouldn't those few light cues be startling as well?

Albee Directs Beckett

EDWARD ALBEE

February 12, 1991

RS: I must confess, I did tell that *New York Times* writer that I was surprised by the clutter on the set.

Albee: This is *Krapp's Last Tape!* I've noticed as I get older, and my mind becomes more soup-like, that I keep things out and around so I can remember to do them. I tidy up and put things away, and I lose contact with them completely. This might also be true to a far greater extent for Krapp.

RS: Could you explain that a little more?

Albee: If I have something I have to do, like a whole group of telephone calls to make, if I put them all neatly on one piece of paper and put it nice and neatly in my desk I'll never make the telephone calls. I'm a very busy person, and if they're out, I will see them: "Aha, I have to do this." And I notice that I keep more things out all the time, and I'm sure this is true of Krapp also. So he finds things, knows where they are. I'm just puzzled that you were puzzled at the many things on the set . . .

RS: Of course, no specific stage direction or textual reference in the play indicates an uncluttered stage.

Albee: It does not. [*Pause.*] I think we're a little overcluttered at the moment.

RS: That was my concern.

Albee: You should see it today. The detritus has given birth to detritus. And I plan to unclutter it a little bit.

RS: But the thrust of that question—a puzzlement, as you kindly put it—was about stylistic appropriateness for a Beckett play. As you said on the first day of rehearsals, Beckett is essences.

Albee: But that doesn't mean that the environment should be unnatural—unnatural to the character.

RS: No, no. But a "natural environment" doesn't necessarily mean a naturalistic environment.

Albee: Krapp's Last Tape is a naturalistic play. Absolutely naturalistic, as naturalistic as any play you could ever see.

RS: I suppose it's a matter of—

Albee: No, no, just look at it. It is a naturalistic play about a man who is playing tapes back. It is a real home; these are real tapes; he's a real man.

RS: Would you, then, have preferred to stage it in a box set?

Albee: No, this is fine. A box set is not naturalistic.

RS: It goes a step towards total naturalism.

Albee: I don't think it does at all. You've just imagined walls here. The actor is imagining the walls.

RS: Then why the jagged edges in the two sides of the stage?

Albee: That's the set designer. Don't talk to me about that.

RS: You accepted it. You're the director.

Albee: I may. I'll accept it at this point. I'm not sure yet.

RS: Well, talking of naturalism, which, of course, is a historical term apart from an aesthetic one, when Alan Schneider was directing *The Lady From Dubuque*, for example, that was set in a home. Do you consider that a naturalistic play?

Albee: Yes.

RS: But you were not very happy with all the clutter Alan wanted on that stage, so much so that—

Albee: Because *those* people living in—

RS: I had anticipated that answer!

Albee: Those people living in that environment had the kind of design they had— the Bauhaus style they had—you don't have clutter in Bauhaus. That's why—

RS: Even after parties and during parties?

Albee: But you don't. You would not have as much clutter as you have in *Krapp's Last Tape*. Naturalistic clutter is O.K. in a naturalistic play. Yes. But I don't believe I'm finally going to end up with everything that's onstage now. I will remind you that what you are seeing now is not what you would see if you were here for the opening.

RS: Yes. I'll be here for the previews.

Albee: Don't even assume that what you see in the previews is what you're going to see by the time we open.

RS: Oh, God. You mean I've wasted my time here.

Albee: No, not necessarily. But I make changes right on through. I made some profound changes in some staging yesterday. Anyhow, I think Krapp keeps a lot of clutter around.

RS: That I understand. But could you not suggest that without so much clutter?

Albee: What do you mean? Brechtian? Brechtian clutter?

RS: Beckettian clutter!

Albee: But that would be naturalistic.

RS: Only if you insisted on it being a naturalistic play that must be done naturalistically.

Albee: It is a naturalistic play as far as I'm concerned. Now you notice there is no clutter in *Ohio Impromptu*. Also I was interested in contrast: the two plays, the two manners.

RS: Why did you choose these two plays? It's a matter of taste, of course, but what kind of things did you have in mind when picking these particular plays?

Albee: Well, I began by persuading the Alley Theatre. They were derelict in their responsibilities . . . two Beckett productions in thirty-one years! I mean, ridiculous. And I wanted to do some plays that weren't as well known. I knew I was going to be directing down here in this small theatre. *Godot* and *Endgame* are quite well known. They're done a lot. *Happy Days* is one of my favorite Beckett plays, very difficult to do. Unless you have a revolve here slowly in the mountain, or have a track and revolve mound. Which you could do, which would be interesting. I'd like to do that sometime. That could be done down here, no problem. And I thought these two plays are not as well known. *Embers* crossed my mind but, nah. And my great affection for *Krapp's Last Tape*. My personal experience. Sentimental attachment too: *The Zoo Story* in Berlin and all that [Albee's first play was staged on a double bill with *Krapp's Last Tape* in Berlin in 1958.] And originally I had planned to do *Krapp's Last Tape* and *Eh Joe*.

RS: The television play, right?

Albee: Yes. Well, I've seen it on stage with a television camera and four projectors. But then it turned out the budget would not permit, I would have to have a projector, a big projector, at each vomitorium and project, a big screen, rear projection. Prohibitively expensive. And since I had seen and admired *Ohio Impromptu*—

RS: You saw the first production?

Albee: It was the Alan Schneider production. I was quite impressed by that. And I said, "I want to do that one."

RS: How many minutes did that last, do you remember? Reviews seemed to say it lasted fourteen minutes.

Albee: It lasted longer than logic would have it, and I don't know why. If they had slowed it down even more, it may well have . . .

RS: There may have been many more silences, prolonged silences.

Albee: It could have been. But I don't know why, and I can't understand how. I know the next question: why thrice?

RS: Why thrice?

Albee: All right, I will go through it the way my mind works. Why thrice, eh? Well, I think I'm quite respectful to Samuel Beckett in my admiration for the work. I believe the only time I've ever altered a play for production was when Lanford Wilson gave me permission to cut twenty minutes' worth.

RS: I'm told that you cut it and then you asked for permission.

Albee: No, sir.

RS: O.K.

Albee: I don't believe so.

RS: But you did call him from Vienna.

Albee: I talked to him in New York during rehearsal when we rehearsed that in New York. I made the cuts in New York. I knew the cuts I wanted to make. I made some experiments with cuts to see if it worked better. I discovered that it did. Lanford wanted to meet with me and said, "Show me the cuts that you want to make." I could only say, "Well, I haven't made them yet, but I think I want to." So I knew what cuts I wanted to make, so that if he wanted to meet, wanted me to show him the cuts, I would have them. I would even have been able to show him a run-through with cuts. But I did not make the cuts until Lanford said, "Oh, Edward, I trust you. You go ahead and make them." And I did. It turned out that they were the cuts that I had planned to make. But that made it official, O.K. I could make the cuts. So, I do respect the playwright's text, and I think it's my job as a director to represent a play as accurately and as clearly as I possibly can. But I think that I've done that in *Ohio Impromptu*.

There are a number of intellectual reasons as to why; it is an intellectual play, of intellectual value. I don't think that what I have done is an afterthought. It is, what, eight minutes, eight and a half minutes, it goes by very quickly. I wanted the audience to have the opportunity to dwell on it, brood on it, while it's occurring. And then I started thinking more, and the Listener and the Reader are the same person. That would allow twice.

RS: Once to read and once to listen.

Albee: Yes. Since it's the same person. And I have seen Beckett's plays before done twice. And then I added the third time through because I thought that was a logical extension—because they are the same person. A logical extension of the repetition.

RS: You have to clarify how that is logical?

Albee: That amplifies for the audience the fact that they are the same person.

RS: Why a black actor and a white actor?

Albee: Now as to white and black, black and white. Black is not a color, white is not a color. They are identical. Black and white are identical. Matter and anti-matter are identical. Why not do that?

RS: But in terms of race?

Albee: No. I don't see a black man on that stage, nor a white man. I don't see it. I'd like to think, and I—especially, I would think—the wigs, the lighting, the non-naturalistic quality of what's happening there. I don't think that they see a black man and a white man. Now, look, there are some people who see a black man and that trails with all sorts of terrible stuff. And this happens with others, too—Japanese people come in and people see and associate certain things. I'm sure it happens with people from India too. I'm sure people from India see somebody else and feel exactly the same way. But I don't see a black man on stage there in this. I don't see a black person. I see black. Black and white are identical.

RS: Can you explain that a little more? Comment on that? What do you mean?

Albee: Neither is a color. White is the absence of all color. Black is the presence of all color. And they become non. Now there is a color. They become non. And opposites are mirror images. You can think of it as a mirror image if you like. They become the same thing.

RS: Also, all of Beckett is full of the interplay of black and white, and light and dark.

Albee: Yes.

RS: Including *Krapp*.

Albee: And that seemed an absolutely natural thing to want to do.

RS: I think it works. I will grant you that. You know, you don't notice the race of the black actor.

Albee: I don't. I don't notice the black man there.

RS: The focus is more, it seems to me, almost emblematic of opposites.

Albee: Yes, exactly.

RS: May I turn the light on so that I can read my questions?

Albee: That would be a good idea. You seem to have read mine. After all these years, why not?

[*Long pause.*] I was able to accommodate my worry that the play would just go right past the audience. So I was glad to be able to justify what I should do to make the audience listen more carefully. As I say, amplification, rather than distortion. I was happy to be able to find a way to do that. Now, there are going to be some people who are going to say, "It's the same thing over and over again. My God!" But you know there are people like that, nothing to be done about it. I think I'm giving the play a fairer shake than it would have on Broadway.

RS: Would you, then, perhaps do it in New York?

Albee: Well, it depends on how happy I am with this. Normally, I'm perfectly happy with what we're doing. If I ever get the exact right balance that I want. The actors are still working on it.

RS: Any play of yours that you have seen with black and white actors?

Albee: I've seen *The Zoo Story* done with black and white actors.

RS: Who was black, Jerry or Peter?

Albee: I've seen both. You know there's an upper middle class of both—black business people in New York. I've seen Mrs. Barker in *The American Dream* performed by a black actress. I can conceive of the Young Man being performed by a black actor.

RS: And a black actor as Grandma in *The Sandbox*.

Albee: Sure. I went to a seminar at Julliard a few weeks ago. A young black actor there started talking about casting blacks in theoretically white roles. And he would not accept the fact that the more naturalistic the play, the more difficult it is to accommodate this. I tried to point out to him—how would Martha played by a black actor work in *Who's Afraid of Virginia Woolf?* I would like to cast a black actress, but that would instantly raise a lot of questions, since it's a totally naturalistic play. Is this a black college? Do we have a black president of a white college? Not very likely. Is it a black college? Then why is there all this white faculty around? And I started bringing up the fact that the more stylized a play, the easier it would be to do such a casting. But he wouldn't accept that anyway.

RS: No?

Albee: No, of course not. He was a militant.

RS: I have my own explanation for your decision about *Ohio Impromptu*. Doing *Ohio Impromptu* thrice encapsulates your work as a playwright-director. As a playwright, you won't change a text you respect, but as a director, you wish to create—not consciously, but simply working as a creative person when you're directing. I thought the solution, therefore, was brilliant. You don't change the text—you replay it with alternating black and white actors. That's why you did it.

Albee: Probably some practical reasons in there too.

RS: Yes. I thought about that, though not in a crass way.

Albee: Eight minutes? That's it?! Well, you know, that's part of it. I realized after I said I wanted to do that play. I said to myself, "Oh my God!"

RS: That's quite a money maker!

Albee: Eight minutes. How can I possibly do this?

Marriage Play

MARK WRIGHT, STAGE MANAGER

Marriage Play, Alley Theatre, 1992

Who's Afraid of Virginia Woolf? Mark Taper Forum, 1989; Broadway, 1976 and 1962

Seascape, Broadway, 1975

A Delicate Balance, Broadway, 1967

Tiny Alice, Broadway, 1965

January 5, 1992

RS: As Albee's stage manager, what changes have you noticed in his working methods since his directing of *Seascape* in 1975?

Wright: Well, he's much more facile in his ability to communicate with the actors on an actor's terms. Not having been trained as a director, it's something he has had to learn as he's come along. He does it very well. He does it *very* well, indeed. It's not that he wasn't able to communicate before, but he does it better now.

RS: Is it often a drawback if you're not an actor prior to being a director?

Wright: Well, yes. In a sense it is because many playwrights—at least the playwrights I have worked with—at the outset think only in terms of the writing, not in terms of the actor's ability or inability to express. You just don't say, "You walk over stage left and you slap him," or "You walk over stage left, and you kiss him," or "You're angry with him." There's another way of going at an actor to help him get to that point. He's learned to be a director. He's instinctively a playwright, but he has learned over the years to be a director and to deal with those technical things that a director has to deal with. He knows when to seek the advice of people about things which he doesn't know. He knows that he is not omnipotent.

RS: Impressionistically, does Albee give more of those external directions compared to internal, character-driven motivation?

Wright: There is indeed a balance. I don't think he gives more or less, or puts more focus on it. As a matter of fact, he generally allows an actor more freedom to move where he would prefer to move on the stage. You've seen the way he worked with Shirley Knight in *Marriage Play*. She would change a move—not the broad outlines of a move—but she would change things within that move to suit herself, and she would not be consistent each time until she found the right way to do it. He is very generous in allowing that. Many directors are very pragmatic and say, "No, you cross on that word and you end the cross on another word." He's not that way at all.

RS: So he allows actors freedom to explore?

Wright: He is very explicit about what he wants in terms of the characterization. How the actor achieves that is another matter. There are several ways to achieve character, as many ways as there are actors. The first thing to do is to cast properly. The second thing to do is for the director to allow the actor to create the character as best he or she can. Edward gives them that freedom, but he does not allow them to move just wherever they feel like moving and do whatever they feel like doing. They can explore, but within the framework that he is setting up.

RS: And he changes his own framework as he goes along?

Wright: Yes, sure. Another word for the theatre should be change, because everything in the theatre changes. And the text changes also as you're shaping it. You saw today the reaction of one of the actors to a cut he had made. And when the actor explained that the lines were necessary for her, he restored them.

RS: What was that change at the very end of *Marriage Play*?

Wright: It's directorial, but it's also something that could've only come from the playwright. During the last four lines of the play He reaches out his hand,

and She takes it. Now, that's not in the script. It's a glimmer of hope that this couple will move forward to face whatever they have together, although at the same time it's totally possible that they won't.

RS: Compared to other directors, is there an Albee signature to his productions?

Wright: Only to the extent that he, of course, knows the intent that he is after. That's what a good director tries to elicit—to find the intent of the playwright. And since he doesn't have to ask himself what a certain line means, it's much easier for him to help the actors find the intent in the words. I don't think there is a particular signature other than, he does not fill his plays with a great deal of movement. He's much more interested in hearing the words. So there is perhaps less physicality in the work, but that, again, is a question of degree.

RS: As compared to other directors, in the productions he has directed Edward seems to prefer symmetrical stage designs and arrangements.

Wright: I am not sure—this set is somewhat symmetrical, clean and simple.

RS: Since you were stage manager for all three productions of Who's Afraid of Virginia Woolf? how different were Edward's 1976 and 1989 productions physically and visually as compared to Alan's 1962 original staging?

Wright: Well, physically both of them were pretty much the same, because basically we used the same ground plan, the same furniture arrangement. The physical set itself was somewhat different. The difference is in the companies.

RS: Was he, in your view, trying to achieve anything different in his 1976 and 1989 productions?

Wright: No. I would say that in 1962 Schneider was able to achieve, as far as I could tell, most of Edward's intent—you'd have to ask Edward how successful he was. When Edward did it, the variation is obviously in the casting. That '76 production with Colleen Dewhurst and Ben Gazzara was perhaps a more successful production than the Glenda Jackson production, because Miss Jackson was not as vulnerable—didn't have the vulnerability that Colleen Dewhurst had. Colleen was a very strong actress, but you felt that she could be moved, she could be touched. You didn't feel that about Glenda. You felt that Glenda could survive anything. She was perhaps miscast. But that happens to everyone. For the most part, I think the casting has been excellent.

RS: Glenda Jackson seemed a bit mannered.

Wright: She's an English actress, and they tend to be more mannered, I think, than Americans.

RS: But beyond that, too. Did Edward try to get her out of her mannerisms?

Wright: She is very firm in her convictions and stuck by her own interpretation, and we were stuck with that interpretation. John Lithgow was another matter; he made an eminently interesting and a very well-rounded George.

RS: During both the 1976 and 1989 productions Edward relied on you a lot to recall details of the original production.

Wright: Well, only to recall certain things in the staging that he had liked, which he recreated—but not exactly the same way. I was helpful in remembering the road map that we used, that's about it.

RS: These things get exaggerated in retelling.

Wright: That's right, they do indeed. Each director is his own man, and Edward certainly is his own man. Regardless of what had happened before, if he saw something new that was happening, he was very quick to not only accept that, but to use it.

RS: You worked with Alan a lot more than you have worked with Edward. How different would an Alan-directed *Marriage Play* have looked?

Wright: I can't even *imagine* at this particular stage what it might have been like. It might have been more realistic, that is, a setting which was really indicative of this couple—with more of an ambience. Something which indicated that there was a real room. Edward doesn't want this to be a symbolic play, but it's very spare, very high-tech. I think Alan might have wanted something which was a bit more—certainly not opulent, but a bit more . . .

RS: Lived-in?

Wright: More lived-in. Yes, more comfortable. Perhaps. Although this couple, as we know, is not George and Martha of *Virginia Woolf.* The interesting thing about this set is that it does recall, for me, the sets Bill Ritman used to make for Edward's plays and for other plays, in that it uses the space of the stage really beautifully. So, while you have the feeling that you are in an endless space, it does make a particular place. The use of space is really important in this one, especially this platform that seems to float in space, but is anchored by these very heavy pieces of furniture.

RS: Do you think the movement and business are too minimal in this production of *Marriage Play*? Would Alan's production have had more movement, business, and props?

Wright: Possibly more props; possibly more business. Although Alan's production of *Waiting for Godot,* which he actually directed for me and I produced off-

Broadway, was very minimalistic, very minimalistic. I think he would have, if Edward would have said to him, this is what I want, that's exactly what he would have given him. The most brilliant thing about Alan was that he always tried to fulfill the playwright's intent. He didn't put any dots in or pause in any of the Beckett plays unless Sam Beckett had written it, and the same thing with Edward. Many directors today impose their own structure, their own ideas, their own format on almost any piece they do. I never saw Alan do that.

RS: What would you list as Edward's strengths?

Wright: His ability to achieve what he wants because he knows what he's written. I haven't watched him direct or been around when he's directed any Beckett, for instance. I would imagine he would be just as truthful to Beckett's intent as indeed he is to his own. And he's certainly bright enough to know the intent of those plays.

RS: Are there any shortcomings that you noticed?

Wright: Well, the only shortcoming that he has ever had—and he increasingly overcomes that—is his ability, as I have said, to communicate with the actors in terms that the actors can understand. And sometimes that's difficult for any director. Some directors bludgeon their actors. Edward kind of nudges his actors. He's learned to be a director. He's instinctively a playwright, but he has learned over the years to be a director and to deal with those technical things that a director has to deal with. He knows when to seek advice. He knows that he is not omnipotent.

RS: Does he discuss subtext with his actors?

Wright: In general, he may discuss the subtext of a line, but he does not take a great amount of time, except the odd remark which, of course, leads an intelligent actor off on the right path.

RS: Occasionally an actor will say that Edward only wants to hear the words and that he feels business and movement get in the way.

Wright: I think it is somewhat unfair, because I've never seen him reject out of hand any business that an actor wanted to do. I think if Shirley wanted to knit during *Marriage Play,* he would try to dissuade her and probably say flatly, "No." But she wouldn't have wanted to, because she's an intelligent actress. I think a comment like that—I mean if actors think that he's trying to just get them to say the words and not do anything—that comes from an actor who really doesn't have anything more to supply other than some business. And actors hide behind business sometimes. I've heard many terribly unfair comments about Alan Schneider . . . but he was a great director.

Understudy for B, *Three Tall Women,* New York, 1994; Woodstock, 1992

Gillian, *Marriage Play,* New York, 1992; Vienna's English Theatre, 1987

B, *Three Tall Women,* Vienna's English Theatre, 1991

November 23, 1994

RS: How did Edward select you for the Vienna production of *Marriage Play*?

Butler: He literally picked me out of a chorus! I had finished a play off-Broadway, and I went up to the Equity office to check my pension, and the stage manager told me, "They are casting an Edward Albee play with two people of forty or over, but nobody is there." Well, nobody will admit they're over forty in this business, so I went down, and that's how I got *Marriage Play.* It was an open call. An open call! When I had the callback, of course, everybody was there, and Edward said, "You're the only one I believed." But prior to that I hadn't worked in fifteen years, as I had semiretired to raise a family. That's how I became associated with him.

RS: Equity rules require some open calls.

Butler: He also did open calls for the Signature's season of Albee plays.

RS: At the first rehearsal in Vienna, did Edward provide any broad guidelines for the play or your character?

KB: He didn't really give us many overall instructions or anything like that. Of course, with Edward's writing you don't have to build terribly hard, because it grows from what's on the written page. His writing is so rich that you just find things as you go along. One interesting thing: he'll never sit through the rehearsal when you're off-book for the first time! As an author he finds it very difficult to see actors mess up his lines.

RS: But he often cuts his scripts during rehearsals.

Butler: He takes pages out! With *Marriage Play* as well as later with *Three Tall Women* he would say, "That's not working here. It has nothing to do with the acting—it just doesn't belong in this play." As a director he's smart enough, brilliant man, to know what's playing and what isn't. That's very good about him: he writes it, but as a director when he sees it's not playing, there's no fiddling around with it, he just yanks it.

RS: He is practical enough to realize what worked theoretically in his head may not on stage.

Butler: That's right. So he pulls big chunks out, and somehow they aren't missed.

They're wonderful speeches, but the arc is maintained. Maybe that's one of the reasons he always rehearses from beginning to middle to end.

RS: Some directors—not playwright-directors—ask you to disregard stage directions about mood, feelings, atmosphere, and so on.

Butler: Well, he doesn't really write anything about mood, except he might put "angry."

RS: He likes "rue."

Butler: Yes, "rue," "with rue." But it's usually absolutely on target, so it shouldn't be disregarded in his texts. Sometimes he'll say, "You might do it a different way." If he likes it better, he says, "That's good. Leave it in." He does give tremendous latitude to actors he trusts. But if you're too far off, he'll certainly let you know, as any good director will.

RS: During the *Marriage Play* rehearsals, were the daily sessions relatively short?

Butler: Very short. We'd get through it, and that would be it. *Marriage Play* is a two-person play, and Tom Klunis and I would be rehearsing, and he'd say, "All right, now go home and learn it."

RS: He does not overwork people. But was the period unusually short?

Butler: He just realizes that four or five hours is about enough for any day.

RS: Especially in two-character or three-character plays.

Butler: He doesn't tend to go over and over. A lot of directors will chop a piece of an act and run it about three times until they feel the actors are getting it. Edward doesn't do that. He might do the whole first part of the first act or the whole first act, but never just little sections. Even that long speech I had, we didn't.

RS: Personally, you don't feel the need for that kind of work on short segments?

Butler: It depends on the play, but not on his stuff. I would go home and work on a certain thing and break it down my way. And he doesn't direct your movement; he lets you find your own physical language.

RS: During the Vienna *Marriage Play* rehearsals, did you sometimes want some more guidance than he gave you?

Butler: No, I like as little as possible, to tell you the truth. When I worked with him in *Marriage Play* it was difficult because I hadn't worked with him before, and I didn't know him. He had things in his head, and it took me a while to get on the same wavelength. But once we did, once he trusted me and I trusted him, it worked fine. Edward tends more to leave actors alone. He always says—it's what most good directors will tell you—hiring the actors is the first thing of being a good director. Knowing that your actors will deliver for you. It's a double whammy with him because we're saying his words—he wants to make sure he's got actors that know what he's talking about. He's very open to creative contributions if he trusts you, and he usually works with actors he trusts.

RS: Are there times you think if Edward has not cast too well?

Butler: You know, it's part of the business. It's nothing you can do anything about.

RS: During his *Marriage Play* rehearsals at the Alley Theatre in Houston, he did some scene-by-scene work with Shirley Knight and Tom Klunis. I remember that, with the complicated fight scene.

Butler: Well, we too rehearsed that a lot, but mostly without Edward. Tom and I rehearsed that in New York before leaving for Vienna. Of course, there was an intermission in Vienna because they have to have schnapps at the bar.

RS: There was an intermission in Houston as well.

Butler: Oh, they did have one in Houston? But in New York at the Signature they took it out, which is much better. In fact, in Vienna Edward was afraid that people wouldn't get it, so he had us, as you may already know, repeat the last few minutes of act 1 at the beginning of act 2. We repeated it exactly—the same lines, the same position. So people would wonder if we'd made a mistake, or say, "What are they doing?" We found it was wonderful just to repeat the whole fight.

Originally he did not want an intermission, and the reason for the intermission was so that the theatre could sell liquor at the bar. In Vienna people take their intermission very seriously—twenty minutes seriously. It's a long intermission!

RS: Sometimes he's also very good with solving physical problems, like those in the fight scene, and also with technical matters.

Butler: Edward is extremely well skilled in technical matters. He's very particular about physical details. Down to a doily on a table. In Vienna they changed the color of the wall four times. He wanted just that particular shade. With the technical stuff he knows exactly what he wants. With lighting he doesn't want any changes; for the most part he doesn't like that. But, something very interesting, he is also very generous, as I saw at that marvelous season down at the Signature Company. They have a very limited budget, and he was so giving to those people, and he spent so much time down there. And really with the technical stuff. He worked with the artistic director; he really gave a lot of time and energy to that season down there. He's wonderful. He's generous, and also, so, that was his stuff and he directed two of the plays. But he's really very kind. People don't know that about him. He's a very good, kind, and loyal man. He was tremendous.

RS: How was your experience with the Signature Theatre Company's *Marriage Play*?

Butler: Edward had first talked about doing *Counting the Ways* with *Marriage Play* for that season. But *Marriage Play* can stand on its own, especially the way it is now. With Jim Houghton directing and Edward guiding us, it was such a good production. It worked very well. We were very pleased with it.

Three Tall Women

EDWARD ALBEE

August 18, 2002

RS: I have talked with various members of the Vienna and New York City casts and wanted your views on the rehearsal process, first in Vienna and then in New York.

Albee: Well, you remember in New York, before leaving for Vienna, we only had the first act. I finished the second act in New York and on the plane going over, and I gave them the second act the first day of rehearsal in Vienna. Sort of an odd way of doing things, but that's the way it was.

RS: Cynthia Bassham, who played C in Vienna, recalled that you gave it to them in the second week. Myra Carter [A in Vienna and New York] also recalled that you gave the second act much later.

Albee: No, I gave them the second act when we got to Vienna—because we only had, I think, three weeks to rehearse in Vienna. Everybody remembers things differently.

RS: That's true. According to the actors, on the first day you merely told them what was going to happen in the second act.

Albee: And I gave them the text.

RS: I have this really long interview with probably your favorite actor, Myra Carter, who kept saying that act 2 was not ready at all during much of Vienna. As you know, she exaggerates.

Albee: I gave it to them the first day of rehearsal, and they learned it, and we opened on time!

RS: Myra kept saying, "It was not written"; "I helped him *write* it"; "It wasn't there." So I am surprised by your answer.

Albee: Well, I think I remember correctly, but I may not. You may want to talk about this to Glyn O'Malley [the American producing director in Vienna].

RS: I am told you emphasized that act 1 and act 2 were two different plays, and that you were, according to different actors, adamant about that. I was surprised by that.

Albee: I don't remember that at all. . . . What I was suggesting to them was that the *characters* the two of them played—that B and C played in act 2—were different characters than the characters they played in act 1. But it is all part of one play. I wanted B and C—A is the same person, of course—but I wanted B and C to remember that they were different people in acts 1 and 2; not that these were different plays, but that they were different characters, of course.

RS: That makes eminent sense. I was surprised by their statements. Both Cynthia and Jordan, who played C in New York, claimed that you kept saying, "These are different plays—don't connect them."

Albee: I never said that, because they weren't different plays.

RS: I am glad I am talking to you.

Albee: I too am glad that you are.

RS: Of course, I talked to Larry [Sacharow, who directed the New York production] as well. He said, "We kept them totally separate," which makes sense. But to characterize them as separate plays did not make sense to me.

Albee: That makes no sense at all.

RS: Cynthia remembers that in Vienna you de-emphasized the autobiographical aspect of the play. In fact, she believes that, had the actors asked you up front about it, you would have probably denied it was autobiographical.

Albee: What does she mean by autobiographical?

RS: I suspect that it was based on your biography.

Albee: Biography, not autobiography. It's based on my adoptive mother.

RS: Well, I was surprised by these comments, because in newspaper and television interviews during the New York production you have never denied that that was the fact. I thought you de-emphasized the biographical aspects during rehearsals in order to make the actors less self-conscious. If they feel the play is fictional and not in any way based on your life, they might feel freer in exploring the characters you had drawn?

Albee: Well, it is a portrait of my adoptive mother. There's no question about that, and I never denied it.

RS: As you said, people remember things differently. Jordan Baker told me she heard that at some stage you took notes when visiting your mother, or even tape-recorded her.

Albee: No, that's not true. Mind you, whenever I see anybody, I take mental notes. Mental notes. But I never tape-recorded the woman. Goodness, the things people remember. You know, I didn't even know I was going to write that play until after my adoptive mother died. I had no plan to write it at all. And then she died, and I realized I was going to. So, obviously, while she was alive I wouldn't take notes, since I wasn't planning to write a play about her.

Albee and His Collaborators on Staging Albee | 241

RS: Were the characters always named A, B, and C? Did their names change?

Albee: They were always A, B, and C, because if I gave them names in the first act, I couldn't give them names in the second act.

RS: Were they not Old Woman, Young Woman, Middle-Aged Woman?

Albee: No, I *think* they were always A, B, and C in both acts. It's just that B and C changed their identities in act 2.

RS: Were there substantial deletions in C's lines in the last quarter of the play?

Albee: Oh. In the last three speeches, I cut some from everybody. It was a little too long. I made some cuts for everybody—equal cuts. Nobody got penalized.

RS: If you can recall the rehearsal period in Vienna, Cynthia and Kathleen Butler [B] felt that they got relatively little attention from you because you had to deal so much with Myra.

Albee: [*Laughs.*] They got enough attention . . . they got enough attention to play the roles properly.

RS: But Myra was a problem, right?

Albee: She was a problem. Yes, of course—not learning her lines and being argumentative about everything. But she's such a good actress that it was worth it.

RS: Cynthia and Kathleen thought they got less time, and also that sometimes when things got bad with Myra you, in fact, cut rehearsals short.

Albee: Well, I would have to, if I couldn't work, of course. And since she was on stage the entire time it was impossible to work without her.

RS: Their understanding was that you were also going back to the hotel room to just revise act 2 and to even actually write it.

Albee: I was making a few cuts. I always make a few cuts in all my plays in rehearsal.

RS: I have a question about your comments in Vienna and New York City about the young woman in act 1. Cynthia Bassham remembers your telling her that you liked her interpretation of C as an "ice bitch," but Jordan remembers your asking her, "Why is she being so nasty? She's only a nervous little attorney!"

Albee: That's pretty much the same thing. Really, if you're insecure, you come across that way. Also, you tell different actresses different things.

RS: One of the actors remembers your coming back during the Vienna run and listening to the play on the audio monitor or squawkbox, rather than watching the play. Is that an accurate recollection? I have seen you do that in other productions too.

Albee: I can learn how a production is going by listening to it. I don't have to look at it, because actors don't change the blocking at all; they just change interpretation. So by listening I can tell whether they've changed interpretation or not.

RS: Myra felt that during the Vienna rehearsals you offered the subtext too often.

Albee: Oh, really? Well.

RS: Which is not something I've heard from anyone else.

Albee: No. I don't think that's true. Always believe the playwright, never the actor!

RS: I understand you were, as usual, very involved in the New York City production, deciding details about sets, costumes, and lighting.

Albee: Oh yeah, yeah . . . and I have that in my contract.

RS: Did you have any disagreements with Larry Sacharow?

Albee: Only one. He wanted to do the early part of act 2 far more stylized than I did. I kept saying it's naturalistic. And then he tried to make it more stylized! We had some arguments about that, but I won my point.

RS: Larry, too, thought that was the main point of disagreement.

Albee: That was the main problem we had between us. For some reason he thought that act 2 wasn't as naturalistic as act 1.

RS: He didn't want to tell you this, but he devised several stylized circular and triangular movements to interlink the three characters. Some actors thought that at times you cringed at some of Larry's stylizations.

Albee: Yeah, he wanted it more stylized, and I wanted it more naturalistic.

RS: You don't remember the stylized movement—the sort of circles and triangles?

Albee: Well, we did them so quickly; we didn't have time to look at them. It began much more stylized than I allowed it to continue.

RS: During the rehearsal stage you attended only run-throughs—once a week or so?

Albee: I would come in and see something new had been added, and I would complain about it. But by the time we opened in New York, at the Promenade, anyway, I think we had gotten most of that nonsense out. The way I had it in Vienna wasn't stylized.

RS: You were able to get what you wanted? You were happy with the production overall?

Albee: Yeah.

RS: How different was the New York City production from the Vienna one?

Albee: Well, the play was completely finished by the time we got to the New York production. It was not all that different, I guess. It was the same play, certainly.

RS: So the New York City production was not different from your Vienna production?

Albee: Well, it was different from Vienna because we had different people working in New York.

RS: But overall it was the same production, the same play, you saw in Vienna, except for some degree of stylization?

Albee: Yeah, of course.

RS: I guess some specifics may have changed. Was the set in New York essentially similar to the one in Vienna?

Albee: Basically. Well, the play didn't change all that much, nor did the intention—the intention did not change at all.

RS: Wasn't the lighting fairly unchanging in Vienna?

Albee: I don't remember any vast adjustment going on. We didn't have as much opportunity for complex lighting in Vienna.

RS: What do you mean?

Albee: Well, we didn't have much equipment. It's a very small proscenium stage . . . no place to put a lot of lighting equipment. But it was enough; it was all right.

RS: Technically, fairly up-to-date stage?

Albee: Well, you don't have to have candles—they had electric lights and things like that. It's all right.

RS: How big is the house?

Albee: Two hundred-plus, I think. [It seats 220.]

RS: And the River Arts Repertory in Woodstock is also a proscenium stage?

Albee: That was proscenium . . . a little bit thrust, mostly proscenium, that curtain, as I remember.

RS: The Vineyard is a thrust?

Albee: The Vineyard Theatre is three-quarters round. And by the time we moved from the Vineyard to the Promenade Theatre, where we played most of the run, that was not quite a proscenium but a thrust.

RS: Did you revise the text much in New York or was it almost all done by then?

Albee: I think, pretty much, it was done. I may have cut a little bit more. I don't remember. Nothing major.

RS: Did you have a role in Myra being cast as A in New York over some other actress?

Albee: I wanted her from beginning.

RS: I know, but was Larry considering Marian Seldes over her?

Albee: Marian was cast as B, and then graduated to A when Myra had to leave.

RS: Was Uta Hagen considered at all?

Albee: I don't remember; I don't think so.

RS: Myra thought that she had to fight to get into the production, since Larry wanted somebody else.

Albee: That may have been; I don't recall that. He didn't get his way, if he did, did he?

RS: Would you work with Myra again?

Albee: Well, Myra right now is playing the Nurse in *All Over.* She's getting older, and she's getting more difficult each year. And she has not been terribly well. I don't know—I can't answer that. Whether I'd like to give her a huge role in anything now, I don't know.

Lawrence Sacharow, director

Three Tall Women, New York, 1994; Woodstock, 1992

Derek Walcott's *Viva Detroit*, River Arts Repertory, 1990

Terry Johnson's *Insignificance*, River Arts Repertory, 1986

Janusz Glowacki's *Hunting Cockroaches*, River Arts Repertory, 1985

Len Jenkin's *Five of Us*, River Arts Repertory, 1983

(all American premieres)

November 21 and 23, 1994

RS: What is your connection to Edward's first director, Alan Schneider?

Sacharow: Alan was my first directing teacher after college—I studied with him professionally, and admired him tremendously. I was also in the Directors Unit at Lee Strasberg's Actors Studio for about five years, but I started directing at Caffé Cino, Café La Mama, and the Judson Poets' Theater, and I did a lot of experimental work with dancers, poets, and writers at the beginning of off-off-Broadway.

RS: The kind of plays you have done remind me of Alan.

Sacharow: I was always intrigued that Alan could have a career directing Albee and Beckett and Pinter. That's what I wanted to do also. I never accepted directing jobs for plays below a certain standard. I've been quite fortunate, especially in meeting Edward and directing *Three Tall Women.* I've admired Edward Albee's plays since *The Zoo Story*, which I saw in college and which really got me excited about the theatre.

RS: I am interested in the nature of your collaboration as well as your differences with Edward during the *Three Tall Women* rehearsals at River Arts and Vineyard. I assume you did not see his Vienna production.

Sacharow: Right, I never saw the Vienna production.

RS: But certainly Edward was wanting something similar in New York, and you might have wanted things a little different.

Sacharow: I had no idea what Edward wanted in Vienna, especially the staging. We never spoke about it, so I can't comment about it. The relationship with Edward started when he gave me the rights to do the play at my theatre in Woodstock, at River Arts Repertory. I had a meeting with him, and I asked him what the play was about for him. When the playwright can articulate what the play is about, it usually gives me a huge amount of information.

RS: What did he say the play was about?

Sacharow: He told me that for him the play was about a woman who you don't like a lot in act 1 and who you get to like a little bit better in act 2. That was very telling about the character, because all the themes in the play are so clear: it's about death and identity and personal transformations over many years. It's not necessary for him to articulate that, because any intelligent person can see the play and talk about those themes. So it's not as interesting for the playwright to restate that. But that was a very personal comment. For me that illuminated the whole nature of that character, and not only the character but the environment and the context of the tensions between them. That comment I found enormously helpful in setting up a dynamic of psychology and helping with understanding the subtext of the play. The philosophical themes are there, but you can't act them. But what you can act is what's happening in the dynamics between the people, and that's mostly what we concentrated on.

RS: I talked to Jordan this morning, and apparently Edward hardly ever talked to the actors directly. He always communicated through you. That's how he worked with Alan too.

Sacharow: Edward and I had several meetings. I told him some of my ideas, and he agreed with most. He agreed with my request that we have a united front in rehearsals. Edward had approval of all the sets and costumes and designs. So he was very instrumental in how the production looks visually. So it was a real collaboration between Edward, the set designer, and myself, with Edward having a lot of input. In Woodstock he came for the first reading; he watched and heard and then he went away. We agreed that he would come back in about ten days and watch a run-through. During those ten days we worked on the subtext and the intentions, and I did a first rough draft of staging. When he came back he watched it and gave me extensive notes privately about what he liked and what he didn't like, and what he felt was successful and what wasn't successful. He didn't give me a lot of information prior to rehearsal, which I felt was very good. But once rehearsals began, his perceptions of how the staging, the subtext, and the characterization worked were very useful. He had a very fixed idea in his head about these people, so he would give me very clear comments on them. In particular I had seen B as being solicitous of the older woman, and he said, "She's hovering around the back of her chair too much. This woman is a battleaxe; she can take care of herself. It should be relaxed. She can lie on the bed. She doesn't have to hover and take care of her." That was very, very helpful. So I basically restaged a lot of the middle character's stuff in act 1 and made it much less formal, which helped a lot. I also wanted the two middle people to have a settled-in quality. I asked them to move really slowly and be very precise with each gesture, with each movement. In the beginning they tended to do it very fast with a lot of emotion. The image I gave them was "Think you're just like a series of snapshots, and you're just, like, settling in to these snapshots." It created a sort of interesting rhythm, and then Edward came in and said, "What's going on? What are you trying to do there?" I said, I've been working with the image of snapshots, and they're sort of settling into these snapshots. He said, "Oh!" and thought about it for a minute and said, "The problem is I *see* the pictures." That was a great comment—just a wonderful note for a director. I just made sure that there were transitions in and out of the snapshots, so they were continuously in this movement pattern, and the photographs in a sense became a motion picture. His comments were astute and telling—without his telling me what to do or how to do it. He gave me his perception, and then I was able to solve the problem, but his perceptions and his insights were enormously useful in helping me solve the problems. So I loved his notes. He's a real artist, and a real artist knows how to talk about art and can talk in terms of unlocking creativity rather than dictating how it should be done. He opened up possibilities.

RS: Did you have disagreements with Edward about things you felt strongly in terms of staging?

Sacharow: He doesn't like a lot of movement, and I've staged act 2 with a lot of movement as the women walk around as models. He objected to it, and I toned it down somewhat. Now I think it has the right tone, but he never said get rid of it. To this day I still don't know whether he likes it or not. He doesn't love a huge amount of movement, and sometimes actors get too impulsive and start going overboard with it.

RS: Any disagreements about props? With Alan props were often an issue.

Sacharow: Oh, really? Well, I didn't want any props. The only props we have are the essential ones, the coffee pourer and the cups. We never had a disagreement about that, because I hate cluttered stages. Everything I direct is spare and clean. I wanted the actors' bodies to sculpt the space and create rhythmic patterns that defined the action. I work very physically. My whole approach is a physical approach—orchestrating energies to support the text, rather than using objects to support the text.

RS: I guess Alan used them much more.

Sacharow: Alan came from more of an Actors Studio tradition with a tendency towards naturalistic staging. I was in the Studio for a number of years, and there were a huge number of props. Then when I met Grotowski I really changed my way of working.

RS: Was there similar agreement about the set?

Sacharow: My first impulse was to do something more stylized, and he felt 'no, that's wrong; it has to be realistic.' Once we got the design he helped with fabric and color. He described the woman's house to the set designer and me. He knew exactly what— the period furniture and all. We basically got whatever he wanted. One disagreement we had was about a little table for C to put papers on. He said, "I didn't have a table in Vienna. Why are you having that table?" I said, "C needs to have a place to spread out some of these legal papers." He agreed but wasn't too happy about it. That was the one piece of furniture that he didn't really visualize in the script but sort of let us have. But he pretty much had the final decision—on the fabrics, materials, all that kind of thing.

RS: If Alan had directed *Three Tall Women,* the production would have been more naturalistic than yours.

Sacharow: Probably, because I work a lot more with movement and movement patterns and a sense of choreography that illuminates action, rather than with naturalistic behavior per se. The ultimate goal is to get realism, but it's just how you approach getting it. In act 2 in particular I worked with triangles—when one person moves, somebody else moves, too. So one feels a ripple in the space. You feel they are connected by the way they move in the space. In act 2 they are all variations of triangle forms that they move in.

RS: Did you talk about that aspect of the movement with Edward?

Sacharow: Never! It's the first time he'll ever hear about it. No, I never spoke to anybody about it because it's not anything that anybody is conscious of. This is the first time I'm actually ever saying it to anybody.

RS: I wasn't conscious of it, but now that you mention it, it's very true, because they were moving so fluidly. It was dance-like to me, and I actually asked Jordan if it was choreographed in some way, and she wasn't aware of it. She said, "No, I don't think it was choreographed or orchestrated by Larry." But clearly you had that in mind.

Sacharow: I had that in mind, but I never told anybody what I was doing, because then they get self-conscious about it and start playing your idea rather than their character. So even to this day I wouldn't tell them while they're still performing it. I never spoke to Edward about it because as long as he didn't mind. . . . It's not about interpreting the text—it doesn't mean anything except that it creates an experience. It's expressing energies in the space—energies which act upon the audience kinetically and physically and subconsciously.

RS: Were there any changes made in the script?

Sacharow: Very, very little. Mostly, the script was pretty tight by the time I got it; Edward had made most of his cuts and changes in Vienna. In Woodstock he cut the three speeches at the end slightly. There were some minor trims but not a lot. When we moved to the Vineyard I asked him to add a line in act 1 to bring up the son just a little bit earlier, because I felt the audience wasn't prepared for him. So Edward added one line about the son.

RS: Did the actors want any changes in the lines?

Sacharow: No, just the last three monologues at the end of act 2 were too long.

RS: Those were cut by about half?

Sacharow: No, I would say a paragraph was taken out of each. Edward would watch a dress rehearsal and then he would make the cuts. He knew what he wanted, and he could hear it and feel it. By the time we got to the Vineyard the script needed very little work, except just a bit of trimming in Myra's last speech. That was it.

RS: Did Edward complain about excessive or unnecessary movement?

Sacharow: Occasionally he would say that they were moving too much. I would just tone it down and keep the movement but not as exaggerated. So he did sort of pull it in somewhat. It still communicated what I felt was important about the play but in a more subtle way. He never said don't do any movement. He always felt if the movement gets over, goes overboard, it's a problem.

RS: Was that one of the recurring concerns he might have had?

Sacharow: Yes, it came up several times.

RS: More than the delivery of the lines?

Sacharow: Mostly, yeah, much more than the delivery of the lines.

RS: Did he say that the two acts should be treated as separate plays?

Sacharow: Yeah, he said they were two separate plays, and he said not to think about the characters in the first act when doing the second act. We just kept them totally separate. We never, never tried to connect them at all. We treated B and C in act 1 as two very different people from those in act 2.

RS: Did you direct them to be physically different too?

Sacharow: Yeah, their whole physical life was totally different. In act 1 it's sort of circles because they're circling each other. In act 2 they're really on diagonal lines, where one feels that you could be looking at one and listening to another and so on—it is physically designed around triangles so that there's always an energy line that connects them in the space and to the audience. It was to try to get a subconscious connection without being heavy-handed and literal about it.

KATHLEEN BUTLER, ACTOR

Understudy for B, *Three Tall Women,* New York, 1994; Woodstock, 1992
Gillian, *Marriage Play,* New York, 1992; Vienna's English Theatre, 1987
B, *Three Tall Women,* Vienna's English Theatre, 1991

November 23, 1994

RS: When did you have your first rehearsal?

Butler: Well, we did the first rehearsal around the table. Of course, just reading the play. After we read through the first act, I said, "Well, how does it sound— it's the first time you've heard it?" And, as always, he said, "No, I've heard it before." Because he hears it as he writes. He's probably told you that he hears it, but he tells his actors that, too. The way he writes his script, everything— emphasis, italics, quotations—is written down as he hears it. And he wants it done so. In Vienna in the beginning we only had the first act. He was still working on the second act, but he found it important that we get our characters established, especially for B and C, who were very different characters in the first act as opposed to the second. So we didn't see the second act until about two and a half weeks into rehearsal, which was surprising since I had all these long speeches in act 2.

RS: How many weeks of rehearsals did you have in Vienna?

Butler: We had five or maybe five and a half weeks.

RS: At the start did he give you any overall advice about your characters?

KB: He certainly . . . didn't talk about his goals, really. He had worked with all of us before and knew that we would be very true to his text and what he wanted.

RS: I was told he wanted you to consider the two acts as two separate plays?

Butler: Yes, he did. He told us that originally. But whether he still feels that way I don't know, since he has seen it performed by different companies. He may have changed his mind. But he did tell us that; he absolutely did.

RS: What are some things that stand out in your mind as particularly helpful?

Butler: He let us pretty much find things. He was very interested in what I had come up with for B's background, but the subtext he leaves up to the actors. Wisely, as a good director he let us find most of it.

RS: Did he agree or disagree with your subtextual readings?

Butler: He'd say "hmm" or "okay," but once we started rehearsal, if he saw something popping up—or even an emphasis or a line that wasn't ringing the way he wanted it to—he would certainly bring it up, and we'd work on that. He did pull reams out of act 1 in Vienna. The second-act coda was initially much longer—several pages; he shortened it to a few sentences in Vienna. Here in New York it's about that long. That's very good about him: he writes it, but as a director when he sees it's not playing, there's no fiddling around with it, he just yanks it. The Vienna production was longer: A went on a lot more about horses; there was a fellow named Bob, and she went on about that and about another fellow too.

RS: Bob was the character who stole.

Butler: Yes. So you've read the typescript. My signal to Myra for any lines she missed was, "Well, what about Bob?"

RS: Did Edward offer many specifics? Did he say, for instance, "B would never do this," or did he suggest a tone or coloration or pitch or line reading?

Butler: No, he didn't do that. I remember one speech, which is still in there, only shorter, about going into town to see the doctor with the arm. I said, "I'm having some difficulty with this. I know we're giving this information to the audience, but how do you think she feels about it?" He said, "Well, it's like she's just shaking her head about that." And that was his direction to give me the clue to how to do it. So to bring it alive, I explored a lot of things about that: whether she was tired and disgusted with it or whether she was just relating it. But that was a very good direction. It stuck with me. He knew what he wanted. He didn't really talk about music, although it was musical. The rhythms of his speech are very musical, and as with any good playwright if you say one word wrong it's very noticeable, especially for the actors. It's jarring because it's not his language, and it stands out. And he's very careful about that. I know where the pauses are.

RS: What was the rehearsal atmosphere like in Vienna?

Butler: It was very nice working with him in *Three Tall Women* because we had worked together before. He knew my work, and he knew he could trust me. He felt the same way with Myra and Cynthia. He was wonderfully skillful personally with the actors in Vienna. It was very difficult for Myra: she wasn't well, and it was very difficult for her to learn this tremendous piece of work which went on and on, and he was just wonderful with her. He knew how good she was, and he stayed with her, and it was wonderful.

RS: It requires a skill—particularly with some actors.

Butler: Yes, and he has it. Personally I thought he was enormously patient and tremendously supportive.

RS: In the first few weeks in Vienna did you not utilize the entire rehearsal period?

Butler: Very short rehearsal periods—every time I've worked with Edward.

RS: Cynthia [who played C] said it was about three hours a day.

Butler: Yeah, very short. It was a lot about Myra's needing to learn this enormous text, and also he didn't want us to get tired. He was very careful about that.

RS: I've noticed that about him. But also Cynthia's impression was he needed time to go write act 2.

Butler: He may have. He was scurrying off to the Hilton pretty quickly. But also with *Marriage Play*, which was handed to us in a complete text, we had very short rehearsal periods.

RS: He doesn't like too many lighting changes.

Butler: Certainly in Vienna there weren't many. There was one basic lighting design for act 1 and one for act 2. As always, he was very particular about our costumes. He just knew exactly the colors, but he was also very nice and would ask, "Do you look good in this color?" He was very much involved with the costumes, props, everything. He knew exactly what he wanted.

RS: How different was the set in Vienna?

Butler: Not terribly different. A little more as the Viennese would do it. Elaborate but quite similar. He's very particular about it.

RS: The walls and arches and windows?

Butler: No, they were a bit different. The walls had this fancy material on them, so you would know immediately that a very wealthy woman lived there. But not terribly unlike this.

RS: Were the costumes different in Vienna?

Butler: The colors were very different, and the designs of each dress were very different. Overall, on the technical stuff, Edward is absolutely right on the nose. Exactly what he wants, and is very, very demanding and fussy. Very. Which is good.

RS: And finally when he realizes he can't get something, he'll be practical and so okay.

Butler: He usually gets it. He certainly does in Vienna. People were standing on their heads to get things right.

RS: Cynthia was happy with the rehearsals, but as a young actress could she have benefited from more help?

Butler: It was just a matter of Edward having to focus on Myra. She pulls it. She made it be the focus because she was having such difficulties with the lines in act 1. She was feeling very insecure, and she consequently complained or had ailments. So Cynthia and I didn't get as much work. I'm sure you've heard that, and I'm sure Myra told you. But we all knew she'd be brilliant. It was wonderful to work with somebody like that—you have to just get by that stuff. Also we knew it was a major play. It was difficult for Edward; he was worn out, too; dealing with that was very tedious. But he showed great patience and restraint, and he knew how good she would be.

RS: Movements in this production directed by Larry are sort of fluid and dance-like. Was that the case in Vienna?

Butler: No, I did not do any of that. I just made a few adjustments to my body—my back was almost straight. I did certain things in act 1 that I thought were indicative of someone taking care of an older person. And then in act 2 something slightly different—not a huge difference—with my body. And that seemed to work fine. But he lets you find it, which is great.

RS: Edward doesn't like a lot of movement.

Butler: He's not big on movement. The lines play themselves. I don't think you need extraneous moves. That's the way I feel. For all characters in Vienna there was much less movement. For the most part it was very still. The second act was a little metaphorical in one movement. But none of the dancing and modeling stuff you see in New York. Actually in the first act we tried all sorts of strange, funny things—I stuck things up under my skirt as Marian [Seldes] does here, and I wound up doing things sitting on the bed. I mean, these were interesting choices, but after I tried them, Edward pulled it back, way back.

RS: Any other differences in the production's look?

Butler: Maybe it's the lighting and maybe it's the costuming: the second act has a different look. A more realistic look than Vienna's slightly out of the ordinary realm.

RS: Is Myra by and large the same as she was in Vienna?

Butler: She grounded this in Vienna, and she has worked and developed. She has enhanced it, but she is still true to exactly what she started to do and what

Edward wanted her to do. Watching Myra is incredible. She's very much what she was in Vienna—only it's so much more, and it's so seamless. Everything she does is always true, and that's the beauty of her acting.

RS: Was A as likeable in Vienna as she is here?

Butler: Well, she's so cute. She's so damn funny! You know Edward would say, "No. We've got to really hate her," because he was working through this stuff with his mother. But, of course, you would never hate her—what's written on the paper, anyway. You can't dislike the character. She was always likeable. You know she's young: she's just turned sixty-five. She's younger than Marion. She's younger than Edward.

RS: People can't believe she is only sixty-five.

Butler: Edward originally thought of her as a real dragon lady.

RS: So did the character change during the Vienna rehearsals?

Butler: No. He didn't realize then that he had written this wonderful—

RS: But didn't the script change? Didn't the character change?

Butler: No. He took stuff out that was too long, but it wasn't a character choice. The character was pretty much there throughout, and the things he took out would not affect it. It was just less talk.

RS: Her facial expressions from line to line just add so much to the character and make her so endearing, too.

Butler: That's how he writes as well: "after a pause," "aside," "chiding," "amused," "ugly," "weeping," "sniveling." When he put that in, he had to get an actress like Myra who could do that, and do it in seven words! She does it. That's Myra. But sometimes she's too endearing. That's Myra too.

The Goat, or, Who Is Sylvia?

Edward Albee

August 20, 2002

RS: Another director you have worked with recently is David Esbjornson—on *The Goat, or, Who Is Sylvia?*

Albee: We had worked on two plays before that, of course.

RS: *Who's Afraid of Virginia Woolf?* at the Guthrie and . . .

Albee: *The Play About the Baby* in New York.

RS: What was it like to work with David on *The Goat, or, Who is Sylvia?*

Albee: Oh, we had a fine time. Got along very well.

RS: The overall approach of another of your directors, Lawrence Sacharow, during *Three Tall Women,* seemed largely in tune with your aesthetic—that's the way it seemed to me. Was that true with David's approach in *The Goat, or Who Is Sylvia?* as well?

Albee: I think so. Yes, sufficiently so that I wasn't unhappy with either of their productions.

RS: How does the experience of working with David and Larry compare to your experience with Alan Schneider, whom you worked with for so long?

Albee: Well, as you know, all directors have their own ideas and their own personalities. But . . . there are some I can work with and some I can't. Some who will do things the way the playwright wants, and some who won't. I have had disagreements, some minor disagreements with every director I've worked with. The ones I've worked with more than once, or plan to, we get along—and they change according to my needs!

RS: Congratulations on the Tony for *The Goat.*

Albee: Thank you. Good play!

RS: I saw the opening night performance and liked it very much.

Albee: It actually got better a month or so in.

RS: With such a controversial subject, how is the production doing financially?

Albee: Well enough that we have a new cast coming in.

RS: How soon is the new cast coming in?

Albee: They start on September 13. We had Mercedes Ruehl and Bill Pullman for six months, now they have to go away. So now we have an actress named Sally Field. And an actor named Bill Irwin.

RS: The vaudevillian.

Albee: Yeah, and Shakespeare and Beckett also. It's going to be a very interesting cast.

RS: And Stephen Rowe and Jeffery Carlson will remain?

Albee: Yes, we have them for a year.

RS: It's going to be quite a different production with these new leads.

Albee: Well, it will be the same play, but approached slightly differently, sure.

DAVID ESBJORNSON, DIRECTOR

The Goat, or, Who Is Sylvia? Broadway, 2002

The Play About the Baby, off-Broadway, 2001

Who's Afraid of Virginia Woolf? Guthrie Theatre, 2001

Arthur Miller's *The Ride down Mt. Morgan,* Broadway, 2002, and *Resurrection Blues,* Guthrie Theatre, 2002

Tony Kushner's *Angels in America: Millennium Approaches,* world premiere,

Eureka Theatre, 1991, and *Homebody/Kabul,* Chelsea Theatre Centre, London, 1999

March 11, 2002

RS: You have worked with Arthur Miller when staging his plays. How is working with Edward different from working with Arthur Miller?

Esbjornson: Arthur's work is a little bit different; his writing tends to be in larger gestures. Both men have big intellectual and political ideas. There is no question about that. Edward tends to work in a lot of nuance and detail. Arthur does too, but he has a kind of overarching boldness that is of a different quality or rhythm than Edward's. Edward's seems to be. . . . It's so hard to talk about two writers.

RS: Could you compare them in terms of their participation in the rehearsal process?

Esbjornson: Arthur understand the process very well. He is similar to Edward in that he just lets me work and then show him things as I develop them, as I get things staged, and he responds to them. Arthur is extremely open to theatricality. Edward, for instance, doesn't like other things—such as music—to overpower his language, whereas Arthur is kind of supportive of that. That's what I mean by Arthur's embracing the large gesture—he doesn't seem to mind if things go to an almost slightly operatic place, whereas Edward wants his world to be more realistic or more tightly constructed.

RS: When did you get the script of *The Goat?*

Esbjornson: I had just opened *The Play About the Baby* with Marion Seldes and Brian Murray [February 1, 2001], and I was also rehearsing *Who's Afraid of Virginia Woolf?* at the Guthrie Theatre with Mercedes Ruehl and Patrick Stewart, whom I had worked with earlier on Arthur's *The Ride down Mount Morgan.* Edward gave me the script of *The Goat* at the first preview of *The Play About the Baby,* or maybe a bit earlier. In any case, I had read it by then. We had breakfast the next morning, and he asked what I thought of it, and I said, I think it's brilliant. And he said, would you like to do it? And I said, of course. I went from not knowing Edward at all to working on three major shows with him within about a year and a half. I found the script very funny and very bold at the same time, and I saw it as a wonderful challenge. I could sense that right away.

RS: Before beginning rehearsals, what kind of preparation do you undertake—make notes for yourself, a director's book, or something like that?

Esbjornson: Well, I would like to be able to say that I am really interesting in that way, but I'm not. [*Laughs.*] Let me just talk about my approach to Edward, because it's too hard to lump everybody together. I find with Edward that I just want to take it in; I just want to understand it intuitively. He's such a careful writer; he's so precise. He thinks about things for so long, and his characters are really fully developed in the situations. And the language, the rhythms, the structures of the play—he pays attention to those things because he's a really wonderful writer. So when you get his play, you are already starting way ahead of what you often get with a new script. You're not, in a sense, "saving" the script or working to fix it right off the bat. You really are just taking it in, and allowing yourself to understand and come up to the place where he is. That's the way I approach his work. It doesn't mean that I can't sense that a particular beat may need some attention, or maybe we may need to talk about it. But I never make prior assumptions, because until I get into the rehearsal room and start working on it and until I understand it from the inside out, I don't want to make any judgments about it.

RS: But do you jot down your first reactions? Alan Schneider used to do that.

Esbjornson: I don't jot them down because I don't ever think they are for anybody. I don't act like it's going to be picked up and read or consumed in the future by someone. I tend to let things percolate; I take information in, and I think about it all for a long period of time. And the longer I have to contemplate it and to get a sense of the world of the play and how it will function, then the easier it is to come to a conclusion about its physical production and how I might want to approach it. But I really have to say that once I understand the physical parameters—the setting and the characters—I really want the rehearsal process to be that of discovery. And I want to understand the play as I go along without too many preconceived notions. And so I kind of go in blank to some extent, but with having thought about it for a long time.

RS: Did the script change a lot during the rehearsal process?

Esbjornson: Not too much during the rehearsal process. During the rehearsal process, I put it on its feet. And we tried to detail the moments and discover the complexities or certain nuances that we wanted to bring to it, or some interpretations that we wanted to try; sometimes playing against the comedy, sometimes going further with it, but wanting to put it on its feet so that we could then look at it together and say, well, where does it need to go now? And in this particular instance, I don't think I even did a run-through for him. I did sections. We worked, and we showed him scene 1; then we worked on scene 2 for a couple of days, and then we showed him scene 2. We went through it that way, whereas in other situations I have done run-throughs. Actually, for instance, with *The Play About the Baby,* he came and saw it fully blocked, fully staged, with run-throughs coming at about the two-week mark.

RS: When did Edward first come in during *The Goat* rehearsals?

Esbjornson: Probably in the last half of the second or early third week. But we talked occasionally. But he really, just in this particular instance, gave us a certain amount of freedom to explore, because it's tough material, and it needs a lot of time. We showed him different sections of it, because we didn't feel like we understood how to put it all together. And then we did one or two run-throughs before going into the theatre.

RS: So when did the script begin to change?

Esbjornson: The script began to change more in previews. We did almost three weeks of previews—it was something that I had worked out with Liz McCann [the producer]. It's very unusual to open a straight play like this cold on Broadway. I felt we needed our best chance to do the work, and we knew we were going to learn a lot in front of an audience. So the majority of changes and cuts came after the first week.

RS: Any changes since the opening?

Esbjornson: No, not since opening. But every day of the previews.

RS: Any major changes come to mind from the preview period?

Esbjornson: Well, there was a speech about Martin's relationship with an Irish wolfhound during his childhood. That used to be where the alien speech is now in scene 2—"an alien came out of whatever it was and took me with it." That used to be the wolfhound speech.

RS: Why did you cut that?

Esbjornson: Because we felt that information—which was at that point way into act 3—was more important for Stevie to hear. It was important for Martin to have a connection with Stevie and go that far with her and not with Ross. Also the speech about the baby on the lap went out of the play for one or two nights, but we put it back in. A lot of editing for little snips of things. Some of those the actors and I wanted. But the majority of the cuts were just Edward's very careful editing of his own work.

RS: In response to his own reactions during the previews?

Esbjornson: Yeah, and in response to audience reaction. Yes, he's very good about that.

RS: Yes, he's very practical. Sometimes he has to be stopped from cutting, too!

Esbjornson: Exactly. There were a couple of instances where we said, don't do that because it's very important, and we feel we need it. And he was also very respectful of that.

RS: What about the look of the set? I guess the set is Edward's visualization of it?

Esbjornson: To some extent. John [Arnone] and I basically created the whole idea of the columns and the upper level. And we wanted it to have a little bit of classical quality to it, a Greek-tragedy quality. So we had that basic plan. When I first read the script I was a little confused by the dialogue that suggested they were in the city. It talked about city needs and all this stuff. And so my original design with John was more oriented towards an apartment, and then Edward said, "Oh no, they are in the suburbs." And then he talked about the Bauhaus style and what an architect would do. At first we were afraid that anything we did would not suggest an architect's home, or that it would suggest it too specifically, and that people would then take issue with it. For a while we had lines in the play which Edward added about now that he's famous he can move into another house, a house that he's designed. As we actually saw the set, I became convinced that it was doing a great job of suggesting an architect's home. I felt that we just didn't need those lines in the script anymore. And I asked him if they could be gone, and he said he thought so.

RS: So when did that decision occur—after you saw the model or the designs or . . . ?

Esbjornson: No it happened in preliminary. We just showed him our process along the way. And once we made the decision about the nature of it, it didn't change very much. What he did accept from John and me was the fragmentation that the set has towards the top, a kind of an abstraction which I was very pleased with because I think Edward's plays can sustain something other than pure realism. I know that's one thing we were able to break into during our collaboration on *The Play About the Baby* as well, a more abstract way of presenting it, and that was very useful to people's appreciation of the play.

RS: Since we are on the subject of the set, in terms of color, did you want a little more color or a little less color? The columns are grey, but the rugs have more color. Occasionally with some directors there have been tussles, with Edward wanting less color and the director wanting more.

Esbjornson: I wanted much more of a neutral quality. In the end we found there was more complexity of color, especially in the floor area. So that became difficult.

RS: Difficult for you, or difficult for someone else?

Esbjornson: For a number of reasons. Some of Edward's taste; some of John's taste; some of what I needed; some of what Elizabeth [Clancy, the costume designer] needed. And she had the hardest job because she was trying to find colors that fit into these characters' world. So her choice was to play the colors off the set and make them of that world. Edward felt strongly that these people were very well off, and so the quality of their clothing had to be very good. But at the same time there was a kind of intellectual, artistic casualness to things too. So they are not uptight people; they have nice things and look great but they are comfortable too. So it's a really tricky balance we were trying to achieve, and an even trickier balance trying to make the palette work. With all the browns and muted colors, we were trying to figure out how to make the characters pop. We really didn't want to put them in pastels, but we really wanted it earthy and warm.

RS: What about the number of props? Obviously, Stevie has to break things and throw things. But Edward usually prefers somewhat minimal props and sets.

Esbjornson: Well, I think that's true, and my aesthetic tends to mirror Edward's in that regard. I really don't like to have a lot of stuff on stage. I'm not particularly fond of this kind of furniture—sitcom kind of ground plan either— but there is a kind of normalcy that we are trying to achieve, and a feeling that these people are surrounded by good taste and good art. So when Stevie starts breaking these things, we know she is willing to destroy some precious things.

RS: But even within that logic, did you and Edward on occasion disagree about the number of objects on stage?

Esbjornson: Well, there was a point at which he said, "There is too much on stage," and I said, "I think you're right." And the next time he came he said, "That's better." But we didn't tussle over it, it was really that he was right; we just had brought in all this stuff, and then we sort of had to select what we wanted to keep up there. But still it ended up being more than usual.

RS: One of the points of contention between Edward and some of his directors is the amount of movement. He often peppers directors with questions like "Why is she moving?" "Can't he convey that without moving?" and so on. Did you have similar disagreements?

Esbjornson: That's very interesting. I have *not* had that problem on any of the three shows that I have worked with him on. I imagine that could be true. He had mentioned at some point that he doesn't necessarily see the need for movement . . . but I've tried to make all the movement feel natural and organic and come out of the text. And when it doesn't, I try to change it; or if it feels false, I try to do something about it. Maybe that's why; or maybe he's just decided that that isn't something he's going to police. But he seems to have been satisfied with the staging choices that I've made in these three productions, or at least he hasn't brought it up with me.

RS: He would have brought it up with you if he was unhappy. He's not exactly bashful.

Esbjornson: No, he's not bashful at all! That's one of the things I like so much about working with him: we can say things to each other. If I want to say something about the writing, and he wants to say something about the directing, we're not precious about it. We're just trying to get the play on in the best possible way. I feel tremendously supported by him; at the same time, he can be critical of something or say that's not working.

RS: Were there any major differences of opinion or disagreements?

Esbjornson: I probably pushed for less realism. I've had this discussion with him. I've said to him, "Your plays—something about the writing—can support abstraction and can support a non-realistic set." But I do think that the elements that the characters touch need to be real, because often the writing takes us into a place that's more absurd or abstract. So you don't want to telegraph that with the physical setting. That's what he's concerned about. Someone might use a big white set or something, and it becomes symbolic. He really doesn't want his plays to smack of symbolism or metaphor. That is already there in the writing, so if you underline that, then you are doing the play a disservice. Actually, you should work against it a bit. That's why he insists on a more realistic approach. In *Who's Afraid of Virginia Woolf?* you show a real house with real people—books, drinking, very tangible things—and *then* show that they have created this abstraction, this imaginary child. If the whole thing is imaginary and abstracted to begin with, then there's nothing . . .

RS: You began to answer my question about disagreements—

Esbjornson: No, what I'm trying to say—if I have a tendency to push, it is in that direction, and he sort of pulls the other way. We seem to have found, thus far at least, a happy compromise. He let us take the set and break it apart at the top, and he let us make a surreal nursery for *The Play About the Baby*. Now it was his notion of how that should be, but it wasn't the way he had originally done it. So when I asked Edward to consider doing *The Play About the Baby* with more than just chairs and flats, he took that in and came back with another thought about his own play that allowed us to articulate an abstract nursery in which the play could take place.

RS: With Alan—in the productions I saw and in my conversations with both him and Edward—I found Alan leaning much more toward naturalistic settings and Edward pulling the other way. Edward would say, "You don't need that many things on stage!" and Alan would respond, "But you need to convey an impression of real people and a real house." And that would go on.

Esbjornson: I think the aesthetic has changed a little bit too, and theatre audiences accept less now. They don't need us filling them in on every single detail. In fact, when you can bring the imagination along, it's a wonderful thing. But it's interesting to hear that about Alan and Edward. I guess Edward's role has been different in different situations!

RS: The view of the goat's head at the end startled me for a second! Was even more of the goat visible earlier in the rehearsals?

Esbjornson: We had several endings. At one point we brought out the entire goat—bloody and everything—and Stevie carried it to Martin. When we did that we were getting too much laughter. The prop didn't exactly look real; it wasn't bad, but it didn't look real; and it wasn't beautiful. One of the most important things about that image of the goat is that it be benign, a rather gorgeous creature with beautiful eyes. Our goat's head now is closer to that. But we also realized that if we didn't reveal so much of the goat, the audience stayed with us a little bit better. My only problem now is the sightline, because we can't quite get the goat in fast enough. So we have left it up there and tried to make it much less about the goat and more about the characters. We had to make that choice at a certain point. We said this isn't about crying over the goat; it is really about what's going to happen now with this family. So we evolved toward that choice. We also felt—and Edward worked on this quite a bit with us—that the play began to make another kind of shift. It started to become a different style at the end, and we needed to ensure that it didn't somehow go into major tragic mode but simply became an extension of the play that had gone before. That involved cutting, tightening, sharpening the end of the play. Cradling the goat had made it into a big presentation—a sacrifice—and was slowly turning the play into something else. Edward sensed that that wasn't working for the play, that we were not taking the realistic style all the way to the end. Now I feel we have at least done that.

RS: What was the sound effect at the end of act 2? Was that Edward's choice?

Esbjornson: No, that was the sound designer's and my choice. We wanted something that felt as though we were in a world of epiphany, and yet at the same time we had the flapping of birds—the Eumenides flying into that world. We kept that out of the second transition: we took the birds away and just had the single tone, which took us into the evening when we wanted a time passage.

RS: Did you ever consider that this whole thing may be happening in one character's mind?

Esbjornson: Oh, I tend not to think too much like that. I could see such an interpretation. Sure. Like a big dream—a big fevered dream. The reason it doesn't come up is that we don't want the audience to say, "Oh, that was all a dream."

RS: But did you ever discuss this with Edward?

Esbjornson: No. No, I never perceived the play that way, and I don't think he has.

RS: How did you visualize the movement of the play? Did you see some sort of arcs, especially in view of the balancing of comedy and tragedy?

Esbjornson: I don't know that I have a plot in my head. Generally you start out with a problem, which Stevie, the wife, tries to push away. Then it becomes clear that there is something there: a little affair and the joke about that. The friend comes in, and little by little the situation unfolds, but it also becomes more humorous as it goes on and leads to the inevitable confession that he is actually having an affair with a goat. So act 1 ends up in a kind of comic moment: "You're fucking a goat!" and the audience is laughing like crazy. The top of act 2: "You're doing what? You're fucking a goat." Right after that. Comedy. Comedy. All the stuff that you say, "Let's read Ross's letter." There's a comic quality to all of this stuff even though underneath there's a kind of edge and pain. And then it goes through a kind of reactive mode for a while where it dips, but then Stevie's need to use comedy to push away the problem keeps coming up, and so the audience ends up hooking on to her and identifying with her. Then about two-thirds of the way through act 2 we try to switch it, and we start to kill some of the jokes a little bit, to play them differently. We need to control the audience a little bit, so Stevie underplays certain jokes or does them bitterly, so that we begin to move toward his epiphany and her howls, where she feels her greatest pain, and then her rage coming out of that. Act 3, you end up in a place of despair for a while that then becomes a little bit funny with Billy, and then it begins to turn very, very dark as you realize that Billy's sexuality is being threatened from the outside and that Martin is trying to support and protect his son and be a father and yet at the same time fight for his own life. Then, of course, it turns dark and deeply tragic as she drags Sylvia in. There are pockets of humor—surprises—that still crop up later, but generally speaking we are trying to move towards tragedy as we get into the final section of it. So that's what we are trying to do.

RS: Your comments do trace a kind of movement of the play's action. Was this intermixing of humor and tragedy hard on the actors?

Esbjornson: What's hard is to keep the rudder in the water. That's the metaphor we use: making sure that even though it's turbulent on top, the course is clear and we don't lose the embarrassment or the pain, because that really is the heart of it. . . .Some critics have already said they're not convinced about that, but I think generally the actors are doing a wonderful job in that regard, because I see people devastated. I see people in tears. I see lots of reactions besides the laughter. And in some ways a lot of the laughter we're getting is uncomfortable. In some ways the laugher is seductive: it opens you up, and then the more serious issues can flow in.

RS: To some extent this description reminds me of *The Ride down Mount Morgan*.

Esbjornson: Yes, we had the same kind of thing with that. It was very interesting. This is harder to play sometimes, but it has a similar sort of ring to it and a similar sort of challenge.

RS: Lyman is very funny, even though what he's done is not.

Esbjornson: Right!

RS: That's a very funny play. But this is a darker play.

Esbjornson: I think so, because it's even pushing farther than that in terms of taboo. But I certainly understand what you're saying, and I certainly felt the same kind of challenge with that play, and both men were after a similar sort of response.

RS: From what you've told me so far, I understand working with Edward has been a good experience.

Esbjornson: I feel very good about working with Edward. I think he's very careful, he's very smart, he's very respectful, and I think very generous, too. I know he has a reputation with some people, but I haven't found it difficult to work with him at all. I really enjoyed it.

RS: He's very practical.

Esbjornson: Very practical.

RS: Understands how theatre works.

Esbjornson: He knows how theatre works; he understands the world and what theatre is in the world, and what it isn't; he understands the world of theatre.

RS: Speaking of the world of theatre, what concerns did the producers who invested their money have in terms of opening this on Broadway?

Esbjornson: This is probably one of the most vulnerable plays that I've come across—it's wide open to attack. It's brave, and everybody involved wanted to be as brave as the play. We realized that we could put it in an off-Broadway theatre where the audience had already been trained to accept that kind of extreme vision, or we could take this play and give it the stature it deserves and put it on Broadway—an arena where you would have a really strong reaction. A varied reaction. That comes with the good and the bad; you can't have it both ways. The spectrum of response has to do with the venue, and that's incredibly exciting.

RS: How has the reception been, and how are the producers feeling about it?

Esbjornson: It's been fantastic: people are talking about it, debating it; some are angry; some are delighted; some find it funny; some find it devastating; some find it challenging to their notions of sexuality and love. This is what theatre should be. The form that he's chosen to express this in is under debate. When was the last time you went to a show on Broadway where everyone was struggling over how or even whether or not you can mix comedy and tragedy?

RS: The critics were unable to really call it what it is.

Esbjornson: Yes. They were unable to articulate their feelings about it. Their response to the experience is so varied, so individual, so exciting that you can't put it in a box, wrap it up, and send it off. I have people calling me saying, "I can't get that play out of my head; I've been thinking about it all week; the characters are talking to me."

STEPHEN ROWE, ACTOR

Ross, *The Goat, or, Who Is Sylvia?* 2002

Lawyer, *Tiny Alice*, 2001

Albee's Men (one-man show), American Repertory Theater, 1998

Jerry, *The Zoo Story*, Vienna's English Theatre, 1984; *Albee Directs Albee*, 1978

Chairman Mao Tse-Tung, *Quotations from Chairman Mao Tse-Tung, Albee Directs Albee*, 1978

The Young Man, *The American Dream, Albee Directs Albee*, 1978

The Young Man, *The Sandbox, Albee Directs Albee*, 1978

March 11, 2002

RS: I am interested in understanding the nature of Edward's involvement in the staging process of *The Goat*.

Rowe: Edward had a sort of jolly sense of asking David permission for when he should come again. They have a working relationship that way from their work on *The Play About the Baby*. Edward came when David thought it was right to come, and it was a very respectful process. David is very good at letting people know when he thinks it's best for them to come, and people really respect his expertise in that way.

RS: Stylistically they seem to see eye to eye. That's the impression I got.

Rowe: Edward said many times that he considers *The Goat* a naturalistic play. To me that says let's create scenes with people talking and listening and seeing what's at stake. David said many times, "Work through the love and embarrassment." Those two poles: love and embarrassment. My approach to scenes kind of bounces off of those two poles.

RS: Was there any disagreement about the set, props, colors, etc.?

Rowe: Not that we ever saw. There were discussions about that, certainly. There were discussions about the nature of the goat itself.

RS: You had the whole goat at first.

Rowe: That just didn't seem right. Apparently, Edward was very unhappy with the size of it. So that had to be adjusted.

RS: Was it too large or too small?

Rowe: Too large. It was unwieldy. For a while we thought it was important to have the animal brought downstage, so that Bill [Pullman] was left holding it, cradling the goat for the last image of the play. That was with us for quite a while until Mercedes [Ruehl] suggested that the upstage area instead was more of a formal location for a sacrifice. But because of sightline problems we resisted having it happen there. Eventually they reconciled to the upstage area, because bringing it down required either that Sylvie drag the body down or that there was a handoff. The handoff seemed awkward and maybe funny. It wasn't funny, but people didn't know what to do with it.

RS: Was Edward happy with the set?

Rowe: I think so. Played around with the rugs a little bit. Those primitive statues on the set are his!

RS: Edward's loft does have primitive sculpture. So they were borrowed from him. Sometimes he buys the stuff used on a set! Did the script undergo a lot of changes?

Rowe: Yes, yes. There was a reference to Ross and Martin having a gay dalliance when they were kids. And that sort of ruffled Ross's feathers before the interview in the first act. I always get the impression that Martin was just trying to throw Ross off. But that storyline didn't really go anywhere; it didn't really pay off. It's fair to say that Edward wanted to get rid of it because he didn't want us to relate to Martin as having these prior experimental experiences in his life. So that it might give people an opportunity to think, well, he started with boys when he was a boy . . . like the whole argument, if you start with marijuana you end up on heroin.

RS: Any other changes?

Rowe: The speech where he explains to Stevie about how it was like an alien came to me. That was originally part of his explanation to Ross in the third act. It replaced a beautiful speech which was used with the same intention, to explain to Stevie how this happened to him—a speech about an Irish wolfhound he had as a child. There is a story about burying an Irish wolfhound in *Fragments* too: the body gets frozen, and the tail is too long for the grave and they're in a quandary whether to break the tail off.[1] I think there must have been an Irish wolfhound somewhere in Albee's life.

RS: Yes, Edward actually had a wolfhound named Harry, and the burial story in *Fragments* is closely autobiographical.[2]

Rowe: Well, I have a feeling that it was the same the dog here in *The Goat*.

RS: You began to talk about Bill Pullman's improvisational approach in his work.

Rowe: Well, it's not really so much improvisation; he's really so very much in the moment that he's just experiencing the text really immediately all the time. I have a feeling that a lot of film work encourages that kind of work and that kind of approach, and it's very exciting to be in the presence of that. It's very fresh, and because he's the center of the play, we all, or at least I, feel like my performance is in his body. It's my job to find my performance in him, in the dynamic of trying to get at him and depending on how elusive he is from day to day.

RS: In the fiction of the play, too, you really have to dig into his psyche to get at the truth.

Rowe: That's a very exciting possibility every night.

RS: Tell me more about David's process of working during these rehearsals.

Rowe: An actor up at ART [the American Repertory Theater] who had worked with David at CSC [the Classic Stage Company] and at the Guthrie called him the greatest blocker you've ever seen, and that's my experience too. He is *very* good at articulating the beats of the text through movement. I don't mean necessarily big movement, but just very small things, like sitting forward on a chair or something like that. Given the furniture in this set, there are only a finite number of possibilities for every encounter, and so it's always like a chess match. He's very good at tweaking where actors are in relation to one another, without imposing movement on you, in order to punctuate text and to punctuate each actor's intention from moment to moment.

RS: I noticed a lot of movement, although it seemed organic and natural. Did Edward object to any of it? He doesn't like too much movement.

Rowe: I never got the feeling that there was much argument about that. My sense is that David had free rein. He's very good at keeping a sort of balance between giving the actors a sense of real freedom and at the same time slowly but surely and consistently blending into the actor's rehearsal process a sense of discipline and a sense of the rigors that the text requires. Basically with this material that translates into: you just keep it [*claps*] moving. These jokes and ideas requires a certain velocity. That was also certainly true in our off-Broadway production of *Tiny Alice,* directed by Mark Lamos at the Second Stage Theatre last year.

Notes

1. Albee in the Theatre

1. Appia, in *L'oeuvre d'art vivant*, quoted in Cole and Chinoy, *Directors on Directing*, 42.

2. Copeau, "La mise en scene," 125–126.

3. Guthrie, "Directing a Play," 94.

4. Williams, *Drama in Performance*, 160, 162.

5. Shaw, letter to Louis Wilkinson, December 6, 1909, in Harris, *Bernard Shaw*, 254.

6. Albee has mentioned this production on several occasions; for example, see the account of his press conference in Selvin, *"Albee Directs Albee."*

7. Barnes, "Albee's *Seascape* Is a Major Event"; Rich, "Drama by Albee: *Man Who Had Three Arms*"; Sullivan, "Albee's *Bessie Smith* and *Dream* Revived"; and Barnes, *"Virginia Woolf."*

8. Albee, *"Counting the Ways" and "Listening"*; "Morning Report . . . Stage," *Los Angeles Times*, May 14, 1987; and Richards, "Edward Albee and the Road Not Taken."

9. *Sand* consisted of revised versions of three earlier plays: *Box, The Sandbox,* and *Finding the Sun.* Signature Theatre Company program, 1993–1994.

10. Solomon, "Albee Directs *Ohio Impromptu* and *Krapp's Last Tape*," 1–2; "Notizen"; and Ottavino, interview by author, January 6, 1990.

11. The date at the initial mention of an Albee play indicates the year it was first staged.

12. Feingold, "Albeecentric"; and Canby, "A Season of Albee."

13. For nearly fifty years now, the role of authorial intention has been a central and contentious issue in literary studies. For a recent discussion of intentionalism, see E. D. Hirsch, *Validity in Interpretation;* also see Newton-de Molina, *On Literary Intention;* and Shawcross, *Intentionality and the New Traditionalism.*

14. Wimsatt and Beardsley, "Intention," 229.

15. In conjunction with Derrida's *De la grammatologie* (1967), which initiated deconstruction, Foucault's *The Archaeology of Knowledge* (1969) provided the most influential and lucid articulation of this position. Derrida's and Foucault's participation also gave the discussion of intentionalism unprecedented philosophical weight.

16. Albee, preface to Schneider, *Entrances,* ix–x.

17. Schneider's production, with professional actors in the leads, opened at Stanford University on August 10, 1975.

18. Brook, "The Old Vic to Vincennes," 90.

19. Shaw, *Shaw on Theatre,* 53.

20. La Fontaine, "Triple Threat."

21. Albee, "Edward Albee Talks About: What Does a Playwright Do?" 13.

22. Schneider, *Entrances,* 275.

23. Ibid., 374.

24. Albee, letter to author, November 13, 1994. Schneider's autobiography is silent about the reason Albee asked for other actors. Albee's letter also explains why the Lunt-Fontanne team was uncertain: "They were scared & hesitated—'London, perhaps?'—to the point we had to go elsewhere."

25. Schneider, *Entrances,* 375.

26. Sullivan, "Albee's *Bessie Smith* and *Dream* Revived."

27. Barnes, "Albee's *Seascape* Is a Major Event."

28. Kerr, "Albee's Unwritten Part; McNally's Missing Joke."

29. Gottfried, "*Woolf* Returns with Same Bite."

30. Kerr, "*Virginia Woolf*—Sparks Still Fly."

31. Kroll, "Albee's Blackjack."

32. Kalem, "Till Death Do Us Part: *Who's Afraid of Virginia Woolf?* by Edward Albee"; and Glover, quoted in publicity brochure, 1978, Albee Papers, University of California, Davis.

33. Barnes, "Double Bill by Albee"; and Boyer, "Premier Albee: Irresistible Rhythms, Unnatural Acts."

34. Johnson, "*Albee Directs Albee*" and "Albee Mixes Humor, Pain."

35. Canby, "A Season of Albee."

36. Feingold, "Albeecentric."

37. Albee, interview by Peter Adam, in Kolin, *Conversations with Edward Albee,* 137.

38. Albee, interview by author, September 14, 1978; and Sullivan, "Edward Albee: Playwright with More Than One Act."

39. Albee, interview by Jeanne Wolf, in Kolin, *Conversations with Edward Albee,* 116.

40. Albee, quoted in Selvin, "*Albee Directs Albee.*"

41. Jouvet, "The Profession of the Producer, II," 59.

42. Marowitz, *Directing the Action,* 11.

43. Jones, *Great Directors at Work,* 160; and Murphy, *Tennessee Williams and Elia Kazan,* xii-xiii.

44. Kazan, quoted in Jones, *Great Directors at Work,* 171.

45. Schneider, interview by author, February 14, 1980.

46. Anouilh, interview, in Hayman, *Playback,* 28.

47. Shaw, *Shaw on Theatre,* 279.

48. Sullivan, "Edward Albee: Playwright with More Than One Act."

49. Albee, interview by author, January 6, 1990, excerpted in Solomon, "Text, Subtext, and Performance," 98.

50. Gaskill, interview by author, February 25, 1983.

51. Beckett, quoted in McMillan and Fehsenfeld, *Beckett in the Theatre,* 88; and Cohn, *Just Play,* 258.

52. Clurman, quoted in Cole and Chinoy, *Directors on Directing,* 272.

53. Albee, quoted in Shirley, "An Audience with Albee."

54. A notable exception is Stephen J. Bottoms, *Albee: "Who's Afraid of Virginia Woolf?"*

(Cambridge: Cambridge University Press, 2000), which examines multiple productions of a single play.

55. Nemirovich-Danchenko, quoted in Cole and Chinoy, *Directors on Directing*, 120.

2. Casting Practices and Director's Preparation

1. Five years later Albee changed the names from He and She to Jack and Gillian, respectively, during rehearsals for the play's second production.

2. Albee, conversation with author, September 14, 1978.

3. Dukore, *Bernard Shaw, Director*, 42.

4. Brecht, quoted in Willet, *Theatre of Bertolt Brecht*, 155; and Kazan, quoted in Ciment, *Kazan on Kazan*, 41.

5. Clurman, *On Directing*, 68–69.

6. Butler, interview by author, November 23, 1994.

7. For example, Marjorie Austrian and Rebecca Laure, two actors not offered a role, comment on this in separate letters in the *Albee Directs Albee* Collection, D-131, University of California, Davis.

8. Albee, conversation with author, August 16, 1978.

9. Albee, quoted in McColm, "The Mystery of Edward Albee"; and Pendleton, interview by author, February 20, 1980.

10. Albee, "Edward Albee Talks About: What Does a Playwright Do?" 10.

11. Albee, interview by Joe Pollack, in Kolin, *Conversations with Edward Albee*, 214.

12. Ibid., 13; and Pendleton, interview by author, February 20, 1980.

13. Pendleton, interview by author, February 20, 1980.

14. Schneider, *Entrances*, 374; and Albee, letter to author, November 13, 1994.

15. Carter, interview by author, November 20, 1994; and Sacharow, interview by author, November 23, 1994. For additional details see chapter 9, on *Three Tall Women*, and my interview of Lawrence Sacharow in chapter 11.

16. Schneider, "What Does a Director Do?" 16–17.

17. Cohn, *Just Play*, 237, 271.

18. Smilgis, "Edward Albee Blames His Newest Broadway Flop on the Critics," 70–73.

19. See, for instance, Albee's comments in Stern, "I Want My Intent Clear."

20. Clurman, *On Directing*, 64.

21. Kazan, quoted in Jones, *Great Directors at Work*, 138.

22. Clurman, *On Directing*, 10.

23. Gottfried, "Edward Albee's Latest."

24. Barnes, "Albee's *Seascape* Is a Major Event"; and Hewes, "Albee Surfaces."

25. Barnes, "*Virginia Woolf*."

26. Kerr, "*Virginia Woolf*—Sparks Still Fly."

27. Gussow, "What's New? Old Shows."

28. Albee, interview by author, September 14, 1978.

29. Albee, "Edward Albee Talks About: What Does a Playwright Do?" 10.

30. Albee, interview by author, September 14, 1978.

31. Dukore, *Bernard Shaw, Director*, 39, 59, 61, 189.

32. Albee, interview by author, September 14, 1978.

33. Albee, quoted in Jalon, "Edward Albee: 'Let Actor Be Creative.'"

34. Albee, interview by author, September 14, 1978.

35. Vilar, quoted in Cole and Chinoy, *Directors on Directing*, 267. Later, however, Vilar seems to have amended his opinion. Clurman's *On Directing* mentions that Vilar "recommended" a director's book and a "written analysis" of a play (26).

36. Shaw, letter to Siegfried Trebitsch, December 10, 1902, Berg Collection, New York Public Library, quoted in Dukore, *Bernard Shaw, Director*, 29.

37. Cohn, *Just Play*, 230–279. For a thorough analysis of Beckett's prerehearsal preparation, see McMillan and Fehsenfeld, *Beckett in the Theatre*.

38. Cohn, *Just Play*, 236.

39. Bergman, quoted in Marker and Marker, *Four Decades in the Theater*, 8; also see 9–12.

40. Agneta Ekmanner and Anita Bjork, respectively, quoted in Carlson and Helander, "Ingmar Bergman," 15.

41. Anita Bjork, quoted in ibid.

42. Freedman, "He Knows the Author, But . . . "

43. Kazan, quoted in Ciment, *Kazan on Kazan*, 175.

44. Guthrie, "An Audience of One," 245.

45. Schneider, "What Does a Director Do?" 16.

46. Albee, quoted in Stern, "I Want My Intent Clear."

47. Ibid.

48. Albee, interview by author, September 14, 1978.

49. Albee, quoted in Stern, "I Want My Intent Clear."

3. *The American Dream*

1. Albee, Preface, *"The American Dream" and "The Zoo Story,"* 53–54. Subsequent page numbers are given in the text.

2. Albee, quoted in Booth, "Albee and Schneider Observe," 79.

3. Albee, quoted in Shirley, "An Audience with Albee."

4. Drake, *"Albee Directs Albee* at UCLA."

5. Jalon, "Edward Albee: 'Let Actor Be Creative'"; and Collins, "Definitive Albee."

6. Weiner, *"Albee Directs Albee."*

7. Albee, quoted in Jalon, "Edward Albee: 'Let Actor Be Creative.'"

8. Undated press release, brochure, and copy of contract, *Albee Directs Albee* Collection, D-131, University of California, Davis.

9. Pendleton, interview by author, February 15, 1980.

10. Albee divided the twenty-two roles into the following categories. The Older Man included Daddy (*The American Dream* and *The Sandbox*), Peter (*The Zoo Story*), Fam (*Fam and Yam*), He (*Counting the Ways*), and Man (*Listening*). The Young Man united Jerry (*The Zoo Story*), Young Man (*The American Dream* and *The Sandbox*), Yam (*Fam and Yam*), and Chairman Mao (*Quotations from Chairman Mao Tse-Tung*). The third category, Older Woman 1 and 2, embraced Mommy (*The American Dream* and *The Sandbox*), Mrs. Barker (*The American Dream*), the Voice (*Box*), the Long-Winded Lady (*Quotations from Chairman Mao Tse-Tung*), She (*Counting the Ways*), and the Woman (*Listening*). The final type, the Young Woman, included the Girl (*Listening*) but, in order to keep costs down, also Grandma (*The American Dream* and *The Sandbox*) and the Old Woman (*Quotations from Chairman Mao Tse-Tung*). Albee also reasoned that acting skill would ultimately trump physical features and age, but when this assumption proved too optimistic in actual practice, he hired a sixth actor, veteran Albee actor Sudie Bond, as Old Woman 3 to play the older woman roles initially played by the Young Woman.

11. Albee, interview by Dick Cavett, *The Dick Cavett Show*, PBS, June 1, 1979.

12. Albee announced the 450 figure at a press conference a month later: Selvin, "*Albee Directs Albee*"; and Freedman, "He Knows the Author, But . . ." In an undated note circa 1980 Mark Amitin includes two additional dates (July 15 and 16) and lists 550 as the number of actors interviewed, suggesting that the producer and the director might have used the weekend preceding the announced dates to informally screen additional actors unavailable on the scheduled dates (*Albee Directs Albee* Collection, D-131, University of California, Davis).

13. Here too the number that Amitin gives (90) is at variance with Albee's figure given at the press conference.

14. Throughout this book, when I enumerate the professional experience of actors, designers, and stage managers, I do so only up to the date of the production under discussion, in order to accurately convey their experience and standing at the time of that production. Also, unless otherwise indicated, all biographical information comes from my copies of the program notes for the production(s) under discussion. That said, the following are brief biographies of the *Albee Directs Albee* actors:

Wyman Pendleton (Older Man) had appeared on Broadway in *Othello, Henry V, There's One in Every Marriage* (Feydeau), and *Cat on a Hot Tin Roof* (Tennessee Williams). His Albee plays included *Tiny Alice, Malcolm, Box* and *Quotations from Chairman Mao Tse-Tung*, and *All Over* (all on Broadway), *A Delicate Balance* (national company), and *The American Dream* and *The Zoo Story* (off-Broadway). His other off-Broadway productions were *Summer and Smoke, Gallows Humor, The Child Buyer*, and *The Giants' Dance*. Besides doing film and TV work, Pendleton had performed with almost every important regional theatre in North America, including, among others, the Goodman Theatre, the American Shakespeare Festival, the Theatre Company of Boston, and the Stratford Shakespeare Festival, Ontario.

Stephen Rowe (Young Man) had trained at the Yale School of Drama and worked for three seasons at the Yale Repertory Theatre. His credits included Andrei Serban's production of *The Ghost Sonata*, Alvin Epstein's *A Midsummer Night's Dream*, and Ron Daniel's Obie Award–winning production of Edward Bond's *Bingo*. Under Polish filmmaker and stage director Andrzej Wajda, he had played principal roles in *The Possessed* and *White Marriage*. His experience also included two seasons at the Williamstown Theatre Festival, the American premiere of Christopher Durang's *The Vietnamization of New Jersey* at Yale, and Richard Nelson's *Jungle Coup* off-Broadway.

Patricia Kilgarriff (Older Woman 1) had trained at the Royal Academy of Dramatic Art and had performed in the West End in *Candide, Oliver, The Most Happy Fella*, and *The Beggar's Opera* (Royal Shakespeare Company). Besides performing with scores of English repertory companies, she had also worked in American regional theatre, television, and film (*Oliver!* and *The Amorous Adventures of Moll Flanders*).

Eileen Burns (Older Woman 2) came with a long theatrical career that had begun with Orson Welles's *Native Son* on Broadway. Her other Broadway credits included *Daughters of Atreus*, Kaufman and Hart's *The Fabulous Invalid* and *The American Way*, Clare Booth Luce's *The Women*, and the Circle in the Square revival of O'Neill's *Mourning Becomes Electra*. She had also performed with Maureen O'Sullivan and Arlene Francis in *Sabrina Fair* and Lana Turner in *Bell, Book and Candle*. Her other credits included the off-off-Broadway one-woman show *The Women of Henry James* and Oliver Hailey's *The Use of the Hall* as well as extensive radio and TV work (*Broadway TV Theatre, U.S. Steel Hour, Studio One, and Love of Life*).

Catherine Bruno (Young Woman) had earned an MFA from New York University, studied with Joseph Chaikin and Paul Sills, and performed off-Broadway at the Playwrights Horizons and off-off-Broadway at the Performance Group (*The Marilyn Project*) and the Open Space.

James Knobeloch (Young Man understudy, non-speaking parts, and assistant stage manager) had previously worked at the Ohio Repertory Theatre in Columbus (*When You Comin' Back, Red Ryder?* premiere), at Sugar Loaf Mountain Theatre in Chillicothe, Ohio, and at Ohio State University in Columbus and Southern Illinois University in Edwardsville.

Michael Miller (understudy, Older Man) had appeared on Broadway in *No Man's Land* (with Sir John Gielgud and Sir Ralph Richardson), *Ivanov* (with Vivien Leigh), *Black Comedy, Trial of Lee Harvey Oswald,* and *Morning, Noon and Night.* His off-Broadway work included *Under Milkwood, Little Murders,* and *Macbeth.* He had created a one-man show, *Process,* based on Kafka's *A Report to the Academy,* and acted with the New York Shakespeare Festival, the American Shakespeare Festival, the Arena Stage, the Alley Theatre, and Stage West, among others. He had made seven feature films, and his television credits ranged from Arthur Miller's *After the Fall* to most of the daytime soap operas.

At this time producer Mark Amitin hired Michael Bartuccio as production stage manager. He had served as the production manager for two years at the Open Theatre, where he had also designed the set for *Nightwalk.* In addition, he had been the touring manager for the Belgian company Theatre Laboratoire Vicinal and worked as the production manager for McGill University's Pollack Concert Hall. Having toured with the Belafonte Show, Bartuccio brought some experience in the commercial theatre as well.

15. Pendleton, interview by author, February 20, 1980.

16. The other understudy hired was Michael Miller, for the Older Man roles. No understudies were hired for the three women actors, since the order of the repertory allowed them to cover each other's roles.

17. Schneider, "What Does a Director Do?" 16, and *Entrances,* 289.

18. Agneta Ekmanner, quoted in Carlson and Helander, "Ingmar Bergman," 15.

19. Cohn, *Just Play,* 237.

20. Rossi, *Minneapolis Rehearsals,* 5–6.

21. Hayman, *Playback,* 31–59.

22. Selbourne, *The Making of "A Midsummer Night's Dream,"* 1–7.

23. Gaskill, interviews by author, February 25 and March 9, 1983.

24. Hardwick, who acted under Shaw's direction, quoted in Dukore, *Bernard Shaw, Director,* 44.

25. Clurman, *On Directing,* 88.

26. Shaw, quoted in Dukore, *Bernard Shaw, Director,* 44.

27. Vilar, quoted in Clurman, *On Directing,* ix–x.

28. Albee, quoted in Jalon, "Edward Albee: 'Let Actor Be Creative.'"

29. Selbourne, *The Making of "A Midsummer Night's Dream,"* 27.

30. Gaskill, interviews by author, February 25 and March 9, 1983.

31. Schneider, *Entrances,* 288, 286.

32. Armstrong, "George Bernard Shaw," 352.

33. Shaw, letter to Louis Wilkinson, quoted in Dukore, *Bernard Shaw, Director,* 49.

34. Stanislavsky, quoted in Clurman, *On Directing,* 115.

35. Weber, "Brecht as Director," 109.

36. Rutenberg, *Edward Albee,* 75.

37. Albee, "Edward Albee," 32.

38. Schneider, paraphrased in Rutenberg, *Edward Albee,* 75.

39. Sudie Bond (Old Woman 3) had appeared on Broadway in *The Waltz of the Toreadors; Harold; My Mother, My Father and Me; Thieves; Hay Fever* (revival); *The Impossible Years;* and *Keep It in the Family.* Her Albee plays included the original productions of *The Sandbox* and *The American Dream* (as well as the latter's Broadway revival) and the Broadway premiere of *Quotations from Chairman Mao Tse-Tung.* Her off-Broadway work included *Summer and Smoke* (Circle in the Square), *The Memorandum* (Public Theater), *The Great Western Union* (Bouwerie Lane Theatre), *The Local Stigmatic* (Actors Playhouse), *New York! New York!* (Playwrights Horizons), and *The Cherry Orchard* (Roundabout Theatre) and earned her three Obie Awards, including two for the Albee plays. In addition to working off-off-Broadway, she acted in numerous popular TV shows and a few films.

40. Schneider, *Entrances,* 310.

41. Albee, "Promptbook," 4.

42. Schneider, *Entrances,* 347.

43. Schneider, quoted in Knowlson, *Samuel Beckett,* 55.

44. Schneider, *Entrances,* 123–124.

45. Ibid., 123.

46. Bergman, quoted in Marker and Marker, *Four Decades in the Theater,* 230.

47. Albee, interview by author, February 14, 1980.

48. Meehan, quoted in Stenz, *Edward Albee,* 29.

49. Paolucci, *From Tension to Tonic,* 31. Paolucci's assessment of the Young Man as a "redeemer" echoes Howard Taubman's view of him as a "sacrificial lamb" in his review of the original production in the *New York Times,* January 25, 1961.

50. Hirsch, *Who's Afraid of Edward Albee?* 20–21.

51. Hayman, *Edward Albee,* 28; and Stenz, *Edward Albee,* 32.

52. Roudane, *Understanding Edward Albee,* 57.

53. Ucciardo, *"Albee Directs Albee."*

54. Albee, "An Interview with Edward Albee, March 18, 1981," 20.

55. Albee, "An Interview with Edward Albee," 120.

56. Albee, "An Interview with Edward Albee, March 18, 1981," 20.

57. Cohn, *Just Play,* 237, 240.

58. Ibid., 240.

59. See, for instance, Cohn, *Edward Albee,* 13; and Paolucci, *From Tension to Tonic,* 31.

60. Albee, "Edward Albee," 32.

61. Cohn, *Edward Albee,* 14; and Roudane, *Understanding Edward Albee,* 53.

62. Schneider, *Entrances,* 289.

63. Albee, "On Making Authors Happy."

64. Albee, interview by author, February 14, 1980.

65. Taubman, "Albee's *The American Dream*"; and Schneider, *Entrances,* 289 and photograph of the set following 224.

66. Karl Eigsti was a veteran Broadway and regional theatre designer. At the time of these productions, Eigsti's work was represented on Broadway by *Eubie* and *Grease,* and during the preceding two seasons he had designed *Cold Storage, Yentl,* and the revivals of *Once in a Lifetime* and *Sweet Bird of Youth.* Besides other New York credits, Eigsti had extensive experience designing for theatres like the Tyrone Guthrie Theatre, the American Shakespeare Festival, the Long Wharf Theatre, the Kennedy Center, and, above all, the Arena Stage,

where, like Albee director Alan Schneider, he had worked frequently, having designed a total of twenty-six productions. Eigsti also taught design at the New York University School of the Arts.

67. Taubman, "Albee's *The American Dream*"; and Schneider, *Entrances,* 288.

68. The set, with its frames, tension towers, cloth drapes, and furniture—freshly covered and painted—was on stage for the first preview on August 27, 1978, even though a copy of Eigsti's "Composite Ground Plan—*Albee Directs Albee*" is curiously dated September 1, 1978 (author's possession).

69. Balliet, "Three Cheers for Albee."

70. Cohn, *Edward Albee,* 11.

71. Stephen Pollock's lighting design credits at that time included the Obie Award–winning production of Edward Bond's *Bingo* at the Yale Repertory Theatre and the premiere of *Night Riders* at the Berkshire Theatre Festival.

72. Eichelbaum, "Strong and Purposeful Staging"; and Drake, "*Albee Directs Albee* at UCLA."

73. Burchard, "*Albee by Albee.*"

74. Wallach, "Albee on Albee."

75. O'Haire, "Art Center Premiers First Season"; "Albee: The Double Takes"; Ucciardo, "*Albee Directs Albee*"; and Kass, "Albee: A Cynic's Look at Society."

76. Burchard, "*Albee by Albee.*"

77. Coe, "Albee Directing Albee."

78. Weiner, "*Albee Directs Albee*"; and Eichelbaum, "Strong and Purposeful Staging."

79. Bowman, "Warm Audience for Albee."

80. Feingold, "All Fugued Up."

81. Collins, "Definitive Albee."

82. Wallach, "Albee on Albee"; Kass, "Albee: A Cynic's Look at Society"; and O'Haire, "Art Center Premiers First Season."

83. Chriss, "Albee Directs Albee with Much Passion"; and "Albee: The Double Takes."

84. Schier, "Albee Revival Stands"; and Collins, "Definitive Albee."

85. Weiner, "*Albee Directs Albee.*"

86. Eichelbaum, "Strong and Purposeful Staging."

87. Bowman, "Warm Audience for Albee"; and Drake, "*Albee Directs Albee* at UCLA."

4. *The Zoo Story*

1. Bloom, introduction to *Edward Albee,* 2.

2. Photocopy of the stage manager's book, in author's possession.

3. Max Reinhardt, *Schriften: Briefe, Reden, Aufsätze, Interviews, Gespräche, Auszüge aus Regiebüchern,* ed. Hugo Fetting (East Berlin: Henschelverlag Kunst und Gesellschaft, 1974), 258–259, quoted in Esslin, "Max Reinhardt," 16; and Clurman, *On Directing,* 16.

4. Albee, *"The American Dream" and "The Zoo Story,"* 41. Subsequent page numbers are given in the text.

5. Willet, *Brecht in Context,* 226.

6. Bergman, quoted in Marker and Marker, *Four Decades in the Theater,* 48.

7. Ibid., 47.

8. Hiley, *Theatre at Work,* 122, 55.

9. Stein, quoted in Patterson, *Peter Stein,* 165. Stein made this comment while directing Botho Strauss's *Gross und klein* in West Berlin in 1978.

10. Goorney, *The Theatre Workshop Story,* 122, 164–165, 167.

11. Stern, "I Want My Intent Clear."

12. Albee, *The Lady From Dubuque* (New York: Atheneum, 1980). All page numbers are given in the text. I draw on my observation and daily record of the rehearsals of *The Lady From Dubuque,* January 2–31, 1980, Morosco Theatre, New York, and on my audiotaped interviews with Albee and Schneider.

13. Just before opening, Baxter Harris replaced Kevin O'Connor, whose recovery from throat surgery proved much slower than anticipated.

14. Albee, interview by author, February 14, 1980.

15. Bergman, quoted in Marker and Marker, *Four Decades in the Theater,* 217.

16. Goorney, *The Theatre Workshop Story,* 167.

17. Atkinson, "A Double Bill Off Broadway"; and Driver, "Bucketful of Dregs."

18. Funke, "Albee Revivals."

19. Heide, "Samuel Beckett's Children"; and Debusscher, *Edward Albee,* 13.

20. Collins, "Definitive Albee."

21. Bloom, introduction to *Edward Albee,* 2.

22. Such misreadings pale in comparison with that of the play's 1963 production in Paris, where, according to the *New York Times* reviewer, from start to finish the entire audience rooted for Peter (Lenoir, "2 Plays by Albee Offered in Paris.")

23. Clurman, *On Directing,* 16.

24. Marker and Marker, *Four Decades in the Theater,* 214.

25. Steger, "Albee Directs Albee."

26. Bentley, "The Brecht Memoir," 21.

27. *Theaterarbeit,* a first-hand account of the Berliner Ensemble's first six productions, edited by Ruth Berlau et al. (3rd ed., Berlin: Henschelverlag Kunst und Gesellschaft, 1967), 315, quoted in Willet, *Theatre of Bertolt Brecht,* 164.

28. Stern, "I Want My Intent Clear"; and Schneider, "What Does a Director Do?" 16.

29. See chapter 3 for Pendleton's major credits.

30. Pendleton, interview by author, February 20, 1980.

31. Drake, "*Albee Directs Albee* at UCLA." Because of the young actor's difficulties in portraying such old characters, as also mentioned in the previous chapter, Albee later replaced her in the Old Woman roles (Grandma in *The American Dream* and *The Sandbox* and the Old Woman in *Quotations from Chairman Mao Tse-Tung*) with veteran actor Sudie Bond, the original Grandma in both *The American Dream* and *The Sandbox.*

32. Shaw, *Shaw on Theatre,* 285.

33. Weber, "Brecht as Director," 109.

34. Max Reinhardt, *Schriften: Briefe, Reden, Aufsätze, Interviews, Gespräche, Auszüge aus Regiebüchern,* ed. Hugo Fetting (East Berlin: Henschelverlag Kunst und Gesellschaft, 1974), 258–259, quoted in Esslin, *Max Reinhardt,* 16.

35. Cohn, *Just Play,* 237.

36. Pendleton, interview by author, February 20, 1980. Nonetheless, it must be reiterated that in this instance Albee allowed actors to work without him more often than usual, because of the extraordinarily tight rehearsal schedule imposed by the production budget.

37. Pendleton, interview by author, February 20, 1980.

38. Schneider, "What Does a Director Do?" 17.

39. Rowe, letter to author, December 8, 1978; and Knobeloch, letter to author, November 13, 1978.

40. Pendleton, interview by author, February 20, 1980.

41. Rowe, letter to author, December 8, 1978.

42. Knobeloch, letter to author, November 13, 1978.

43. Reinhardt, *Schriften,* 258–259, quoted in Esslin, *Max Reinhardt,* 17; and Clurman, *On Directing,* 111.

44. Chriss, "Albee Directs Albee with Much Passion."

45. Steger, "Albee Directs Albee."

46. Wallach, "Albee on Albee"; and "Albee: The Double Takes."

47. O'Haire, "Art Center Premiers First Season"; and Kass, "Albee: A Cynic's Look at Society."

48. Cohn, "On Playwrights Directing."

49. Eichelbaum, "Strong and Purposeful Staging."

50. Weiner, *"Albee Directs Albee."*

51. Bowman, "Warm Audience for Albee"; and Coe, "Albee Directing Albee."

52. Schier, "Albee Revival Stands."

53. Drake, *"Albee Directs Albee* at UCLA."

5. *Fam and Yam* and *The Sandbox*

1. Albee, interview by Dick Cavett, *The Dick Cavett Show,* PBS, June 1, 1979.

2. These plays—together with *Nekros* by Harry Tierney—were produced on a bill simply entitled "Three One-Acts." Gelb, "Plays by Beckett and Albee in ANTA Series." The play's original performance occurred on August 27, 1960, at The White Barn, Westport, CT.

3. Albee, *"The Sandbox"; "The Death of Bessie Smith" (with "Fam and Yam"),* 82. Subsequent page numbers are given in the text.

4. Albee's new preferences were realized in the set by designer Karl Eigsti.

5. Albee, interview by author, February 14, 1980.

6. Ibid.

7. Gelb, "Plays by Beckett and Albee in ANTA Series."

8. Rutenberg, *Edward Albee,* 52–53, 51.

9. American Conservatory Theatre, Marines' Memorial Theatre, San Francisco, November 4, 1978.

10. The first performance of *The Sandbox* occurred on a bill called "4 in 1" at the Jazz Gallery in New York City. In addition to *The Sandbox,* the four-play bill consisted of Fernando Arrabal's *The Two Executioners* and *Picnic on the Battlefield* and H. B. Lutz's *The Chip.* Gelb, *"4 in 1* Bill of One-Act Plays"; and Hewes, *The Best Plays of 1961–1962,* 323.

11. Albee, "Edward Albee," 67.

12. Albee, interview by Dick Cavett, *The Dick Cavett Show,* PBS, June 1, 1979.

13. This reading occurred on the afternoon of August 21, 1978.

14. Albee, Preface, *"The American Dream"* and *"The Zoo Story,"* 9.

15. Rutenberg, *Edward Albee,* 43.

16. *The Sandbox,* One-Act Theatre Company, San Francisco, June 17, 1979.

17. Debusscher, *Edward Albee,* 34.

18. Paolucci, *From Tension to Tonic,* 27. Subsequent page numbers are given in the text.

19. Rutenberg, *Edward Albee,* 48; Bigsby, *Albee,* 30; and Debusscher, *Edward Albee,* 33.

20. Debusscher, *Edward Albee,* 33; and Bigsby, *Albee,* 30.

21. McCarthy, *Edward Albee,* 47.

22. Shaw, *Shaw on Theatre,* 267.

23. Willet, *The Theatre of Bertolt Brecht,* 161.

24. Weber, "Brecht as Director," 105.

25. Cohn, *Just Play,* 258.

26. Dark, "Production Casebook No. 5," 31.

27. Bentley, "The Brecht Memoir," 21–22.

28. Dukore, *Bernard Shaw, Director,* 13.

29. Arrabal, quoted in Amoia, *Off-Stage Voices,* 89.

30. Albee, quoted in Stern, "I Want My Intent Clear."

31. Albee, interview by Dick Cavett, *The Dick Cavett Show,* PBS, June 1, 1979.

32. Dukore, *Bernard Shaw, Director,* 45.

33. Vilar, quoted in Cole and Chinoy, *Directors on Directing,* 267.

6. *Box* and *Quotations from Chairman Mao Tse-Tung*

1. Gottfried, *"Box* and *Mao"*; and Kerr, "Mao—But What Message?"

2. Reprinted as the introduction to Albee, *"Box" and "Quotations from Chairman Mao Tse-Tung": Two Inter-related Plays,* ix–xi. Subsequent page numbers are given in the text, including for quotations from Albee's introductory material.

3. During the rehearsals and interviews Albee customarily abbreviated the longer title as *Mao Tse-Tung,* a practice I follow here. Most critics, in contrast, use the abbreviation *Quotations.*

4. McCarthy, *Edward Albee,* 43; and Paolucci, *From Tension to Tonic,* 127.

5. Such a directorial approach toward humanizing the Voice in *Box* eventually culminated in his introducing a silent, shrouded female figure into the cube when he directed the play at the Signature Theatre in 1994. With her back to the audience, this black-clad figure sat on her knees in the center of the square, stared into the void, and occasionally moved her torso in a wave-like motion. Canby, "A Season of Albee"; and Richards, "3 Albee One-Acters."

6. Pendleton, interview by author, February 15, 1980.

7. Pendleton, rehearsal notations in typescript. All information about the Broadway rehearsals comes from notations in this script, which is in my possession.

8. Albee's preference for a simple set and minimal movement for *Mao* in the auditorium was principally an aesthetic one, although a contributing pragmatic consideration was a projected tour involving travel as well as playing in theatres with very different auditoria.

9. Nearly two decades later he published this untruncated speech as "Monologue of the Long-Winded Lady" in Albee, *Selected Plays of Edward Albee,* 293–304.

10. Cohn, "Albee's *Box* and Ours," 141–142; and Bigsby, *"Box* and *Quotations from Chairman Mao Tse-Tung,"* 159.

11. Albee, interview by author, February 14, 1980.

12. Albee, interview by Dick Cavett, *The Dick Cavett Show,* PBS, June 1, 1979. Also see Jalon, "Edward Albee: 'Let Actor Be Creative.'"

13. Jack MacGowran, quoted in McMillan and Fehsenfeld, *Beckett in the Theatre,* 67.

14. Schneider, "Reality Is Not Enough," 72.

15. Author's observations.

16. Bergman, quoted in Marker and Marker, *Four Decades in the Theater,* 1, 9.

17. Bergman, quoted in Marker and Marker, *A Project for the Theatre,* 5.

18. Brook, quoted in Selbourne, *The Making of "A Midsummer Night's Dream,"* 23.

19. Fletcher, "Roger Blin at Work," 404.

20. Schneider, interview by author, January 31, 1980.

21. Ibid.

1. Quoted in Coe, "Lone Star over Lithuania," 26.

2. Kochanskyte, quoted in ibid., 26.

3. Bruce Gray had appeared in *Androcles and the Lion*, *The Complaisant Lover*, *The Rehearsal*, *The Beggar's Opera*, *The Philadelphia Story*, *The Matchmaker*, and *Hamlet* in such theatres as the Mermaid (London, U.K.), the Theatre Royal (Bath, U.K.). the Studio Arena Theatre (Buffalo), and the Circle Repertory Company (New York City). Gray also had extensive television and movie credits. He was a guest star on *Dallas*, *Matlock*, *Falcon Crest*, *Silver Spoons*, *Hitchcock*, and *Murder, She Wrote*, and he had recurring roles on *Knots Landing*, *Head of the Class*, *Emerald Point N.A.S.*, and *Murphy's Law*. His movies included *L.B.J.*, *Drop-Out Father*, *Dragnet*, *Let's Get Harry*, *Between Friends*, *A Fan's Notes*, and *The Club*.

Carol Mayo Jenkins had appeared on Broadway in *The Three Sisters*, *Oedipus Rex*, *There's One in Every Marriage*, *First Monday in October*, and *The Suicide*. Her off-Broadway credits included *The Old Ones*, *Little Eyolf*, *Zinnia* (Drama Desk nomination, Outstanding Actress), *Moliere in Spite of Himself*, and *The Lady's Not for Burning*. She had also done extensive work in regional theatres and had a recurring role on the television series *Fame*.

John Ottavino had appeared in New York in *The Open Boat* at the Ensemble Studio Theatre, in *The Crucible* at the Roundabout Theatre Conservatory, and in *Dandy Dick* at the Roundabout Theatre. He had acted in several Albee-directed productions, including *All Men Are Whores*, *Hawk Moon*, and *The Sandbox* at Vienna's English Theatre, *The Death of Bessie Smith* at the Alley Theatre, and *Seascape* at the Coconut Grove Playhouse. On television, he had worked on *The Equalizer*, *The Guiding Light*, and *As the World Turns*. His films included *Falling in Love* and *See You in the Morning*.

Cynthia Bassham was a recent graduate of the American Conservatory Theatre in San Francisco. She had appeared in *A Funny Thing Happened on the Way to the Forum*, *A Christmas Carol*, *Marco Millions*, and *Feathers* at the Geary Theater in San Francisco and in *All My Sons* at the San Jose Repertory Company.

4. For further details, see Evans, "Alley's *Virginia Woolf* to play in Soviet Union"; and Coe, "Lone Star over Lithuania." Politics caused a last-minute cancellation of the engagement at the Sovremennik Theatre, where artistic director Galina Volchek had herself played Martha in a Russian production of *Who's Afraid of Virginia Woolf?* Coe, "Lone Star over Lithuania," 24.

5. The following discussion focuses on these Alley Theatre rehearsals, held from December 19, 1989, to January 10, 1990.

6. Albee, letter to author, September 11, 1989.

7. Edward Albee, *Who's Afraid of Virginia Woolf?* (New York: Atheneum, 1962), 242. Subsequent page numbers are given in the text.

8. For an excellent discussion of five major productions of *Who's Afraid of Virginia Woolf?* see Bottoms, *Albee: "Who's Afraid of Virginia Woolf?"* Additional analyses of this and other Albee plays can be found in Bottoms's fine collection of essays, *The Cambridge Companion to Edward Albee*.

9. Sagal, "Albee Directs Albee in Los Angeles," 17.

10. Stenz, *Edward Albee*, 49.

11. Schneider, quoted in Shelton, "Alan Schneider's Direction," 40.

12. Ibid., 45.

13. Albee, interview by author, September 14, 1978.

14. Schneider, interview by author, January 31, 1980.

15. Baxandall, "The Theatre of Edward Albee," 30.

16. Albee, quoted in Rutenberg, *Edward Albee,* 230.

17. Schneider, "Reality Is Not Enough," 72.

18. Nadel, "*Who's Afraid* at Billy Rose," 254.

19. Hill, interview by author, January 5, 1990.

20. "Landmark Symposium: *Who's Afraid of Virginia Woolf?*" 10.

21. Ottavino, interview by author, January 6, 1990.

22. Carlson and Helander, "Ingmar Bergman," 16, 15.

23. Lindblom, quoted in ibid., 15.

24. Roudane, *Understanding Edward Albee,* 70.

25. Bigsby, *Twentieth-Century American Drama,* 268, and *Modern American Drama,* 134.

26. Hirsch, *Who's Afraid of Edward Albee?* 29.

27. Schneider, quoted in Shelton, "Alan Schneider's Direction," 44–45.

28. Stenz, *Edward Albee,* 39, 43.

29. Schneider, quoted in Shelton, "Alan Schneider's Direction," 43.

30. Ibid.

31. Roudane, "*Who's Afraid of Virginia Woolf?*" 75; and Stenz, *Edward Albee,* 50.

32. Cohn, *Edward Albee,* 23; and Roudane, "*Who's Afraid of Virginia Woolf?*" 87.

33. Albee firmly refused requests by public relations staff at the Los Angeles Music Center to remove George's Oriental references (PCI).

34. Kazan, quoted in Jones, *Great Directors at Work,* 142.

35. Schneider, "What Does a Director Do?" 17.

36. Cohn, *Edward Albee,* 24.

37. Hirsch, *Who's Afraid of Edward Albee?* 30.

38. McCarthy, *Edward Albee,* 68, 75.

39. Albee, interview by Kathy Sullivan, *Conversations with Edward Albee,* 185.

40. Ibid., 98.

41. Schneider in *Playbill* (October 1964), quoted in Shelton, "Alan Schneider's Direction," 40.

8. *Marriage Play*

1. Albee, *Marriage Play* (New York: Dramatists Play Service, 1995), 38. Subsequent page numbers are given in the text.

2. Kathleen Butler had appeared on the New York stage in *Triangles, Craig's Wife,* and *Hiding on the Outside,* and in the film *A League of Their Own.* Tom Klunis had appeared in eleven Broadway and twenty-three off-Broadway productions, as well as performing in such major venues as Joseph Papp's New York Shakespeare Festival and Public Theater, the Alley Theatre, the Arena Stage, the Hartford Stage, the Yale Repertory Theatre, and the McCarter Theatre. Among his Broadway plays were *Henry V, The Devils, The Bacchae, Ghosts,* and *The Little Foxes.* He had worked with playwrights Paddy Chayefsky on *Gideon* (Broadway), William Gibson on *The Miracle Worker* (off-Broadway), and David Hare on *Plenty* (Broadway) and *A Map of the World* (off-Broadway), and had previously worked with Albee on *Counting the Ways* (Alley Theatre).

3. Shirley Knight came with a distinguished list of theatre, film, and television honors: a Tony Award, an Emmy Award, a London Critics Award, a Venice Film Festival award for Best Actress, a Critics' Prize at the Cannes Film Festival, and nominations for two Academy Awards. Her major theatre productions included *The Three Sisters* (directed by

Lee Strasberg), *The Cherry Orchard, A Touch of the Poet, The Glass Menagerie, A Streetcar Named Desire, A Lovely Afternoon for Creve Coeur* (written for her by Tennessee Williams), *Kennedy's Children,* and *Landscape of the Body.*

4. The Alley Theatre production was, in fact, produced in collaboration with the McCarter Theatre.

5. For a humorous account of Albee's dictating the details of director James Houghton's production of *Marriage Play* at the Signature Theatre Company, especially the number of couches that Albee rejected for the set, see Blum, "What's It All About, Albee?"

6. Spencer, "Echoes from the Wilderness Years"; and Nightingale, "Unholy Deadlock."

7. These productions are listed in a press release from the Alley Theatre, December 11, 1991, in my possession.

8. In addition to my record of the rehearsals and early performances and conversations with Albee, this account is also based on conversations and interviews with the four actors and with Derek Mclane, who designed the set, as well as the costumes (January 3 and 4, 1992).

9. Shewey, "The Persistence of Edward Albee," 19.

10. Shaw, *Shaw on Theatre,* 153.

11. *Who's Afraid of Virginia Woolf?* Doolittle Theatre, Hollywood, CA, 1989.

12. Albee retained this version, with his name and the play's title equally emphasized, on the cover and title pages of the printed version of the play as well. This decision has misled most libraries into listing the title not as *Marriage Play* but as *Edward Albee's Marriage Play.*

9. *Three Tall Women*

1. Unless otherwise indicated, information about the various *Three Tall Women* productions discussed in this chapter comes from my interviews with the principal participants: Edward Albee, Myra Carter (A in Vienna, Woodstock, and New York), Kathleen Butler (B in Vienna and understudy for B in Woodstock and New York), Cynthia Bassham (C in Vienna), Jordan Baker (C in Woodstock and New York), and Lawrence Sacharow (director of the Woodstock, New York, and Houston productions). Direct quotations from these interviews are given full citations.

2. Lawrence Sacharow won a Lucille Lortel Award for his direction of *Three Tall Women* and an Obie Award for Len Jenkin's *Five of Us.* He also directed the 1995 Alley Theatre production of *Three Tall Women* in Houston. An off- and off-off-Broadway director since the early 1960s, Sacharow was a pioneer of biographical theatre and had directed at such venues as the Caffé Cino, the Judson Poets' Theater, Café La Mama, the Classic Stage Company, and the Hudson Guild. In 1979 he established the non-profit River Arts Repertory and served as its artistic director. That theatre eventually began to serve as a first stop for new work that went on to off-Broadway and even Broadway (Taitz, "Off-Broadway Plays Sprout in Summer Theater"). Sacharow's other notable productions were the American premieres of Derek Walcott's *Viva Detroit,* Terry Johnson's *Insignificance,* and Janusz Glowacki's *Hunting Cockroaches.*

3. Albee, *Three Tall Women,* 15. Subsequent page numbers are given in the text.

4. Albee's device resembles even more closely Peter Barnes's method in *Three Visions.*

5. Myra Carter, a British actor who had spent most of her career in the United States, had appeared on Broadway in *The Chalk Circle, Major Barbara, Georgy, Maybe Tuesday, Present Laughter, Suddenly Last Summer,* and *Something Unspoken.* Her earlier Albee plays included *All Over* at the Hartford Stage Company and on PBS (for which she received an Emmy nomination) and *A Delicate Balance* at the Arena Stage. Her off-Broadway credits include

King John, Abingdon Square, Helen, and *The Secret Concubine.* For her performance in *Three Tall Women,* Carter went on to win numerous awards, including a Drama Desk Award, an OBIE Award, an Outer Critics Circle Award, and a Lucille Lortel Award.

Kathleen Butler's stage and film credits are given in note 2 to chapter 8. As discussed in that chapter, she had also originated the role of Gillian in Albee's production of *Marriage Play* in Vienna and reprised it during the Signature Theatre Company's Albee season.

6. For the sake of consistency, I use the letter names that Albee finally settled on.

7. The Young Man was played by Vienna-based British actor Howard Nightingall, who had trained at London's Academy of Live and Recorded Arts. Because of his relative youth, Nightingall came with few major credits.

8. Butler, interviews by author, November 10 and 23, 1994.

9. Albee, quoted in Wise, "Being Misunderstood Has Kept Albee Far from Home."

10. Richards, "Edward Albee and the Road Not Taken" (includes the quotation from Hoess).

11. Bassham, interview by author, November 10, 1994.

12. Butler, interview by author, November 23, 1994.

13. Bassham, interview by author, November 10, 1994.

14. Butler, interview by author, November 23, 1994.

15. Bassham, interview by author, November 10, 1994.

16. Sacharow, interview by author, November 21 and 23, 1994.

17. Bassham, interview by author, November 10, 1994; and Butler, interview by author, November 23, 1994.

18. Albee, interview by author, August 18, 2002. In this interview, possibly because of the time that had elapsed since the rehearsals, Albee did not recall characterizing the two acts as two different plays.

19. Sacharow, interview by author, November 21 and 23, 1994.

20. Baker, interview by author, November 21, 1994.

21. Sacharow, interview by author, November 21 and 23, 1994.

22. Butler, interview by author, November 23, 1994.

23. Bassham, interview by author, November 10, 1994.

24. Butler, interview by author, November 23, 1994.

25. Albee, interview by author, August 18, 2002.

26. Cole, "Probing inside the Bone."

27. Canby, "A Season of Albee."

28. Butler, interview by author, November 23, 1994.

29. Baker, interview by author, November 21, 1994; and Bassham, interview by author, November 10, 1994.

30. Albee, interview by author, August 18, 2002.

31. Baker, interview by author, November 21, 1994.

32. Albee, "Yes Is Better Than No," 38.

33. Albee, interview by author, August 18, 2002.

34. Sacharow, interview by author, November 21 and 23, 1994.

35. Baker, interview by author, November 21, 1994.

36. Albee, interview by author, August 18, 2002.

37. Sacharow, interview by author, November 21 and 23, 1994.

38. Carter, interview by author, November 20, 1994; and Baker, interview by author, November 21, 1994. Nonetheless, the part had been earlier offered to Uta Hagen, who had played Martha in the original *Who's Afraid of Virginia Woolf?* Sacharow had also offered the

part to Marian Seldes, a Broadway star and veteran Albee actor going back to *A Delicate Balance* in 1966; she, however, chose to play B, a decision she occasionally second-guessed during the Promenade run. Baker, interview by author, November 21, 1994.

39. Sacharow, interview by author, November 21 and 23, 1994.

40. Albee, "Yes Is Better Than No," 38.

41. Butler, interview by author, November 23, 1994.

42. Carter, interview by author, November 20, 1994.

43. Bassham, interview by author, November 10, 1994.

44. Baker, interview with author, November 21, 1994.

45. Albee, interview by author, August 18, 2002.

46. In this and the next paragraph, all rehearsal details and quotations come from Bassham, interview by author, November 10, 1994.

47. Ibid.

48. Albee, interview by author, August 18, 2002.

49. Baker, interview by author, November 21, 1994.

50. Albee, interview by author, August 18, 2002.

51. Bassham, interview by author, November 10, 1994.

52. Butler, interview by author, November 23, 1994.

53. In this and the next paragraph, all quotations are from Carter, interview by author, November 20, 1994, unless otherwise indicated. Because of some internal contradictions in Carter's comments and a radical divergence between her statements and those of other interviewees, I quote only remarks that I can crosscheck against my own observation, my conversations with Albee, other actors, and director Lawrence Sacharow, or a published source.

54. Lahr, "Sons and Mothers."

55. Appelo, review of *Three Tall Women*.

56. Bassham, interview by author, November 10, 1994; and Butler, interview by author, November 23, 1994.

57. Albee, interview by author, August 18, 2002.

58. Butler, interview by author, November 23, 1994.

59. Lahr, "Sons and Mothers."

60. All quotations in this and the following four paragraphs are from Sacharow, interview by author, November 21 and 23, 1994, unless otherwise indicated.

61. Dukore, *Bernard Shaw, Director,* 121.

62. Albee, interview by author, February 14, 1980.

63. Hall, "A Director's Approach."

64. Albee, interview by author, February 14, 1980.

65. Albee, quoted in Klein, "Awaiting a Death, Longing for Love."

66. Albee, interview by Joe Pollack, in Kolin, *Conversations with Edward Albee,* 212.

67. Albee, interview by author, January 4, 1992.

68. In this and the following paragraph, unless otherwise indicated, all quotations are from Sacharow, interview by author, November 21 and 23, 1994.

69. Canby, "A Season of Albee."

70. In this and the following paragraph, all quotations are from Sacharow, interview by author, November 21 and 23, 1994, unless otherwise indicated.

71. Albee, interview by author, August 18, 2002.

72. Albee, "Yes Is Better Than No," 38.

73. Albee, interview by author, August 18, 2002.

74. Sacharow, interview by author, November 21 and 23, 1994.

75. Albee, interview by author, August 18, 2002.

76. Sacharow, interview by author, November 21 and 23, 1994.

77. Albee, interview by Alan Wallach, in Kolin, *Conversations with Edward Albee,* 131.

78. Albee, "Yes Is Better Than No," 38.

79. Albee, interviews by William Flanagan and Adrienne Clarkson, in Kolin, *Conversations with Edward Albee,* 58, 90.

80. Clurman, "Albee on Balance."

81. The actors differ with each other and with Albee about the exact date the cast received act 2. I follow Cynthia Bassham's date—May 20, 1991—because it is confirmed by a contemporaneous record in her careful and detailed daily journal.

82. Albee, interview by author, August 18, 2002.

83. Baker, interview by author, November 21, 1994.

84. Butler, interview by author, November 23, 1994.

85. Carter, interview by author, November 20, 1994.

86. Butler, interview by author, November 23, 1994.

10. Albee's Double Authoring

1. Arden, *To Present the Pretence,* 210–211.

2. Styan, *Drama, Stage and Audience,* 6; and Meyerhold, quoted in Clurman, *On Directing,* 84.

3. Albee, interview by author, January 6, 1990

4. Schneider, interview by author, January 31, 1980.

5. Albee, interview by author, September 14, 1978.

6. Schneider, interview by author, January 31, 1980.

7. Albee, interview by Dick Cavett, *The Dick Cavett Show,* PBS, June 1, 1979.

8. Williams, *Drama in Performance,* 162.

11. Albee and His Collaborators on Staging Albee

1. Albee, *Fragments,* 25–31.

2. Gussow, *Edward Albee,* 349–350.

Works Cited

Interviews by author

Albee, Edward. August 16, 1978; September 14, 1978; February 14, 1980; January 6, 1990; February 12, 1991; January 4, 1992; January 5, 1992; August 18, 2002; August 20, 2002.

Baker, Jordan. November 21, 1994.

Bassham, Cynthia. November 10, 1994.

Butler, Kathleen. November 10, 1994; November 23, 1994.

Carter, Myra. November 20, 1994.

Esbjornson, David. March 11, 2002.

Gaskill, William. February 25, 1983; March 9, 1983.

Hill, Robert. January 5, 1990.

Ottavino, John. January 6, 1990.

Pendleton, Wyman. February 15, 1980; February 20, 1980.

Rowe, Stephen. March 11, 2002.

Sacharow, Lawrence. November 21, 1994; November 23, 1994.

Schneider, Alan. August 6, 1975; January 31, 1980; February 14, 1980.

Wright, Mark. January 5, 1992.

Works by Edward Albee

"The American Dream" and "The Zoo Story." New York: Signet, 1963.

"Box" and "Quotations from Chairman Mao Tse-Tung": Two Inter-related Plays. New York: Atheneum, 1969.

"Box" and "Quotations from Chairman Mao Tse-Tung." Broadway premiere. Directed by Alan Schneider, Billy Rose Theatre, New York City, September 1968. Manuscript in the author's possession.

"Counting the Ways" and "Listening": Two Plays. New York: Atheneum.

"Edward Albee." Interview. In Walter Wager, ed., The Playwrights Speak, 25–67. New York: Delacorte, 1967. (Originally published in Beverwyck [Siena College, New York], Winter 1965.)

"Edward Albee Talks About: What Does a Playwright Do?" *New York Theatre Review,* October 1978, 10–13.

Fragments: A Sit-Around. New York: Dramatists Play Service, 1995.

"An Interview with Edward Albee." In Alan Downer, *The American Theatre Today,* 110–123. Voice of America *Forum* Series. New York: Basic Books, 1967.

"An Interview with Edward Albee, March 18, 1981." Interview by Charles S. Krohn and Julian N. Wasserman. In Julian N. Wasserman, ed., *Edward Albee: An Interview and Essays,* 1–27. Syracuse, N.Y.: Syracuse University Press, 1983.

"Promptbook: Edward Albee: Auto, If Not Biographical." Interview. *Dramatics,* November–December 1979, 3–4.

"Yes Is Better Than No: An Interview with the Playwright by Steven Samuels." *American Theater,* September 1994, 38.

Interview by Dick Cavett. *The Dick Cavett Show.* PBS, KVIE, Sacramento, Calif., June 1, 1979.

The Lady From Dubuque. New York: Atheneum, 1980.

The Lady From Dubuque. Broadway premiere. Directed by Alan Schneider, Morosco Theatre, New York City, January 30, 1980. Manuscript in the author's possession.

Letter to author, September 11, 1989.

Letter to author, November 13, 1994.

Letter to Mark Hall Amitin. n.d. [circa late 1978–early 1979]. Photocopy in the author's possession.

The Man Who Had Three Arms. Broadway premiere. Directed by Edward Albee, Lyceum Theatre, New York City, April 5, 1983. Manuscript in the author's possession.

Marriage Play. New York: Dramatists Play Service, 1995.

Marriage Play. American premiere. Directed by Edward Albee, Alley Theatre, Houston, January 2, 1992. Manuscript in the author's possession.

"On Making Authors Happy." *Cinebill* 1, no. 3 (October 1973). [Program, *A Delicate Balance,* dir. Tony Richardson, American Film Theatre.]

Papers. *Albee Directs Albee* Collection. D-131, Department of Special Collections, General Library, University of California, Davis.

"The Sandbox"; "The Death of Bessie Smith" (with "Fam and Yam"). New York: Signet–New American Library, 1963.

Selected Plays of Edward Albee. With an introduction by Edward Albee. Garden City, N.J.: Doubleday, 1987.

Three Tall Women. New York: Plume, 1995.

Who's Afraid of Virginia Woolf? New York: Atheneum, 1962.

Who's Afraid of Virginia Woolf? Mark Taper Forum and Alley Theatre productions, 1989 and 1990. Directed by Edward Albee, Dolittle Theatre, Los Angeles, and Alley Theatre, Houston, 1989–1990. Manuscript in the author's possession.

Works by Others

"Albee: The Double Takes." *Three Village Herald,* August 30, 1978.

Amacher, Richard E. *Edward Albee.* 2nd ed. Boston: Twayne, 1982.

Amoia, Alba, ed. *Off-Stage Voices: Interviews with Modern French Dramatists.* Troy, N.Y.: Whitson Publishing Co., 1975.

Appelo, Tim. Review of *Three Tall Women. Nation,* March 14, 1994.

Arden, John. *To Present the Pretence: Essays on the Theatre and Its Public.* London: Methuen, 1975.

Armstrong, William. "George Bernard Shaw: The Playwright as Producer." *Modern Drama* 8, no. 4 (February 1966): 347–361.

Atkinson, Brooks. "Theatre: A Double Bill Off Broadway." Review of *The Zoo Story* and *Krapp's Last Tape. New York Times,* January 15, 1960.

Balliet, Whitney. "Three Cheers for Albee." Review of *The American Dream. New Yorker,* February 4, 1961.

Barnes, Clive. "Albee's *Seascape* Is a Major Event." *New York Times,* January 27, 1975. Reprinted in *New York Theatre Critics' Reviews,* 1975, 368.

———. "Stage: Double Bill by Albee." *New York Times,* February 4, 1977.

———. "Stage: *Virginia Woolf." New York Times,* April 2, 1976. Reprinted in *New York Theatre Critics' Reviews,* 1976, 310.

Baxandall, Lee. "The Theatre of Edward Albee." *Tulane Drama Review* 9, no. 4 (Summer 1965): 19–40.

Beckerman, Bernard. *Dynamics of Drama: Theory and Method of Analysis.* New York: Drama Book Specialists, 1979.

Bentley, Eric. "The Brecht Memoir." *Theater* 14 (Spring 1983): 4–26.

Bigsby, C. W. E. *Albee.* Edinburgh: Oliver & Boyd, 1969.

———. "*Box* and *Quotations from Chairman Mao Tse-Tung*: Albee's Diptych." In *Edward Albee: A Collection of Critical Essays,* ed. C. W. E. Bigsby, 151–164. Englewood Cliffs, N.J.: Prentice-Hall, 1975.

———. *A Critical Introduction to Twentieth-Century American Drama.* Vol. 2. Cambridge: Cambridge University Press, 1984.

———. *Modern American Drama, 1945–1990.* Cambridge: Cambridge University Press, 1992.

Bloom, Harold. Introduction to *Edward Albee,* ed. Harold Bloom, 1–8. Modern Critical Views. New York: Chelsea House, 1987.

Blum, David. "What's It All About, Albee?" *New York,* November 15, 1993, 70–78.

Booth, John E. "Albee and Schneider Observe: Something's Stirring." *Theatre Arts* 45, no. 3 (March 1961): 22–24, 78–79.

Bottoms, Stephen J. *Albee: "Who's Afraid of Virginia Woolf?"* Cambridge: Cambridge University Press, 2000.

———. *Cambridge Companion to Edward Albee.* Cambridge: Cambridge University Press, 2005.

Bowman, Pierre. "Warm Audience for Albee." *Honolulu Star Bulletin,* November 11, 1978.

Boyer, Mark. "Premier Albee: Irresistible Rhythms, Unnatural Acts." *Hartford (Conn.) Advocate,* February 6, 1977.

Brook, Peter. "The Old Vic to Vincennes: Interviews with Michael Kuslow and Peter Brook." Interview by Stephen R. Lawson. *Yale/Theater* 7, no. 1 (Fall 1975): 82–95.

Burchard, Hank. "*Albee by Albee* Is, Uh, Albee by Albee." *Washington Post,* February 23, 1979.

Canby, Vincent. "A Season of Albee, Obsessions Safely Intact." *New York Times,* February 6, 1994.

Carlson, Harry G., and Karin Helander. "Ingmar Bergman—Filmic Theatre Man and Actors' Director: Swedish Perspectives on Ingmar Bergman." *Western European Stages* 12, no. 1 (Winter 2000): 11–16.

Chriss, Joel. "Albee Directs Albee with Much Passion." *New York Statesman,* August 30, 1978.

Ciment, Michael. *Kazan on Kazan.* London: Secker and Warburg, 1973.

Clurman, Harold. "Albee on Balance." *New York Times,* November 13, 1966.

———. *On Directing.* New York: Collier, 1974.

Coe, Richard. "Albee Directing Albee." *Washington Post,* February 25, 1979.

———. "Lone Star over Lithuania." *American Theatre,* September 1990, 22–27.

Cohn, Ruby. "Albee's *Box* and Ours." *Modern Drama* 14, no. 2 (September 1971): 137–143.

———. *Edward Albee.* Minneapolis: University of Minnesota, 1969.

———. *Just Play: Beckett's Theatre.* Princeton, N.J.: Princeton University Press, 1980.

———. "On Playwrights Directing." *Bay Arts Review* 3, no. 21 (November 21–29, 1979).

Cole, L. C. "Theatre Review: Probing inside the Bone." *New York Native,* May 2, 1994.

Cole, Toby, and Helen Krich Chinoy. *Directors on Directing: A Source Book of the Modern Theatre.* 2nd rev. ed. New York: Macmillan, 1976.

Collins, William B. "Definitive Albee: We Get What He Sees." *Philadelphia Inquirer,* April 22, 1979.

Copeau, Jacques. "La mise en scene." In *Copeau: Texts on Theatre,* ed. and trans. John Rudlin and Norman H. Paul, 124–126. London: Routledge, 1990. Partially reprinted from the *Encylopedie Française.*

Dark, Gregory. "Production Casebook No. 5: Edward Bond's *Lear* at the Royal Court." *Theatre Quarterly* 2, no. 5 (January–March 1972): 20–31.

Debusscher, Gilbert. *Edward Albee: Tradition and Renewal.* Trans. Anne D. Williams. Brussels: American Studies Center, 1967.

De La Fuente, Patricia. *Edward Albee: Planned Wilderness.* Edinburgh, Tex.: Pan American University, 1980.

Derrida, Jacques. *Of Grammatology.* Trans. Gayatri C. Spivak. Baltimore, Md.: Johns Hopkins University Press, 1976.

Drake, Sylvie. "*Albee Directs Albee* at UCLA." *Los Angeles Times,* October 18, 1978.

Driver, Tom F. "Bucketful of Dregs." Review of *The Zoo Story. Christian Century,* February 17, 1960.

Dukore, Bernard F. *Bernard Shaw, Director.* Seattle: University of Washington Press, 1971.

———. Letter to author, January 3, 1979

Eichelbaum, Stanley. "Strong and Purposeful Staging of Albee One-Acts." *San Francisco Examiner,* October 25, 1978.

Eigsti, Karl. Composite ground plan for New York City and touring productions of *The Zoo Story* and *The American Dream.* September 1, 1978. Photocopy in the author's possession.

Esslin, Martin. "Max Reinhardt: High Priest of Theatricality." *Drama Review* 21, no. 2 (T74, June 1977): 3–24.

———. *The Theatre of the Absurd.* New York: Doubleday, 1961.

Evans, Everett. "Alley's *Virginia Woolf* to Play in Soviet Union." *Houston Chronicle,* January 3, 1990.

Feingold, Michael. "Albeecentric." *Village Voice,* March 1, 1994.

———. "All Fugued Up." *Village Voice,* February 19, 1979.

Fletcher, John. "Roger Blin at Work." *Modern Drama* 8, no. 4 (February 1966): 401–409.

Foucault, Michel. *The Archaeology of Knowledge.* Trans. A. M. Sheridan-Smith. New York: Pantheon, 1972.

Freedman, Mitchell. "An Albee Last Act Still Unwritten." *Long Island (N.Y.) Newsday,* Nassau ed., August 8, 1978.

———. "He Knows the Author, But . . ." *Long Island (N.Y.) Newsday,* Suffolk ed., August 23, 1978.

Fuegi, John. *The Essential Brecht.* University of Southern California Studies in Comparative Literature, vol. 4. Los Angeles: Hennessey and Ingalls, 1972.

Funke, Lewis. "Albee Revivals." Review of *The American Dream* and *The Zoo Story. New York Times,* May 29, 1963.

Gelb, Arthur. "Plays by Beckett and Albee in ANTA Series." *New York Times,* October 26, 1960.

———. "*4 in 1* Bill of One-Act Plays Opens at the Jazz Gallery." Review of Edward Albee's *The Sandbox,* Fernando Arrabal's *The Two Executioners* and *Picnic on the Battlefield,* and H. B. Lutz's *The Chip. New York Times,* May 17, 1960.

Goorney, Howard. *The Theatre Workshop Story.* London: Methuen, 1981.

Gottfried, Martin. "Theatre: *Box* and *Mao.*" *Women's Wear Daily,* October 1, 1968.

———. "Theatre: Edward Albee's Latest." *New York Post,* January 27, 1975. Reprinted in *New York Theatre Critics' Reviews,* 1975, 368.

———. "*Woolf* Returns with Same Bite." *New York Post,* April 2, 1976.

Gussow, Mel. "Alan Schneider, 66, Director of Beckett, Dies." *New York Times,* May 4, 1984.

———. *Edward Albee: A Singular Journey; A Biography.* New York: Applause, 2001.

———. "What's New? Old Shows." *New York Times,* May 9, 1976.

Guthrie, Tyrone. "An Audience of One." In Toby Cole and Helen Krich Chinoy, eds., *Directors on Directing: A Source Book of the Modern Theatre,* 245–256. New York: Macmillan, 1976.

———. "Directing a Play." In *The Director in a Changing Theatre: Essays on Theory and Practice, with New Plays for Performance,* ed. J. Robert Wills, 85–100. Palo Alto: Mayfield, 1976.

Hall, Peter. "A Director's Approach." In John Lahr, ed., *A Casebook on Harold Pinter's "The Homecoming."* 9–25. New York: Grove, 1971.

Harris, Frank. *Bernard Shaw.* Garden City, N.Y.: Garden City Publishing, 1931.

Hayman, Ronald. *Edward Albee.* London: Heinemann, 1971.

———. *Playback.* London: Davis-Poynter, 1973.

Heide, Robert. "Samuel Beckett's Children." *Other Stages* 2, no. 11 (February 7–20, 1980), 6.

Hewes, Henry. "Albee Surfaces." *Saturday Review,* March 8, 1975.

———, ed. *The Best Plays of 1961–62.* New York: Dodd, Mead, 1962.

Hiley, Jim. *Theatre at Work: The Story of the National Theatre's Production of Brecht's "Galileo."* London: Routledge & Kegan Paul, 1981.

Hirsch, E. D. *Validity in Interpretation.* New Haven: Yale University Press, 1967.

Hirsch, Foster. *Who's Afraid of Edward Albee?* Berkeley: Creative Arts Book, 1978.

Jalon, Alan. "Edward Albee: 'Let Actor Be Creative, Have His Head for a While.'" *New York Westsider,* February 1, 1979.

Johnson, Malcolm L. "*Albee Directs Albee.*" *Hartford (Conn.) Courant,* February 6, 1977.

———. "Albee Mixes Humor, Pain." *Hartford (Conn.) Courant,* February 3, 1977.

Jones, David Richard. *Great Directors at Work: Stanislavsky, Brecht, Kazan, Brook.* Berkeley: University of California Press, 1986.

Jouvet, Louis. "The Profession of the Producer, II." *Theatre Arts Monthly* 21 (January 1937): 57–64.

Kalb, Jonathan. *Beckett in Performance.* Cambridge: Cambridge University Press, 1989.

Kalem, T. E. "The Theater: Till Death Do Us Part: *Who's Afraid Of Virginia Woolf?* by Edward Albee." *Time,* April 12, 1976.

Kass, Susan. "Albee: A Cynic's Look at Society." *New York Statesman,* September 12, 1978.

Kerr, Walter. "Mao—But What Message?" *New York Times,* March 17, 1968.

———. "Stage View: Albee's Unwritten Part; McNally's Missing Joke." *New York Times,* February 2, 1975.

———. "Stage View: '—Sparks Still Fly.'" *New York Times,* April 11, 1976.

Klein, Alvin. "Theatre Review: Awaiting a Death, Longing for Love." Review of *All Over. New York Times,* February 24, 2002.

Knapp, Bettina. *Off-Stage Voices: Interviews with Modern French Dramatists.* Troy, N.Y.: Whitston, 1975.

Knobeloch, James. Letter to author. November 13, 1978.

Knowlson, James, ed. and intro. *"Happy Days": The Production Notebook of Samuel Beckett.* London: Faber and Faber, 1985.

———, ed. *Samuel Beckett: "Krapp's Last Tape." Theatre Notebook 1.* London: Brutus Books, 1980.

Kolin, Philip C., ed. *Conversations with Edward Albee.* Jackson: University of Mississippi Press, 1988.

Kroll, Jack. "Theater: Albee's Blackjack." *Newsweek,* April 12, 1976.

La Fontaine, Barbara. "Triple Threat On, Off and Off-Off Broadway." *New York Times,* February 25, 1968.

Lahr, John. "Sons and Mothers." *New Yorker* 70, no. 13 (May 16, 1994): 102–105.

"Landmark Symposium: *Who's Afraid of Virginia Woolf?" Dramatists Guild Quarterly* 19, no. 1 (Spring 1982): 8–23.

Laure, Rebecca. Letter to Edward Albee. August 9, 1978. Photocopy in the author's possession.

Lenoir, Jean-Pierre. "2 Plays by Albee Offered in Paris." *New York Times,* January 11, 1963.

Marker, Frederick J., and Lise-Lone Marker, ed. and intro. *Ingmar Bergman: A Project for the Theatre.* New York: Frederick Ungar, 1983.

———. *Ingmar Bergman: Four Decades in the Theater.* Directors in Perspective. Cambridge: Cambridge University Press, 1982.

Marowitz, Charles. *Directing the Action: Acting and Directing in the Contemporary Theatre.* New York: Applause, 1991. Reprint of *Prospero's Staff: Acting and Directing in the Contemporary Theatre* (Bloomington: Indiana University Press, 1986).

McCarthy, Gerry. *Edward Albee.* Macmillan Modern Dramatists. London: Macmillan, 1987.

McColm, Del. "The Mystery of Edward Albee: Controversial Playwright Attacks Critics, Defends Arts, Government." *Davis (Calif.) Enterprise,* April 21, 1977.

McMillan, Dougald, and Martha Fehsenfeld. *Beckett in the Theatre.* London: Calder, 1988.

"Morning Report . . . Stage." *Los Angeles Times,* May 14, 1987.

Murphy, Brenda. *Tennessee Williams and Elia Kazan: A Collaboration in the Theatre.* Cambridge: Cambridge University Press, 1992.

Nadel, Alan. "*Who's Afraid* at Billy Rose." *New York World-Telegram and Sun,* October 15, 1962, 14. Reprinted in *New York Theatre Critics' Reviews,* 1962, 254.

Newton-de Molina, David, ed. *On Literary Intention: Critical Essays.* Edinburgh: University Press, 1976.

Nightingale, Benedict. "Unholy Deadlock." *London Times,* May 10, 2001.

"Notizen." *Theater heute,* no. 26 (November 1985): 67.

O'Haire, Hugh, Jr. "Theatre: Art Center Premiers First Season." *Suffolk County (N.Y.) News,* September 21, 1978.

O'Malley, Glyn [assistant to Edward Albee]. Letter to Mark Amitin, October 31, 1978, personal copy.

Paolucci, Anne. *From Tension to Tonic: The Plays of Edward Albee.* Carbondale: Southern Illinois University Press, 1972.

Patterson, Michael. *Peter Stein: Germany's Leading Theatre Director.* Directors in Perspective. Cambridge: Cambridge University Press, 1981.

Pendleton, Wyman. Rehearsal notations for his role as Chairman Mao in a typescript of Edward Albee's *Quotations from Chairman Mao Tse-Tung,* with loose sheets of director Alan Schneider's rehearsal notes to Pendleton. Broadway premiere production, Billy Rose Theatre, September 1968. In the author's possession.

Rich, Frank. "Stage: Drama by Albee: *Man Who Had Three Arms.*" *New York Times,* April 6, 1983.

Richards, David. "Edward Albee and the Road Not Taken." *New York Times,* June 16, 1991.

———. "Review/Theater: 3 Albee One-Acters about People Boxed In." *New York Times,* February 10, 1994.

Rossi, Alfred. *Minneapolis Rehearsals: Tyrone Guthrie Directs "Hamlet."* Berkeley: University of California Press, 1980.

Roudane, Matthew C. *Understanding Edward Albee.* Columbia: University of South Carolina Press, 1987.

———. *"Who's Afraid of Virginia Woolf?" Necessary Fictions, Terrifying Realities.* Boston: Twayne, 1990.

Rowe, Stephen. Letter to author, December 8, 1978.

Rutenberg, Michael E. *Edward Albee: Playwright in Protest.* New York: Discuss/Avon, 1970.

Sagal, Peter. "Albee Directs Albee in Los Angeles." *Theater Week* 3, no. 11 (October 23, 1989): 16–19.

Schier, Ernest. "Albee Revival Stands, Untarnished by Time." *Philadelphia Bulletin,* April 21, 1979.

Schneider, Alan. *Entrances: An American Director's Journey.* New York: Viking, 1986.

———. "Reality Is Not Enough: An Interview with Alan Schneider." In *Edward Albee: A Collection of Critical Essays,* ed. C. W. E. Bigsby, 69–75. Englewood Cliffs, N.J.: Prentice-Hall, 1975. Reprinted from *Tulane Drama Review* 9, no. 3 (Spring 1965): 143–150.

———. "What Does a Director Do?" *New York Theatre Review* (Spring 1977): 16–17.

Selbourne, David. *The Making of "A Midsummer Night's Dream."* London: Methuen, 1982.

Selvin, Barbara. *"Albee Directs Albee." Village Times* (New York), August 24, 1978.

Shaw, George Bernard. *Shaw on Theatre.* Ed. E. J. West. New York: Hill and Wang, 1959.

Shawcross, John T. *Intentionality and the New Traditionalism: Some Liminal Means to Literary Revisionism.* University Park: Pennsylvania State University Press, 1991.

Shelton, Lewis E. "Alan Schneider's Direction of *Who's Afraid of Virginia Woolf?*" *Journal of American Drama and Theatre* 3, no. 3 (Fall 1991): 39–50.

Shewey, Don. "The Persistence of Edward Albee." *American Theatre,* April 1992, 14–21, 60–62.

Shirley, Don. "An Audience with Albee: Up the Freight Elevator to the Playwright's Roost." *Washington Post,* February 18, 1979.

Smilgis, Martha. "Stage: Edward Albee Blames His Newest Broadway Flop on the Critics— and Casts for *Lolita* on Subways." *People,* February 25, 1980, 70–73.

Solomon, Rakesh H. "Albee Directs *Ohio Impromptu* and *Krapp's Last Tape.*" *Beckett Circle* 12, no. 2 (Spring 1991): 1–2.

———. "Crafting Script into Performance: Edward Albee in Rehearsal." *American Drama* 2, no. 2 (Spring 1993): 76–99.

———. "Text, Subtext, and Performance: Edward Albee on Directing *Who's Afraid of Virginia Woolf?*" *Theatre Survey* 34, no. 2 (November 1993): 94–110.

Spencer, Charles. "Echoes from the Wilderness Years." *Daily Telegraph,* May 10, 2001.

Steger, B. L. "Review: Albee Directs Albee: *The Zoo Story.*" *Island Odyssey: A Leisure Review* (New York), September 11, 1978.

Stenz, Anita Maria. *Edward Albee: The Poet of Loss.* Studies in American Literature 32. The Hague: Mouton, 1978.

Stern, Daniel. "I Want My Intent Clear." *New York Times,* March 28, 1976.

Styan, J. L. *Drama, Stage and Audience.* London: Cambridge University Press, 1975.

———. *Elements of Drama.* Cambridge: Cambridge University Press, 1969.

———. *Max Reinhardt.* Cambridge: Cambridge University Press, 1982.

Sullivan, Dan. "Edward Albee: Playwright with More Than One Act." *Los Angeles Times,* October 15, 1979.

———. "Theater: Albee's *Bessie Smith* and *Dream* Revived." *New York Times,* October 3, 1968.

Taitz, Sonia. "Theatre: Off-Broadway Plays Sprout in Summer Theater." *New York Times,* June 11, 1989.

Taubman, Howard. "The Theatre: Albee's *The American Dream.*" *New York Times,* January 25, 1961.

Ucciardo, Frank. "Review: *Albee Directs Albee.*" *Island Odyssey: A Leisure Review* (New York), September 11, 1978.

Wallach, Allan. "Theater: Albee on Albee." *Newsday,* September 11, 1978.

Weber, Carl. "Brecht as Director." In *Brecht,* ed. Erika Munk, 101–110. New York: Bantam, 1972. Reprinted from *TDR: The Drama Review* 12, no. 1 (Fall 1967).

Weiner, Bernard. "*Albee Directs Albee:* Playwright at the Helm." *San Francisco Chronicle,* October 26, 1979.

Willet, John. *Brecht in Context: Comparative Approaches.* London: Methuen, 1983.

———. *The Theatre of Bertolt Brecht: A Study from Eight Aspects.* London: Methuen, 1959.

Williams, Raymond. *Drama in Performance.* New York: Basic Books, 1968.

Wimsatt, W. K., and Monroe Beardsley. "Intention." In *Dictionary of World Literature,* rev. ed., ed. Joseph T. Shipley, 229–232. New York: Philosophical Library, 1953.

Wise, Michael Z. "Being Misunderstood Has Kept Albee Far from Home." *Tampa Tribune,* July 8, 1991.

Index

Note: Page references in *italics* indicate information contained in photographs. Some quotations in the text are attributed in the endnotes. Where necessary these are indexed with reference to the text page cited. E.g., 269n12 (3)

Williams, Raymond, 2, 196
Williams, Tennessee, 5, 7, 11, 18
Wilson, Robert, 8
Wimsatt, W. K., 5
Wolcott, Derek, 180
Worth, Irene, 26–27, 112
Wright, Mark, 232–236

The Zoo Story: acting in, 58, 64–66, 71; blocking, 63; casting, 54, 67; character interpretation, 58–62, 64–65, 277n22; characterization in, 56–57, 64; critical scholarship, 218; directorial method, 70–71; external direction, 57–59; introductory remarks, 55; limited supervision of, 67–68, 203–204; line readings, 56, 57; pacing, 58; Pendleton on, 203–204; photographs, *73;* previews, 67; productions of, 54; reviews, 71–72; set and stage decor, 55–56, 195; stage business, 56, 63–64, 65; summary of, 54–55; textual revisions, 62–63, 195; themes and interpretation, 55, 61–64; vocal orchestration, 64; vocal rhythm, 57

Rakesh H. Solomon teaches in the Department of Theatre and Drama at Indiana University, Bloomington. He specializes in both American theatre and Indian theatre, with additional expertise in contemporary British theatre and theatre historiography. He has published on these subjects in *Theatre Journal; TDR: The Drama Review; Theatre Survey; Theatre Research International; American Drama; Forum for Modern Language Studies, International Journal of the Humanities;* and *International Journal of Interdisciplinary Social Sciences.* His articles have also appeared in *The Cambridge Companion to Edward Albee; Edward Albee: A Casebook; Alan Ayckbourn: A Casebook; Writing and Rewriting National Theatre Histories; Modern Indian Theatre: A Reader; Comparative Literature Now; Reader's Guide to Literature in English;* and *In Search of the Historical Scene: Perspectives on Theater Historiography.* His forthcoming book is *Political Plays and Colonial Censorship: Documents, Commentary, and Text of Kichaka-Vadha.*